Table of Contents

Introduction to the First Edition

To international students planning to enter a university in the United States on either the graduate or undergraduate level, the TOEFL (Test of English as a Foreign Language) may seem an almost insurmountable obstacle. Though it may indeed be an obstacle, we believe it is one that can be overcome with the right kinds of practice. The exercises we present here are expressly designed to help students develop the skills necessary for this task. These exercises, however, will be equally useful to students with other types of goals in mind.

This book is geared towards students with at least low intermediate English proficiency, which in TOEFL terms would be a score in the 400 to 420 range. The book is better suited, however, to students with high intermediate to advanced proficiency.

We see three ways in which this book can be utilized. First, the student studying independently or with a tutor will find clear guidance in the self-explanatory objectives, directions, and examples. Second, the book provides a straightforward format for a special TOEFL preparation course. Some of the material, especially the introductory, review, and timed exercises, should be done in class. As many exercises as time permits would be assigned for independent homework. Even in a course as short as thirty classroom hours, this book will provide a worthwhile basis for study. A seventy-five hour course would give more than ample time to deal with the material effectively. Finally, in intensive English programs operating on a semester basis, teachers sharing responsibility for teaching a single group of students could use the book as a primary or secondary text. Each teacher would use that portion of the book suited to the subject matter of his or her course. It is with these latter two purposes in mind that the Tapescript and Key have been published in a separate book: teachers may wish to retain this book until the end of the course, distributing it only as necessary during the course for independent in-class checking.

We believe this book has the requisite flexibility to meet these and other goals. In fact, the ideal approach would not be to start at the beginning and work doggedly to the last page. Like exercises, though grouped together, might be spread over a number of days or weeks. "Hard" exercises can be mixed with "easy" ones: analytical structure exercises may be lightened with short listening tasks. In other words, a teacher can use the material in any order, depending on the level, the needs, or even the mood of the class.

Carol E. King
Nancy A. Stanley
1982

Introduction to the Second Edition

Since 1986, a new section has been added to the TOEFL, which allows students to demonstrate their ability to write in English: the Test of Written English (TWE).

The Test of Written English requires examinees to compose a short essay showing their ability to organize ideas, support these with examples or evidence, and to write in standard English. To help students taking the writing test, this edition of **Building Skills for the TOEFL** includes a new section, Section 4, which discusses and analyzes the two types of essay question in the Test of Written English, and offers practice questions in the TWE style. A TWE question is now included in each Practice Test in Section 5.

Nancy A. Stanley
Carol E. King
1988

Acknowledgements

Directions to sample questions reprinted by permission of Educational Testing Service. However, the sample test questions were neither provided nor approved by Educational Testing Service.

I gratefully acknowledge the support and assistance I received from the students, faculty, and administration of the Intensive English Program of the University of Texas at Austin, Texas. In particular, I would like to thank Ray Cowart, Marianne Miller, Charles Seltzer, Patti Shadburn, Barbara Singh, and Leslie Wiseman, each of whom helped me in special ways. I also appreciate the patience and understanding of the TOEFL special course teachers who suffered through early drafts of some portions of the manuscript. Without the help of all of these people, this book might never have come into being.

Carol E. King
March 1982
Austin, Texas

To SBJ, his book—NS

Nancy A. Stanley
March 1982
Mexico City

TOEFL Tactics for the Practice Exercises and Tests

Apart from the two complete TOEFL Practice Tests in Section 5 of this book, there are various TOEFL Practice Exercises interspersed throughout Sections 2 and 3. These are clearly marked as such, and they contain questions similar to those you will find on the relevant section of the actual TOEFL.

All the exercises in *Building Skills for the TOEFL* are designed to help you to develop the skills required to be successful on the actual TOEFL: the following advice on "TOEFL Tactics" will help you to make the best use of all the material presented throughout the book.

i) TOEFL Tactics: Keeping the TOEFL in perspective

When some students become aware of the importance of the TOEFL to their academic future in the United States, they become obsessed with studying the TOEFL, and only the TOEFL. Such students may become blind to the importance of following a well-rounded program of English study. Avoid becoming one of these students by keeping the following suggestions in mind:

1   You need to remember that a program of TOEFL preparation can never take the place of an integrated program of study in a reputable institute or school. Do not fall into the trap of thinking that **only** study materials and books labeled TOEFL will help you prepare for the test. All good language books can help you.

2   You need to think about how other aspects of your English study relate to your TOEFL preparation. If you are a student in a language program in the United States, you should consider how your courses in grammar, reading, writing, and listening relate to the TOEFL test. Most language schools carefully plan their courses with the demands of the TOEFL in mind. If you are taking an English course in your home country, you should also think about the ways in which your program of study relates to the TOEFL.

3   You need to remember that being a fluent speaker of English does not necessarily mean that you will get a good TOEFL score. Some students who have excellent conversational English are surprised and angry when they receive low TOEFL scores. Although good speaking ability will help you succeed in the United States, good reading and writing ability are even more important for academic success.

4   You need to remember that people who write well in English make the best scores on the TOEFL. It is difficult for some students to understand that the TOEFL tests writing ability in the Structure and Written Expression Section as well as in the Test of Written English. If you cannot write good compositions in English, you will probably not get a good TOEFL score. Learn to write well.

ii) TOEFL Tactics: Planning your program

Since you are using these practice materials at home or with a class, you are obviously very interested in getting your best score on the TOEFL. These practice materials can help you if you use them in a systematic program of study. Here are some ideas for you to consider as you plan your TOEFL preparation program:

1   You need a clear overview of the materials. You can get an overview by referring to the table of contents and by skimming through the different sections before you begin to study and periodically as you proceed through the exercises and practice tests.

2   You need to spread your study over as many weeks as possible. It is not a good idea to do a lot of studying in a short amount of time.

3   You need to study each day, on a regular basis. One hour of study on each of six days is more beneficial than six hours of study on one day.

4   You need to use all the materials for **each section**. Avoid the temptation to omit some or all of the exercises and to focus on the practice tests. The practice tests help you only if you do all the exercises that precede them, even if you think that the exercises are too easy or too difficult. If they are really easy for you, you will be able to do them quickly. If they are really difficult, you will need to do them carefully, study your errors and in some cases repeat the exercises more than once.

5   Some students find it very helpful to study with friends. If you know someone else who is preparing for the TOEFL, it might be good for the two of you to plan to study together on a regular basis. In this way you can help each other and also be more regular and systematic in your study program.

6   If you are studying with a class, it is very important for you to do your homework carefully every day. What you do at home is sometimes more important than what you do in class. You cannot benefit from the teacher's presentation unless you are prepared for the class.

iii) TOEFL Tactics: Using practice tests

1   Put your answers in the blanks. Do not write directly on the questions unless you are directed to do so.

2   Do not look at the answer key until you have finished all the questions.

3   When you compare your answers to the correct answers, mark what is wrong but do not write down the correct answers.

4   As you compare your answers to the correct answers, put a small dot (.) beside your incorrect answers. Do not erase your first answer. Instead of erasing, write your second answer beside the small dot.

5   Examine each question carefully before you mark your second answer. Allow yourself the appropriate amount of time for your second answer by calculating the number of seconds allowed for each question in the original time limit.

6   Compare your second answers with the correct answers. Again, mark your wrong second answers with another small dot. Then, answer some questions for a third time if necessary.

7   Only after three attempts at answering the question should you transfer the

correct answer from the answer key to your practice test.

8   If you mark all your answers in or near the blanks (on the left side of the paper), you can easily cover your old answers when you review the practice tests at a later date.

iv) TOEFL Tactics: Timing

1   Wear a watch when you practice and when you take a real TOEFL. Your test room may not have a clock.

2   Remember the average time per question on each section of the test. You can calculate the average time by dividing the number of minutes for a section by the number of questions in the section.

3   Budget your time carefully. You should finish a section just before the time is over. If you work too quickly or too slowly, you will not get your best score.

4   Speed can be your enemy. Students who finish the Structure and Written Expression or the Reading Comprehension and Vocabulary sections too quickly and have a lot of extra time left over rarely get good scores.

5   The TOEFL Practice Exercises in Sections 2 and 3 of this book have ideal time limits indicated. You should regard these as a goal to aim for and mark the point you reach each time you do one of these exercises in order to check your progress.

6   Remember that you can move around inside one section beginning with either type of question. Control the test; don't let the test control you.

7   Easy questions and difficult questions are mixed together. If you spend too much time on a difficult question, you may not have enough time for some easier questions that appear later on in the test.

v) TOEFL Tactics: Do you know when you know?

It is very important for you to have a clear understanding of yourself and how you are answering TOEFL questions. If you are a good language student, then you are probably very good at guessing intelligently about the meaning of written and spoken language. But do you know when you are guessing and when you are sure of an answer? Try this process on a practice test to find out whether you know when you know and when you are guessing.

1   As you answer the questions on the practice test, put a small check(ˏ) beside those answers about which you are 100 percent certain you are correct.

2   When you compare your answers with the correct answers, calculate what percentage of your "100 percent certain" answers were actually correct.

3   Are you usually correct when you are "100 percent certain" that your answers are correct?

4   You may want to repeat this process on several exercises and practice tests.

vi) TOEFL Tactics: Tricky questions

Some of the questions on the TOEFL are definitely tricky. The TOEFL writers are very clever about making all the wrong answers appear right in some way.

Some students fall for the TOEFL tricks while others do not. You need to know how often the TOEFL is tricking you into choosing the wrong answer. Try this process.

1   Put two answers in the blank beside each question. Think about each question carefully, then write your first answer followed by your second answer.

2   Always put your two answers in the same order: first answer first, and second answer second.

3   Compare your two answers with the correct answers. Count how many of your first answers were correct. Count how many of your second answers were correct. Compare these two numbers.

4   Consider these questions: Which were better — your first answers or your second answers? Why? Was the TOEFL able to trick you into choosing some wrong answers? How should you answer on a real TOEFL?

5   You may want to repeat this process on several exercises or practice tests.

vii) TOEFL Tactics: Changing answers

Some students try to finish a section of the test quickly so that they can go back and think again about the answers to some of the difficult questions. This tactic of reconsidering answers and possibly changing some of them is good for some students, but bad for others. If you ever use this answering tactic, you should check whether it is good for you by following the answering process below for the practice tests and exercises in this book.

1   Answer all the questions on the practice test in order as quickly as you can. When you find a difficult question, put a question mark (?) beside your answer.

2   Then, go back to each question mark and think about the question again. Do not erase your first answer.

3   If you think your first answer is correct, put a check (√) beside the question mark.

4   If you think that another answer is correct, do not erase your first answer. Instead of erasing, write your second answer beside the question mark.

5   Compare your answers with the correct answers. Count how many of your first answers were correct and count how many of your second answers were correct. Compare these two numbers. Which is better?

6   Consider these questions: Is it a good idea for you to change your first answer? Should you work quickly and return to difficult questions or not? Are your first answers or your second answers usually better?

7   You may want to repeat this process on other exercises or practice tests.

viii) TOEFL Tactics: Posture and performance

1   When you practice and when you take a real TOEFL, sit up straight, lean forward slightly, and keep both feet on the floor. Never lean back in the chair.

2   Sit in a straight chair at a table or desk when you practice. Do not lie on the floor or the bed, or lean back in a comfortable chair when you practice. A

position which is too comfortable will not help you learn: when you sit in a studious position, you can concentrate better.

3   Use both hands when you practice. Use your pencil hand to answer the questions. Use your other hand to mark your place on the questions.

4   Keep your eyes on the questions and answer sheet. Don't look around the room or at other people if you are working with a group. The key to answering the question is always on the page.

5   If you are working in a class or with your friends, you can ask one person to watch you while you do a practice test or exercise. The observer can tell you about your posture while you practice and can possibly give you some suggestions about improving your posture and therefore your performance.

BUILDING SKILLS FOR THE
TOEFL

Section I: Listening Comprehension

Introduction

The Listening Comprehension Section of the TOEFL tests your knowledge of **spoken English** such as might be heard in a classroom or other public place in the United States. The English is delivered at normal conversational speed by speakers who have clear North American pronunciation. The vocabulary and grammatical patterns are typical of those used by an educated speaker in a relaxed situation.

The Listening Comprehension Section is the first section of the TOEFL. Depending on the facilities available, a test center may use either a record or a tape. At centers with language laboratories, each person will listen through a pair of earphones. There are always fifty listening items organized into three groups, Parts A, B, and C, each having separate directions. It takes approximately forty minutes to complete all the items.

In all three parts, each item and question is spoken only once. The test, however, is preceded by a very complete introduction, which includes sample items from each part. It is important to pay close attention to this introduction, even if you are familiar with the format of the test. Careful listening will help you determine if your seating is satisfactory for comfortable listening. In addition, it will enable you to get accustomed to the voices of the speakers and the volume of the recording.

Part A: Similar Sentences: There are twenty items in the first part. For each item, you hear one sentence. You have about thirteen seconds to read four sentences in the test booklet and choose the written sentence that is similar in meaning to the spoken sentence. The many sight-sound confusions contained in the answers make these items difficult.

Part B: Short Conversations: The second part consists of fifteen short conversations between two speakers, usually a man and a woman. After each conversation, a third speaker asks one question about the conversation. Many different types of questions are asked, but most require you to draw conclusions from the information in the conversation. You have about thirteen seconds to read four phrases or sentences and choose the one that answers the spoken question.

Part C: Longer Conversations and Mini-Talks: This part consists of fifteen questions based on three or four selections. During the thirteen-second pause after each question, you must read four phrases or sentences and mark the answer. The **longer conversations** often take place in an academic setting such as a university library or classroom, but they may also concern some other topic. The **mini-talks**, like the longer conversations, usually last less than two minutes. They are informative talks or classroom lectures of a non-technical nature. Previous knowledge of the topics is not required in order to answer the questions. Notetaking during the talks is neither necessary nor permitted.

In the following pages, the three parts of the Listening Comprehension Section are approached through ten objectives covering specific problem areas of this section of the TOEFL. If you study these objectives systematically, you should develop an effective strategy for dealing with the Listening Comprehension questions in the actual TOEFL.

Note on using the taped exercises:
The **Objectives, Directions, and Examples** for the **Listening Comprehension** exercises in **Section 1** of this book have not been recorded. They are printed clearly at the beginning of the exercises and should be studied carefully before starting the tape, which gives the exercise number only, followed immediately by the main part of the exercise.

However, the **Listening Comprehension** sections of **Practice Tests I and II** in **Section 5** of this book have been recorded in full, including **Directions and Examples**, in order to simulate the test situation as closely as possible.

Part A: Similar Sentences

In **Part A, Similar Sentences**, you hear one sentence. You have thirteen seconds to read four sentences and choose the one that is **similar in meaning** to the sentence you heard. All four written sentences are similar to the spoken sentence in some way, but only one written sentence is similar in the right way: **similar in meaning**.

To be successful on Part A, you must focus on similarity in meaning and avoid being tricked by the similarities in grammar, sound, and vocabulary that are contained in the wrong answers.

The **correct** answer is	similar in meaning.
The **wrong** answers may be {	similar in sound. similar in vocabulary. similar in grammar.

It is important that you understand and recognize these four types of similarities. Look at the following sample question. Can you tell how each of the four answers is similar to the spoken sentence?

You hear:	[Planes have grown more popular than trains in recent years.]
You read:	(A) There are fewer planes than trains.
	(B) Traveling by train is popular.
	(C) They have owned it for three years.
	(D) Air travel is now very common.

Answer (A) is **similar in grammar** to the spoken sentence. Both are comparative sentences, but there is no similarity in meaning.

Answer (B) is **similar in vocabulary** because the words *train* and *popular* are found in both sentences, but the meaning of the two sentences is different.

Answer (C) is **similar in sound** to the spoken sentence. The words *have owned* sound like *have grown*, and *in recent years* sounds like *three years*.

Answer (D) is **correct** because it is **similar in meaning** to the spoken sentence even though it is not similar in grammar, vocabulary, or sound.

It is important to note that the correct answer may not only be similar in meaning to the spoken sentence but may be similar in grammar, vocabulary, or sound as well. Likewise, a wrong answer may be similar in more than one way, but it is not similar in the correct way, **similar in meaning**.

Exercise L-1

Objective: To determine which sentences are similar in meaning to a key sentence and which are merely similar in grammar or similar in sound.

Directions: Read the key sentence **aloud** to yourself several times. Then tell how each sentence that follows is similar to the key sentence by writing:
> **M** if it is similar in **meaning**
> **G** if it is similar in **grammar**
> **S** if it is similar in **sound**

Example:
> **key sentence:** Planes have grown more popular than trains in recent years.

> _G_   There are fewer planes than trains.

> _S_   They have owned it for three years.

> _M_   Air travel is now very common.

key sentence: Bill would have come if he'd known you were here.

_____ 1 Won't you have some, Bill?

_____ 2 Bill is not here.

_____ 3 If you were here, Bill would come.

_____ 4 Bill wants to see you.

_____ 5 Bill brought some wood.

_____ 6 Unless you're here, Bill won't come.

_____ 7 Did you hear about Bill?

_____ 8 Someone should have told Bill you were here.

_____ 9 If Bill had come, you would have known.

_____ 10 No one heard you and Bill were coming.

Exercise L-2

Objective: To determine which sentences are similar in meaning to a key sentence and which are merely similar in vocabulary or similar in sound.

Directions: Read the key sentence **aloud** to yourself several times. Then tell how each sentence that follows is similar to the key sentence by writing:
   M if it is similar in **meaning**
   V if it is similar in **vocabulary**
   S if it is similar in **sound**

Example:

   key sentence: Planes have grown more popular than trains in recent years.

   _V_ Traveling by train is popular.

   _M_ Air travel is now very common.

   _S_ They have owned it for three years.

key sentence: Sue flipped through her cookbook, looking for an easy recipe for lamb.

_____ 1 Sue was looking for her cookbook.

_____ 2 Sue was planning the menu.

_____ 3 Sue threw her book on the floor.

_____ 4 Sue didn't know how to prepare the meat.

_____ 5 Lamb is not easy to cook.

_____ 6 Sue tripped over the cookbook.

_____ 7 Sue wanted to prepare something simple.

_____ 8 Sue was through reading the book.

_____ 9 Sue received four new books.

_____ 10 Sue ripped out the recipe.

Objectives for Listening Comprehension Section

Part A: Similar Sentences

▶ 1 Derive meaning via grammatical structure.
2 Hear sounds accurately.
3 Interpret the meaning of multiple-definition words.
4 Match sounds and meaning to letter combinations.

Part B: Short Conversations

5 Identify the speakers.
6 Avoid sight-sound problems.
7 Recognize language functions.
8 Relate vocabulary to context.

Part C: Mini-Talks and Longer Conversations

9 Anticipate the topics and the questions.
10 Recognize paraphrases of words and phrases.

Objective 1: Derive Meaning via Grammatical Structure

Part A, Similar Sentences, presents spoken sentences and questions of all types. Some are short; others are long. Some are affirmative; some are negative. Some contain only one clause; some contain two or three clauses. The variety of types of spoken sentences that you might hear is large. There are, however, five types that you can reasonably expect to hear. These five types, along with some examples, are listed below in order of frequency.

1 Comparative sentences
Jack is a lot taller than I'd imagined.
This typewriter works better than the newer one.

2 Conditional sentences
If you want to get well, you'd better take your medicine every day.
Pete will never improve his speed unless he runs every day.

3 Sentences telling a sequence of events
Would you buy me some stamps on your way to the grocery store?
When the concert ended, the crowd demanded an encore.

4 Sentences of cause and result

Sam got stopped by the police because his tail light was burned out.

We moved to Texas to avoid the severe winter weather.

5 Sentences containing perfect modals

Fred might have gone to the tennis match.

We shouldn't have eaten so much ice cream.

The exercises which follow will focus on one or more of these types of sentences, both in spoken and written form. The purpose of these exercises is to help you improve your ability to **derive meaning via grammatical structure**.

Exercise L-3

Objective: To recognize whether two comparative sentences have the same meaning.

Directions: For each item, you will **hear** a comparative sentence. Then, you will **read** another comparative sentence and decide whether it has the same meaning as the comparison you heard. In the blank, write **S** if the meaning is the **same**. Write **D** if the meaning is **different**.

Example: **You hear:** [It rains less in summer than in winter.]
You read and answer: _D_ It doesn't rain as much in winter as in summer.

_____ 1 Calculators used to be less expensive than they are now.

_____ 2 Bicycles aren't quite as dangerous as motorcycles.

_____ 3 Television documentaries receive lower ratings than comedies.

_____ 4 Hand tools are much less costly to maintain than electric ones.

_____ 5 Liberal arts courses are much more popular than engineering courses.

_____ 6 Retired people usually have lower incomes than working people.

_____ 7 Late model cars don't have as many breakdowns as older models.

_____ 8 Synthetic materials aren't usually as expensive as natural materials.

_____ 9 Walking fast doesn't burn quite as many calories as running slowly.

_____ 10 Alkaline batteries last longer than ordinary batteries.

Exercise L-4

_____

Objective: To recognize restatements of comparative sentences.

Directions: For each item, you will **hear** a comparative sentence. In the blank, write the letter of the sentence that is similar in meaning to the sentence you heard.

Example: **You hear:**   [Jane's a good bit taller than her brother.]

> **You read and answer:**
>   _B_ (A) Jane's not as tall as her brother.
>   (B) Jane's brother is much shorter.

_____ 1 (A) Less water is needed for a bath.
           (B) A shower requires less water.

_____ 2 (A) Peter's older than his cousin.
           (B) His cousin is older.

_____ 3 (A) Motorcycles outnumber bicycles.
           (B) More students ride bicycles.

_____ 4 (A) They used to be popular.
           (B) They have become more popular.

_____ 5 (A) More people play tennis.
           (B) Soccer is as popular as tennis.

_____ 6 (A) George's grades are never as good as Sue's.
           (B) Sue's grades have gotten better than George's.

_____ 7 (A) Vanilla is twice as popular as chocolate.
           (B) Two chocolate cones are sold for every one of vanilla.

_____ 8 (A) They used to be happier.
           (B) Fred isn't as happy as Alice.

_____ 9 (A) Betty thought she would earn more.
           (B) Betty didn't expect to make as much.

_____ 10 (A) Nevada has more people per square mile.
            (B) Arkansas has more people per square mile.

Exercise L-5

Objective: To recognize similarities in meaning in comparative sentences.

Directions: For each item you will **hear** a sentence. In the blank, write the letter of the sentence which is similar in meaning to the comparative sentence you hear.

Example: **You hear:** ⎡It's better to complete your basic requirements in⎤
⎢your first two years than put them off until your⎥
⎣junior and senior years.⎦

You read and answer:

_*B*_ (A) It's better to wait until your junior and senior years to complete basic requirements.

(B) It's not as good to wait until your junior and senior years to complete basic requirements.

_____ 1 (A) Biology students take more math courses.
(B) Business students take more math courses.

_____ 2 (A) More people attend basketball games.
(B) Baseball games are attended by more people.

_____ 3 (A) Fraternities are becoming less popular.
(B) Fraternities are becoming more popular.

_____ 4 (A) Most students don't like French and Spanish.
(B) French and Spanish are more popular than any other foreign languages.

_____ 5 (A) No one has had tenure longer than Professor Thomas.
(B) Professor Thomas hasn't had tenure very long.

_____ 6 (A) Today's students are better prepared.
(B) Students from former years were better prepared.

_____ 7 (A) Other electives are more popular than physical education courses.
(B) No other elective attracts as many students as physical education courses.

_____ 8 (A) More students are applying now than before.
(B) The number of students applying is lower now.

_____ 9 (A) Undergraduates have the fewest privileges of all.
(B) Undergraduates have many more privileges than others.

_____ 10 (A) Tuition won't cost as much as last year.
(B) Tuition will remain about the same.

Exercise L-6

<u>Objective:</u> To interpret the meaning of some types of conditional sentences.

<u>Directions:</u> For each item, you will **hear** a sentence and **see** a statement associated with it. Write the letter **T** in the blank if the associated statement is true according to the spoken sentence. Write **F** if it is false.

> <u>Example:</u> **You hear:** [We would've been there if the baby hadn't got sick.]
>
> **You read and answer:** __T__ The baby got sick.

_____ 1 I'm on the wrestling team.

_____ 2 She didn't know her lines.

_____ 3 They didn't go on vacation.

_____ 4 She's a volunteer at the hospital.

_____ 5 I heard about your accident immediately.

_____ 6 He didn't have enough money to stay.

_____ 7 We're not satisfied with what we've done.

_____ 8 I think you should be very happy.

_____ 9 Jack is very mad.

_____ 10 I stayed home because I'm sick.

_____ 11 The train left without us.

_____ 12 I'm going to audition for the band.

_____ 13 She gets angry easily.

_____ 14 I didn't get the invitation on time.

_____ 15 He is a generous person.

Exercise L-7

<u>Objective and Directions:</u> see Exercise L-6.

_____ 1 We assumed you would be asleep.

_____ 2 We went to the museum.

_____ 3 He thinks he can find a better job.

_____ 4 We took a cab.

_____ 5 I can't call my roommate.

_____ 6 Dallas is too expensive for her.

_____ 7 Coffee makes Thelma nervous.

_____ 8 The soup needed salt.

_____ 9 I'm too tired to go out.

_____ 10 I'm going to purchase a sailboat.

_____ 11 John has been asked to do it.

_____ 12 His drinking was regarded as a problem.

_____ 13 They are not sowing.

_____ 14 I'm going to apply for the job.

_____ 15 The result is certain.

Exercise L-8

<u>Objective and Directions:</u> see Exercise L-6.

_____ 1 I was invited.

_____ 2 Bill is more talented than Tony.

_____ 3 The plan was not adopted.

_____ 4 The policemen didn't arrive.

_____ 5 He is polite.

_____ 6 They did cooperate.

_____ 7 He realized the consequences.

_____ 8 He didn't do it the way I did it.

_____ 9 You haven't tried it.

_____ 10 She told me.

_____ 11 The idea of buying occurred to him.

_____ 12 Elizabeth is not as tall as Mary.

_____ 13 John arrived.

_____ 14 I think it would be good to reconsider.

_____ 15 He is my friend.

Exercise L-9

Objective: To determine the sequence of events in a sentence by interpreting time signal words and grammatical structures.

Directions: For each item, you will **hear** a sentence. In the blank, write the letter, (A) or (B), which corresponds to the action which occurred first or is likely to occur first.

Example: **You hear:** [Go straight for two blocks before turning left.]

You read and answer: _B_ (A) turning left
(B) going straight

The correct answer is (B) because this action is likely to occur first.

_____ 1	(A) making a call		_____ 12	(A) leaving	
	(B) returning home			(B) ending	
_____ 2	(A) seeing Mike		_____ 13	(A) finishing a degree	
	(B) starting school			(B) starting a degree	
_____ 3	(A) getting married		_____ 14	(A) finishing the talk	
	(B) living in Texas			(B) having coffee	
_____ 4	(A) visiting		_____ 15	(A) wrapping	
	(B) shopping			(B) going to the post office	
_____ 5	(A) feeling good		_____ 16	(A) the ending of the war	
	(B) sleeping			(B) leaving England	
_____ 6	(A) leaving		_____ 17	(A) opening a book	
	(B) discussing			(B) making coffee	
_____ 7	(A) arriving		_____ 18	(A) going out	
	(B) going to bed			(B) finishing homework	
_____ 8	(A) ringing		_____ 19	(A) causing trouble	
	(B) leaving			(B) reaching second birthday	
_____ 9	(A) graduating		_____ 20	(A) sorting mail	
	(B) reading			(B) being promoted	
_____ 10	(A) playing golf		_____ 21	(A) improving my game	
	(B) playing tennis			(B) taking lessons	
_____ 11	(A) having lunch		_____ 22	(A) meeting you	
	(B) going to the lab			(B) putting the cake in the oven	

_____ 23 (A) completing requirements
          (B) registering

_____ 24 (A) receiving the money
          (B) returning

_____ 25 (A) going to the movies five times
          (B) beginning of the month

Exercise L-10

<u>Objective and Directions:</u> see Exercise L-9.

_____ 1 (A) talking with me
          (B) accepting an offer

_____ 2 (A) completing the typing
          (B) going to the post office

_____ 3 (A) working at this job
          (B) meeting interesting people

_____ 4 (A) buying new clothes
          (B) losing 20 pounds

_____ 5 (A) hearing from you
          (B) staying here

_____ 6 (A) bell ringing
          (B) leaving

_____ 7 (A) going to a job interview
          (B) getting a haircut

_____ 8 (A) asking her out
          (B) your breaking up with her

_____ 9 (A) returning home
          (B) receiving the mail

_____ 10 (A) taking this road
          (B) being directed by police

_____ 11 (A) running a mile
          (B) exercising

_____ 12 (A) not getting into college
          (B) joining the armed services

_____ 13　(A)　looking at new houses
　　　　(B)　having enough money for a down payment

_____ 14　(A)　starting to rain
　　　　(B)　finding the game has changed

_____ 15　(A)　repairing the washer
　　　　(B)　greeting the repairman

_____ 16　(A)　graduating
　　　　(B)　visiting parents every weekend

_____ 17　(A)　borrowing the novel
　　　　(B)　getting the novel back from Donna

_____ 18　(A)　talking to your father
　　　　(B)　leaving

_____ 19　(A)　deadline passing
　　　　(B)　submitting their application

_____ 20　(A)　reading more novels
　　　　(B)　making better grades

_____ 21　(A)　hearing the alarm
　　　　(B)　falling asleep

_____ 22　(A)　coming home
　　　　(B)　getting dark

_____ 23　(A)　hearing the bell ring
　　　　(B)　completing the test

_____ 24　(A)　deciding on the menu
　　　　(B)　going to the supermarket

_____ 25　(A)　Milton's leaving the station
　　　　(B)　Hodge's escaping

Exercise L-11

Objective: To identify the cause in a cause and result sentence.

Directions: For each item, you will **hear** a sentence expressing a cause and result. In the blank, write the letter, (A) or (B), which corresponds to the **cause**.

Example: **You hear:** ⎡The harsh weather last year was the result of⎤
⎣turbulence in the upper atmosphere.⎦

You read and answer: _A_ (A) turbulence in the upper
atmosphere
(B) harsh weather last year

The correct answer is (A), since turbulence in the upper atmosphere caused the harsh weather.

_____ 1 (A) his appearance
(B) his diet

_____ 2 (A) flooding
(B) late snows

_____ 3 (A) overripe fruit
(B) Animals become intoxicated.

_____ 4 (A) feel flabby
(B) begin an exercise program

_____ 5 (A) damaging rumors
(B) malicious gossip

_____ 6 (A) She stopped dating him.
(B) He drank too much.

_____ 7 (A) drilled in the southeastern corner
(B) found oil

_____ 8 (A) overexposure to the sun
(B) skin rash

_____ 9 (A) nervousness
(B) demanding surveillance

_____ 10 (A) put extra locks on
(B) Several neighbor's homes had been burglarized.

_____ 11 (A) crippling paralysis
(B) disease

_____ 12 (A) police enquiries
        (B) man taken into custody

_____ 13 (A) became friends with board members
        (B) admitted to the club

_____ 14 (A) Wankler Effect
        (B) phenomenon

_____ 15 (A) undisciplined attitude
        (B) problem

_____ 16 (A) became more popular
        (B) made into a movie

_____ 17 (A) certain diets
        (B) high cholesterol levels

_____ 18 (A) prolonged fasting
        (B) death

_____ 19 (A) automation
        (B) lost his job

_____ 20 (A) drowsiness or nausea
        (B) failure to follow the instructions

Exercise L-12

Objective: To identify the result in a cause and result sentence.

Directions: For each item, you will **hear** a sentence expressing a cause and result. In the blank, write the letter, (A) or (B), which corresponds to the **result**.

Example: **You hear:** ⎡The team's victory in the divisional playoffs was⎤
⎢due to their fitness and to the skill of the quarter-⎥
⎣back.⎦

You read and answer: *B* (A) fitness and skill of the quarterback
(B) team's victory in the divisional playoffs

The correct answer is (B), since the result was the team's victory.

_____ 1 (A) The waiter was rude.
(B) I haven't gone there again.

_____ 2 (A) out of breath
(B) stopped running

_____ 3 (A) the prevalence of high interest rates
(B) no immediate improvement

_____ 4 (A) The dog bit their son.
(B) They filed a formal complaint.

_____ 5 (A) sold his car
(B) paid for his operation

_____ 6 (A) overwork and poor health care
(B) nervous collapse

_____ 7 (A) a rise in the price of orange juice
(B) harsh frosts in Florida

_____ 8 (A) a vigorous advertising campaign
(B) increased sales

_____ 9 (A) a number of diseases
(B) smoking

_____ 10 (A) knocking in the engine
(B) using the wrong grade of gasoline

_____ 11 (A) the complaint
        (B) increased vigilance

_____ 12 (A) a stronger cardiovascular system
        (B) regular aerobic exercise

_____ 13 (A) The earthquake started.
        (B) Everyone rushed out of their houses.

_____ 14 (A) adverse living conditions
        (B) physical adaptations

_____ 15 (A) viewing evidence
        (B) a case against the defendant

_____ 16 (A) condensation
        (B) lower temperatures

_____ 17 (A) a real recovery
        (B) sacrifice and hard work

_____ 18 (A) warping
        (B) dampness in the wood

_____ 19 (A) dependence
        (B) unsupervised use

_____ 20 (A) lack of self-confidence
        (B) chronic skin infections

Exercise L-13

Objective: To interpret the meaning of sentences containing perfect modals.

Directions: For each item, you will **hear** a sentence and **see** a statement associated with it. In the blank, write the letter **T** if the associated statement is true according to the sentence you heard; write **F** if it is false.

Example: **You hear:** [I might have gone if you'd asked me.]

        You read and answer: _T_ It's possible I would've gone if I'd been invited.

_____ 1 I'm confident John got a raise.

_____ 2 I didn't do that.

_____ 3 Karen won an Olympic gold medal.

_____ 4 She realized that Joe wouldn't do it.

19

_____ 5 It's possible that I know him.

_____ 6 It probably wasn't difficult.

_____ 7 It possibly wasn't the first time.

_____ 8 Somebody helped them.

_____ 9 Perhaps you explained it.

_____ 10 She did consider it.

_____ 11 It's possible he didn't think of that.

_____ 12 It's fairly likely that you were a beautiful baby.

_____ 13 Perhaps I would have.

_____ 14 No one knows if it would've worked.

_____ 15 They were lucky this time.

Exercise L-14

<u>Objective and Directions:</u> see Exercise L-13.

_____ 1 It's a good thing you called the police.

_____ 2 Somebody helped me carry the desk.

_____ 3 It was obviously the right color.

_____ 4 I did go.

_____ 5 Jennifer rode the horse too fast.

_____ 6 Their behavior was indistinguishable from everybody else's.

_____ 7 We definitely had an enjoyable evening.

_____ 8 I'm sure she was very upset.

_____ 9 He didn't mind being reminded of his father's death.

_____ 10 Perhaps taking the job was a bad idea.

_____ 11 With more information, he would possibly have thought it over.

_____ 12 The price didn't bother the prince.

_____ 13 I needed your help to finish it.

_____ 14 They've got the best seats in the place.

_____ 15 Tim hasn't learned a thing in the last six months.

Objectives for Listening Comprehension Section

Part A: Similar Sentences

    1 Derive meaning via grammatical structure.
▶ 2 Hear sounds accurately.
    3 Interpret the meaning of multiple-definition words.
    4 Match sounds and meaning to letter combinations.

Part B: Short Conversations

    5 Identify the speakers.
    6 Avoid sight-sound problems.
    7 Recognize language functions.
    8 Relate vocabulary to context.

Part C: Mini-Talks and Longer Conversations

    9 Anticipate the topics and the questions.
  10 Recognize paraphrases of words and phrases.

Objective 2: Hear Sounds Accurately

You are probably aware from your listening experience, both while studying English and while using English in the real world, that it is possible to grasp the main idea of what someone says without understanding all the words. One reason for this is that each sentence you hear is spoken within the context of a particular situation. It is this context that enables you to guess at what is said with great accuracy. Another reason that the meaning may be clear, even when the words and sounds are not, is that a speaker often repeats or restates key words and ideas.

In Part A of the TOEFL listening comprehension, however, sentences are spoken **only once** and **out of context**. The sentences you hear do not relate to any particular situation and are not part of a longer exchange. There is no repetition of important words or phrases. Therefore, to catch the meaning, you need to listen much more carefully to each sentence in Part A than you would need to if you encountered the same sentence in a normal conversation.

Although your primary focus must always be on meaning, you need to hear individual sounds and words accurately. If you misunderstand one key word in the spoken sentence, you may be led to choose one of the wrong answers. The wrong answers are full of sight-sound confusions and are purposefully misleading and tricky.

The exercises that follow will give you practice in discriminating between words with similar sounds. Many of the words in these exercises will be familiar to you, but you will encounter others that you have never seen or whose meaning you do not know. Before beginning an exercise, examine the words carefully and use a dictionary to find the meaning of any unfamiliar ones.

**Note on using Exercises L-15 through L-50:

Each of the exercises for Objective 2 (L-15 through L-50) has two parts, Set A and Set B. **The key words in each Set A exercise correspond to the related words and phrases in the Set B exercise of the same number, but their order is not necessarily the same.** For example, **Exercise L-17 Set A** question 4, (A) jam (B) gem, corresponds to Exercise L-17 Set B question 4, (A) marmalade (B) jewel.

There is only **one exercise on tape called Exercise L-17.** The students will listen to the taped exercise **two times, once for Set A** and **again for Set B**.

For review purposes, however, the teacher can create a completely different exercise for the students by reading aloud from the **tapescript** and randomly changing some of the key words. The tapescript for this example (Exercise L-17, question 4) says *That jam is expensive. (gem)* thus indicating the alternative exercise.

First exercise, the tape: [That jam is expensive.]

Further exercise, the teacher: [That gem is expensive.]

Many of the words in these exercises are common, everyday words that will be familiar to the students. All students, however, will encounter new words in the exercises. Students should be encouraged to look up in a dictionary any unfamiliar words they find in a Set A exercise, and study these words before attempting the corresponding Set B exercise. *The Heritage Illustrated Dictionary of The English Language, International Edition* (published by American Heritage Publishing Co., Inc. and Houghton Mifflin) was used as the major source for verification of pronunciation and meaning.

Also, the students need to know that the related words or phrases in the Set B exercises are not meant to be exact synonyms for the words they will hear, nor can they always be substituted for the key words in the sentences they hear. The words are related in some way, or are synonyms.

The following chart shows the interrelationship of these exercises, giving examples of the sound confusions dealt with. Exercises L-15 through L-29 concentrate on **vowel** distinctions which form minimal pairs, and these are extended in Exercises L-46 through L-50, as shown on the chart. Exercises L-30 through L-45, on the other hand, deal with **consonant** distinctions which form minimal pairs. Using the chart, you may wish to use the exercises in a sequence that is different from the one in this book.

	SET A	SET B
L-15	peel/pill	skin/capsule
L-16	tin/ten	almost a dozen/metal
L-17	man/men	adult male/adult males
L-18	cup/cap	mug/headgear
L-19	hot/hat	burning/headwear
L-20	knot/nut	tree fruit/tie up
L-21	bat/bought	purchased/hit
L-22	sew/saw	mend/looked
L-23	the/though	even if/(def. article)
L-24	bird/board	feathered animal/plank
L-25	beast/burst	animal/break
L-26	burn/barn	farm building/fire wound
L-27	pray/pry	address a deity/snoop
L-28	tie/toy	cravat/plaything
L-29	toy/toe	plaything/digit of foot
L-30	pin/bin	container/needle
L-31	tin/bin	noise/metal
L-32	cold/gold	precious metal/low temperature
L-33	busing/buzzing	transportation/noise
L-34	sheep/cheap	inexpensive/animal
L-35	cheep/jeep	car/noise
L-36	fine/vine	punishment/plant
L-37	bet/vet	veterinary surgeon/wager
L-38	mouse/mouth	animal/opening
L-39	load/road	burden/way
L-40	fry/fly	pilot/cook
L-41	day/they	those (people)/dawn
L-42	win/wing	victory/part of bird
L-43	stings/stinks	hurts/smells
L-44	vine/wine	plant/drink
L-45	yam/jam	sweet potato/marmalade

	SET A	SET B
L-46	seal/sill/Sal/sell	girl's name/purvey/ledge/stick
L-47	cap/cop/cup	small container/policeman/headgear
L-48	bad/bawd/bode/bud	begin to grow/augur/prostitute/unfortunate
L-49	borne/bean/burn/barn	kept/farm building/vegetable/incinerate
L-50	bay/buy/boy/bow	lad/curved weapon/purchase/reddish brown

Exercises L-15 through L-29, Set A

Exercise L-15, Set A

Objective: To identify words heard in a sentence on the basis of sound.

Directions: For each item, you will **see** two words and you will **hear** a sentence which contains one of the words. In the blank, write the letter, (A) or (B), of the word you have heard in the sentence. (**See note** on page 22.)

Example: **You hear:** [Did you get a good slip?]

You read and answer: __A__ (A) slip
(B) sleep

____ 1	(A) peel	(B) pill	____ 6	(A) seeping	(B) sipping
____ 2	(A) ship	(B) sheep	____ 7	(A) cheeks	(B) chicks
____ 3	(A) beat	(B) bit	____ 8	(A) bins	(B) beans
____ 4	(A) hills	(B) heels	____ 9	(A) leap	(B) lip
____ 5	(A) hitting	(B) heating	____ 10	(A) bid	(B) bead

Exercise L-16, Set A

Objective and Directions: see Exercise L-15, Set A.

____ 1	(A) tin	(B) ten	____ 6	(A) den	(B) din
____ 2	(A) well	(B) will	____ 7	(A) penned	(B) pinned
____ 3	(A) chicks	(B) checks	____ 8	(A) wrist	(B) rest
____ 4	(A) felled	(B) filled	____ 9	(A) tilling	(B) telling
____ 5	(A) bill	(B) bell	____ 10	(A) bet	(B) bit

Exercise L-17, Set A

Objective and Directions: see Exercise L-15, Set A.

_____ 1 (A) man
     (B) men

_____ 6 (A) head
     (B) had

_____ 2 (A) ten
     (B) tan

_____ 7 (A) pen
     (B) pan

_____ 3 (A) said
     (B) sad

_____ 8 (A) bet
     (B) bat

_____ 4 (A) jam
     (B) gem

_____ 9 (A) slapped
     (B) slept

_____ 5 (A) sanding
     (B) sending

_____ 10 (A) landing
     (B) lending

Exercise L-18, Set A

Objective and Directions: see Exercise L-15, Set A.

_____ 1 (A) cup
     (B) cap

_____ 6 (A) bus
     (B) bass

_____ 2 (A) hat
     (B) hut

_____ 7 (A) gnats
     (B) nuts

_____ 3 (A) bag
     (B) bug

_____ 8 (A) sudden
     (B) sadden

_____ 4 (A) brash
     (B) brush

_____ 9 (A) mat
     (B) mutt

_____ 5 (A) luck
     (B) lack

_____ 10 (A) lamp
     (B) lump

Exercise L-19, Set A

Objective and Directions: see Exercise L-15, Set A.

_____ 1 (A) hot
     (B) hat

_____ 3 (A) sock
     (B) sack

_____ 2 (A) cat
     (B) cot

_____ 4 (A) topped
     (B) tapped

_____ 5 (A) backs
     (B) box

_____ 8 (A) lock
     (B) lack

_____ 6 (A) clack
     (B) clock

_____ 9 (A) caps
     (B) cops

_____ 7 (A) lost
     (B) last

_____ 10 (A) knack
     (B) knock

Exercise L-20, Set A

Objective and Directions: see Exercise L-15, Set A.

_____ 1 (A) knot
     (B) nut

_____ 6 (A) putt
     (B) pot

_____ 2 (A) cud
     (B) cod

_____ 7 (A) doll
     (B) dull

_____ 3 (A) boss
     (B) bus

_____ 8 (A) duck
     (B) dock

_____ 4 (A) cut
     (B) cot

_____ 9 (A) long
     (B) lung

_____ 5 (A) luck
     (B) lock

_____ 10 (A) robbed
     (B) rubbed

Exercise L-21, Set A

Objective and Directions: see Exercise L-15, Set A.

_____ 1 (A) bat
     (B) bought

_____ 6 (A) spawned
     (B) spanned

_____ 2 (A) sat
     (B) sought

_____ 7 (A) facet
     (B) faucet

_____ 3 (A) pawn
     (B) pan

_____ 8 (A) fawn
     (B) fan

_____ 4 (A) loss
     (B) lass

_____ 9 (A) clad
     (B) clawed

_____ 5 (A) crass
     (B) cross

_____ 10 (A) bran
     (B) brawn

Exercise L-22, Set A

<u>Objective and Directions:</u> see Exercise L-15, Set A.

_____ 1 (A) sew   _____ 6 (A) naught
    (B) saw   (B) note

_____ 2 (A) bought   _____ 7 (A) wrought
    (B) boat   (B) wrote

_____ 3 (A) cold   _____ 8 (A) owed
    (B) called   (B) awed

_____ 4 (A) gnaw   _____ 9 (A) law
    (B) know   (B) low

_____ 5 (A) roe   _____ 10 (A) coast
    (B) raw   (B) cost

Exercise L-23, Set A

<u>Objective and Directions:</u> see Exercise L-15, Set A.

_____ 1 (A) the   _____ 6 (A) humming
    (B) though   (B) homing

_____ 2 (A) bun   _____ 7 (A) rub
    (B) bone   (B) robe

_____ 3 (A) nut   _____ 8 (A) puck
    (B) note   (B) poke

_____ 4 (A) comb   _____ 9 (A) hole
    (B) come   (B) hull

_____ 5 (A) coal   _____ 10 (A) boat
    (B) cull   (B) butt

Exercise L-24, Set A

<u>Objective and Directions:</u> see Exercise L-15, Set A.

_____ 1 (A) bird   _____ 3 (A) sore
    (B) board   (B) sir

_____ 2 (A) fur   _____ 4 (A) herb
    (B) fore   (B) orb

_____ 5 (A) herd
  (B) hoard

_____ 8 (A) store
  (B) stir

_____ 6 (A) word
  (B) ward

_____ 9 (A) curds
  (B) cords

_____ 7 (A) warm
  (B) worm

_____ 10 (A) core
  (B) cur

Exercise L-25, Set A

Objective and Directions: see Exercise L-15, Set A.

_____ 1 (A) beast
  (B) burst

_____ 6 (A) teams
  (B) terms

_____ 2 (A) bead
  (B) bird

_____ 7 (A) fur
  (B) fee

_____ 3 (A) heard
  (B) heed

_____ 8 (A) burrs
  (B) bees

_____ 4 (A) lurking
  (B) leaking

_____ 9 (A) shirt
  (B) sheet

_____ 5 (A) word
  (B) weed

_____ 10 (A) week
  (B) work

Exercise L-26, Set A

Objective and Directions: see Exercise L-15, Set A.

_____ 1 (A) burn
  (B) barn

_____ 6 (A) car
  (B) cur

_____ 2 (A) curt
  (B) cart

_____ 7 (A) bard
  (B) bird

_____ 3 (A) dart
  (B) dirt

_____ 8 (A) carve
  (B) curve

_____ 4 (A) hurts
  (B) hearts

_____ 9 (A) fir
  (B) far

_____ 5 (A) firm
  (B) farm

_____ 10 (A) star
  (B) stir

Exercise L-27, Set A

Objective and Directions: see Exercise L-15, Set A.

_____ 1 (A) pray   _____ 6 (A) "why"
    (B) pry   (B) way

_____ 2 (A) plate   _____ 7 (A) white
    (B) plight   (B) wait

_____ 3 (A) lie   _____ 8 (A) tray
    (B) lay   (B) try

_____ 4 (A) pay   _____ 9 (A) flying
    (B) pie   (B) flaying

_____ 5 (A) say   _____ 10 (A) high
    (B) sigh   (B) hay

Exercise L-28, Set A

Objective and Directions: see Exercise L-15, Set A.

_____ 1 (A) tie   _____ 6 (A) foil
    (B) toy   (B) file

_____ 2 (A) soy   _____ 7 (A) tiling
    (B) sigh   (B) toiling

_____ 3 (A) Roy   _____ 8 (A) bile
    (B) rye   (B) boil

_____ 4 (A) isle   _____ 9 (A) points
    (B) oil   (B) pints

_____ 5 (A) vice   _____ 10 (A) poise
    (B) voice   (B) pies

Exercise L-29, Set A

Objective and Directions: see Exericse L-15, Set A.

_____ 1 (A) toy   _____ 3 (A) coal
    (B) toe   (B) coil

_____ 2 (A) bowl   _____ 4 (A) soil
    (B) boil   (B) soul

_____ 5 (A) toil   _____ 8 (A) roll
       (B) toll   (B) royal

_____ 6 (A) foal   _____ 9 (A) bow
       (B) foil   (B) boy

_____ 7 (A) buoyed   _____ 10 (A) loins
       (B) bode   (B) loans

Exercises L-15 through L-29, Set B

Exercise L-15, Set B

Objective: To identify the meaning of a word heard in a sentence by selecting a closely related word or synonym.

Directions: For each item, you will **see** two words or phrases and you will **hear** one sentence. In the blank, write the letter, (A) or (B), of the word or phrase more closely paralleling a word that you have heard in the sentence. (****See note** on page 22.)

   Example: **You hear:** [Did you get a good slip?]

           You read and answer: __A__ (A) undergarment
                              (B) rest

_____ 1 (A) skin   _____ 6 (A) leaking
       (B) capsule   (B) drinking

_____ 2 (A) boat   _____ 7 (A) baby chickens
       (B) animal   (B) parts of faces

_____ 3 (A) hit   _____ 8 (A) food
       (B) chomped   (B) containers

_____ 4 (A) parts of shoes   _____ 9 (A) part of the mouth
       (B) small mountains   (B) jump

_____ 5 (A) warming   _____ 10 (A) round ornament
       (B) striking   (B) offer

Exercise L-16, Set B

Objective and Directions: see Exercise L-15, Set B.

_____ 1 (A) almost a dozen
       (B) metal

_____ 2 (A) testament
       (B) water hole

_____ 3 (A) baby chickens
       (B) validations

_____ 4 (A) made full
       (B) knocked down

_____ 5 (A) object that rings
       (B) check

_____ 6 (A) noise
       (B) study

_____ 7 (A) affixed
       (B) wrote

_____ 8 (A) lower arm joint
       (B) remainder

_____ 9 (A) plowing
       (B) talking

_____ 10 (A) gambled
       (B) cut with teeth

Exercise L-17, Set B

Objective and Directions: see Exercise L-15, Set B.

_____ 1 (A) adult males
       (B) adult male

_____ 2 (A) ten-dollar bill
       (B) browned skin

_____ 3 (A) unhappy
       (B) reputed

_____ 4 (A) marmalade
       (B) jewel

_____ 5 (A) delivering
       (B) polishing

_____ 6 (A) preside over
       (B) owned

_____ 7 (A) writing instrument
       (B) cooking utensil

_____ 8 (A) wager
       (B) be the batter

_____ 9 (A) dozed
       (B) struck

_____ 10 (A) bringing down
       (B) loaning

Exercise L-18, Set B

Objective and Directions: see Exercise L-15, Set B.

_____ 1 (A) mug
       (B) headgear

_____ 2 (A) shack
       (B) headgear

_____ 3 (A) purse
       (B) insect

_____ 4 (A) brooms and such
       (B) bold

——— 5 (A) fortune ——— 8 (A) make unhappy
      (B) shortage   (B) abrupt

——— 6 (A) vehicle ——— 9 (A) mongrel
      (B) fish   (B) floor covering

——— 7 (A) tree fruits ——— 10 (A) light fixture
      (B) insects   (B) swelling

Exercise L-19, Set B

<u>Objective and Directions:</u> see Exercise L-15, Set B.

——— 1 (A) burning ——— 6 (A) timepiece
      (B) headwear   (B) abrupt sound

——— 2 (A) kitten ——— 7 (A) at the end
      (B) bed   (B) missing

——— 3 (A) stocking ——— 8 (A) secure
      (B) bag   (B) don't have

——— 4 (A) outdid ——— 9 (A) headgear
      (B) struck gently   (B) police

——— 5 (A) rears ——— 10 (A) rap
      (B) container   (B) talent

Exercise L-20, Set B

<u>Objective and Directions:</u> see Exercise L-15, Set B.

——— 1 (A) tree fruit ——— 6 (A) golf stroke
      (B) tied up cord   (B) container

——— 2 (A) chewing quid ——— 7 (A) toy
      (B) marine fish   (B) boring

——— 3 (A) chief ——— 8 (A) pier
      (B) vehicle   (B) bird

——— 4 (A) bed ——— 9 (A) lengthy
      (B) incision   (B) breathing organ

——— 5 (A) fastener ——— 10 (A) polished
      (B) fortune   (B) stole

Exercise L-21, Set B

Objective and Directions: see Exercise L-15, Set B.

_____ 1 (A) purchased
     (B) hit

_____ 2 (A) put
     (B) looked for

_____ 3 (A) cooking utensil
     (B) hock

_____ 4 (A) girl
     (B) deficit

_____ 5 (A) vulgar
     (B) irritable

_____ 6 (A) engendered
     (B) embraced

_____ 7 (A) aspect
     (B) tap

_____ 8 (A) young deer
     (B) admirer

_____ 9 (A) clothed
     (B) with claws

_____ 10 (A) muscle
     (B) cereal

Exercise L-22, Set B

Objective and Directions: see Exercise L-15, Set B.

_____ 1 (A) mend
     (B) looked at

_____ 2 (A) ship
     (B) bribed

_____ 3 (A) chilly
     (B) summoned

_____ 4 (A) understand
     (B) chew

_____ 5 (A) uncooked
     (B) eggs

_____ 6 (A) letter
     (B) zero

_____ 7 (A) made
     (B) inscribed

_____ 8 (A) impressed
     (B) creditors (of)

_____ 9 (A) legal
     (B) not high

_____ 10 (A) expense
     (B) shoreline

Exercise L-23, Set B

Objective and Directions: see Exercise L-15, Set B.

_____ 1 (A) even if
     (B) (definite article)

_____ 2 (A) part of skeleton
     (B) bread roll

_____ 3 (A) letter
     (B) tree fruit

_____ 4 (A) arrange hair
     (B) visit

_____ 5 (A) fossil fuel
    (B) item eliminated

_____ 6 (A) birds that return to
    their coop
    (B) birds that are tiny and
    colorful

_____ 7 (A) garment
    (B) massage

_____ 8 (A) hockey equipment
    (B) punch

_____ 9 (A) outer shell
    (B) opening

_____ 10 (A) ship
    (B) stub

Exercise L-24, Set B

Objective and Directions: see Exercise L-15, Set B.

_____ 1 (A) feathered animal
    (B) plank

_____ 2 (A) front
    (B) animal hair

_____ 3 (A) lesion
    (B) (form of address)

_____ 4 (A) sphere
    (B) plant

_____ 5 (A) drive
    (B) accumulate

_____ 6 (A) district
    (B) promise

_____ 7 (A) wriggle
    (B) make hotter

_____ 8 (A) put away
    (B) mix

_____ 9 (A) small ropes
    (B) coagulated milk

_____ 10 (A) apple center
    (B) dog

Exercise L-25, Set B

Objective and Directions: see Exercise L-15, Set B.

_____ 1 (A) animal
    (B) break

_____ 2 (A) feathered animal
    (B) round ornament

_____ 3 (A) follow
    (B) perceived

_____ 4 (A) dripping
    (B) lying in wait

_____ 5 (A) plant
    (B) utterance

_____ 6 (A) groups of players
    (B) semesters

_____ 7 (A) animal hair
    (B) charge

_____ 8 (A) insects
    (B) prickly plant

_____ 9 (A) garment
    (B) bedcover

_____ 10 (A) task
    (B) seven days

Exercise L-26, Set B

Objective and Directions: see Exercise L-15, Set B.

_____ 1 (A) farm building
     (B) fire wound

_____ 2 (A) wagon
     (B) uncommunicative

_____ 3 (A) earth
     (B) arrow

_____ 4 (A) injuries
     (B) bodily organ

_____ 5 (A) ranch
     (B) company

_____ 6 (A) dog
     (B) vehicle

_____ 7 (A) feathered animal
     (B) poet

_____ 8 (A) bend
     (B) cut

_____ 9 (A) tree
     (B) distant

_____ 10 (A) upheaval
     (B) heavenly body

Exercise L-27, Set B

Objective and Directions: see Exercise L-15, Set B.

_____ 1 (A) address a deity
     (B) snoop

_____ 2 (A) shallow dish
     (B) difficult condition

_____ 3 (A) prevaricate
     (B) rested

_____ 4 (A) salary
     (B) pastry

_____ 5 (A) speak
     (B) exhale audibly

_____ 6 (A) reason
     (B) route

_____ 7 (A) uncolored
     (B) delay

_____ 8 (A) attempt
     (B) serving utensil

_____ 9 (A) skinning
     (B) airborne

_____ 10 (A) upper
     (B) grass

Exercise L-28, Set B

Objective and Directions: see Exercise L-15, Set B.

_____ 1 (A) cravat
     (B) plaything

_____ 2 (A) exhale audibly
     (B) sauce

_____ 3 (A) (man's name)
     (B) bread

_____ 4 (A) petroleum
     (B) small island

_____ 5 (A) clamp
        (B) speaking

_____ 8 (A) temper
        (B) large pimple

_____ 6 (A) steel tool
        (B) sword

_____ 9 (A) tankards
        (B) ideas

_____ 7 (A) shingles
        (B) working

_____ 10 (A) pastries
         (B) composure

Exercise L-29, Set B

Objective and Directions: see Exercise L-15, Set B.

_____ 1 (A) plaything
        (B) digit of foot

_____ 6 (A) sword
        (B) young horse

_____ 2 (A) roll
        (B) clean in hot water

_____ 7 (A) augured
        (B) floated

_____ 3 (A) fossil fuel
        (B) spiral

_____ 8 (A) monarch
        (B) bread

_____ 4 (A) vital core
        (B) land

_____ 9. (A) type of weapon
         (B) lad

_____ 5 (A) work
        (B) charge

_____ 10 (A) borrowings
         (B) thighs and groin

Exercises L-30 through L-45, Set A

Exercise L-30, Set A

Objective: To identify words heard in a sentence on the basis of sound.

Directions: For each item, you will **see** two words and you will **hear** a sentence which contains one of the words. In the blank, write the letter, (A) or (B), of the word you have heard in the sentence. (****See note** on page 22.)

Example: **You hear:** [If we tried it, I'm sure it would work.]

You read and answer: _A_ (A) tried
                               (B) dried

_____ 1 (A) pin
        (B) bin

_____ 3 (A) post
        (B) boast

_____ 2 (A) bear
        (B) pear

_____ 4 (A) pie
        (B) buy

_____ 5 (A) cub
     (B) cup

_____ 6 (A) cap
     (B) cab

_____ 7 (A) big
     (B) pig

_____ 8 (A) back
     (B) pack

_____ 9 (A) peaches
     (B) beaches

_____ 10 (A) putter
     (B) butter

Exercise L-31, Set A

Objective and Directions: see Exercise L-30, Set A.

_____ 1 (A) tin
     (B) din

_____ 2 (A) teens
     (B) deans

_____ 3 (A) dent
     (B) tent

_____ 4 (A) coat
     (B) code

_____ 5 (A) let
     (B) led

_____ 6 (A) fat
     (B) fad

_____ 7 (A) drunk
     (B) trunk

_____ 8 (A) drain
     (B) train

_____ 9 (A) write
     (B) ride

_____ 10 (A) cards
     (B) carts

Exercise L-32, Set A

Objective and Directions: see Exercise L-30, Set A.

_____ 1 (A) cold
     (B) gold

_____ 2 (A) goat
     (B) coat

_____ 3 (A) girl
     (B) curl

_____ 4 (A) class
     (B) glass

_____ 5 (A) bag
     (B) back

_____ 6 (A) clocks
     (B) clogs

_____ 7 (A) frock
     (B) frog

_____ 8 (A) glue
     (B) clue

_____ 9 (A) dogs
     (B) docks

_____ 10 (A) cane
     (B) gain

Exercise L-33, Set A

<u>Objective and Directions:</u> see Exercise L-30, Set A.

_____ 1 (A) busing
          (B) buzzing

_____ 2 (A) piece
          (B) peas

_____ 3 (A) price
          (B) prize

_____ 4 (A) pens
          (B) pence

_____ 5 (A) his
          (B) hiss

_____ 6 (A) lose
          (B) loose

_____ 7 (A) sip
          (B) zip

_____ 8 (A) noose
          (B) news

_____ 9 (A) lies
          (B) lice

_____ 10 (A) spies
          (B) spice

Exercise L-34, Set A

<u>Objective and Directions:</u> see Exercise L-30, Set A.

_____ 1 (A) sheep
          (B) cheap

_____ 2 (A) chewing
          (B) shoeing

_____ 3 (A) ships
          (B) chips

_____ 4 (A) cheat
          (B) sheet

_____ 5 (A) chops
          (B) shops

_____ 6 (A) wash
          (B) watch

_____ 7 (A) witches
          (B) wishes

_____ 8 (A) sherry
          (B) cherry

_____ 9 (A) cash
          (B) catch

_____ 10 (A) match
          (B) mash

Exercise L-35, Set A

<u>Objective and Directions:</u> see Exercise L-30, Set A.

_____ 1 (A) cheep
          (B) jeep

_____ 2 (A) joking
          (B) choking

_____ 3 (A) gin
          (B) chin

_____ 4 (A) large
          (B) larch

—— 5 (A) H
(B) age

—— 6 (A) jeering
(B) cheering

—— 7 (A) britches
(B) bridges

—— 8 (A) etch
(B) edge

—— 9 (A) jar
(B) char

—— 10 (A) lunch
(B) lunge

Exercise L-36, Set A

<u>Objective and Directions:</u> see Exercise L-30, Set A.

—— 1 (A) fine
(B) vine

—— 2 (A) feel
(B) veal

—— 3 (A) veiled
(B) failed

—— 4 (A) view
(B) few

—— 5 (A) leaf
(B) leave

—— 6 (A) vat
(B) fat

—— 7 (A) van
(B) fan

—— 8 (A) fast
(B) vast

—— 9 (A) fowls
(B) vowels

—— 10 (A) very
(B) ferry

Exercise L-37, Set A

<u>Objective and Directions:</u> see Exercise L-30, Set A.

—— 1 (A) bet
(B) vet

—— 2 (A) vest
(B) best

—— 3 (A) van
(B) ban

—— 4 (A) volts
(B) bolts

—— 5 (A) boats
(B) votes

—— 6 (A) bat
(B) vat

—— 7 (A) vowels
(B) bowels

—— 8 (A) saber
(B) savor

—— 9 (A) jibed
(B) jived

—— 10 (A) livers
(B) libbers

Exercise L-38, Set A

Objective and Directions: see Exercise L-30, Set A.

_____ 1 (A) mouse   _____ 6 (A) sin
       (B) mouth   (B) thin

_____ 2 (A) sums   _____ 7 (A) moth
       (B) thumbs   (B) moss

_____ 3 (A) thick   _____ 8 (A) thought
       (B) sick   (B) sought

_____ 4 (A) think   _____ 9 (A) mass
       (B) sink   (B) math

_____ 5 (A) pass   _____ 10 (A) northmen
       (B) path   (B) norsemen

Exercise L-39, Set A

Objective and Directions: see Exercise L-30, Set A.

_____ 1 (A) load   _____ 6 (A) lot
       (B) road   (B) rot

_____ 2 (A) rice   _____ 7 (A) wrong
       (B) lice   (B) long

_____ 3 (A) right   _____ 8 (A) rust
       (B) light   (B) lust

_____ 4 (A) wrist   _____ 9 (A) lung
       (B) list   (B) rung

_____ 5 (A) lie   _____ 10 (A) loom
       (B) rye   (B) room

Exercise L-40, Set A

Objective and Directions: see Exercise L-30, Set A.

_____ 1 (A) fry   _____ 3 (A) fright
       (B) fly   (B) flight

_____ 2 (A) collect   _____ 4 (A) prow
       (B) correct   (B) plow

_____ 5 (A) climb   _____ 8 (A) claw
       (B) crime   (B) craw

_____ 6 (A) glows   _____ 9 (A) blue
       (B) grows   (B) brew

_____ 7 (A) grass   _____ 10 (A) free
       (B) glass   (B) flea

Exercise L-41, Set A

Objective and Directions: see Exercise L-30, Set A.

_____ 1 (A) day   _____ 4 (A) udder
       (B) they   (B) other

_____ 2 (A) side   _____ 5 (A) thighs
       (B) scythe   (B) dyes

_____ 3 (A) breathe
       (B) breed

Exercise L-42, Set A

Objective and Directions: see Exercise L-30, Set A.

_____ 1 (A) win   _____ 4 (A) rung
       (B) wing   (B) run

_____ 2 (A) ban   _____ 5 (A) sin
       (B) bang   (B) sing

_____ 3 (A) rang
       (B) ran

Exercise L-43, Set A

Objective and Directions: see Exercise L-30, Set A.

_____ 1 (A) stings   _____ 4 (A) sing
       (B) stinks   (B) sink

_____ 2 (A) thing   _____ 5 (A) rink
       (B) think   (B) ring

_____ 3 (A) slink
       (B) sling

Exercise L-44, Set A

Objective and Directions: see Exercise L-30, Set A.

_____ 1 (A) vine   _____ 4 (A) vales
      (B) wine   (B) whales

_____ 2 (A) wheel   _____ 5 (A) wipers
      (B) veal   (B) vipers

_____ 3 (A) vest
      (B) west

Exercise L-45, Set A

Objective and Directions: see Exercise L-30, Set A.

_____ 1 (A) yam   _____ 4 (A) jet
      (B) jam   (B) yet

_____ 2 (A) yolk   _____ 5 (A) jello
      (B) joke   (B) yellow

_____ 3 (A) years
      (B) jeers

Exercises L-30 through L-45, Set B

Exercise L-30, Set B

Objective: To identify the meaning of a word heard in a sentence by selecting a closely related word or synonym.

Directions: For each item, you will **see** two words or phrases and you will **hear** one sentence. Write the letter, (A) or (B), of the word or phrase more closely paralleling a word that you have heard in the sentence. (****See note** on page 22.)

Example: **You hear:** [If we tried it, I'm sure it would work.]

You read and answer: _B_ (A) made dry
                                 (B) attempted

_____ 1 (A) container   _____ 3 (A) claim
      (B) needle   (B) position

_____ 2 (A) fruit   _____ 4 (A) pastry
      (B) animal   (B) purchase

_____ 5 (A) baby animal
     (B) container

_____ 6 (A) headgear
     (B) taxi

_____ 7 (A) animal
     (B) large

_____ 8 (A) rucksack
     (B) part of body

_____ 9 (A) fruit
     (B) shores

_____ 10 (A) golf club
     (B) dairy product

Exercise L-31, Set B

Objective and Directions: see Exercise L-30, Set B.

_____ 1 (A) noise
     (B) metal

_____ 2 (A) teenagers
     (B) faculty heads

_____ 3 (A) indentation
     (B) canvas shelter

_____ 4 (A) postal number
     (B) garment

_____ 5 (A) conducted
     (B) allowed

_____ 6 (A) temporary fashion
     (B) excess weight

_____ 7 (A) bole of tree
     (B) inebriated person

_____ 8 (A) locomotive
     (B) water system

_____ 9 (A) travel
     (B) send a letter

_____ 10 (A) pieces of paper
     (B) wagons

Exercise L-32, Set B

Objective and Directions: see Exercise L-30, Set B.

_____ 1 (A) precious metal
     (B) low temperature

_____ 2 (A) animal
     (B) garment

_____ 3 (A) wave
     (B) child

_____ 4 (A) category
     (B) container

_____ 5 (A) purse
     (B) part of body

_____ 6 (A) timepieces
     (B) shoes

_____ 7 (A) garment
     (B) animal

_____ 8 (A) indication
     (B) sticking agent

_____ 9 (A) animals
     (B) wharves

_____ 10 (A) improvement
     (B) walking stick

Exercise L-33, Set B

Objective and Directions: see Exercise L-30, Set B.

____ 1	(A) transportation (B) noise	____ 6	(A) let go (B) become unable to keep

____ 1   (A) transportation   ____ 6   (A) let go
           (B) noise   (B) become unable to keep

____ 2   (A) vegetables   ____ 7   (A) short drink
           (B) bit   (B) fastener

____ 3   (A) cost   ____ 8   (A) loop in rope
           (B) award   (B) information

____ 4   (A) writing instruments   ____ 9   (A) body parasites
           (B) money   (B) untruths

____ 5   (A) possessed by him   ____ 10   (A) seasoning
           (B) boo   (B) intelligence agents

Exercise L-34, Set B

Objective and Directions: see Exercise L-30, Set B.

____ 1   (A) inexpensive   ____ 6   (A) clean
           (B) animal   (B) observe

____ 2   (A) masticating   ____ 7   (A) desires
           (B) nailing horseshoes   (B) sorceresses

____ 3   (A) boats   ____ 8   (A) fruit
           (B) pieces   (B) wine

____ 4   (A) bed linen   ____ 9   (A) trick
           (B) dishonest person   (B) money

____ 5   (A) pieces of meat   ____ 10   (A) equal
           (B) stores   (B) pulp

Exercise L-35, Set B

Objective and Directions: see Exercise L-30, Set B.

____ 1   (A) car   ____ 3   (A) alcoholic drink
           (B) noise   (B) part of face

____ 2   (A) suffocating   ____ 4   (A) big
           (B) making fun   (B) type of tree

_____ 5 (A) long time
         (B) letter of the alphabet

_____ 6 (A) applause
         (B) insults

_____ 7 (A) civil engineering
             structures
         (B) pants

_____ 8 (A) put a border on
         (B) engrave

_____ 9 (A) container
         (B) burn

_____ 10 (A) meal
          (B) physical movement

Exercise L-36, Set B

Objective and Directions: see Exercise L-30, Set B.

_____ 1 (A) punishment
         (B) plant

_____ 2 (A) meat
         (B) how it feels

_____ 3 (A) with face covered
         (B) unsuccessful

_____ 4 (A) vista
         (B) small number

_____ 5 (A) part of tree
         (B) departure

_____ 6 (A) weight
         (B) container

_____ 7 (A) vehicle
         (B) ventilator

_____ 8 (A) huge
         (B) fashionable

_____ 9 (A) sounds
         (B) birds

_____ 10 (A) water vehicle
          (B) adverb

Exercise L-37, Set B

Objective and Directions: see Exercise L-30, Set B.

_____ 1 (A) veterinary surgeon
         (B) wager

_____ 2 (A) superior quality
         (B) waistcoat

_____ 3 (A) prohibition
         (B) vehicle

_____ 4 (A) electrical power
         (B) rolls of cloth

_____ 5 (A) ships
         (B) electoral support

_____ 6 (A) stick
         (B) container

_____ 7 (A) sounds
         (B) part of body

_____ 8 (A) taste
         (B) sword

_____ 9 (A) complained
         (B) danced

_____ 10 (A) bodily organs
          (B) liberationists

Exercise L-38, Set B

<u>**Objective and Directions:**</u> see Exercise L-30, Set B.

_____ 1 (A) animal
       (B) opening

_____ 2 (A) part of hand
       (B) totals

_____ 3 (A) ill
       (B) large

_____ 4 (A) go under
       (B) consider

_____ 5 (A) road
       (B) crossing

_____ 6 (A) immorality
       (B) slender

_____ 7 (A) lichen
       (B) insect

_____ 8 (A) looked for
       (B) believed

_____ 9 (A) mathematics
       (B) religious service

_____ 10 (A) men from the north
       (B) men from Norway

Exercise L-39, Set B

<u>**Objective and Directions:**</u> see Exercise L-30, Set B.

_____ 1 (A) burden
       (B) way

_____ 2 (A) cereal
       (B) body parasite

_____ 3 (A) correct
       (B) not dark

_____ 4 (A) enumeration
       (B) arm joint

_____ 5 (A) untruth
       (B) cereal

_____ 6 (A) mold
       (B) all

_____ 7 (A) too lengthy
       (B) incorrect

_____ 8 (A) lasciviousness
       (B) oxidization

_____ 9 (A) part of ladder
       (B) bodily organ

_____ 10 (A) weaving instrument
       (B) enclosed space

Exercise L-40, Set B

<u>**Objective and Directions:**</u> see Exercise L-30, Set B.

_____ 1 (A) pilot
       (B) cook

_____ 2 (A) mark mistakes
       (B) gather

_____ 3 (A) trip by air
       (B) scare

_____ 4 (A) part of ship
       (B) agricultural implement

_____ 5 (A) ascent
     (B) offense

_____ 6 (A) shines
     (B) increases in size

_____ 7 (A) transparent material
     (B) lawn

_____ 8 (A) gullet
     (B) foot

_____ 9 (A) color
     (B) fermented drink

_____ 10 (A) secondhand (*lit.* insect)
     (B) unrestricted

Exercise L-41, Set B

Objective and Directions: see Exercise L-30, Set B.

_____ 1 (A) those (people)
     (B) dawn

_____ 2 (A) position
     (B) cutting tool

_____ 3 (A) reproduce
     (B) respire

_____ 4 (A) not this one
     (B) teat

_____ 5 (A) coloring agents
     (B) upper part of the legs

Exercise L-42, Set B

Objective and Directions: see Exercise L-30, Set B.

_____ 1 (A) victory
     (B) part of bird

_____ 2 (A) prohibition
     (B) noise

_____ 3 (A) sounded
     (B) continued

_____ 4 (A) race
     (B) part of ladder

_____ 5 (A) behave immorally
     (B) chant

Exercise L-43, Set B

Objective and Directions: see Exercise L-30, Set B.

_____ 1 (A) hurts
     (B) smells

_____ 2 (A) anything
     (B) reflection

_____ 3 (A) throw
     (B) creep

_____ 4 (A) go under
     (B) chant

_____ 5 (A) ice skating facility
     (B) boxing facility

Exercise L-44, Set B

Objective and Directions: see Exercise L-30, Set B.

_____ 1 (A) plant   _____ 4 (A) sea mammals
       (B) drink   (B) valleys

_____ 2 (A) circular ring   _____ 5 (A) snakes
       (B) meat   (B) cleaners

_____ 3 (A) waistcoat
       (B) direction

Exercise L-45, Set B

Objective and Directions: see Exercise L-30, Set B.

_____ 1 (A) sweet potato   _____ 4 (A) all the same
       (B) marmalade   (B) jet-propelled

_____ 2 (A) funny story   _____ 5 (A) color
       (B) egg yellow   (B) dessert

_____ 3 (A) insults
       (B) passing time

Exercises L-46 through L-50, Set A

Exercise L-46, Set A

Objective: To identify words heard in a sentence on the basis of sound and meaning.

Directions: For each item, you will **hear** a sentence containing one of the written words, (A), (B), (C), or (D). In the blank, write the letter of the word contained in the sentence. (****See note** on page 22.)

    Example: **You hear:** [He has a peck of tomatoes.]

          You read and answer: _D_ (A) peek
                                 (B) pick
                                 (C) pack
                                 (D) peck

_____ 1 (A) seal   _____ 2 (A) seat
       (B) sill   (B) sit
       (C) Sal   (C) sat
       (D) sell   (D) set

_____ 3   (A)   beat
          (B)   bit
          (C)   bat
          (D)   bet

_____ 7   (A)   heed
          (B)   hid
          (C)   had
          (D)   head

_____ 4   (A)   teen
          (B)   tin
          (C)   tan
          (D)   ten

_____ 8   (A)   meat
          (B)   mitt
          (C)   mat
          (D)   met

_____ 5   (A)   bead
          (B)   bid
          (C)   bad
          (D)   bed

_____ 9   (A)   lead
          (B)   lid
          (C)   lad
          (D)   led

_____ 6   (A)   neat
          (B)   knit
          (C)   gnat
          (D)   net

_____ 10   (A)   peat
          (B)   pit
          (C)   pat
          (D)   pet

Exercise L-47, Set A

<u>Objective and Directions:</u> see Exercise L-46, Set A.

_____ 1   (A)   cap
          (B)   cop
          (C)   cup

_____ 6   (A)   rat
          (B)   rot
          (C)   rut

_____ 2   (A)   sack
          (B)   sock
          (C)   suck

_____ 7   (A)   shack
          (B)   shock
          (C)   shuck

_____ 3   (A)   gnats
          (B)   knots
          (C)   nuts

_____ 8   (A)   last
          (B)   lost
          (C)   lust

_____ 4   (A)   backs
          (B)   box
          (C)   bucks

_____ 9   (A)   hat
          (B)   hot
          (C)   hut

_____ 5   (A)   sadden
          (B)   sodden
          (C)   sudden

_____ 10   (A)   cats
          (B)   cots
          (C)   cuts

Exercise L-48, Set A

Objective and Directions: see Exercise L-46, Set A.

_____ 1 (A) bad
      (B) bawd
      (C) bode
      (D) bud

_____ 6 (A) bast
      (B) bossed
      (C) boast
      (D) bust

_____ 2 (A) pan
      (B) pawn
      (C) pone
      (D) pun

_____ 7 (A) Cal
      (B) call
      (C) coal
      (D) cull

_____ 3 (A) cat
      (B) caught
      (C) coat
      (D) cut

_____ 8 (A) bat
      (B) bought
      (C) boat
      (D) butt

_____ 4 (A) Hal
      (B) haul
      (C) whole
      (D) hull

_____ 9 (A) fan
      (B) fawn
      (C) phone
      (D) fun

_____ 5 (A) mad
      (B) Maud
      (C) mode
      (D) mud

_____ 10 (A) Mal
      (B) maul
      (C) mole
      (D) mull

Exercise L-49, Set A

Objective and Directions: see Exercise L-46, Set A.

_____ 1 (A) borne
      (B) bean
      (C) burn
      (D) barn

_____ 4 (A) core
      (B) key
      (C) cur
      (D) car

_____ 2 (A) stored
      (B) steed
      (C) stirred
      (D) starred

_____ 5 (A) bored
      (B) bead
      (C) bird
      (D) barred

_____ 3 (A) four
      (B) fee
      (C) fur
      (D) far

_____ 6 (A) hoard
      (B) he'd
      (C) herd
      (D) hard

_____ 7 (A) spored
    (B) speed
    (C) spurred
    (D) sparred

_____ 9 (A) bore
    (B) bee
    (C) burr
    (D) bar

_____ 8 (A) port
    (B) peat
    (C) pert
    (D) part

_____ 10 (A) sore
    (B) see
    (C) sir
    (D) Saar

Exercise L-50, Set A

Objective and Directions: see Exercise L-46, Set A.

_____ 1 (A) bay
    (B) buy
    (C) boy
    (D) bow

_____ 6 (A) bale
    (B) bile
    (C) boil
    (D) bowl

_____ 2 (A) say
    (B) sigh
    (C) soy
    (D) sew

_____ 7 (A) cane
    (B) kine
    (C) coin
    (D) cone

_____ 3 (A) fail
    (B) file
    (C) foil
    (D) foal

_____ 8 (A) lane
    (B) line
    (C) loin
    (D) lone

_____ 4 (A) tail
    (B) tile
    (C) toil
    (D) toll

_____ 9 (A) mail
    (B) mile
    (C) moil
    (D) mole

_____ 5 (A) ray
    (B) rye
    (C) Roy
    (D) row

_____ 10 (A) vale
    (B) vile
    (C) voile
    (D) vole

Exercises L-46 through L-50, Set B

Exercise L-46, Set B

Objective: To identify the meaning of a word heard in a sentence by selecting a closely related word or synonym.

Directions: For each item you will **see** four words or phrases and you will **hear** one sentence. Write the letter, (A), (B), (C), or (D), of the word or phrase most closely paralleling a word that you have heard in the sentence. (****See note** on page 22.)

Example: **You hear:** [They peek at the baby every hour.]

You read and answer: _D_   (A) group
(B) measure
(C) cut
(D) look

_____ 1   (A) girl's name
(B) purvey
(C) ledge
(D) stick

_____ 2   (A) took a chair
(B) congealed
(C) take a seat
(D) place

_____ 3   (A) wagered
(B) rhythm
(C) "flying mouse"
(D) piece

_____ 4   (A) browned skin
(B) metal
(C) adolescent
(D) one more than nine

_____ 5   (A) patch
(B) drop
(C) offer
(D) naughty

_____ 6   (A) furrow
(B) small insect
(C) loosely-woven fabric
(D) tidy

_____ 7   (A) secreted
(B) owned
(C) chairman
(D) pay attention to

_____ 8   (A) small rug
(B) glove
(C) animal flesh
(D) became acquainted

_____ 9   (A) cover
(B) boy
(C) major role
(D) conducted

_____ 10   (A) small portion
(B) stone
(C) house animal
(D) turf

Exercise L-47, Set B

<u>Objective and Directions:</u> see Exercise L-46, Set B.

_____ 1 (A) small container
      (B) policeman
      (C) headgear

_____ 6 (A) routine
      (B) decay
      (C) rodent

_____ 2 (A) bag
      (B) draw
      (C) punch

_____ 7 (A) surprise
      (B) hut
      (C) de-husk

_____ 3 (A) tangles
      (B) insects
      (C) tree fruits

_____ 8 (A) final
      (B) craving
      (C) mislaid

_____ 4 (A) money
      (B) container
      (C) supports

_____ 9 (A) very warm
      (B) headgear
      (C) shack

_____ 5 (A) soaking
      (B) unforeseen
      (C) make unhappy

_____ 10 (A) beds
      (B) incisions
      (C) mature kittens

Exercise L-48, Set B

<u>Objective and Directions:</u> see Exercise L-46, Set B.

_____ 1 (A) begin to grow
      (B) augur
      (C) prostitute
      (D) unfortunate

_____ 4 (A) husk
      (B) move (away)
      (C) (masculine name)
      (D) entire

_____ 2 (A) cooking utensil
      (B) hock
      (C) play on words
      (D) bread

_____ 5 (A) wet earth
      (B) angry
      (C) means
      (D) (feminine name)

_____ 3 (A) secret
      (B) incision
      (C) outer garment
      (D) apprehended

_____ 6 (A) raffia
      (B) statue
      (C) ordered
      (D) brag

_____ 7 (A) telephone
     (B) thin out
     (C) California
     (D) fossil fuel

_____ 8 (A) ship
     (B) wooden club
     (C) stock
     (D) purchased

_____ 9 (A) grayish-brown
     (B) ventilator
     (C) call
     (D) enjoyable

_____ 10 (A) reflect (on)
     (B) injure
     (C) burrowing animal
     (D) (indicates bad, badly)

Exercise L-49, Set B

<u>Objective and Directions:</u> see Exercise L-46, Set B.

_____ 1 (A) kept
     (B) farm building
     (C) vegetable
     (D) incinerate

_____ 2 (A) horse
     (B) kept
     (C) asterisked
     (D) provoked

_____ 3 (A) number
     (B) charge
     (C) animal hair
     (D) distant

_____ 4 (A) crux
     (B) automobile
     (C) crucial
     (D) dog

_____ 5 (A) round ornament
     (B) feathered animal
     (C) drilled
     (D) striped

_____ 6 (A) (he would)
     (B) group
     (C) treasure
     (D) difficult

_____ 7 (A) boxed
     (B) urged
     (C) produced spores
     (D) velocity

_____ 8 (A) harbor
     (B) turf
     (C) role
     (D) high-spirited

_____ 9 (A) insect
     (B) tedious person
     (C) prickly seed
     (D) saloon

_____ 10 (A) (form of address)
     (B) understand
     (C) place in Germany
     (D) inflamed

Exercise L-50, Set B

<u>Objective and Directions:</u> see Exercise L-46, Set B.

_____ 1 (A) lad
     (B) curved weapon
     (C) purchase
     (D) reddish-brown

_____ 2 (A) fasten
     (B) brown sauce
     (C) exhale audibly
     (D) recite

_____ 3 (A) be doomed
        (B) young horse
        (C) smooth and shape
        (D) fencing weapon

_____ 4 (A) charge
        (B) playing piece
        (C) labor
        (D) rear portion

_____ 5 (A) (masculine name)
        (B) line
        (C) trace
        (D) whiskey

_____ 6 (A) dish
        (B) temper
        (C) reach boiling point
        (D) large package

_____ 7 (A) (cattle)
        (B) pine fruit
        (C) invent
        (D) rattan

_____ 8 (A) row
        (B) cut of meat
        (C) solitary
        (D) narrow road

_____ 9 (A) post
        (B) mill
        (C) burrowing animal
        (D) 1,760 yards

_____ 10 (A) sheer fabric
        (B) disgusting
        (C) valley
        (D) rodent

Objectives for Listening Comprehension Section

Part A: Similar Sentences

    1 Derive meaning via grammatical structure.
    2 Hear sounds accurately.
▶   3 Interpret the meaning of multiple-definition words.
    4 Match sounds and meaning to letter combinations.

Part B: Short Conversations

    5 Identify the speakers.
    6 Avoid sight-sound problems.
    7 Recognize language functions.
    8 Relate vocabulary to context.

Part C: Mini-Talks and Longer Conversations

    9 Anticipate the topics and the questions.
   10 Recognize paraphrases of words and phrases.

Objective 3: Interpret the Meaning of Multiple-Definition Words

After you have heard the sounds accurately and can identify the words in the spoken sentence, your next step is to interpret the meaning of the words correctly. Some words always have the same meaning and function, while others have several possible meanings and functions. We shall call these words **multiple-definition words.**

Multiple-definition words pose interesting listening problems. The meaning of the key word must be determined from its use in a sentence. Therefore, you need to focus on the overall meaning of the sentence in order to decide the proper definition of the key word.

In the following exercises, only a few multiple-definition words will be used. While there is no guarantee that any of the words you encounter here will occur on an actual TOEFL test, it would be a good idea for you to learn their various meanings, particularly the new meanings for familiar words. You should refer to a good American English dictionary whenever necessary.

Exercise L-5 I

Objectives: (i) To recognize that a word can have multiple meanings.
(ii) To identify the meaning of a word from its context.

Directions: For each item, you will **see** four sentences. In each sentence, one word is underlined. In the blank, write the letter, (A), (B), or (C), of the sentence in which the underlined word is used in the same sense as in the original sentence, though not necessarily in the same form.

Example: _C_ May I borrow your lecture notes?

(A) I got the note you sent.

(B) She can't hit all the high notes.

(C) He never takes any notes.

_____ 1 You'll need a coat.

(A) This room will need a second coat.

(B) There's a coat in the closet.

(C) You're coated with grease.

_____ 2 She's exhausted all other alternatives.

(A) Smog is caused by vehicle exhaust.

(B) She's completely exhausted.

(C) Our fuel supply will soon be exhausted.

_____ 3 They long for their families.

(A) John will return before long.

(B) That skirt is too long for her.

(C) How I long to see you.

_____ 4 He is doing his military training.

(A) Flower girls carried the bride's train.

(B) Board the train at the next platform.

(C) He trains long-distance runners.

_____ 5 I've just started studying.

(A) He has just arrived from London.

(B) He's a very just leader.

(C) We invited just close friends.

_____ 6   The tires are almost worn out.

   (A) She tires very quickly.
   (B) You must be tired.
   (C) Have you got a spare tire?

_____ 7   Would you please pass the salt?

   (A) Don't try to pass on a curve.
   (B) They pass notes in class.
   (C) I think I may pass out.

_____ 8   His hot temper is a major problem.

   (A) He plans to major in psychology.
   (B) Our major concern is the location.
   (C) He's been promoted to major.

_____ 9   Did you enjoy your trip?

   (A) The trip was a disaster.
   (B) He tripped on the stairs.
   (C) Did you trip the switch?

_____ 10 She runs a small shop.

   (A) Look how fast he's running.
   (B) He plans on running for public office.
   (C) The charity was run by an old man.

Exercise L-52

<u>Objective:</u> To identify from context which of a word's several possible meanings fits a given sentence.

<u>Directions:</u> For each item, you will **see** one key word and four associations of that word, and you will **hear** a sentence containing the key word. In the blank, write the letter, (A), (B), (C), or (D), of the relevant association.

Example: **You hear:** [He mounted his horse and rode off.]

You read and answer: __C__ mounted

(A) assembled
(B) climbed
(C) got on
(D) framed

_____ 1 **blow**

(A) disaster
(B) punch
(C) inflate
(D) move

_____ 2 **take**

(A) require
(B) steal
(C) regard
(D) record

_____ 3 **picture**

(A) photograph
(B) model
(C) movie
(D) imagine

_____ 4 **jam**

(A) fruit preserves
(B) become immovable
(C) interfere with
(D) difficult situation

_____ 5 **associate**

(A) colleague
(B) assistant
(C) relate
(D) hang out with

_____ 6 **exercise**

(A) physical, muscular activity
(B) school work
(C) make use of
(D) form of training

_____ 7 **under**

(A) covered by
(B) lower than
(C) in process of
(D) less than

_____ 8 **class**

(A) school group
(B) social rank
(C) category
(D) high quality

_____ 9 **light**

(A) lamp
(B) not heavy
(C) not dark
(D) illuminate

_____ 10 **shower**

(A) a light rainfall
(B) bath
(C) heap with
(D) bathe

Exercise L-53

<u>Objective and Directions:</u> see Exercise L-52.

_____ 1 **quarter**

(A) fourth part
(B) coin (U.S.)
(C) district
(D) part of school year

_____ 2 **note**

(A) paper money
(B) musical symbol
(C) short letter
(D) take account of

_____ 3 **kid**

(A) child
(B) young goat
(C) type of leather
(D) pull someone's leg

_____ 4 **works**

(A) functions
(B) factory
(C) mechanism
(D) author's opus

_____ 5 **check**

(A) bill
(B) bank order
(C) test
(D) pattern of crossed
     lines

_____ 6 **degree**

(A) indication of an angle
(B) indication of heat
(C) university qualification
(D) small steps

_____ 7 **hard**

(A) not soft
(B) difficult
(C) heavily
(D) severe

_____ 8 **bridge**

(A) part of a ship
(B) construction
     connecting two points
(C) game of cards
(D) dental work

_____ 9 **hot**

(A) having heat
(B) spicy
(C) angry
(D) on form

_____ 10 **dear**

(A) expression of concern
(B) expensive
(C) much loved
(D) salutation

Exercise L-54

<u>Objective and Directions:</u> see Exercise L-52.

_____ 1 **fly**

    (A) insect
    (B) travel through the air
    (C) transport by air
    (D) go quickly

_____ 2 **bar**

    (A) saloon
    (B) metal rod
    (C) prohibit
    (D) piece of candy

_____ 3 **date**

    (A) designation of the day
    (B) fruit
    (C) social engagement
    (D) mark with the date

_____ 4 **branch**

    (A) part of a tree
    (B) division of a subject
    (C) subsidiary of a
         company
    (D) diverge

_____ 5 **season**

    (A) time of year for
         specific activity
    (B) flavor
    (C) mature
    (D) division of a year

_____ 6 **volume**

    (A) amount
    (B) space occupied
    (C) loudness
    (D) tome

_____ 7 **press**

    (A) periodical
         publications
    (B) push
    (C) reporters as a group
    (D) extracting machine

_____ 8 **court**

    (A) woo
    (B) legal judgment site
    (C) sovereign's
         entourage
    (D) sports place

_____ 9 **box**

    (A) martial art
    (B) container
    (C) type of hedge
    (D) theater seat location

_____ 10 **call**

    (A) bird noise
    (B) telephone
    (C) give a name
    (D) shout

Exercise L-55

Objective: To correlate two sentences (one heard, one seen) in which a word is being used in the same sense.

Directions: For each item, you will **see** one key word and four sentences in which that word is used; you will **hear** the word used in a fifth sentence. In the blank, write the letter, (A), (B), (C), or (D), of the sentence in which the key word is used in the same sense as in the sentence you hear.

Example: **You hear:** ⎡The scar ran along her shoulder and down her right⎤
⎣side.   ⎦

You read and answer: _D_ side

(A) There was no writing on the other side of the piece of paper.
(B) Whose side are you on in this argument?
(C) There's a tall building on the other side of the road.
(D) He had a pain in his side.

_____ 1 **board**

(A) Liz sublet her apartment by advertising on the notice board.
(B) The board nailed across the hole failed to keep out the rain.
(C) As treasurer, he automatically became a member of the board.
(D) Dormitory fees cover room and board.

_____ 2 **play**

(A) The coach alternated his tight ends to take in the next play to the quarterback.
(B) *The Mousetrap* is probably the world's longest-running play.
(C) If you find there's too much play in the joint, you'll have to have it tightened.
(D) All work and no play makes Jack a dull boy.

_____ 3 **stall**

(A) The horse must be taken out while its stall is being cleaned.
(B) If the negotiations stall, we'll be in serious trouble.
(C) You stall for time while I check his references.
(D) On Sunday mornings, he sold magazines from a stall in the French market.

_____ 4 **bank**

(A) The houses along the northern bank suffered most from the floods.
(B) They always bank the proceeds on Monday morning.
(C) In the face of any crisis, we know we can bank on Thelma.
(D) You can be sure that the money is still in the bank.

_____ 5 **game**

   (A) The forest is full of game.
   (B) The football game is the crowning point to a week of celebrations.
   (C) Dan's behaving very strangely; I wonder what his game is.
   (D) Don't get so worked up about it; it's only a game.

_____ 6 **shot**

   (A) This remarkable shot shows this rarest of birds landing on its nest.
   (B) A shot rang out as they walked towards the building.
   (C) You'll need a shot once a week for the next two months.
   (D) Jack gave it his best shot but lost the race.

_____ 7 **paper**

   (A) I usually buy the morning paper on the way to work.
   (B) The price of paper has gone up alarmingly.
   (C) I think we should paper this room rather than paint it.
   (D) He read a paper on the country's economic options.

_____ 8 **stroke**

   (A) Smoking almost certainly increases the chances of suffering a stroke.
   (B) The overhead backhand is probably the most difficult stroke in the game.
   (C) It doesn't like anyone to stroke it.
   (D) With one stroke of the pen, he made the colony a state.

_____ 9 **plain**

   (A) Samantha was quite plain compared with her extraordinarily handsome brothers and sisters.
   (B) The hotel's cuisine is unexceptional, but includes good plain food.
   (C) The rains do indeed fall mainly on the plain.
   (D) It was plain to me from his account that he was lying.

_____ 10 **yield**

   (A) Thanks to the new strains, the yield per acre has risen sharply.
   (B) These trees will yield enough fruit for the entire summer.
   (C) Steam vessels must traditionally yield to sailing vessels.
   (D) Unable to fight on, the king yielded his kingdom to the invaders.

Exercise L-56

Objective and Directions: see Exercise **L-55.**

_____ 1 **match**

   (A) His work is so delicate that no one in this country can match it.
   (B) You can't strike that on the wall, it's a safety match.
   (C) The man at the paint store will match the color for you.
   (D) The match was billed as the fight of the century.

_____ 2 **mean**

   (A) The mean temperature in summer goes as high as 74 degrees.
   (B) What does that word mean?
   (C) Cinderella's sisters were always mean to her.
   (D) Before he became famous, he lived in a mean house near the center of town.

_____ 3 **round**

   (A) The leaders met in Mexico City for a round of talks on nuclear disarmament.
   (B) By the second round of the fight, it was clear who the winner would be.
   (C) Let me get this one; you paid for the last round.
   (D) We're trying to find a round table for our living room.

_____ 4 **account**

   (A) The accused man couldn't account for his whereabouts on the night of the murder.
   (B) The shareholders asked to be given all the details related to the company's government account.
   (C) The picnic was cancelled on account of rain.
   (D) The president of the club presented an account of his trip to Arizona at the last meeting.

_____ 5 **body**

   (A) The engine is still good; it's too bad the body has rusted out.
   (B) Detectives found the body in a clump of bushes beside the river.
   (C) As a religious body, this church is tax-exempt.
   (D) The moon is the only other heavenly body man has yet managed to visit.

_____ 6 **well**

    (A) What a relief it is that the children always behave so well at other people's houses.

    (B) Shake the bottle well before use.

    (C) He's well over forty, no matter what he says.

    (D) The doctor says she's well enough to go back to work.

_____ 7 **spring**

    (A) The hillside spring provided fresh water the year round.

    (B) There must be a spring broken in this car.

    (C) As spring approaches, the sense of nature's renewal is felt everywhere.

    (D) The prison guards watched, ready to spring into action at any moment.

_____ 8 **right**

    (A) The right answer is 20.3.

    (B) You have the right to remain silent.

    (C) Visiting the bereaved family was the right thing to do.

    (D) He fell right to the bottom of the well.

_____ 9 **fast**

    (A) At that time, no one in the world could run as fast as Jesse Owens.

    (B) It's not that late, your watch must be fast.

    (C) He ended his fast on the thirty-fifth day.

    (D) These are fast colors, madam; they will not run.

_____ 10 **beat**

    (A) In the nineteenth century, teachers often beat their students.

    (B) I didn't expect to beat you home.

    (C) After adding the flour, beat in two eggs.

    (D) Her heart skipped a beat every time she saw him.

Exercise L-57

Objective and Directions: see Exercise L-55.

_____ 1 **chance**

    (A) Competitors have three chances to win a prize.

    (B) As a general, he was always ready to take chances.

    (C) The weatherman says there is a ten percent chance of rain this evening.

    (D) If you chance to meet her, give her my regards.

_____ 2 **file**

    (A) The carpenter didn't have the cross-grained file he needed.

    (B) You'll find an account of the meeting in the top-secret file.

    (C) At the end of the performance, please file out calmly.

    (D) If you file a complaint, the police will be forced to prosecute.

_____ 3 **charge**

    (A) Please charge that to my account.

    (B) The Poles are said to have mounted the last cavalry charge in history.

    (C) The charge against him was reduced to manslaughter.

    (D) I'd like to speak to the person in charge if you don't mind.

_____ 4 **time**

    (A) How much time do you need to complete the job?

    (B) If you want to break the record, you must time your jump perfectly.

    (C) The last time I saw you, we were in Athens.

    (D) What time is it?

_____ 5 **sound**

    (A) When the trumpets sound, the procession will begin.

    (B) His judgment in these matters is always sound.

    (C) The sound we heard was terrifying.

    (D) Those people sound angry.

_____ 6 **keep**

    (A) You need a lot more money these days to keep a family of four.

    (B) I wish you'd learn to keep still during class.

    (C) Will you keep this for me until I return?

    (D) Mrs. Moffett keeps chickens and sells the eggs daily.

_____ 7 **wave**

    (A) Long thought to be the wave of the future, electric cars have proved extremely difficult to develop.

    (B) How much does your beautician charge for a permanent wave?

    (C) With a wave of his hand, he was gone.

    (D) Krakatoa caused a huge tidal wave when it erupted.

_____ 8 **medium**

    (A) Television has proved to be an extraordinarily potent advertising medium.

    (B) I'll have my steak medium rare.

    (C) He was a famous spiritualist medium.

    (D) Though of only medium height, he is extremely strong.

_____ 9 **rich**

    (A) I find the food here too rich for my taste.

    (B) The soil is so rich that it produces several crops a year.

    (C) When his patent was granted, he became a rich man overnight.

    (D) The rich texture of this fabric makes it unique.

_____ 10 **stand**

    (A) Spectators at baseball games stand and sing the national anthem.

    (B) We've decided to rent a stand in the exhibition hall.

    (C) His was not a popular view, but he decided he had to take a stand.

    (D) Although many thought it unfair, the higher courts decided that the decision must stand.

Objectives for Listening Comprehension Section

Part A: Similar Sentences

    1 Derive meaning via grammatical structure.
    2 Hear sounds accurately.
    3 Interpret the meaning of multiple-definition words.
►   4 Match sounds and meaning to letter combinations.

Part B: Short Conversations

    5 Identify the speakers.
    6 Avoid sight-sound problems.
    7 Recognize language functions.
    8 Relate vocabulary to context.

Part C: Mini-Talks and Longer Conversations

    9 Anticipate the topics and the questions.
  10 Recognize paraphrases of words and phrases.

Objective 4: Match Sounds and Meaning to Letter Combinations

The relationship between how a word sounds and how it is spelled seems arbitrary and confusing. While it is true that some very common, as well as less common, words have irregular spellings, the vast majority of English words follow regular spelling patterns.

On a TOEFL listening test, you do not have much time to ponder how a particular word that you heard might appear when written. Therefore, you need to be able to match sounds to letter combinations almost instantaneously.

In the **first** group of exercises, you will learn to recognize groups of common letter combinations that produce the same vowel sound. If you are already familiar with the sound system of English, you can complete these exercises very quickly for review purposes. If the sound system is somewhat new to you, however, you will need to work more thoughtfully. In either case, a good American English dictionary will be useful. Do not hesitate to look up the meaning of all new words before or while doing an exercise.

In the **second** group of exercises, you will encounter pairs of **homonyms.** Homonyms are words that have exactly the same pronunciation, but different meanings and different spellings. In both Parts A and B of the TOEFL Listening Comprehension homonyms may create sound/meaning/spelling problems. To identify a homonym, you must think about the general meaning of the sentence and match the meaning of the word with the appropriate spelling. Use a dictionary and study all the new homonyms you encounter.

Exercise L-58

<u>Objective:</u> To identify words that follow specific sound-spelling patterns.

<u>Directions:</u> Among the 23 words in the box, you will find 4 examples of each of the 5 common spellings for the **long a sound.** Keeping in mind that these 5 spelling patterns produce the same vowel sound, pronounce each word and notice its spelling. Find and circle the 3 words that have a different pronunciation. Arrange the other 20 words in the appropriate columns.
Note: * means consonant.

✓ face	wait	mail	weigh	they
✓ prey	page	pay	say	freight
lay	have	fade	hey	age
are	brain	eight	key	grey
	neighbor	delay	raise	

1 -a*e	2 -ai-	3 -ay	4 -ei-	5 -ey
face				*prey*

Think of at least 10 more words that you know that have this **long a sound.** Write each word in the appropriate column according to its spelling. Consult a dictionary to check your work.

Exercise L-59

Objective: To identify words that follow specific sound-spelling patterns.

Directions: Among the 23 words in the box, you will find 4 examples of each of the 5 common spellings for the **long** e **sound**. Keeping in mind that these 5 patterns produce the same vowel sound, pronounce each word and notice its spelling. Find and circle the 3 words that have a different pronunciation. Arrange the other 20 words in the appropriate columns.
Note: * means consonant.

✓ these	flee	grease	lien	flea
✓ heel	niece	seize	gene	fee
yield	breathe	either	theme	breeze
steak	lease	chief	protein	scene
	great	ceiling	friend	

1 -e*e-	2 -ee-	3 -ea-	4 -ie-	5 -ei-
these	heel			

Think of at least 10 more words that you know that have this **long** e **sound**. Write each word in the appropriate column according to its spelling. Consult a dictionary to check your work.

Exercise L-60

Objective: To identify words that follow specific sound-spelling patterns.

Directions: Among the 23 words in the box, you will find 4 examples of each of the 5 common spellings for the **long** ⓘ **sound**. Keeping in mind that these patterns produce the same vowel sound, pronounce each word and notice its spelling. Find and circle the 3 words that have a different pronunciation. Arrange the other 20 words in the appropriate columns.
Note: * means consonant.

✓ spine	lie	recline	machine	comply
✓ sigh	file	delight	died	rye
my	bye	pie	rely	sunny
dye	give	thigh	slight	spy
	eye	hive	vie	

1 -i*e	2 -igh(t)	3 -y	4 -ie-	5 -ye
spine	sigh			

Think of at least 10 more words that you know that have this **long** ⓘ **sound**. Write each word in the appropriate column according to its spelling. Consult a dictionary to check your work.

Exercise L-61

Objective: To identify words that follow specific sound-spelling patterns.

Directions: Among the 23 words in the box, there are 4 examples of each of the 5 common spellings for the **long o sound**. Keeping in mind that these patterns produce the same vowel sound, pronounce each word and notice its spelling. Find and circle the 3 words that have a different pronunciation. Arrange the other 20 words in the appropriate columns.

Note: * means consonant.

✓ note	coat	flow	loan	don't
✓ most	spoke	yolk	owe	cost
foe	how	oats	globe	float
know	toe	doe	now	hoe
	cone	bowl	roll	

1 -o*e	2 -o**	3 -oa-	4 -oe	5 -ow-
note	*most*			

Think of at least 10 more words that you know that have this **long o sound**. Write each word in the appropriate column according to its spelling. Consult a dictionary to check your work.

Exercise L-62

Objective: To identify words that follow specific sound-spelling patterns.

Directions: Among the 23 words in the box, there are 4 examples of each of the 5 common spellings for the **long ⓤ sound**. Keeping in mind that these patterns produce the same vowel sound, pronounce each word and notice its spelling. Find and circle the 3 words that have a different pronunciation. Arrange the other 20 words in the appropriate columns.

Note: * means consonant.

✓ cute	true	pull	due	neuter
✓ few	neutral	stew	but	fruit
feud	suit	juice	ruler	hue
built	huge	clue	spew	crude
	crew	eulogy	cruise	

1 -u*e-	2 -ue	3 -ew	4 -ui-	5 -eu-
cute		*few*		

Think of at least 10 more words that you know that have this **long ⓤ sound**. Write each word in the appropriate column according to its spelling. Consult a dictionary to check your work.

Exercise L-63

<u>Objective:</u> To identify on the basis of context which of two homonyms appears in a sentence.

<u>Directions:</u> For each item, you will **see** two homonyms and **hear** a sentence containing one of them. In the blank, write the letter of the homonym, (A) or (B), which corresponds to the meaning of the word in the spoken sentence.

<u>Example:</u> **You hear:** [Terry read the entire novel in two days.]

   You read and answer: _A_ (A) read
              (B) red

_____ 1 (A) daze   _____ 6 (A) due
         (B) days   (B) dew

_____ 2 (A) scents   _____ 7 (A) bare
         (B) cents   (B) bear

_____ 3 (A) rain   _____ 8 (A) souls
         (B) reign   (B) soles

_____ 4 (A) lie   _____ 9 (A) steel
         (B) lye   (B) steal

_____ 5 (A) pain   _____ 10 (A) dear
         (B) pane   (B) deer

Exercise L-64

<u>Objective and Directions:</u> see Exercise L-63.

_____ 1 (A) vein   _____ 6 (A) steak
         (B) vain   (B) stake

_____ 2 (A) peal   _____ 7 (A) knights
         (B) peel   (B) nights

_____ 3 (A) tale   _____ 8 (A) hares
         (B) tail   (B) hairs

_____ 4 (A) dough   _____ 9 (A) wine
         (B) doe   (B) whine

_____ 5 (A) sell   _____ 10 (A) beach
         (B) cell   (B) beech

Exercise L-65

<u>Objective and Directions:</u> see Exercise L-63.

_____ 1 (A) bells   _____ 6 (A) site
        (B) belles   (B) sight

_____ 2 (A) fainted   _____ 7 (A) break
        (B) feinted   (B) brake

_____ 3 (A) bow   _____ 8 (A) rode
        (B) bough   (B) rowed

_____ 4 (A) male   _____ 9 (A) wear
        (B) mail   (B) ware

_____ 5 (A) peace   _____ 10 (A) file
        (B) piece   (B) phial

Exercise L-66

<u>Objective and Directions:</u> see Exercise L-63.

_____ 1 (A) grate   _____ 6 (A) born
        (B) great   (B) borne

_____ 2 (A) stile   _____ 7 (A) fair
        (B) style   (B) fare

_____ 3 (A) feet   _____ 8 (A) right
        (B) feat   (B) rite

_____ 4 (A) sows   _____ 9 (A) beau
        (B) sews   (B) bow

_____ 5 (A) wait   _____ 10 (A) one
        (B) weight   (B) won

Exercise L-67

<u>Objective and Directions:</u> see Exercise L-63.

_____ 1 (A) byes   _____ 3 (A) hose
        (B) buys   (B) hoes

_____ 2 (A) plane   _____ 4 (A) sail
        (B) plain   (B) sale

_____ 5 (A) time   _____ 8 (A) heir
      (B) thyme   (B) air

_____ 6 (A) need   _____ 9 (A) corps
      (B) knead   (B) core

_____ 7 (A) toe   _____ 10 (A) weighed
      (B) tow   (B) wade

Exercise L-68

<u>Objective:</u> To distinguish between homonyms by associating a sentence with the meaning of one of the words.

<u>Directions:</u> For each item, you will **see** two homonyms and you will **hear** a sentence. In the blank, write the letter, (A) or (B), of the homonym which is related in meaning to a word or phrase in the sentence you hear.

    <u>Example:</u> **You hear:** ⎡The sister who taught Latin was the oldest member⎤
                    ⎣of that religious order.   ⎦

        You read and answer: _B_ (A) none
                              (B) nun

_____ 1 (A) rough   _____ 6 (A) ate
      (B) ruff   (B) eight

_____ 2 (A) pale   _____ 7 (A) hear
      (B) pail   (B) here

_____ 3 (A) seen   _____ 8 (A) course
      (B) scene   (B) coarse

_____ 4 (A) rote   _____ 9 (A) their
      (B) wrote   (B) there

_____ 5 (A) we'd   _____ 10 (A) new
      (B) weed   (B) knew

Exercise L-69

<u>Objective and Directions:</u> see Exercise L-68.

_____ 1 (A) not   _____ 3 (A) butt
      (B) knot   (B) but

_____ 2 (A) slay   _____ 4 (A) would
      (B) sleigh   (B) wood

_____ 5 (A) week   _____ 8 (A) waist
      (B) weak   (B) waste

_____ 6 (A) horse   _____ 9 (A) meat
      (B) hoarse   (B) meet

_____ 7 (A) blew   _____ 10 (A) lone
      (B) blue   (B) loan

Exercise L-70

Objective and Directions: see Exercise L-68.

_____ 1 (A) seam   _____ 6 (A) heel
      (B) seem   (B) heal

_____ 2 (A) hour   _____ 7 (A) bate
      (B) our   (B) bait

_____ 3 (A) bridal   _____ 8 (A) hole
      (B) bridle   (B) whole

_____ 4 (A) prey   _____ 9 (A) we'll
      (B) pray   (B) wheel

_____ 5 (A) flew   _____ 10 (A) four
      (B) flu   (B) for

Exercise L-71

Objective and Directions: see Exercise L-68.

_____ 1 (A) nose   _____ 6 (A) been
      (B) knows   (B) bin

_____ 2 (A) sea   _____ 7 (A) maid
      (B) see   (B) made

_____ 3 (A) whale   _____ 8 (A) ant
      (B) wail   (B) aunt

_____ 4 (A) your   _____ 9 (A) mite
      (B) you're   (B) might

_____ 5 (A) threw   _____ 10 (A) reeds
      (B) through   (B) reads

Exercise L-72

<u>**Objective and Directions:**</u> see Exercise L-68.

_____ 1 (A) groan
     (B) grown

_____ 2 (A) please
     (B) pleas

_____ 3 (A) way
     (B) weigh

_____ 4 (A) know
     (B) no

_____ 5 (A) teems
     (B) teams

_____ 6 (A) pour
     (B) poor

_____ 7 (A) mane
     (B) main

_____ 8 (A) too
     (B) two

_____ 9 (A) wry
     (B) rye

_____ 10 (A) beat
     (B) beet

Part B: Short Conversations

Part B presents short conversations between two speakers that are followed by a single question. The conversation is frequently between a man and a woman but sometimes between two men or two women. The voices of the speakers are always clearly distinguishable. The question is always asked by a third speaker. You have about thirteen seconds to read four choices and mark the answer to the question on your answer sheet.

The conversations are on many different topics, and there are many types of questions. Therefore, you must:

> **Focus on the speakers** → Who is talking?
> **Focus on the topic** → What are they talking about?

By focusing your attention on these two aspects of each conversation, you will also pick up enough information to answer any question that might be asked.

Many TOEFL students, especially those who have lived in the United States for a time, feel that Part B is easier than Parts A or C. It is true that hearing words and ideas in the context of a conversation makes this listening task somewhat more realistic than the one in Part A. For most students, the conversation and the question are understandable, but it is often still difficult to choose the correct answer. Each wrong answer, as well as the right answer, is related in some way to the words in the conversation. The same types of similarities discussed in Part A occur in Part B: similarities in sound, similarities in vocabulary, and similarities in grammar. You can avoid choosing an incorrect answer by focusing your attention on meaning.

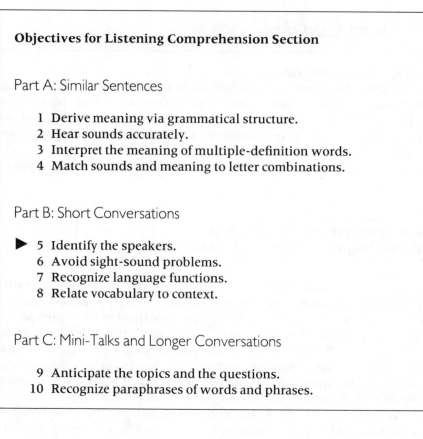

Objectives for Listening Comprehension Section

Part A: Similar Sentences

1 Derive meaning via grammatical structure.
2 Hear sounds accurately.
3 Interpret the meaning of multiple-definition words.
4 Match sounds and meaning to letter combinations.

Part B: Short Conversations

▶ 5 Identify the speakers.
6 Avoid sight-sound problems.
7 Recognize language functions.
8 Relate vocabulary to context.

Part C: Mini-Talks and Longer Conversations

9 Anticipate the topics and the questions.
10 Recognize paraphrases of words and phrases.

Objective 5: Identify the Speakers

Consider the first focus: **Who is talking?** There is always a clear relationship between the two speakers in the conversation. Some examples of possible relationships are those that exist between two friends, two classmates, a husband and a wife, a customer and a service person, a doctor and a patient, or a student and a professor. If you can determine how the two speakers are related, then you are more likely to be able to figure out what they are talking about. Conversely, if you are able to determine what they are talking about, you can probably infer what type of relationship exists between the two speakers.

Consider the second focus: **What are the people talking about?** The topic of conversation is always characteristic of the relationship of the speakers. In other words, if the speakers have a doctor-patient relationship, then you can assume they will be discussing a topic related to health care. If one speaker is a professor and the other a student, they will discuss a topic related to classwork. Conversely, you will never hear a doctor and a patient discussing a movie they have both seen because such a topic would not be appropriate to their relationship. Neither should you expect to hear a boss and an employee discussing a trip to the zoo because topics concerning office business are more appropriate to their relationship.

Exercise L-73

Objective: To identify vocabulary items associated with a profession.

Directions: Identify the **two** items in each group that would **not** be appropriate in a conversation about or with a member of the profession.

Example: *F,G* A conversation with an auto mechanic.

(A) fan belt	(E) wiper blade
(B) battery	(F) ceiling fan
(C) brakes	(G) pan
(D) clutch	(H) radiator

_____ 1 A conversation about a plumber.

(A) wrench	(E) drain
(B) sink	(F) leak
(C) stationery	(G) ceramic vase
(D) dripping faucet	(H) pipe

_____ 2 A conversation with a police officer.

(A) ambulance	(E) a ticket
(B) driver's license	(F) emergency
(C) traffic citation	(G) speeding
(D) industry	(H) melody

_____ 3 A conversation with a postman.

(A) stamps	(E) envelope
(B) lecture	(F) first class
(C) mail	(G) recipe
(D) package	(H) special delivery

_____ 4 A conversation about a waiter.

(A) menu	(E) check
(B) chimney	(F) garbage
(C) wine list	(G) change
(D) tip	(H) catsup

_____ 5 A conversation with a hotel desk clerk.

(A) clothing	(E) room service
(B) register	(F) luggage
(C) sculpture	(G) checking out
(D) bellhop	(H) keys

_____ 6 A conversation about a florist.

        (A) schedule   (E) corsage
        (B) bouquet   (F) long-stemmed
        (C) carnations   (G) roses
        (D) arrangement   (H) shovel

_____ 7 A conversation with a travel agent.

        (A) reservations   (E) tour
        (B) couch   (F) fare
        (C) lodgings   (G) boulder
        (D) ticket   (H) cruise

_____ 8 A conversation with a librarian.

        (A) reference   (E) reserve desk
        (B) fiction   (F) stacks
        (C) hooks   (G) periodicals
        (D) microfiche   (H) take-out service

_____ 9 A conversation with an apartment manager.

        (A) lease   (E) contacts
        (B) index   (F) thirty-day notice
        (C) sublet   (G) parking
        (D) deposit   (H) rent

_____ 10 A conversation about a nurse.

        (A) medication   (E) shoot
        (B) prescription   (F) appointment
        (C) physical exam   (G) penicillin
        (D) injection   (H) peel

Exercise L-74

<u>Objective:</u> To determine the identity of a speaker in a given situation.

<u>Directions:</u> For each item you will hear a phrase or sentence. **Check (✓)** the appropriate box to identify the speaker. **Note:** You will hear unconnected phrases or sentences, not a conversation.

<u>Example:</u> **You read:** The location is a classroom.
Check **T** if the **teacher** is speaking.
Check **S** if the **student** is speaking.

You hear: ⌈1 Your essay is already two days late.
2 Could you recommend some additional reading? ⌋

You answer: 1 (✓) ( )   2 ( ) (✓)
                        T   S   T   S

The location is a dentist's office.
Check **D** if the **dentist** is speaking.
Check **P** if the **patient** is speaking.

1 ( ) ( )   6 ( ) ( )
      D   P   D   P

2 ( ) ( )   7 ( ) ( )
      D   P   D   P

3 ( ) ( )   8 ( ) ( )
      D   P   D   P

4 ( ) ( )   9 ( ) ( )
      D   P   D   P

5 ( ) ( )   10 ( ) ( )
      D   P   D   P

The location is a library.
Check **L** if the **librarian** is speaking.
Check **U** if the library **user** is speaking.

11 ( ) ( )   16 ( ) ( )
       L   U   L   U

12 ( ) ( )   17 ( ) ( )
       L   U   L   U

13 ( ) ( )   18 ( ) ( )
       L   U   L   U

14 ( ) ( )   19 ( ) ( )
       L   U   L   U

15 ( ) ( )   20 ( ) ( )
       L   U   L   U

Exercise L-75

<u>Objective and Directions:</u> see Exercise L-74.

The location is the student advisor's office.
Check **A** if the **advisor** is speaking.
Check **S** if the **student** is speaking.

1 ( ) ( )   6 ( ) ( )
  A   S   A   S

2 ( ) ( )   7 ( ) ( )
  A   S   A   S

3 ( ) ( )   8 ( ) ( )
  A   S   A   S

4 ( ) ( )   9 ( ) ( )
  A   S   A   S

5 ( ) ( )   10 ( ) ( )
  A   S   A   S

The location is beside a highway. The policeman has stopped the speeding motorist.
Check **P** if the **policeman** is speaking.
Check **M** if the speeding **motorist** is speaking.

11 ( ) ( )   16 ( ) ( )
   P   M   P   M

12 ( ) ( )   17 ( ) ( )
   P   M   P   M

13 ( ) ( )   18 ( ) ( )
   P   M   P   M

14 ( ) ( )   19 ( ) ( )
   P   M   P   M

15 ( ) ( )   20 ( ) ( )
   P   M   P   M

Exercise L-76

<u>Objective and Directions:</u> see Exercise L-74.

The location is the customer's home.
Check **R** if the **repairman** is speaking.
Check **C** if the **customer** is speaking.

1 ( ) ( )
  R   C
			6 ( ) ( )
			   R C	

2 ( ) ( )
  R   C
			7 ( ) ( )
			   R C	

3 ( ) ( )
  R   C
			8 ( ) ( )
			   R C	

4 ( ) ( )
  R   C
			9 ( ) ( )
			   R C	

5 ( ) ( )
  R   C
			10 ( ) ( )
			   R C	

The location is a classroom.
Check **T** if the **teacher** is speaking.
Check **S** if the **student** is speaking.

11 ( ) ( )
   T   S
			16 ( ) ( )
			   T S	

12 ( ) ( )
   T   S
			17 ( ) ( )
			   T S	

13 ( ) ( )
   T   S
			18 ( ) ( )
			   T S	

14 ( ) ( )
   T   S
			19 ( ) ( )
			   T S	

15 ( ) ( )
   T   S
			20 ( ) ( )
			   T S	

Exercise L-77

Objective: To identify an individual's occupation or profession.

Directions: For each item, you will hear one sentence which contains enough information for you to infer the speaker's occupation, which is one of the alternatives, (A), (B), (C), or (D), in the box below. In the blank, write the letter of the statement which correctly answers the question, "What does the man do?" The question and alternative answers are not on the tape.

Example: **You hear:** ⌈24 A and B are on the right about half-way down⌉
⌊the aisle. ⌋

You read: The question and alternative answers in the box below.

You answer: _B_

> **What does the man do?**
>
> (A) He sells used cars.
> (B) He's a flight attendant.
> (C) He's a service station attendant.
> (D) He's a tour guide.

1 _____   11 _____

2 _____   12 _____

3 _____   13 _____

4 _____   14 _____

5 _____   15 _____

6 _____   16 _____

7 _____   17 _____

8 _____   18 _____

9 _____   19 _____

10 _____   20 _____

Exercise L-78

Objective: To identify an individual's occupation or profession.

Directions: For each item you will hear one sentence which contains enough information for you to infer the speaker's occupation, which is one of the alternatives, (A), (B), (C), or (D), in the box below. In the blank, write the letter of the statement which correctly answers the question, "What does the woman do?" The question and alternative answers are not on the tape.

Example: **You hear:** If you're not satisfied, you can return it within 30 days.

You read: The question and alternative answers in the box below.

You answer: _A_

> **What does the woman do?**
>
> (A) She's a sales clerk.
> (B) She works at the dry cleaners.
> (C) She drives a taxi.
> (D) She's a bank teller.

1 ____	11 ____
2 ____	12 ____
3 ____	13 ____
4 ____	14 ____
5 ____	15 ____
6 ____	16 ____
7 ____	17 ____
8 ____	18 ____
9 ____	19 ____
10 ____	20 ____

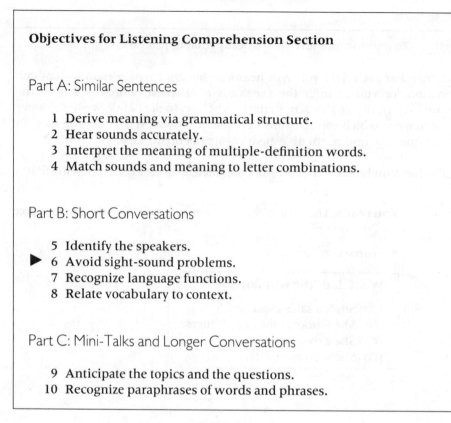

Objectives for Listening Comprehension Section

Part A: Similar Sentences

1 Derive meaning via grammatical structure.
2 Hear sounds accurately.
3 Interpret the meaning of multiple-definition words.
4 Match sounds and meaning to letter combinations.

Part B: Short Conversations

5 Identify the speakers.
► 6 Avoid sight-sound problems.
7 Recognize language functions.
8 Relate vocabulary to context.

Part C: Mini-Talks and Longer Conversations

9 Anticipate the topics and the questions.
10 Recognize paraphrases of words and phrases.

Objective 6: Avoid Sight-Sound Problems

Sight-sound confusions occur as often in Part B, Conversations, as they do in Part A, Similar Sentences. Fortunately, the short conversations provide a fuller context for understanding individual words. While careful word-level listening is still necessary, it is far more important to concentrate on the overall meaning of the complete conversation.

These exercises present a mixture of sound problems. Because meaning is so important, you should use a dictionary before doing an exercise or while checking your answers.

**Note on using Exercises L-79 through L-83:
Each of the next five exercises has two parts, Set A and Set B. **The key words in each Set A exercise correspond to the related words and phrases in the Set B exercise of the same number, but their order is not necessarily the same.** For example, **Exercise L-79 Set A** question 1, (A) bigger, (B) picker, (C) bicker, (D) pickle, corresponds to **Exercise L-79 Set B** question 1, (A) squabble (*see C above*), (B) harvester (*see B above*), (C) larger (*see A above*), (D) preserve (*see D above*).

There is only **one exercise on tape called Exercise L-79.** Students will listen to the taped exercise **two times, once for Set A** and **again for Set B.**

The tapescript shows four sentences for each item, although only one of these sentences is on tape. The taped sentence is marked with an asterisk (*). For review purposes or to provide extra practice on difficult sounds, the teacher can create completely different exercises for the students by reading aloud the alternative sentences to those on tape.

Exercises L-79 through L-83, Set A

Exercise L-79, Set A

Objective: To identify words heard in a sentence on the basis of sound and contextual clues.

Directions: For each item, you will **see** four words and **hear** one sentence containing one of the words. In the blank, write the letter, (A), (B), (C), or (D), of the word contained in the sentence. (**See note** on page 88.)

> Example: **You hear:** [The cart was full of grass clippings.]
>
> **You read and answer:** _B_ (A) cat
> (B) cart
> (C) cut
> (D) curt

___ 1	(A) bigger		___ 6	(A) theme	
	(B) picker			(B) dim	
	(C) bicker			(C) thin	
	(D) pickle			(D) deem	
___ 2	(A) drab		___ 7	(A) jam	
	(B) globe			(B) yarn	
	(C) drape			(C) germ	
	(D) grab			(D) gem	
___ 3	(A) sworn		___ 8	(A) shows	
	(B) sure			(B) chose	
	(C) shorn			(C) choose	
	(D) sore			(D) shoes	
___ 4	(A) finalists		___ 9	(A) tall	
	(B) violins			(B) toil	
	(C) finest			(C) dual	
	(D) violence			(D) tool	
___ 5	(A) gust		___ 10	(A) balloon	
	(B) crust			(B) felon	
	(C) cussed			(C) flown	
	(D) cursed			(D) bloom	

Exercise L-80, Set A

<u>Objective and Directions:</u> see Exercise L-79, Set A.

_____ 1 (A) spirit
　　　　(B) script
　　　　(C) split
　　　　(D) spurt

_____ 2 (A) hanker
　　　　(B) hangar
　　　　(C) hunger
　　　　(D) anger

_____ 3 (A) silver
　　　　(B) savor
　　　　(C) saber
　　　　(D) sliver

_____ 4 (A) floss
　　　　(B) false
　　　　(C) flaws
　　　　(D) falls

_____ 5 (A) those
　　　　(B) dose
　　　　(C) though
　　　　(D) doze

_____ 6 (A) similes
　　　　(B) surmise
　　　　(C) survive
　　　　(D) smiles

_____ 7 (A) grown
　　　　(B) ground
　　　　(C) crowned
　　　　(D) crone

_____ 8 (A) soothe
　　　　(B) south
　　　　(C) suit
　　　　(D) snooze

_____ 9 (A) trade
　　　　(B) tried
　　　　(C) tirade
　　　　(D) trait

_____ 10 (A) honor
　　　　(B) injure
　　　　(C) hour
　　　　(D) owner

Exercise L-81, Set A

<u>Objective and Directions:</u> see Exercise L-79, Set A.

_____ 1 (A) bare
　　　　(B) peer
　　　　(C) beer
　　　　(D) pare

_____ 2 (A) sizzle
　　　　(B) swivel
　　　　(C) swindle
　　　　(D) spindle

_____ 3 (A) thunder
　　　　(B) lumber
　　　　(C) plunder
　　　　(D) blunder

_____ 4 (A) string
　　　　(B) sing
　　　　(C) sting
　　　　(D) sling

_____ 5 (A) picture
    (B) vigor
    (C) pitcher
    (D) vicar

_____ 8 (A) quilt
    (B) quick
    (C) quite
    (D) quit

_____ 6 (A) most
    (B) mast
    (C) mass
    (D) moist

_____ 9 (A) longer
    (B) languor
    (C) latter
    (D) laggard

_____ 7 (A) president
    (B) present
    (C) presence
    (D) precedent

_____ 10 (A) sheik
    (B) shreik
    (C) creek
    (D) cheek

Exercise L-82, Set A

Objective and Directions: see Exercise L-79, Set A.

_____ 1 (A) works
    (B) warts
    (C) waltz
    (D) walks

_____ 6 (A) slept
    (B) slipped
    (C) split
    (D) spelled

_____ 2 (A) first
    (B) flirt
    (C) burst
    (D) birth

_____ 7 (A) jeer
    (B) cheer
    (C) jarred
    (D) charred

_____ 3 (A) whine
    (B) wind
    (C) find
    (D) fine

_____ 8 (A) lurch
    (B) rush
    (C) lush
    (D) lunch

_____ 4 (A) beep
    (B) bleat
    (C) peep
    (D) pleat

_____ 9 (A) respiration
    (B) expiration
    (C) inspiration
    (D) aspiration

_____ 5 (A) thrust
    (B) truce
    (C) thirst
    (D) truest

_____ 10 (A) mash
    (B) mush
    (C) much
    (D) match

Exercise L-83, Set A

Objective and Directions: see Exercise L-79, Set A.

_____ 1 (A) towel
      (B) vow
      (C) bow
      (D) trowel

_____ 6 (A) win
      (B) wan
      (C) wand
      (D) wind

_____ 2 (A) log
      (B) lark
      (C) lug
      (D) luck

_____ 7 (A) din
      (B) knit
      (C) dean
      (D) neat

_____ 3 (A) roast
      (B) wrote
      (C) rode
      (D) lost

_____ 8 (A) farther
      (B) falter
      (C) flatter
      (D) father

_____ 4 (A) coast
      (B) ghosts
      (C) costs
      (D) goats

_____ 9 (A) hone
      (B) old
      (C) hold
      (D) own

_____ 5 (A) just
      (B) gust
      (C) gist
      (D) joist

_____ 10 (A) thin
      (B) there
      (C) tear
      (D) tin

Exercises L-79 through L-83, Set B

Exercise L-79, Set B

Objective: To identify the meaning of a word heard in a sentence by selecting a closely-related word or synonym.

Directions: For each item you will **see** four words or phrases, and you will **hear** one sentence. In the blank, write the letter, (A), (B), (C), or (D), of the word or phrase that most closely parallels a word or phrase that you heard in the sentence. (****See note** on page 88.)

    Example: **You hear:** [The cart was full of grass clippings.]

        You read and answer: __C__ (A) feline
                                    (B) eliminated
                                    (C) wagon
                                    (D) brusque

_____ 1 (A) squabble
       (B) harvester
       (C) larger
       (D) preserve

_____ 2 (A) cloth
       (B) snatch
       (C) sphere
       (D) dreary

_____ 3 (A) depilated
       (B) vowed
       (C) certain
       (D) painful

_____ 4 (A) fiddles
       (B) physical abuse
       (C) runners-up
       (D) best

_____ 5 (A) blast
       (B) afflicted
       (C) swore
       (D) layer

_____ 6 (A) judge
       (B) subject
       (C) faint
       (D) slender

_____ 7 (A) story
       (B) particle
       (C) precious stone
       (D) predicament

_____ 8 (A) select
       (B) picked
       (C) demonstrates
       (D) footwear

_____ 9 (A) instrument
       (B) work
       (C) long
       (D) double

_____ 10 (A) criminal
       (B) traveled by air
       (C) flower
       (D) blow up

Exercise L-80, Set B

Objective and Directions: see Exercise L-79, Set B.

_____ 1 (A) screenplay
       (B) will
       (C) short burst
       (D) separated

_____ 2 (A) appetite
       (B) shed
       (C) indignation
       (D) crave

_____ 3 (A) sword
       (B) aroma
       (C) tiny slice
       (D) gray

_____ 4 (A) loses his balance
       (B) untruthful
       (C) defects
       (D) soft thread

_____ 5 (A) the ones designated
       (B) nap
       (C) measure
       (D) while

_____ 6 (A) grins
       (B) comparisons
       (C) suppose
       (D) remain alive

_____ 7 (A) honored as
        (B) increased
        (C) land
        (D) witch

_____ 9 (A) occupation
        (B) attempted
        (C) diatribe
        (D) characteristic

_____ 8 (A) calm
        (B) nap
        (C) coat and trousers
        (D) southern

_____ 10 (A) privilege
        (B) proprietor
        (C) 60 minutes
        (D) hurt

Exercise L-81, Set B

Objective and Directions: see Exercise L-79, Set B.

_____ 1 (A) gaze
        (B) peel
        (C) drink
        (D) uncovered

_____ 6 (A) pole
        (B) damp
        (C) the majority of
        (D) large amount

_____ 2 (A) crackle
        (B) rotate
        (C) perforate
        (D) cheat

_____ 7 (A) gift
        (B) bearing
        (C) chief executive
        (D) example

_____ 3 (A) wood
        (B) roar
        (C) booty
        (D) mistake

_____ 8 (A) completely
        (B) leave
        (C) speedy
        (D) bedcover

_____ 4 (A) warble
        (B) catapult
        (C) cord
        (D) burn

_____ 9 (A) straggler
        (B) last mentioned
        (C) lengthier
        (D) stillness

_____ 5 (A) clergyman
        (B) forcefulness
        (C) jug
        (D) imagine

_____ 10 (A) chief
        (B) cry
        (C) stream
        (D) impudence

Exercise L-82, Set B

Objective and Directions: see Exercise L-79, Set B.

_____ 1 (A) growths
        (B) dance
        (C) strolls
        (D) functions

_____ 2 (A) top
        (B) broke
        (C) start
        (D) court

94

_____ 3 (A) howl
     (B) coil
     (C) locate
     (D) excellent

_____ 7 (A) mock
     (B) burst of applause
     (C) burned
     (D) unsettled

_____ 4 (A) complain
     (B) sound
     (C) look
     (D) fold

_____ 8 (A) luncheon
     (B) stagger
     (C) luxurious
     (D) hurry

_____ 5 (A) pushed
     (B) most reliable
     (C) ceasefire
     (D) long

_____ 9 (A) breathing
     (B) goal
     (C) closing
     (D) encouragement

_____ 6 (A) slid
     (B) slumbered
     (C) relieved
     (D) divided

_____ 10 (A) contest
     (B) purée
     (C) a lot
     (D) sentimentality

Exercise L-83, Set B

Objective and Directions: see Exercise L-79, Set B.

_____ 1 (A) promise
     (B) small spade
     (C) cloth
     (D) front

_____ 6 (A) pale
     (B) stick
     (C) finish first
     (D) air

_____ 2 (A) frolic
     (B) carry
     (C) good fortune
     (D) piece of wood

_____ 7 (A) make
     (B) tidy
     (C) noise
     (D) chairman

_____ 3 (A) beef
     (B) missing
     (C) composed
     (D) drove

_____ 8 (A) compliment
     (B) founder
     (C) waver
     (D) more distant

_____ 4 (A) prices
     (B) spirits
     (C) shoreline
     (D) animal

_____ 9 (A) possess
     (B) ancient
     (C) contain
     (D) sharpen

_____ 5 (A) beam
     (B) fair
     (C) air
     (D) main idea

_____ 10 (A) metal
     (B) skinny
     (C) at that place
     (D) rip

Exercise L-84

Objective: To avoid sound-alike confusion while searching for proper restatements.

Directions: Listen to each statement carefully. In the blank, write the letter, (A), (B), (C), or (D), of its restatement.

__C__ 1 (A) Our property is near theirs.
        (B) Their bees will sting us.
        (C) The arrival time is still uncertain.
        (D) They didn't know our house was so far.

_____ 2 (A) Your servant said it was chilly.
        (B) The chicken made a nest for its eggs.
        (C) The children miss you.
        (D) Their room needs to be cleaned.

_____ 3 (A) He's too nervous.
        (B) Pete saw some dolphins recently.
        (C) Climbing the hill was taxing.
        (D) He needs some rest.

_____ 4 (A) Let's take the elevator.
        (B) Do you need a ride?
        (C) This gift is too heavy to lift.
        (D) Will you lift up the can?

_____ 5 (A) Stop when you hear the horn.
        (B) There's only enough food for four.
        (C) Your father looks better now.
        (D) It'll taste better with seasoning.

_____ 6 (A) They intend to take a vacation.
        (B) They will either win or lose.
        (C) The crew plans to leave when it's cool.
        (D) They can win if they find the clues.

_____ 7 (A) The view from this seat is distorted.
        (B) There are dozens of stores in this district.
        (C) They get a reduced rate.
        (D) The citizens of the state are proud of its history.

_____ 8 (A) She looked like she had been crying.
        (B) She's happy he repaired the door.
        (C) She was very surprised.
        (D) He won the walking race.

_____ 9 (A) When do you leave for Europe?
         (B) Choose the one you want.
         (C) I'm sorry you're sick.
         (D) Turn left if you can.

_____ 10 (A) Bill always does well.
         (B) Bill has come to look at his grades.
         (C) No one except Bill did well.
         (D) Bill has two good grades.

Objectives for Listening Comprehension Section

Part A: Similar Sentences

    1 Derive meaning via grammatical structure.
    2 Hear sounds accurately.
    3 Interpret the meaning of multiple-definition words.
    4 Match sounds and meaning to letter combinations.

Part B: Short Conversations

    5 Identify the speakers.
    6 Avoid sight-sound problems.
▶ 7 Recognize language functions.
    8 Relate vocabulary to context.

Part C: Mini-Talks and Longer Conversations

    9 Anticipate the topics and the questions.
  10 Recognize paraphrases of words and phrases.

Objective 7: Recognize Language Functions

In Part B, you hear people conversing in everyday situations. The words, phrases, and sentences you hear take on meaning from the context in which they are spoken. A single sentence can function in different ways in different situations.

    These example situations illustrate how a sentence can function in more than one way.

Situation 1:   MAN: What's the matter? You look awful.
                WOMAN: I've got a headache.

In this situation, the sentence *I've got a headache* functions as an expression of the woman's feelings.

Situation 2a: MAN: How about going to a movie later?
                WOMAN: I've got a headache.

In situation 2a, the sentence *I've got a headache*, taken together with the man's suggestion of a movie, functions both as an implied rejection of his suggestion and as an expression of her feelings.

Situation 2b: ⌈ MAN: How about going to a movie later? ⌉
                ⌊ WOMAN: No, thanks. <u>I've got a headache.</u> ⌋

In situation 2b, as you can see, there is no missing link. The woman explicitly rejects the man's suggestion, and then gives an excuse for not accepting the suggestion by expressing her feelings.

   This group of exercises provides practice in recognizing some language functions that might appear in Part B (and Part C) conversations. While the possibilities are enormous, TOEFL frequently presents situations in which **offers**, **requests**, and **suggestions** are important. Included, therefore, is some focused practice in recognizing ways in which these three language functions are often made explicit.

Exercise L-85

Objective: To distinguish between offers and requests. Here are some typical openers.

requests	**offers**
Will you . . .	Can I . . .
Would you . . .	Shall I . . .
Can you . . .	Do you want me to . . .
Could you . . .	Would you like . . .
How about . . .	How about . . .
Would you mind . . .	

Directions: For each item, you will **hear** a question. Write **R** in the blank if you hear a **request**. Write **O** if you hear an **offer**.

Example: **You hear:** [How about lending me a pencil?]

        You answer: _*R*_ because the speaker is requesting a pencil.

1 _____   6 _____

2 _____   7 _____

3 _____   8 _____

4 _____   9 _____

5 _____   10 _____

Exercise L-86

<u>Objectives:</u> (i) To distinguish between offers and requests within the context of a short conversation.

(ii) To gain familiarity with the variety of question types that might be used to elicit information about an offer or a request contained in a conversation.

<u>Directions:</u> For each item, you will **hear** a short conversation containing either an offer or a request. The question that follows focuses on this function. In the blank, write the letter, (A), (B), (C), or (D), of the answer.

Example: **You hear:**

WOMAN:	I'm such a terrible typist that I may never finish this report.
MAN:	Would you like me to take over for a while?
QUESTION:	What does the man offer to do?

You read and answer: _C_ (A) Take her to the airport.
(B) Repair the typewriter.
(C) Type for a few minutes.
(D) Take the report to a typist.

The answer is (C) because the man is offering to help the woman by typing for a few minutes.

_____ 1 (A) Carry the box down.
(B) Take the book upstairs.
(C) Move the bricks.
(D) Help the woman down the stairs.

_____ 2 (A) How to set up camp.
(B) How to become a scout.
(C) How to cut the wood.
(D) How to start a fire.

_____ 3 (A) Offer the man a cigarette.
(B) Air out the room.
(C) Extinguish her cigarette.
(D) Turn on the fan.

_____ 4 (A) Attend the lecture.
(B) Offer the professor a drink.
(C) Stop at the grocery store.
(D) Go to the cafeteria.

_____ 5 (A) An umbrella.
(B) A ride.
(C) A present.
(D) Some directions.

_____ 6 (A) Borrow his notes.
 (B) Take a note to his professor.
 (C) Lend him her notes.
 (D) Pick up his prescription.

_____ 7 (A) More air.
 (B) A raise.
 (C) A room with a window.
 (D) A better view.

_____ 8 (A) Give her a light.
 (B) Turn on the heat.
 (C) Call her that night.
 (D) Practice bird calls.

_____ 9 (A) A red car.
 (B) A factory job.
 (C) A choice of cars.
 (D) A ride to work.

_____ 10 (A) A party invitation.
 (B) To buy a house.
 (C) A tour of the house.
 (D) Something warm to drink.

Exercise L-87

Objectives: (i) To recognize some ways in which **suggestions** are made.

Let's . . .
Shall we . . .
Perhaps we should . . .
Maybe you should . . .
Why don't you/we/I . . .

(ii) To recognize when a suggestion has been accepted or rejected.

acceptance	**rejection**
OK.	(No.) Let's . . .
Sure. Why not?	(No thanks.) I'd better . . .
(That's a) good idea.	Thanks, but . . .
Sounds good to me.	Maybe we should . . .
By all means.	I don't know.

Directions: For each item, you will **hear** a short exchange between two people. Then a question is asked by a third person. In the blank, write the letter, (A), (B), (C), or (D), of the answer.

Example: **You hear:** ⌐ WOMAN: Fred is frequently late, but this is
                                                          ridiculous. Why don't we go
                                                           inside?
            MAN: Let's give him another five
                                                           minutes.
           └ QUESTION: What are the people going to do? ⌐

You read and answer: __D__ (A) Wait in the building.
                                          (B) Leave the gate open.
                                          (C) Give up on Fred.
                                          (D) Stay outside longer.

The correct answer is (D) because the man rejects the woman's suggestion to wait inside and suggests they stay outside longer.

_____ 1 (A) Quitting work early.
      (B) Making a doctor's appointment.
      (C) Going to the drug store.
      (D) Trying to lose weight.

_____ 2 (A) He was annoyed.
      (B) He was sympathetic.
      (C) He was reserved.
      (D) He was enthusiastic.

_____ 3 (A) Go on a diet.
      (B) Talk to her sister.
      (C) Look at a map.
      (D) Try to win first prize.

_____ 4 (A) Arrive early.
      (B) Take a ship.
      (C) Look for the package.
      (D) Use air freight.

_____ 5 (A) Look for the money.
      (B) Hurry to the movie.
      (C) Set the clock.
      (D) Stay for the next film.

Exercises L-88 through L-90, Set A

Exercise L-88, Set A

Objective: To recognize which speaker intends to accomplish a stated purpose.

Directions: For each item, you will **hear** a short dialogue. In the blank, write the letter of the answer to the written question, according to the information in the dialogue.

Example: **You hear:** ⌈ MAN: Why don't we go to a drive-in
movie tonight?
WOMAN: Don't you think it's going to rain? ⌋

You read and answer: _A_ Who is making a suggestion?

(A) the man
(B) the woman

_____ 1 Who is expressing
sympathy?

(A) the man
(B) the woman

_____ 2 Who is apologizing?

(A) the man
(B) the woman

_____ 3 Who is making a request?

(A) the man
(B) the woman

_____ 4 Who is complaining?

(A) the man
(B) the woman

_____ 5 Who is expressing
confusion?

(A) the man
(B) the woman

_____ 6 Who is asking for advice?

(A) the man
(B) the woman

_____ 7 Who is asking for directions?

(A) the man
(B) the woman

_____ 8 Who is declining an
invitation?

(A) the man
(B) the woman

_____ 9 Who is complaining?

(A) the man
(B) the woman

_____ 10 Who is postponing
something?

(A) the man
(B) the woman

Exercise L-89, Set A

Objective and Directions: see Exercise L-88, Set A.

_____ 1 Who is disagreeing?

    (A) the man
    (B) the woman

_____ 2 Who is expressing sarcasm?

    (A) the man
    (B) the woman

_____ 3 Who is expressing admiration?

    (A) the man
    (B) the woman

_____ 4 Who is hinting at something?

    (A) the man
    (B) the woman

_____ 5 Who is giving directions?

    (A) the man
    (B) the woman

_____ 6 Who is taking leave?

    (A) the man
    (B) the woman

_____ 7 Who is gossiping?

    (A) the man
    (B) the woman

_____ 8 Who is excusing himself or herself?

    (A) the man
    (B) the woman

_____ 9 Who is paying a compliment?

    (A) the man
    (B) the woman

_____ 10 Who is offering a warning?

    (A) the man
    (B) the woman

Exercise L-90, Set A

Objective and Directions: see Exercise L-88, Set A.

_____ 1 Who is expressing anxiety?

    (A) the man
    (B) the woman

_____ 2 Who is insulting someone?

    (A) the man
    (B) the woman

_____ 3 Who is giving information?

    (A) the man
    (B) the woman

_____ 4 Who is making an accusation?

    (A) the man
    (B) the woman

_____ 5 Who is making a suggestion?

    (A) the man
    (B) the woman

_____ 6 Who is expressing concern?

    (A) the man
    (B) the woman

_____ 7 Who is making an offer?

(A) the man
(B) the woman

_____ 8 Who is bragging?

(A) the man
(B) the woman

_____ 9 Who is asking for further information?

(A) the man
(B) the woman

_____ 10 Who is identifying someone?

(A) the man
(B) the woman

Exercises L-88 through L-90, Set B

Exercise L-88, Set B

Objective: To gain familiarity with the variety of questions that may follow conversations.

Directions: For each item, you will **hear** a short conversation. **Read** the question, and write your answer in the blank.

Example: **You hear:**

> WOMAN: I feel faint.
> MAN: No wonder. You haven't had a bite all day.

You read and answer: _C_ What is the matter with the woman?

(A) She is sick.
(B) She was bitten by an ant.
(C) She is hungry.
(D) She spilled her paint.

_____ 1 What probably happened to the man's father?

(A) He made a mistake.
(B) He missed the bus.
(C) He is deaf.
(D) He passed away.

_____ 2 Where did this conversation probably take place?

(A) At the toy store.
(B) At school.
(C) At the office.
(D) At the auto mechanic's shop.

_____ 3 What does the woman do?

(A) She's a plumber.
(B) She's a nurse.
(C) She's a maid.
(D) She's a gardener.

105

_____ 4   How does the man feel?

    (A) He is satisfied.
    (B) He is impatient.
    (C) He is exhausted.
    (D) He is amused.

_____ 5   What is the man going to do?

    (A) Explain the homework.
    (B) Repair the steps.
    (C) Get a new job.
    (D) Look for the answer.

_____ 6   Why is the man asking for advice?

    (A) His homework is difficult.
    (B) He doesn't like his professor.
    (C) He's having trouble learning Spanish.
    (D) He has to decide which professor he wants.

_____ 7   What does the woman want?

    (A) A reducing diet.
    (B) The location of the subway.
    (C) Directions to the museum.
    (D) A ride to the museum.

_____ 8   Why can't the man go to the party?

    (A) He needs to catch up on his sleep.
    (B) He is going out of town on business.
    (C) He hasn't finished his homework.
    (D) He has a deadline to meet.

_____ 9   Where did this conversation take place?

    (A) In a hospital.
    (B) At a party.
    (C) In a parking lot.
    (D) In an elevator.

_____ 10   What is the man going to do?

    (A) Get some fresh air.
    (B) Take a taxi to the park.
    (C) Get some parts for his car.
    (D) Go home from work.

Exercise L-89, Set B

<u>Objective and Directions:</u> see Exercise L-88, Set B.

_____ 1 What was the book about?

 (A) Early American ships.
 (B) Exploration of the Americas.
 (C) Famous shipwrecks.
 (D) Principles of shipbuilding.

_____ 2 What did the man just do?

 (A) He made the woman laugh.
 (B) He lied to the woman.
 (C) He told an amusing story.
 (D) He told a bad joke.

_____ 3 What is Jeff like?

 (A) He's easy to get along with.
 (B) He is rarely thoughtless.
 (C) He tries to please everyone.
 (D) He is industrious.

_____ 4 What is the woman doing?

 (A) Shopping for new clothes.
 (B) Cleaning out her closet.
 (C) Getting dressed.
 (D) Looking for her black dress.

_____ 5 Where has the woman just come from?

 (A) The accounting office.
 (B) The post office.
 (C) Class.
 (D) The library.

_____ 6 Why did the woman thank the man?

 (A) He gave her a ride home again.
 (B) He gave her his extra bed.
 (C) She had been a visitor in his home.
 (D) She likes the gift he gave her.

_____ 7 What did the woman say about Mr. Stanley?

 (A) He is unemployed.
 (B) He is wealthy.
 (C) He works at the post office.
 (D) He has just gone bankrupt.

_____ 8 What does the man do?

    (A) He is a cashier.
    (B) He sells books.
    (C) He is a literature professor.
    (D) He works in a library.

_____ 9 What does the woman say about the man?

    (A) He looks tired.
    (B) He works too hard.
    (C) He still looks rested.
    (D) He looks very young.

_____ 10 What does the woman tell the man to do?

    (A) Detour around the construction.
    (B) Get the car repaired.
    (C) Come to supper on Saturday.
    (D) Bring fruit to the picnic.

Exercise L-90, Set B

Objective and Directions: see Exercise L-88, Set B.

_____ 1 What is the man afraid he'll have to do?

    (A) Talk to the landlord.
    (B) Go to the doctor.
    (C) Give a speech.
    (D) Find a new apartment.

_____ 2 What does the man think about the sign?

    (A) It is better than his own.
    (B) It was made by a child.
    (C) It looks terrible.
    (D) It may win a prize.

_____ 3 What will the man probably do?

    (A) Purchase a pair of bluejeans.
    (B) Buy a new boat.
    (C) Try out for the team.
    (D) Go sailing.

_____ 4 What are these people discussing?

    (A) A new clerk at the store.
    (B) An unsolved crime.
    (C) How to open the door.
    (D) How to turn on the closet light.

_____ 5   What's the man's problem?

    (A) He needs a new pair of shoes.
    (B) His record player is unreliable.
    (C) He hasn't been able to sell his stereo.
    (D) He needs to raise some money.

_____ 6   What is the woman going to do?

    (A) Spend a few days out of town.
    (B) Stop at the nearest service station.
    (C) Look for her car keys.
    (D) Have her brakes repaired.

_____ 7   Where did this conversation probably take place?

    (A) At the carwash.
    (B) At a hardware store.
    (C) At the lost-and-found office.
    (D) At a car dealership.

_____ 8   What does the woman say about John?

    (A) He has a bad temper.
    (B) He is the youngest student in school.
    (C) He is a track star.
    (D) He is very immature.

_____ 9   Where did this conversation probably take place?

    (A) At a track meet.
    (B) In a school gymnasium.
    (C) In a gun shop.
    (D) At a book store.

_____ 10   What are thoese people doing?

    (A) Watching television.
    (B) Discussing a news article.
    (C) Considering a trip to the lake.
    (D) Talking about the weather.

Exercise L-91

Objective: To recognize the speaker's purpose on the basis of what the language is intended to accomplish.

Directions: For each item, you will **hear** a short dialogue. In the blanks, write the letters that indicate each speaker's purpose. You must write two answers for each dialogue.

Example: **You hear:** ⌈ MAN: Can I get your coat for you?
                    WOMAN: Yes. That's mine over there on
                                  the rocking chair. ⌉

        You read and answer:

  B   The man is   *D*   The woman is

    (A) making a suggestion.   (A) confirming.
    (B) offering help.   (B) expressing uncertainty.
    (C) offering advice.   (C) expressing gratitude.
    (D) bragging.   (D) identifying something.

1 _____ The woman is   _____ The man is

    (A) expressing concern.   (A) discouraging the woman.
    (B) identifying.   (B) conceding a point.
    (C) starting an argument.   (C) making a suggestion.
    (D) making an accusation.   (D) expressing doubt.

2 _____ The man is   _____ The woman is

    (A) offering help.   (A) giving permission.
    (B) teasing.   (B) insulting the man.
    (C) remembering.   (C) making small talk.
    (D) reminding.   (D) postponing.

3 _____ The woman is   _____ The man is

    (A) making a request.   (A) giving directions.
    (B) asking for information.   (B) responding to a complaint.
    (C) complaining.   (C) providing information.
    (D) asking the time.   (D) telling the woman the time.

4 _____ The man is   _____ The woman is

    (A) selling sandwiches.   (A) accepting.
    (B) asking for a sandwich.   (B) declining.
    (C) making an offer.   (C) giving information.
    (D) requesting information.   (D) describing.

5 _____ The woman is

    (A) identifying.
    (B) flattering.
    (C) complaining.
    (D) planning.

_____ The man is

    (A) making a suggestion.
    (B) telling the woman the time.
    (C) imploring.
    (D) expressing doubt.

6 _____ The man is

    (A) sharing a secret.
    (B) excusing himself.
    (C) refusing to go out.
    (D) bothering the woman.

_____ The woman is

    (A) telling a joke.
    (B) offering a warning.
    (C) advising.
    (D) predicting.

7 _____ The woman is

    (A) asking for information.
    (B) taking leave.
    (C) making a promise.
    (D) apologizing.

_____ The man is

    (A) asking for information.
    (B) complaining.
    (C) compromising.
    (D) bragging.

8 _____ The woman is

    (A) sympathizing.
    (B) elaborating.
    (C) apologizing.
    (D) disagreeing with the judges.

_____ The man is

    (A) sharing a secret.
    (B) expressing thanks.
    (C) complimenting the woman.
    (D) giving advice.

9 _____ The man is

    (A) persuading.
    (B) extending an invitation.
    (C) paying a compliment.
    (D) expressing an opinion.

_____ The woman is

    (A) disagreeing.
    (B) indicating ignorance.
    (C) reporting facts.
    (D) repeating.

10 _____ The woman is

    (A) commenting.
    (B) inviting.
    (C) questioning.
    (D) denying.

_____ The man is

    (A) explaining.
    (B) accepting.
    (C) acknowledging.
    (D) declining.

Exercise L-92

Objective and Directions: see Exercise L-91.

1 _____ The woman is

    (A) selling a product.
    (B) complaining.
    (C) requesting information.
    (D) making a promise.

_____ The man is

    (A) expressing intentions.
    (B) negotiating and apologizing.
    (C) identifying and agreeing.
    (D) explaining and giving information.

2 _____ The man is

    (A) asking for information.
    (B) gossiping.
    (C) fantasizing.
    (D) paying a compliment.

_____ The woman is

    (A) giving information.
    (B) taking leave.
    (C) refusing politely.
    (D) accepting a compliment.

3 _____ The woman is

    (A) planning a trip.
    (B) offering to lend something.
    (C) giving directions.
    (D) making a request.

_____ The man is

    (A) refusing a request.
    (B) offering advice.
    (C) giving permission.
    (D) giving orders.

4 _____ The man is

    (A) telling a joke.
    (B) repeating a joke.
    (C) complaining.
    (D) hiding his feelings.

_____ The woman is

    (A) explaining.
    (B) agreeing.
    (C) recounting events.
    (D) disagreeing.

5 _____ The woman is

    (A) declining an invitation.
    (B) hypothesizing.
    (C) expressing gratitude.
    (D) accepting an invitation.

_____ The man is

    (A) issuing a warning.
    (B) persuading.
    (C) organizing.
    (D) explaining.

6 _____ The man is

    (A) announcing the train.
    (B) making a cautionary statement.
    (C) excusing himself.
    (D) hypothesizing.

_____ The woman is

    (A) acceding to a suggestion.
    (B) making a suggestion.
    (C) quitting her job.
    (D) giving up.

7 _____ The woman is   _____ The man is

    (A) asking whose pots and
         pans are on the table.
    (B) telling Frank to wash
         the pots and pans.
    (C) asking Frank if he's
         ready to eat.
    (D) telling Frank to set the
         table.

    (A) sympathizing.
    (B) identifying.
    (C) apologizing.
    (D) disagreeing.

8 _____ The man is   _____ The woman is

    (A) discussing the time of
         day.
    (B) taking his leave.
    (C) hurrying the woman
         up.
    (D) apologizing.

    (A) expressing optimism.
    (B) threatening.
    (C) breaking a date.
    (D) acquiescing.

9 _____ The woman is   _____ The man is

    (A) expressing admiration.
    (B) calculating a risk.
    (C) introducing.
    (D) emphasizing doubt.

    (A) asking for further
         information.
    (B) expressing doubt.
    (C) disputing an expressed
         opinion.
    (D) expressing agreement.

10 _____ The man is   _____ The woman is

    (A) keeping a secret.
    (B) apologizing.
    (C) expressing
         disappointment.
    (D) thanking the woman.

    (A) trying to leave quickly.
    (B) expressing sympathy.
    (C) saying she was happy to
         help.
    (D) breaking her relationship
         with the man.

Exercise L-93

Objective and Directions: see Exercise L-91.

1 _____ The woman is   _____ The man is

    (A) making excuses.   (A) asking for identification.
    (B) taking leave.   (B) making small talk.
    (C) convincing the man.   (C) disputing.
    (D) introducing herself.   (D) interrogating.

2 _____ The man is   _____ The woman is

    (A) making a suggestion.   (A) imploring.
    (B) bragging.   (B) expressing an opinion.
    (C) conceding a point.   (C) interrogating.
    (D) making accusations.   (D) politely refusing a
                                     suggestion.

3 _____ The woman is   _____ The man is

    (A) making plans.   (A) expressing indecision.
    (B) inquiring.   (B) giving advice.
    (C) making an offer.   (C) expressing intentions.
    (D) selling insurance.   (D) persuading.

4 _____ The man is   _____ The woman is

    (A) trying to borrow   (A) making excuses.
        something.   (B) complaining.
    (B) checking up.   (C) clarifying.
    (C) setting deadlines.   (D) confirming travel plans.
    (D) asking for
        identification.

5 _____ The man is   _____ The woman is

    (A) sympathizing.   (A) instructing.
    (B) disagreeing.   (B) consoling.
    (C) expressing   (C) describing.
        disappointment.   (D) worrying.
    (D) making a supposition.

6 _____ The man is   _____ The woman is

    (A) expressing enthusiasm.   (A) contradicting.
    (B) making a comparison.   (B) making a request.
    (C) questioning.   (C) expressing sarcasm.
    (D) describing.   (D) expressing hope.

7 _____ The woman is   _____ The man is

    (A) sharing beliefs.   (A) giving information.
    (B) expressing anxiety.   (B) expressing certain
    (C) expressing sympathy.   knowledge.
    (D) describing tasks.   (C) encouraging.
                                        (D) setting a deadline.

8 _____ The woman is   _____ The man is

    (A) expressing preference.   (A) making a suggestion.
    (B) ordering a meal.   (B) asking for further
    (C) requesting service.   information.
    (D) bartering.   (C) giving information.
                                          (D) expressing indecision.

9 _____ The man is   _____ The woman is

    (A) imploring.   (A) introducing herself.
    (B) taking leave.   (B) making a pass.
    (C) asking for an opinion.   (C) offering assistance.
    (D) asking for directions.   (D) saying she doesn't know.

10 _____ The woman is   _____ The man is

    (A) asking for a favor.   (A) conceding a point.
    (B) making plans.   (B) making a guess.
    (C) presenting an argument.   (C) expressing probability.
    (D) telling a story.   (D) congratulating the woman.

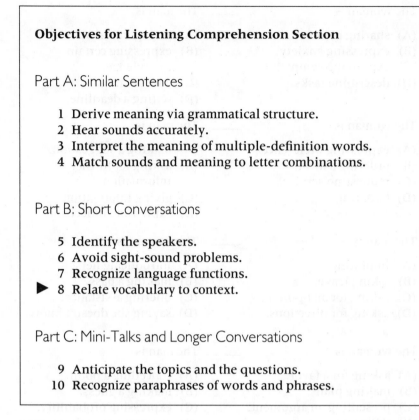

Objectives for Listening Comprehension Section

Part A: Similar Sentences

1 Derive meaning via grammatical structure.
2 Hear sounds accurately.
3 Interpret the meaning of multiple-definition words.
4 Match sounds and meaning to letter combinations.

Part B: Short Conversations

5 Identify the speakers.
6 Avoid sight-sound problems.
7 Recognize language functions.
► 8 Relate vocabulary to context.

Part C: Mini-Talks and Longer Conversations

9 Anticipate the topics and the questions.
10 Recognize paraphrases of words and phrases.

Objective 8: Relate Vocabulary to Context

Part B (and Part C) conversations are frequently, perhaps even usually, followed by questions that were not explicitly answered by the speakers. To answer such questions, you must draw logical conclusions from the stated information. For Objective 5, you practiced making inferences about the speakers. In these exercises, you will be asked to make predictions about the subject matter of the rest of a conversation after hearing only the first sentence. In addition, you will be asked to infer from a single sentence where an entire conversation takes place.

As you are doing these exercises, avoid sight-sound confusions, and remember that single words often have multiple meanings.

Exercise L-94

Objective: To predict from the opening sentence in a conversation what vocabulary items might occur later in the conversation.

Directions: For each item, you will **see** three words or phrases. You will **hear** only the first sentence of the conversation. In the blank, write the letter of the **one** item that might be mentioned in the rest of the conversation.

Example: **You hear:** [I stubbed my toe on the dining room chair.]

> **You read and answer:** _C_ (A) table
> (B) finger
> (C) bandaid

_____ 1 (A) receipts
(B) chalk
(C) past participles

_____ 2 (A) bouquet
(B) merry-go-round
(C) cake

_____ 3 (A) hiking boots
(B) wiring
(C) campaign

_____ 4 (A) tourists
(B) rifle
(C) dishwasher

_____ 5 (A) intern
(B) scaffold
(C) application

_____ 6 (A) profit
(B) television newscast
(C) wrapping paper

_____ 7 (A) error
(B) reservation
(C) secretary

_____ 8 (A) bride
(B) blanket
(C) broom

_____ 9 (A) fuse
(B) cassette
(C) faucet

_____ 10 (A) experiment
(B) earphones
(C) chemicals

Exercise L-95

Objective and Directions: see Exercise L-94.

_____ 1 (A) trial
        (B) brother
        (C) budget

_____ 2 (A) pistol
        (B) uniform
        (C) fertilizer

_____ 3 (A) operation
        (B) spices
        (C) umbrella

_____ 4 (A) departure
        (B) grandfather clock
        (C) refreshments

_____ 5 (A) truck
        (B) growing
        (C) seniority

_____ 6 (A) keys
        (B) suite-mate
        (C) gift

_____ 7 (A) hunting dogs
        (B) automobiles
        (C) shade trees

_____ 8 (A) diamond
        (B) emerald
        (C) quarterback

_____ 9 (A) candles
        (B) sandals
        (C) slippery

_____ 10 (A) groceries
        (B) bed sheets
        (C) bird seed

Exercise L-96

<u>Objective:</u> To identify the place in which a sentence was spoken on the basis of key words.

<u>Directions:</u> Listen to the tape two or more times, once for Column A and at least once for Column B. For each item, you will hear a sentence.

Column A: Identify the place in which the sentence was spoken, and write the letter corresponding to that place in Column A.

Column B: Write the word or words that support your decision in Column B.

<u>Example:</u> **You hear:**
1 You're allowed only one phone call, and I advise you to call a defense lawyer.
2 The defense has saved the game for the home team.
3 We caught him about ten minutes ago running away from the sporting goods store.
4 The defense rests its case.
5 The quarterback misjudged the distance.

You read and answer:
Police station (P)   Football game (F)   Courtroom (C)

	Column A	Column B
1	P	*one phone call*
2	F	*game, home team*
3	P	*caught, running away*
4	C	*defense, case*
5	F	*quarterback, distance*

Airport (A)   Bookstore (B)   Post office (P)

	Column A	Column B
1		
2		
3		
4		
5		
6		
7		
8		
9		
10		

Exercise L-97

<u>Objective and Directions:</u> see Exercise L-96.

Restaurant (R)   **Beach (B)**   **Hospital (H)**

Column A   **Column B**

1 _____   _____

2 _____   _____

3 _____   _____

4 _____   _____

5 _____   _____

6 _____   _____

7 _____   _____

8 _____   _____

9 _____   _____

10 _____   _____

Exercise L-98

<u>Objective and Directions:</u> see Exercise L-96.

Beauty shop (B)   **Hardware shop (H)**   **Laundromat (L)**

Column A   **Column B**

1 _____   _____

2 _____   _____

3 _____   _____

4 _____   _____

5 _____   _____

6 _____   _____

7 _____   _____

8 _____   _____

9 _____   _____

10 _____   _____

Exercise L-99

<u>Objective and Directions:</u> see Exercise L-96.

	Theater (T)	School (S)	Bank (B)

Column A   **Column B**

1 _____   _____

2 _____   _____

3 _____   _____

4 _____   _____

5 _____   _____

6 _____   _____

7 _____   _____

8 _____   _____

9 _____   _____

10 _____   _____

Exercise L-100

<u>Objective and Directions:</u> see Exercise L-96.

	Hotel (H)	Supermarket (S)	Gymnasium (G)

Column A   **Column B**

1 _____   _____

2 _____   _____

3 _____   _____

4 _____   _____

5 _____   _____

6 _____   _____

7 _____   _____

8 _____   _____

9 _____   _____

10 _____   _____

Part C: Mini-Talks and Longer Conversations.

Part C usually consists of three or four listening selections, each lasting approximately one to one and a half minutes.

Longer Conversations: These conversations often take place in a university setting or concern a university topic, but may also take place on a beach, in a store, at home, and so on. All of the exercises for Part B Objectives (5, 6, 7, and 8) are equally useful for Part C. Basically, Part C conversations differ from those in Part B only in length. Therefore, the focus of the following exercises will be the mini-talks.

Mini-Talks: The mini-talks usually fit into one of four categories:

1 Classroom lectures on general subject matter areas.
2 Classroom explanations of course requirements or procedures.
3 Informative talks for new university students.
4 Informative talks for the general public.

One way you can prepare for the mini-talks in Part C is by finding out as much as you can about the operation of universities in the United States. Read at least one university catalog or information booklet in order to familiarize yourself with the vocabulary and subject matter it contains.

Objectives for Listening Comprehension Section

Part A: Similar Sentences

    1 Derive meaning via grammatical structure.
    2 Hear sounds accurately.
    3 Interpret the meaning of multiple-definition words.
    4 Match sounds and meaning to letter combinations.

Part B: Short Conversations

    5 Identify the speakers.
    6 Avoid sight-sound problems.
    7 Recognize language functions.
    8 Relate vocabulary to context.

Part C: Mini-Talks and Longer Conversations

▶   9 Anticipate the topics and the questions.
    10 Recognize paraphrases of words and phrases.

Objective 9: Anticipate the Topics and the Questions

Success on Part C Mini-Talks requires careful concentration and a good memory. Notetaking is neither necessary nor permitted. If you anticipate the types of talks you might hear, you will be able to identify the topic more quickly. If you anticipate the types of questions you might be asked, you will be able to guess which information is important to remember.

Each selection in Part C is preceded by a short spoken statement that gives identification information. For example, [Questions 36 through 41 refer to the following **conversation**.] or [Questions 42 through 48 are based on the following **talk about an unusual bird**.] As soon as you hear [Questions . . .], you must focus your attention. This short statement can help you identify the upcoming listening task and better understand the first sentences of the selection. **The first sentences are extremely important.**

123

There are four catagories of questions that occur regularly. Always anticipate these questions. Anticipation will help you identify and remember the important aspects of the talk.

Categories of Questions

1 Main idea of the talk (central idea, purpose, topic).
2 Information about the speaker and the audience.
3 Facts and reasons contained in the talk.
4 Opinions and feelings expressed by the speaker.

Exercise L-101

Objective: To categorize the listening selection after hearing only the first sentences.

Directions: For each item, you will hear the first sentences of a mini-talk. In the blank, write the letter, (A), (B), (C), or (D), that identifies which type of talk you heard. The alternative answers in the box below are the same for all questions.

Example: **You hear:**   ⌈Registration for informal union classes will begin⌉
             │tomorrow in the union building. Be sure to bring│
             ⌊your student ID.   ⌋

You read: The alternative answers given in the box below.

You answer: _C_

Answers for all questions:

(A) Classroom lecture on specific subject matter.
(B) Classroom talk on course requirements or procedures.
(C) Informative talk for university students.
(D) Informative talk for the general public.

---

1 _____   6 _____

2 _____   7 _____

3 _____   8 _____

4 _____   9 _____

5 _____   10 _____

Exercise L-102

<u>Objective:</u> To identify the subject of a classroom lecture from the first sentences.

<u>Directions:</u> You will hear the first two or three sentences of a professor's remarks on the first day of class. On the chart below, you should answer these two questions about what you heard:

Question 1 What kind of class is the speaker probably addressing?
Question 2 What is the subject matter of the course?

<u>Example:</u> **You hear:** As you probably know, Astronomy 301 is a general introduction to the field. This section, however, is for non-science majors. So, if any of you are in engineering or another applied science field, see me after class to transfer to the other section.

The correct answers are (B) and (F), as shown on the charts below.

Question 1: What kind of class is the speaker probably addressing?

	Ex.	1	2	3	4	5
(A) Art History						
(B) Astronomy	✓					
(C) Biology						
(D) Education						
(E) English						
(F) History						
(G) Physics						

Question 2: What is the subject matter of the course?

	Ex.	1	2	3	4	5
(A) Contemporary American History						
(B) Architecture of early Egypt						
(C) Embryology						
(D) English literature						
(E) Experiments with electricity						
(F) General astronomy	✓					
(G) William Shakespeare						

Exercise L-103

Objective: To focus concentration by anticipating possible questions.

Directions: For each item, you will hear the first sentences of a mini-talk. Listen for the answers to the questions given in the box below. Then, in the blank, write the letters of the questions that were answered in the first sentences you heard.

Note: You may want to listen to this exercise more than once and discuss your answers with your classmates.

Example: **You hear:** The Capitol 10,000-meter race will take place this coming Sunday. Although it's too late to register by mail, you still have time to pick up a registration form at the Chamber of Commerce office.

You read: The questions, (A), (B), (C), (D), (E), in the box below.

You answer: *B, C, E*

Which questions can be answered?

(A) **Who** is speaking?
(B) **What** is the main subject of the talk?
(C) **Who** is the audience?
(D) **Where** does this talk probably take place?
(E) **When** does this talk probably take place?

---

1 _____   6 _____

2 _____   7 _____

3 _____   8 _____

4 _____   9 _____

5 _____   10 _____

Exercise L-104

Objective: To recognize the importance of listening carefully to the questions and the question words.

Directions: For each item, you will hear a question. In the blank, write the letter, (A), (B), (C), or (D), of the correct answer. The answer will be obvious if you think about the question.

> Example: **You hear:** [What characteristic makes birds unique?]
>
> **You read and answer:** _C_ (A) There are many varieties of birds.
> (B) Birds are not the only animals that fly.
> (C) No other animal has feathers.
> (D) Some birds build nests on the ground.

_____ 1 (A) Because of little rainfall.
(B) In two bands around the earth.
(C) After a period of little rain.
(D) In the United States.

_____ 2 (A) Mountains which are old and worn.
(B) Over hundreds of millions of years.
(C) Because of rain, wind and ice.
(D) The process of wearing away land.

_____ 3 (A) They travel at the same speed.
(B) They have different lengths and frequencies.
(C) Two examples are light and X-rays.
(D) Only a few can be perceived by man.

_____ 4 (A) It is a muscular membrane.
(B) It separates the chest cavity from the abdomen.
(C) It lowers to allow air to enter the lungs.
(D) It assists in the breathing process.

_____ 5 (A) They live in large hives.
(B) They rely on a good sense of distance, time, and smell.
(C) They forage on pollen and nectar.
(D) They build homes in hollow trees.

_____ 6 (A) It described social injustices of the day.
(B) It consists of novels and satirical works.
(C) He was a British writer.
(D) He lived in the nineteenth century.

_____ 7 (A) It is a triangular area.
  (B) As a river moves, it deposits sediment.
  (C) It consists of gravel, sand, and silt.
  (D) It is found where a river flows into the sea.

_____ 8 (A) They were painted in the 1930's.
  (B) They depicted common people instead of aristocrats.
  (C) They were painted by Thomas Benton.
  (D) They won many prizes.

_____ 9 (A) He lived in the eighth century B.C.
  (B) He wrote the *Iliad*.
  (C) He was a Greek poet.
  (D) His epic poems are the greatest ever written.

_____ 10 (A) It has been dried.
  (B) It loses some of its taste.
  (C) It does not spoil.
  (D) Its water content is low.

Objectives for Listening Comprehension Section

Part A: Similar Sentences

    1 Derive meaning via grammatical structure.
    2 Hear sounds accurately.
    3 Interpret the meaning of multiple-definition words.
    4 Match sounds and meaning to letter combinations.

Part B: Short Conversations

    5 Identify the speakers.
    6 Avoid sight-sound problems.
    7 Recognize language functions.
    8 Relate vocabulary to context.

Part C: Mini-Talks and Longer Conversations

    9 Anticipate the topics and the questions.
▶ 10 Recognize paraphrases of words and phrases.

Objective 10: Recognize Paraphrases of Words and Phrases

There are always a number of ways to express a single idea.

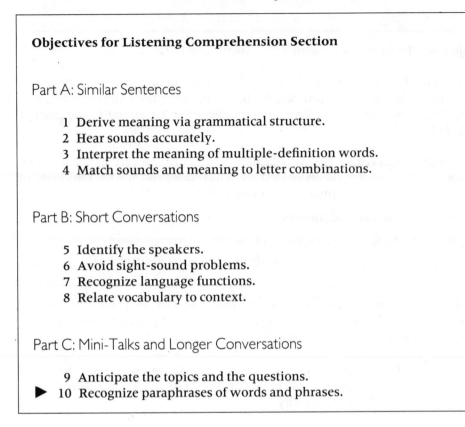

semi-arid regions = {
  semi-desert areas
  desert-like stretches of land
  areas with little rainfall
  regions without much precipitation
  dry terrain
  localities where it rarely rains
  places with sparse rainfall
}

All these phrases convey basically the same meaning. In other words, *areas with little rainfall* is a **paraphrase** of *semi-arid regions.*

    When listening to Part C mini-talks, it is very important to focus on the **ideas** the speaker is discussing rather than just the vocabulary he/she is using. The spoken questions and written answers will test your understanding of the ideas. Only rarely, however, will they contain the same vocabulary that was used by the speaker. Instead, the questions and **the correct answers will often be paraphrases** of the important ideas in the mini-talks.

Exercise L-105

Objective: To recognize paraphrases of words and phrases.

Directions: For each item, you will read one portion of a mini-talk. Below it, you will see five words or phrases. In the blank, write the letters, (A, (B), (C), (D), (E), of the ones that correctly paraphrase ideas contained in the portion you read.

Example: You read: The Appalachian Mountains are very old. They have been eroded by wind, rain, and ice for hundreds of thousands of years.

You see and answer:

B,C,D (A) spared from   (C) ancient
              destruction   (D) transformed
         (B) eons   (E) untouched

Gulls are a common sight all over the world. In fact, they have become so numerous that they are a source of growing concern. The more their population grows, the more problems they cause.

_____ 1 (A) frequently spotted   (D) mounting problems
              (B) increasingly bothersome (E) decreasing concern
              (C) relative rarity

Flocks of gulls cause aircraft crashes and contaminate water supplies. And, perhaps more important, they threaten the survival of other wild birds.

_____ 2 (A) domestic birds   (D) cause of drought
              (B) plane wrecks   (E) source of pollution
              (C) possible extinction

Gulls are sometimes referred to as "rats of the air." They will eat almost anything, from the chicks and eggs of their own and other species to bottle caps and nails; and modern man is inadvertently encouraging them to do so. Careless garbage disposal produces easily accessible trash heaps.

_____ 3 (A) rodent-like habits   (D) metal objects
              (B) discriminating appetite (E) accidently aiding
              (C) careful rubbish disposal

This flexible feeding pattern allows gulls to flourish under even the most adverse conditions. Less adaptable birds simply cannot compete and eventually die off or move on.

_____ 4 (A) unfavorable conditions (D) most suitable situations
              (B) stiff competition   (E) flight patterns
              (C) eating habits

Exercise L-106

Objective: To distinguish between correct paraphrases and phrases that merely contain repeated vocabulary but express the wrong meaning.

Directions: For each item, you will **hear** one portion of an informative talk for new university students. You will **read** five words or phrases. In the blank, write the letters, (A), (B), (C), (D), (E), of the answers which correctly paraphrase something in the portion of the talk you have just heard.

Note: You may want to listen to this exercise more than once and discuss your answers with your classmates.

Example: **You hear:** ⎡The dormitory cafeteria serves three meals daily⎤
during the week, but only breakfast and lunch on
the weekends.⎦

You read and answer:

__A,B,D__ (A) nineteen meals per week   (D) regular schedule
(B) twice on Saturday   (E) no lunch on Sunday
(C) Monday through Thursday

_____ 1 (A) resolve some doubts   (D) college procedures
(B) university personnel   (E) upcoming examinations
(C) week-long registration

_____ 2 (A) free of charge   (D) follow the directions
(B) without any trouble   (E) line up on the steps
(C) this simple process

_____ 3 (A) packet of letters   (D) available at the post office
(B) at the end of the meeting   (E) previously sent
(C) information on orientation

_____ 4 (A) language proficiency   (D) quantitative ability
(B) optional placement tests   (E) mandatory examinations
(C) final step in registration

_____ 5 (A) select your classes   (D) containing your picture
(B) guide for visitors   (E) identification card
(C) schedule of classes

_____ 6 (A) approval of a professor   (D) located at
(B) your official signature   (E) request your professors
(C) advice on your courses

_____ 7   (A) prompt payment of fees   (D) check-cashing procedures
              (B) checks required   (E) remember your money
              (C) cash accepted

_____ 8   (A) best wishes   (D) good attendance
              (B) turn over the program   (E) express my gratitude
              (C) worry and tension

Exercise L-107

Objective: To recognize correct sentence paraphrases.

Directions: The mini-talk you will hear is divided into four portions. After each portion, you will **read two groups** of sentences. Only **one sentence in each group** is correct in meaning. In the blank, write the letter, (A), (B), or (C), of the correct sentence.

__C__ 1.1   (A) The Old West lasted only nineteen years.
            (B) Cowboys contributed to the end of the Old West.
            (C) The period of the Old West wasn't as long as most people think.
_____ 1.2   (A) The Old West couldn't survive the invention of barbed wire.
            (B) Barbed wire was invented by an American cowboy.
            (C) The use of barbed wire ended in the days of the Old West.

_____ 2.1   (A) Dobb wrote a short history of barbed wire.
            (B) Dobb is formally recognized as the inventor of barbed wire.
            (C) Dobb didn't believe that barbed wire would work well.
_____ 2.2   (A) Gillinger was the first to patent barbed wire.
            (B) Gillinger conceived of barbed wire first.
            (C) Gillinger went to see Dobb about the barbed wire.

_____ 3.1   (A) Gillinger's barbs were made of metal and glass.
            (B) Children liked to climb Gillinger's barbed wire fence.
            (C) Gillinger was a cattle rancher.
_____ 3.2   (A) The fencing attracted cattle.
            (B) Cattle trampled the barbed wire fence.
            (C) Cattle shied away from the barbed wire.

_____ 4.1   (A) Gillinger earned $400 from the new fence.
            (B) Gillinger's new fence became widely known.
            (C) Gillinger designed 400 kinds of barbed wire.
_____ 4.2   (A) Today's barbed wire is very similar to Gillinger's.
            (B) Barbed wire was only used in the West.
            (C) Barbed wire was gone by the turn of the century.

Exercise L-108

<u>Objective:</u> To concentrate on the overall meaning of questions.

<u>Directions:</u> The mini-talk you will hear is divided into three portions. After each portion, you will **hear** a series of questions. If a question can be answered with the information you heard, put a **check** (✓) in the blank. If a question is nonsensical in light of the information, or if the answer was not contained in the information you heard, put an **X** in the blank.

Example: **You hear:** ⎡ All animals sleep, but no one is sure exactly why. It's not because they're tired. People sleep about the same amount each night, regardless of how active they have been. ⎤

You hear and answer: ✗ ⎡ How much sleep does the average person need? ⎤

✓ ⎡ According to the speaker, what kind of sleep pattern do most people have? ⎤

✗ ⎡ Why is man the only animal that sleeps? ⎤

There is insufficient information to answer the first question, and the third question is nonsensical.

1 ____	5 ____	9 ____
2 ____	6 ____	10 ____
3 ____	7 ____	11 ____
4 ____	8 ____	12 ____

Section 2: Structure and Written Expression

Introduction

The Structure and Written and Expression Section of the TOEFL concentrates on written English, and in the following exercises we will review the structures and patterns used in **formal written English.** Generally, the structures used in both formal and informal English are the same, but you may find some ways in which formal written English is quite different from the informal English you may be accustomed to hearing and speaking. An individual who studies English sentence structure and becomes skillful in speaking and listening but never becomes a competent writer is unlikely to make a good score on the Structure and Written Expression Section of the TOEFL.

The Structure and Written Expression Section has two parts containing a total of **forty questions** and **twenty-five minutes** is allowed for completing it. If you use your time wisely on practice tests and on the actual test, you will spend approximately **thirty-five seconds** on each question. Successful test-takers are very time-conscious: by working neither too fast nor too slowly, they finish the last question just before the test supervisor tells them to stop working. On each TOEFL practice exercise in these lessons, a time limit is indicated so that you can develop a successful **time strategy** whether you practice alone or with a teacher.

When taking the actual TOEFL, it is not necessary to begin with the first question in this section nor to answer the questions in order. Because you have twenty-five minutes for both parts, you are free to begin with either Part A or Part B and move back and forth between the two parts as you choose. If you begin with Part A you should not stop working when you reach its end, but rather you should begin immediately with Part B and work to the end of the entire Structure and Written Expression Section.

Part A: Sentence Completion: There are fifteen questions in Part A, and about forty percent of them are **simple sentences**, containing only one subject-verb combination. The other sixty percent are generally **complex sentences**, containing at least two subject-verb combinations involving some type of subordination. Each sentence is incomplete, and you must choose the word or phrase given which best completes the sentence. **All the words and phrases in the four answers are grammatically correct when considered independently.** But, when considered in the context of the incomplete sentence – in terms of grammar and meaning – only one of the words or phrases is correct. It is important to remember this fact so that you will not waste time looking for errors in the answers. Instead, you should spend your time carefully examining the incomplete sentence in order to find out what type of structure is needed to form either a simple or a complex sentence.

Part B: Error Identification: There are twenty-five questions in Part B and, as in Part A, about forty percent of these questions are simple sentences and about sixty percent are complex sentences. **But, in Part B, you are looking for an error, the part of the sentence that is wrong.** After you have read a sentence completely and carefully, you should examine each underlined part again. You should not waste your time wondering if there is an error in a part of the sentence that is not underlined. **The error you are looking for is always underlined.** Also, you should not waste your time thinking about a possible correction for the error. On the Structure and Written Expression Section of the TOEFL, you do not need to correct errors, only to find them.

In the following pages, we will examine ten elements of English sentence structure that are covered in the Structure and Written Expression Section of the TOEFL. These ten elements are organized into a list of ten objectives, called the **10-Point Checklist of Problem Areas.** You should study this checklist carefully and memorize the ten points in the order they are presented. Each time you examine a Structure and Written Expression question, go through this list systematically as you look for the best sentence completion or the error.

Parts A and B: Sentence Completion and Error Identification

10-Point Checklist of Problem Areas

1 Check for subject and verb (both present; neither repeated).
   Example of error: *Children they need love and protection.*

2 Check verb agreement, tense, and form.
   Example of error: *That student has living here for ten years.*

3 Check for full subordination.
   Example of error: *Because wanted to learn fast, the girl studied all the time.*

4 Check the verbals.
   Example of error: *This is a very interested book.*

5 Check pronoun form, agreement, and reference.
   Example of error: *It was me who answered the telephone.*

6 Check word form.
   Example of error: *Those roses smell real sweet.*

7 Check word order.
   Example of error: *The policeman asked the man what was he doing.*

8 Check for parallel structure.
   Example of error: *He likes to swim, to play tennis, and riding horses.*

9 Check for unnecessary repetition.
   Example of error: *He is a very fast, quick runner.*

10 Check for correct usage.
   Example of error: *She is interested for learning Arabic.*

Exercise S-1

Objective: To identify the ten important types of structure errors.

Directions: Match each sentence to a problem area from the 10-point checklist above. Write the appropriate number in the blank.

_____ a Johnny Carson he hosts a famous late night talk show.

_____ b That student is creative, conscientious, and does everything carefully.

_____ c The doctor has all ready left the hospital.

_____ d After the sun has rose, the birds begin chirping.

_____ e Alcoholism sometimes results from an emotion problem.

_____ f The players were chosen for their ability to make fast, quick moves.

_____ g The crowd enjoyed the excited movie.

_____ h That man is enough strong to lift three hundred pounds.

_____ i The swimming pool was closed because needed cleaning.

_____ j Some animals protect themself with camouflage.

Exercise S-2

TOEFL Practice: Structure and Written Expression: Time 6 minutes.

Objective: To recognize correct sentence completions and the ten important types of structure errors.

Questions 1–4

Directions: Choose the one word or phrase, (A), (B), (C), or (D), that best completes the sentence. Write your answer in the blank.

_____ 1 The salamander - - - - - - - to the order Candata.

    (A) in   (C) which
    (B) belongs   (D) belonging

_____ 2 It is the metallurgist - - - - - - - studies ways to work metals.

    (A) when   (C) which
    (B) and   (D) who

_____ 3 Although - - - - - - - named until 1782, aluminum was used as early as 5300 B.C.

    (A) it was not   (C) was not
    (B) is   (D) which was

_____ 4 Scientists are studying laetrile to find out if - - - - - - - cancer.

    (A) can it cure   (C) it can cure
    (B) can cure   (D) curing

Questions 5–10

Directions: Identify the <u>one</u> underlined word or phrase, (A), (B), (C), or (D), that should be corrected or rewritten. Write your answer in the blank.

_____ 5 Ride <u>sharing</u> has <u>became</u> more popular <u>since</u> gasoline prices
            A   B   C
      <u>have risen.</u>
        D

_____ 6 The elephant population <u>it has</u> declined <u>rapidly</u> because <u>many</u> of
                          A   B   C
      the animals <u>are killed</u> each year.
              D

_____ 7 When parents allow <u>his</u> children to spend <u>many hours</u> watching
                       A   B
      television, the children are not <u>likely</u> to be <u>physically</u> fit.
                             C   D

_____ 8 Families <u>who</u> are <u>enough fortunate</u> to own a historic home <u>may be</u>
                A   B   C
      able <u>to get</u> restoration funds from the government.
           D

_____ 9 A good sentence <u>in English</u> is <u>one</u> that is <u>brief, short,</u> and <u>easy to</u>
                      A   B   C   D
      understand.

_____ 10 The <u>first things</u> a new <u>international</u> student must do include renting
               A   B
      an apartment, registering <u>for</u> classes, and <u>to get</u> to know the city.
                              C   D

Note: When you have completed the exercise, check the following points:

— Did you put your answers in the blanks?
— Did you use the time wisely?
— Did you answer every question?
— Did you use the 10-point checklist?

Objectives for Structure and Written Expression Section

Parts A and B: Sentence Completion and Error Identification

10-Point Checklist of Problem Areas

▶ 1 Check the subject and verb (both present; neither repeated).
2 Check verb agreement, tense, and form.
3 Check for full subordination.
4 Check the verbals.
5 Check pronoun form, agreement, and reference.
6 Check word form.
7 Check word order.
8 Check for parallel structure.
9 Check for unnecessary repetition.
10 Check for correct usage.

Objective 1: Check the Subject and Verb
Exercise S-3

Objective: To identify the ten important types of structure errors.

Directions: Match each sentence to a problem area from the 10-point checklist above. Write the appropriate number in the blank.

_____ a The zebra as well as other African animals face possible extinction.

_____ b The space shuttle back to earth safely.

_____ c Some people claim that importing wine is better than domestic wine.

_____ d Each of those cars had their tires slashed.

_____ e Teachers are likely to praise correct and accurate answers.

_____ f Will Rogers was known primarily for a humorist.

_____ g Mechanical engineering is an applied scientist.

_____ h The director will see you if will wait a few minutes.

_____ i Never it has rained so much in Austin.

_____ j Many people gave time, money, and their energy to the project.

139

Exercise S-4

Objective: To identify five types of structures which can function as subjects.

Directions: Every sentence has at least one subject and one verb. The subject is usually placed before the verb. The subject is always a noun, pronoun, or one of the other noun structures shown in these examples.

Noun (N)	S <u>Your invitation</u>	
Pronoun (PRO)	S <u>It</u>	
Gerund (G)	S <u>Accepting</u> your invitation	V <u>makes</u> me happy.
Infinitive (INF)	S <u>To accept</u> your invitation	
Noun Clause (NC)	S <u>That you invited me</u>	

   (i) Underline the subject in each sentence.
  (ii) In the blank, write the abbreviation (shown above) that tells which one of the five subject types the sentence contains.

<u>N</u>   1 <u>Courtesy</u> demands a prompt apology.

_____ 2 He is the new director of the institute.

_____ 3 To drive more than fifty-five miles per hour is illegal.

_____ 4 Walking to the university takes twenty minutes.

_____ 5 Whoever wins the race will receive a trophy.

_____ 6 Cemeteries are frightening places at night.

_____ 7 Rollerskating has recently become very popular.

_____ 8 That all the passengers survived the crash is miraculous.

_____ 9 To get angry is not the solution.

_____ 10 These appear to be photographs of a North African village.

_____ 11 Zebras have black and white stripes.

_____ 12 That was a silly remark.

_____ 13 What he said confused me.

_____ 14 Falling in love is a beautiful experience.

_____ 15 To sleep all morning is a waste of time.

Exercise S-5

Objective: To identify the verb(s) in the sentence.

Directions: Every sentence has at least one subject and at least one verb. The subject in each sentence is already underlined. Find all the verbs and all parts of each verb, and put **V** above them. Look at the examples before you begin.

1 The municipal auditorium is located on the shores of Town Lake.

2 That new book will interest football fans.

3 There are several new apartment complexes west of the university.

4 Near the auditorium stand the city coliseum and the fair grounds.

5 Buses depart from the station every half hour.

6 Many career opportunities are available to a lawyer.

7 The cable television company has recently installed lines to the suburbs.

8 That new book has been checked out and read by a dozen people this week.

9 Through the branches of the tree shone the light of the full moon.

10 The new highway will have been completed by January of next year.

11 Here lies the grave of the first mayor of the city.

12 Rice is a popular food all over the world.

13 The children held on to their father's hands and walked quietly beside him.

14 The severe freeze damaged many crops and caused a rise in food prices.

15 Mathematics and history were his favorite subjects.

16 The head of the English department instituted many changes.

17 There should have been more rainfall during the winter months.

18 Deep down in the earth lie deposits of uranium.

19 Both the tulips and the daffodils are already blooming.

20 Those students have obviously studied English for a number of years.

Exercise S-6

Objective: To identify the possible functions of a word.

Directions: Many words in English can function in more than one way while other words can have only one function.
- (i) Put a **check (✓)** beside words that are always verbs.
- (ii) Put an **X** beside words that are never verbs.
- (iii) Put **two checks (✓✓)** beside words that can function both as a verb and as another part of speech (noun, adjective, etc.). Check your dictionary.

✓✓	1 dream	_____	11 laugh
_____	2 window	_____	12 advice
_____	3 seem	_____	13 migrate
_____	4 live	_____	14 passenger
_____	5 cigarette	_____	15 begin
_____	6 house	_____	16 large
_____	7 become	_____	17 continue
_____	8 eat	_____	18 trip
_____	9 can	_____	19 smoke
_____	10 below	_____	20 warm

Exercise S-7

Objective: To identify the function of a word from the context.

Directions: Read each group of words carefully. Put a **check (✓)** in the blank if the underlined word is functioning as a verb. Put an **X** if the underlined word is not functioning as a verb.

_____✓ 1 mittens <u>warm</u> the hands

_____ 2 the smoke <u>rose</u> to the ceiling

_____ 3 those dormitories <u>house</u> the men

_____ 4 her <u>laugh</u> hurt my ears

_____ 5 the <u>will</u> interests the lawyer

_____ 6 his <u>cries</u> fell on deaf ears

_____ 7 one <u>can</u> fell on the floor

_____ 8 the experiments require <u>live</u> organs

_____ 9 secretaries <u>book</u> appointments

_____ 10 her <u>dreams</u> came true

Exercise S-8

<u>Objective:</u> To identify the function of a word from its use in a sentence.

<u>Directions:</u> Each underlined word can function either as a verb or as a noun depending on its use in a sentence. Put **V** in the blank if the word is functioning as a **verb** and **N** if it is functioning as a **noun**.

<u>N</u>   1 In the desert the <u>need</u> for water is of primary importance.

_____ 2 Out of the darkness came a woman's <u>cry</u> for help.

_____ 3 On a dark night <u>dreams</u> can seem larger than life.

_____ 4 A safe place for a <u>will</u> is in a bank deposit box.

_____ 5 Since few classrooms have clocks, instructors <u>time</u> exercises with a watch.

_____ 6 For a novice backpacker, an all-day <u>climb</u> on this mountain is strenuous.

_____ 7 After a day on the <u>slopes</u>, skiers warm their feet by the fire.

_____ 8 An opossum <u>mothers</u> her young carefully during their first weeks.

_____ 9 At the last minute, a swift <u>kick</u> by one player tied the game.

_____ 10 For the engineering student recent <u>studies</u> are the most relevant.

_____ 11 Transatlantic travelers who want time to relax and read <u>book</u> passage on one of the few luxury liners.

_____ 12 Near the living room windows were <u>stands</u> for the houseplants.

_____ 13 When the weather turns warm, youngsters <u>spring</u> from their beds early.

_____ 14 When they are unable to reach an agreement, committee members <u>table</u> the motion.

_____ 15 A country's military <u>might</u> determines its international policies.

_____ 16 Although it takes more money, highway engineers <u>bank</u> sharp curves on all new roads.

_____ 17 When they are trying to improve their time, joggers <u>clock</u> their practice runs.

_____ 18 To ensure maximum growing time for young rosebushes, <u>plant</u> them in early spring.

_____ 19 Unless you place a flat stone under one leg, the picnic table will <u>rock</u>.

_____ 20 While reading her book, the operator <u>pages</u> employees who get calls.

Exercise S-9

Objective: To distinguish between clauses and phrases.

Directions: Every sentence has at least one clause. Every clause contains a subject and a verb. A phrase is a group of words that does not have **both** a subject and a full verb. Put **C** beside each **clause** and **P** beside each **phrase.**

_C_ 1 cars cost a lot of money   _____ 11 radial tires are expensive

_____ 2 in terms of population   _____ 12 from ten to twenty years

_____ 3 walking home takes time   _____ 13 the girl standing outside

_____ 4 spelling irregular verbs   _____ 14 hopping from foot to foot

_____ 5 to dream of better days   _____ 15 acupuncture requires needles

_____ 6 the man ate quickly   _____ 16 swimming develops stamina

_____ 7 cars needing many repairs   _____ 17 to learn English quickly

_____ 8 winter nights chill the bones   _____ 18 time heals all wounds

_____ 9 to enter costs ten dollars   _____ 19 the drive home at night

_____ 10 after the last dance   _____ 20 anger never helps

Exercise S-10

Objective: To distinguish sentences from groups of words with missing or unnecessary elements.

Directions: To be a sentence, a group of words must contain a subject and a verb.
  Mark complete and correct sentences with a **check (✓)** in the blank.
  Mark a group of words with a **minus (−)** if an element is omitted.
  Mark a group of words with a **plus (+)** if an element is repeated.

_✓_ 1 water is precious in the desert

_+_ 2 running ~~it~~ is good exercise

_____ 3 the girl $\overset{\text{is}}{\wedge}$ wearing a large hat

_____ 4 too much alcohol harms the liver

_____ 5 the man he has no driver's license

_____ 6 the couple with their two children

_____ 7 the desert cools off at night

_____ 8 on the wall hung a picture

_____ 9 children playing on the swings

_____ 10 the officers they had guns

_____ 11 the words repeated by the children

_____ 12 eating regularly it helps dieters

_____ 13 swimming develops arm muscles

_____ 14 the dog with its three puppies

_____ 15 the car full of teenagers crashed

_____ 16 the cars parked beside the building

_____ 17 children they laughed and sang

_____ 18 marriages require cooperation

_____ 19 a subject it must not be repeated

_____ 20 this is a simple sentence

Exercise S-11

<u>Objective:</u> To identify phrases that separate the subject and the verb.

<u>Directions:</u> Sometimes the subject and the verb in a sentence are separated by a phrase. In each of the following sentences, circle the phrase that separates the subject from its verb.

1 Influenza, (a common disease,) has no cure.

2 A woman (in my class) has three children.

3 The Volkswagen, a German car, gets good gas mileage.

4 Fruits, such as peaches and watermelon, grow well in Texas.

5 Winston Churchill, a famous prime minister, led the English during the war.

6 The coffee in this jar comes from South America.

7 The authors of this book want to help you.

8 Pélé, the famous soccer player, grew up in Brazil.

9 Cigars from Cuba are expensive.

10 Those chairs, the ones in the hall, need to be repaired.

11 Exercising in the hot sun can cause heat stroke.

12 Caffeine, a stimulant, is found in both coffee and tea.

13 Aspirin, a popular pain-killer, can be purchased without a prescription.

14 Your laughing at me hurt my feelings.

15 A person in his condition should not be driving.

16 Marilyn Monroe, a famous movie star, committed suicide.

17 That fellow with red hair used to work at the radio station.

18 Many vegetables such as tomatoes and lettuce grow in South Texas.

19 Gardening, according to a recent survey, becomes more popular every day.

20 The neighbors across the street have four dogs.

Exercise S-12

<u>TOEFL Practice:</u> Structure and Written Expression: Time 6 minutes.

<u>Objective:</u> To recognize correct sentence completions and structure errors related to the subject and verb, as well as other errors.

Questions 1–2

<u>Directions:</u> Choose the <u>one</u> word or phrase, (A), (B), (C), or (D), that best completes the sentence. Write your answer in the blank.

_____ 1 Buckwheat flour - - - - - - - the seeds of the buckwheat plant.

        (A) is made from   (C) it is from
        (B) from   (D) and

_____ 2 The state of Ohio - - - - - - - name from an Iroquoian word meaning "great river".

        (A) and its   (C) it got its
        (B) along with its   (D) got its

Questions 3–10

<u>Directions:</u> Identify the <u>one</u> underlined word or phrase, (A), (B), (C), or (D), that should be corrected or rewritten. Write your answer in the blank.

_____ 3 Boston, the hub <u>of historic</u> New England, <u>it is</u> the <u>capital of</u>
                    A   B   C
      Massachusetts and <u>the largest</u> city in the area.
                      D

_____ 4 Mixed seeds, such as cracked corn, peanuts, and sunflower seeds, is
          A   B   C
     popular feed for winter birds.
           D

_____ 5 Unlike most capital cities, Brasilia it was constructed specifically
            A   B   C
     to house government offices.
        D

_____ 6 Borax, generally found in the desert, being useful as a water
               A   B   C
     softener in the laundry industry.
        D

_____ 7 After roosting all day in a dark cave, a bat leaves its shelter and
             A   B
     spends the night hunting for their food.
      C   D

_____ 8 Modern buttons, unlike early ones, they are frequently
                                       A   B
     mass-produced and usually made of plastic.
         C   D

_____ 9 The letter "B" probably it originated as a picture sign of a house.
      A   B   C   D

_____ 10 The Dambovita River, a tributary of the Danube, it runs through
      A   B   C   D
     Bucharest.

Objectives for Structure and Written Expression Section

Parts A and B: Sentence Completion and Error Identification

10-Point Checklist of Problem Areas

1 Check the subject and verb (both present; neither repeated).
▶ 2 Check verb agreement, tense, and form.
3 Check for full subordination.
4 Check the verbals.
5 Check pronoun form, agreement, and reference.
6 Check word form.
7 Check word order.
8 Check for parallel structure.
9 Check for unnecessary repetition.
10 Check for correct usage.

Objective 2: Check Verb Agreement, Tense, and Form
Exercise S-13

Objective: To review the ten important types of structure errors.

Directions: Match each sentence to a problem area from the 10-point checklist above. Write the appropriate number in the blank.

_____ a Professor Jamison is extreme well liked by his colleagues.

_____ b The report was concise, and it was succinct.

_____ c The picture had fell behind the sofa.

_____ d They spend their vacations either in Europe or Mexico.

_____ e Beside two houses in the city, he owns a farm in the country.

_____ f Is in the Rio Grande valley that the ruby-red grapefruit is grown.

_____ g After finishing dinner, the telephone rang.

_____ h She had no idea whom had left her the note.

_____ i They agreed tomorrow to make a decision.

_____ j Antique furniture sells well even though is expensive.

Exercise S-14

Objective: To understand three ways in which a verb may be wrong.

Verbs: Key Concepts

Verbs are the most complex part of speech in English. They can take many different forms and function in many different ways. Verbs indicate the person and number of the subject and the tense and voice (active and passive) of the action. Every sentence has at least one clause and every clause has at least one verb. Understanding verbs, therefore, is crucial to success on the TOEFL.

Directions: Identify and correct the errors.

1 **Subject-verb agreement:** Does each verb agree with its subject? Do singular verbs have singular subjects? Do plural verbs have plural subjects?

    a The teacher with her students are viewing a film.
    b It was the neighbor's dogs that was barking last night.
    c Everyone but the janitor have left the building.

2 **Tense:** Is the tense of the verb correct for the intended meaning of the sentence? Are there any time markers which control tense? Do the tenses of all the verbs in the sentence fit logically with one another?

    d The doctor was out of town since last week.
    e John Kennedy has been being dead since 1963.
    f The man said that he will work late tonight.

3 **Form of irregular verbs:** Is the verb regular or irregular? If it is irregular, is the correct one of its three principal parts used?

    g The program has already began.
    h This is the first time a player has broke his arm.
    i The ship sunk ten miles from the coast.

Exercise S-15

Objective: To identify the subject of a sentence in order to choose the correct verb.

Directions: Underline the subject(s) of each sentence. Fill in the blank with *is* if the subject is singular or *are* if the subject is plural.

1 Nylon, like orlon, __is__ synthetic.

2 Either his children or his wife _____ arriving today.

3 Both the chair and the sofa _____ on sale.

4 Every dog and cat _____ vaccinated against rabies.

149

5 There _____ several universities in this city.

6 It _____ the bicyclists who endanger the joggers.

7 *The New York Times* _____ read by many people.

8 Everyone in the class _____ working hard.

9 All of the creeks _____ polluted.

10 All of the water _____ contaminated.

11 The committee _____ having its meeting.

12 The committee _____ separated from their families for long periods of time.

13 Two hundred dollars _____ a lot of money to lose.

14 Mathematics _____ a pure science.

15 A number of doctors _____ employed by the hospital.

16 The number of female doctors _____ growing.

17 The English _____ well known for their love of tea.

18 The hypothesis _____ supported by the data.

19 The young deer _____ staying near their mothers.

20 Those species of fish _____ found in Texas lakes.

Note: The rules for subject-verb agreement which follow will help you determine the accuracy of your answers. If your answer is wrong, it is probably because you did not correctly identify the subject of the sentence.

Exercise S-16

Objective: To improve your understanding of rules 1–3 concerning subject-verb agreement.

Rules for Subject-Verb Agreement: Singular Subjects

1 When the following words are used as **subjects**, they are always singular. Some of these words are **plural in meaning**, but they always require **singular verbs**.

everyone	someone	anyone	no one	each
everybody	somebody	anybody	nobody	either
everything	something	anything	nothing	neither

    S   V
<u>Everyone</u> <u>is</u> here.

    S   V
<u>Neither</u> of these books <u>is</u> very new.

2 When *each* or *every* comes before singular subjects joined by *and*, a **singular verb** is required.

        S   S   V
Every <u>man</u> and <u>woman</u> <u>is</u> eligible to vote.

        S   S   V
Each <u>student</u> and <u>teacher</u> <u>has</u> a locker.

3 Introductory *it* is singular and always followed by a **singular verb**.

   S V
<u>It</u> <u>was</u> the dogs which awakened me.

   S V
<u>It</u> <u>is</u> his grades that worry him.

Questions 1–5

<u>Directions:</u> Underline the subject of the missing verb, and fill in the blank with *was* or *were*.

1 In World War II, it _____ the men who served in combat roles.

2 Neither of the reporters _____ allowed to interview the players.

3 Everyone _____ required to write a composition.

4 Every man, woman, and child _____ given a free ticket.

5 Everything in the house _____ destroyed by the fire.

Questions 6–10

<u>Directions:</u> Underline the subjects and the verbs. Put a **check (✓)** beside correct sentences and an **X** beside incorrect sentences.

_____ 6 Each fruit and vegetable were organically grown.

_____ 7 Everyone have to arrive at 8:30 in the morning.

_____ 8 It was the children who broke the windows.

_____ 9 Everything in the house is for sale.

_____ 10 Every student want to pass the TOEFL.

Exercise S-17

Objective: To improve your understanding of rules 4–5 concerning subject-verb agreement.

Rules for Subject-Verb Agreement (continued)

4 Words that come between a subject and its verb do not change the number of the subject. Prepositional phrases often have this position.

> S   V
> The man | *together with* / *in addition to* / *along with* / *as well as* | his ten children | is leaving soon.

> S   V
> Everyone *except him* has a book.

> S   V
> The teacher *along with her students* is viewing a film.

> S   V
> One *of the most enjoyable parties* was given by Helen.

5 *There, here,* and *where* are **never** subjects (except in a sentence like this one!). When a sentence begins with one of these words, the subject comes after the verb.

> V   S
> There are no dogs in this neighborhood.

> V   S
> Here are the results of the experiments.

Questions 1–5

Directions: Underline the subject of each missing verb. Fill in the blank with *has* or *have.*

1 Wallpaper in addition to new curtains _____ been ordered.

2 There _____ been no new discoveries in that field.

3 Algeria as well as Tunisia and Libya _____ sent students to the United States.

4 Where _____ everyone gone?

5 John but not Mike _____ gone to play soccer at the park.

Questions 6–10

Directions: Underline the subjects and the verbs. Put a **check** (✓) beside correct sentences and an **X** beside incorrect sentences.

_____ 6 There has never been so many joggers in the race.

_____ 7 A box of books as well as a large suitcase are under the bed.

_____ 8 The president together with his assistants has left for Washington.

_____ 9 Here is the music as well as the words to the song.

_____ 10 Everyone in the two classes speak English very well.

Exercise S-18

Objective: To improve your understanding of rules 6–8 concerning subject-verb agreement.

Rules for Subject-Verb Agreement (continued): Plural Subjects

6 Subjects joined by *and* or *both . . . and . . .* take a **plural verb** (but see Rule 2).

$$\underset{\text{S}}{\text{A red \underline{Honda}}} \text{ and a blue } \underset{\text{S}}{\underline{\text{Ford}}} \underset{\text{V}}{\underline{\text{are parked}}} \text{ outside.}$$

A red Honda and a blue Ford are parked outside.
    S   S   V

Both tigers and elephants are becoming extinct.
    S   S   V

7 *Several, many, both, few* are plural words and always take a **plural verb**.

Both are going to attend the University of Texas.
   S   V

Only a few have passed the exam.
      S   V

8 Some nouns are always plural in form and always take **plural verbs**.
    clothes: trousers, pants, jeans, sunglasses
    tools: scissors, pliers, tweezers
    abstract: riches, thanks, means
However, some of them are followed by a singular verb when used in expressions such as *a pair of . . ., a word of . . .*

His pants are still at the cleaners. **but:** That pair of pants is dirty.
   S V   S   V

Your thanks are enough for me. **but:** A word of thanks is enough.
   S   V   S   V

Questions 1–5

Directions: Underline the subject of the missing verb. Fill in the blank with *is* or *are*.

1 Few _____ strong enough to finish the race.

2 There _____ a pair of sunglasses lying on the floor.

3 Both my good trousers and my old jeans _____ at the laundry.

4 Many of you _____ going to score above 500 on the TOEFL.

5 There _____ several on the top shelf of the bookcase.

Questions 6–10

Directions: Underline the subjects and the verbs. Put a **check** (✓) beside correct sentences and an **X** beside incorrect sentences.

_____ 6 That pair of Dior sunglasses must have cost a lot of money.

_____ 7 When the bell rang, a few were still working on the test.

_____ 8 The screwdriver along with the pliers were left out in the rain.

_____ 9 Several of the fish appears to be dying.

_____ 10 The scissors is in the bottom drawer.

Exercise S-19
_____

Objective: To improve your understanding of rules 9–11 concerning subject-verb agreement.

Rules for Subject-Verb Agreement (continued): Alternatives

9 When subjects are joined by the following structures, the verb must agree with the closer subject.

$$S_1 \qquad S_2 \qquad V$$
Neither the students **nor** the teacher is allowed to smoke.

$$S_1 \qquad S_2 \quad V$$
Either the teacher **or** the students have your books.

$$S_1 \qquad S_2 \qquad V$$
Not only the nurses **but also** the doctor is coming soon.

10 Many words may be singular or plural depending on what they refer to: *None, all, some, any, majority, most, half,* etc. When these words are followed by a prepositional phrase, the number of the object of the preposition will determine whether the words are singular or plural.

    S   V
All of the book has been destroyed.

    S   V
All of the books have been thrown away.

    S   V
All of the money is in bank.

11 The expression *a number of* is **plural**, and the expression *the number of* is **singular**.

       S   V
A number of students were missing from class.

       S   V
The number of Mexican students in class is small.

<u>Directions:</u> Underline the subject of the missing verb and fill in the blank with *is* or *are.*

1 Neither the doctor nor the nurses _____ here.

2 The number of nurses in the city _____ very large.

3 All of the nurses _____ very good.

4 All of the medicine _____ gone.

5 Some of the water _____ used for irrigation.

6 Most of the money _____ counterfeit.

7 Not only the money but also the jewels _____ locked up in the safe.

8 Neither the jewels nor the money _____ mine.

9 All of the cookies _____ gone.

10 Half of the furniture _____ in the truck.

Exercise S-20

<u>Objective:</u> To improve your understanding of rules 12–14 concerning subject-verb agreement.

Rules for Subject-Verb Agreement (continued): Unusual Singular Subjects

12 Expressions stating one amount of **time, money, weight, volume,** etc. are plural in form but take a **singular verb.**

      S   V
<u>Two weeks</u> <u>is</u> enough time for a nice vacation.

          S   V
<u>Five hundred dollars</u> <u>is required</u> as a down payment.

      S   V
<u>Ten extra pounds</u> <u>is</u> a lot to lose in a week.

      S   V
<u>Twenty gallons</u> of gasoline <u>costs</u> a lot of money.

13 Some words are always plural in form but singular in meaning. These
words require **singular verbs**.
    academic subjects: mathematics, physics, economics, statistics,
    civics . . .
    diseases: measles, mumps, herpes . . .
    abstract nouns: news, ethics, politics . . .
       S   V
<u>Mathematics</u> <u>is</u> a difficult subject.
         S   V
The <u>news</u> <u>was</u> very good.

14 Titles of books and movies, even if plural in form, take singular verbs.
       S   V
<u>The New York Times</u> <u>is</u> a good newspaper.
      S   V
<u>Star Wars</u> <u>was</u> a good movie.

<u>Directions:</u> Underline the subjects and verbs in each sentence. Put a **check** (✓)
beside correct sentences and an **X** beside incorrect sentences.

_____   1 German measles cause red spots on the chest and arms.

_____   2 News of the peace talks has not yet reached the island.

_____   3 Politics usually attract ambitious individuals.

_____   4 There were extra copies of *The New York Times* in all the offices.

_____   5 Two weeks are ample time for a camping trip to the state park.

_____   6 According to the champion, one hundred pounds are easy to lift.

_____   7 Two thousand dollars is a lot for him to pay for tuition.

_____   8 Both mathematics and physics are interesting.

_____   9 *Jaws*, a movie about sharks, was seen by a record number of people.

_____ 10 Mumps cause inflammation and swelling of the glands.

Exercise S-21

Objective: To improve your understanding of rules 15–16 concerning subject-verb agreement.

Rules for Subject-Verb Agreement (continued): Singular and Plural Subjects with the Same Form

15 Collective nouns are usually singular, but may be plural if the members are functioning independently. Watch the pronouns for clues to the singular or plural nature of the subject. Some of these words are *class, team, police, committee, audience, family, faculty,* etc.

        S   V
That class has its final test on Friday.

        S   V
The class are working on their individual projects today.

16 Some nouns use the same form for both singular and plural meanings. The pronouns and modifiers with these words will indicate whether they are singular or plural in meaning.

    always with s: species, series, etc.

        S   V   S   V
    That species is rare   Those species are common.

    never with s: sheep, deer, etc.

        S   V   S   V
    That deer is young.   Those deer are old.

Directions: Underline the subject of each sentence. If the subject is changeable, circle any clues that tell you whether the subject is singular or plural. Fill in the blank with *is* or *are.*

1 The crew _____ asleep in their bunks down in the hold of the ship.

2 Several unusual species of birds _____ found in this area.

3 When a young deer _____ motionless, its coloring will hide it well.

4 The committee _____ ready to make its recommendations public.

5 Both apparatus _____ available for your use.

6 The family _____ fighting among themselves constantly.

7 The fish in the aquarium _____ waiting for their daily feeding.

8 Each of those species of birds _____ common in Texas.

9 All sheep _____ dipped in the spring to kill the parasites.

10 The press _____ requested to show their credentials to the guard.

Exercise S-22

Objective: To improve your understanding of rules 17–18 concerning subject-verb agreement.

Rules for Subject-Verb Agreement (continued): Nationality and Foreign Words

17 Nouns for nationality that end with *-ese, -ch,* or *-sh* may be singular or plural depending on their meaning. Some of these words are *Chinese, French, English,* etc. When the word refers to *a language,* it takes a singular verb. When the word refers to the *people of the country,* it takes a plural verb and is preceded by the article *the.*

    S   V
    French is a Romance language.

    S   V
    English is spoken in the U.S.

    S   V
    The French are romantic.

    S   V
    The English love tea.

18 English has borrowed words from other languages. Some of these words have unusual singular and plural forms.

origin	singular	plural	singular (plural) examples
Greek	-is	-es	basis (bases), crisis (crises)
Greek	-on	-a	criterion (criteria), phenomenon (phenomena)
Latin (m)	-us	-i	radius (radii), alumnus (alumni)
Latin (f)	-a	-ae	alga (algae), vita (vitae)
Latin (n)	-um	-a	datum (data), medium (media)
Latin	-ix/-ex	-ices	index (indices), appendix (appendices)

    S   V
    The algae in the pool are hard to remove.

    S   V
    The radius of the circle is two inches.

Directions: Underline the subject and fill in the blank with *is* or *are.*

1 Alumni of the university _____ invited to the graduation ceremony.

2 These bacteria _____ being studied by university scientists.

3 English _____ heard all over the world.

4 The Portuguese _____ fortunate to have such a beautiful coastline.

5 Many Vietnamese _____ living in the United States.

6 The criteria for promotion _____ clearly stated.

7 The appendices _____ usually found at the back of a book.

8 Supernatural phenomena _____ of great interest to many people.

Exercise S-23

Objective: To identify the controlling subject and the verb which agrees with it.

Directions: Underline the subject with which the missing verb must agree. Then, fill in the blank with the correct verb form from the two choices in parentheses.

1 No one in this group of contenders ___*stands*___ a chance of beating the current speed record. (*stands, stand*)

2 Neither the education library nor the psychology library _____ the books that the professor recommended. (*has, have*)

3 Restricted ownership and enforced registration _____ two major approaches to handgun legislation. (*is, are*)

4 There _____ no doubt in anyone's mind about the guilt of the defendants. (*was, were*)

5 A gray and white car _____ parked outside the building. (*is, are*)

6 *Sound and Sense* _____ written for college students just beginning serious study of poetry. (*was, were*)

7 Every success and failure _____ to an individual's growth and maturity. (*contributes, contribute*)

8 The news on the local radio stations as well as newspaper accounts _____ that the prison riot was serious. (*confirms, confirm*)

9 It is still the women who _____ the burden of household chores. (*bears, bear*)

10 Neither all of the cookies nor all of the fruit _____ been eaten yet. (*has, have*)

11 Unlike Americans who seem to prefer coffee, the English _____ a great deal of tea. (*drinks, drink*)

12 A family of mockingbirds _____ in the tree every spring. (*nests, nest*)

13 Outside the door _____ several rosebushes. (*stands, stand*)

14 Everything, including the clothes in the closets, _____ stolen from the apartment. (*was, were*)

15 To a do-it-yourself handyman, a pair of pliers _____ very useful. (*is, are*)

16 The number of days of vacation provided to university employees _____ constant from year to year. (*remains, remain*)

17 For intermediate level students, *Steps in Composition* _____ useful reading and writing exercises. (*provides, provide*)

18 Despite the development of a vaccine, measles _____ still a serious danger to adult victims. (*is, are*)

19 Statistics as well as a course in research methodology _____ required of all doctoral candidates (*is, are*)

20 In their statements to the press, the committee _____ expressing several surprising viewpoints. (*is, are*)

Exercise S-24

TOEFL Practice: Structure and Written Expression: Time 6 minutes.

Objective: To recognize when a sentence contains an error in subject-verb agreement, or another type of error.

Directions: Identify the <u>one</u> underlined word or phrase, (A), (B), (C), or (D), that should be corrected or rewritten. Write your answer in the blank.

_____ 1 The ability to conceal <u>themselves</u> by camouflage <u>enable</u> some
                           A   B
    <u>otherwise defenseless animals to survive.</u>
        C   D

_____ 2 The information <u>on</u> the various <u>types of wasps</u> and bees in the area
                        A   B
    <u>were</u> useful to environmentalists who <u>were fighting</u> the use of
      C   D
    pesticides.

_____ 3 Compared to <u>the number</u> of paid holidays enjoyed <u>by most</u>
               A   B
    employees in the company, three weeks of vacation <u>seems</u>
                                            C
    <u>generous.</u>
      D

_____ 4 Sponges, with a <u>structural</u> organization like <u>that</u> of a colony of
                    A   B
    one-celled animals, <u>they stand</u> at the <u>lowest</u> level of the animal
                      C   D
    kingdom.

_____ 5 The large birdhouse together with the <u>numerous</u> birdfeeders under
                                        A
    the eaves <u>attract</u> a <u>considerable</u> number of different species
              B   C
    <u>in the summer.</u>
      D

_____ 6 Since snake eggs are <u>tough</u> and baby snakes can survive alone
                              A

at birth, neither the eggs <u>or</u> newborn snakes <u>need</u> protection from
            B   C   D

the mother.

_____ 7 Digitalis is a drug which is <u>prepared from</u> the seeds <u>and leafs</u> of a
        A   B   C

plant with the same name and is <u>used as</u> a cardiac stimulant.
                                   D

_____ 8 Benjamin Franklin, a famous American statesman, author, and

scientist, <u>he was</u> born in <u>1709</u> and <u>lived</u> to the age <u>of eighty-four.</u>
              A   B   C   D

_____ 9 The most famous alumnus of the college <u>were</u> invited to <u>participate</u>
                                                  A   B

in the graduation ceremony and <u>related</u> activities scheduled
                                   C

for late <u>May.</u>
            D

_____ 10 At <u>present,</u> advertising <u>is</u> one of the <u>most strictly</u> regulated <u>industry</u>
            A   B   C   D

in the United States.

Exercise S-25

<u>Objective:</u> To determine whether the tense of a verb is correct for the meaning of the sentence.

<u>Directions:</u> Each of these sentences contains a time marker, such as *today* or *two years ago*, which controls the tense of the verb. Some of the verbs are correct according to the time markers; others are wrong.
   (i) **Underline** the verb.
   (ii) **Circle** the time marker.
   (iii) Put a **check (✓)** if the verb tense is correct and an **X** if it is wrong.

__X__ 1 (So far) no uniform international policy against terrorism <u>is established.</u>

_____ 2 Some of the city's swimming pools were closed since the end of last summer.

_____ 3 From time to time even the healthiest individual needs to have a complete physical examination.

_____ 4 The city council is for some time now considering widening that street.

_____ 5 By this time next year, most students will leave school and return home.

_____ 6 Up until now, no cure for cancer is found.

_____ 7 It has been raining steadily since yesterday.

_____ 8 At the time of his death, John Kennedy has still been in his forties.

_____ 9 By the end of the hour, most students had finished answering all the questions.

_____ 10 In the early part of the twentieth century, immigrants are coming to America in great numbers.

Exercise S-26

Objective: To identify and correct errors in the forms of irregular verbs.

Directions: Many verbs in English have irregular past and past participle forms. Examine the verbs in these sentences and indicate whether the correct verb forms are used. If the verbs are correct, put a **check** (✓) beside the sentence. If one of the verbs is wrong, **circle** it and write the correct verb form in the blank.

__rung__ 1 After the bells had (rang) the students left the building.

__✓__ 2 A Japanese freighter sank near the coast just after midnight.

_____ 3 Unfortunately, not everyone who tried out for the football team could be chose.

_____ 4 At his inauguration, the new President sworn to uphold the Constitution.

_____ 5 The company's most experienced tree trimmer was rushed to the hospital after he had almost sawed off his leg with the chainsaw.

_____ 6 None of the dead woman's immediate family knew what had became of her will.

_____ 7 The President always sends a delegation of government officials to meet important visitors.

_____ 8 The careless hiker was bit by a poisonous snake.

_____ 9 In the fall, my grandfather always climbed the pecan tree and shaken off as many pecans as he could.

_____ 10 Individuals who have never ridden are advised to select one of the older horses.

_____ 11 Unlike adult dogs, puppies are feed twice a day.

_____ 12 Tomorrow night, the drum major will led the band during the half-time performance at the football game.

_____ 13 Instead of walking down the stairs, the boy swang his leg over the banister and slid down to the first floor.

_____ 14 The fish stank so badly that the refrigerator had to be cleaned to get rid of the smell.

_____ 15 Several inches of snow have fell since the beginning of the year.

_____ 16 A fresh coat of paint will hid all the marks on the walls in the children's room.

_____ 17 The trees in the new park have grown very quickly since they were planted last year.

_____ 18 The woman looked as though she had just came from the beauty salon.

_____ 19 Until the arbiter has hear both sides of the question, he cannot make an intelligent decision.

_____ 20 More poems have been written on the subject of love than on any other subject.

Exercise S-27

TOEFL Practice: Structure and Written Expression: Time 6 minutes.

Objective: To determine whether a sentence contains a verb tense error, or another type of error.

Directions: Identify the <u>one</u> underlined word or phrase, (A), (B), (C), or (D), that should be corrected or rewritten. Write your answer in the blank.

_____ 1 The party could <u>not be called</u> <u>success</u> because so <u>few</u> people that
                       A   B   C
        were <u>invited actually</u> came.
               D

_____ 2 The <u>Johnston family</u> <u>have been</u> living in a <u>tiny</u> apartment since they
                A   B   C
        <u>move</u> to town last September.
         D

_____ 3 Over the <u>past few</u> years medical researchers <u>have searching</u> for a
               A   B
        <u>means</u> to <u>control</u> the herpes virus.
         C   D

_____ 4 The pilot that was killed in the crash maintains an outstanding
           A   B   C
record of safety.
       D

_____ 5 For some time now, television advertising is tightly controlled by
        A   B   C   D
the Federal Communications Commission.

_____ 6 The cost of groceries have risen so rapidly during the past several
                           A   B   C
years that lower-income families can scarcely buy what they need.
                                 D

_____ 7 After the horse had threw the jockey several times, its owners
                      A   B
decided it was best to withdraw it from the upcoming race.
                     C   D

_____ 8 Although Latin was extreme important in its day, it has been
                      A   B   C
considered a dead language since the fall of the Roman Empire.
                                     D

_____ 9 Christianity has become a worldwide religion since it has begun
                      A   B   C
almost two thousand years ago.
       D

_____ 10 Although the students are disliking the material they are studying
                               A   B
right now, their instructor has no authority to change the syllabus.
         C   D

Objectives for Structure and Written Expression Section

Parts A and B: Sentence Completion and Error Identification

10-Point Checklist of Problem Areas

1 Check the subject and verb (both present; neither repeated).
2 Check verb agreement, tense, and form.
► 3 Check for full subordination.
4 Check the verbals.
5 Check pronoun form, agreement, and reference.
6 Check word form.
7 Check word order.
8 Check for parallel structure.
9 Check for unnecessary repetition.
10 Check for correct usage.

Objective 3: Check for Full Subordination
Exercise S-28

Objective: To review the ten important types of structure errors.

Directions: Match each sentence to a problem area from the 10-point checklist above. Write the appropriate number in the blank.

_____ a John Glenn has been a pilot, an astronaut, and in the Senate.

_____ b Women whom study engineering find jobs easily.

_____ c Mathematics, according to many students, are difficult.

_____ d That man tries to attract girls with a gentlemanly approach.

_____ e After to finish class, the group went to lunch.

_____ f Students studying Arabic they have an advantage if they already know Farsi.

_____ g Simultaneously, everyone stood at the same time.

_____ h Classes are held in a three-floors building near the campus.

_____ i Promoters were surprised at the amount of tickets sold.

_____ j The winners got such a big prize that gave a party.

Exercise S-29

Objective: To recognize the various introductory words that are used to begin the three types of subordinate clauses.

The Complex Sentence: Key Concepts

1   A **complex sentence** contains at least two clauses: a **main clause** and a **subordinate clause**.

2   A **subordinate clause**, which is dependent on the main clause for its meaning, may function in a sentence as an **adjective**, an **adverb**, or a **noun**.

  (i)   **An adjective clause** (also called a **relative clause**) usually begins with a pronoun, such as *who, whom, whose, that, which, where,* or *when,* and immediately follows the noun or pronoun which it describes.
 (ii)   **An adverb clause** begins with an adverbial conjunction, such as *because, although, if,* or *while,* and is frequently found at the beginning or the end of a sentence.
(iii)   **A noun clause** begins with the word *that* or a question word, such as *why, what,* or *how,* and can function in a sentence in any of the ways that a noun can.

Directions: Each of these complex sentences will have two clauses: one main clause and one subordinate clause. Fill in the blank with a word which can begin the subordinate clause. Then, underline the subordinate clause.

Adjective clauses:
1 No one knew the men _____ were standing outside the room.
2 Pure gold, _____ is easily bent, is rarely used for jewelry.
3 The girl's family disapproves of the boy _____ she wants to marry.

Adverb clauses:
4 Farmers use irrigation _____ their crops will not die.
5 Copper is a much used conductor_____ it is strong and cheap.
6 The man would have died _____ the doctors had not operated.

Noun clauses:
7 The weatherman predicted _____ it would rain.
8 _____ the magician did surprised the crowd.
9 The policeman asked _____ I lived.

Exercise S-30

Objective: To distinguish between main clauses and subordinate clauses.

Directions: A main clause is a subject-verb combination that can function independently as a sentence. A subordinate clause is a subject-verb combination that begins with a word such as *because, which, after,* or *if* and **cannot** function independently as a sentence. For example:

    main clause: the rain stopped
    subordinate clause: after the rain stopped

    main clause: he lost his wallet
    subordinate clause: which he lost

Decide whether each clause is a **main clause (MC)** or a **subordinate clause (SC)** and put the appropriate abbreviation in the blank.

_MC_   1 it started to rain

_____   2 after the runner fell down

_____   3 before the telephone was invented

_____   4 which no one clearly understood

_____   5 she left because of you

_____   6 what you said to me

_____   7 a singer performed after dinner

_____   8 because the chicken was burned

_____   9 she has been crying a lot

_____ 10 when you left town

_____ 11 the cost of chicken has gone up

_____ 12 whom he saw at the theater

_____ 13 exercise promotes health

_____ 14 walking develops leg muscles

_____ 15 winning is not everything

_____ 16 that apples are very nutritious

_____ 17 while the choir was singing

_____ 18 if prices continue to climb

_____ 19 they arrived after the deadline

_____ 20 although there was ice on the road

Exercise S-31

_____

Objective: To distinguish between subordinate clauses and phrases by looking for a subject and a verb.

Directions: A subordinate clause contains a subject and a full verb; a phrase does not. Indicate whether each item is a **subordinate clause (SC)** or a **phrase (PHR)** by putting the correct abbreviation in the blank.

PHR   1 before finishing dinner

_____   2 if the doctors operate soon

_____   3 whom the committee chose

_____   4 after the last class

_____   5 as the sun set behind the hill

_____   6 because he was born in Texas

_____   7 standing in a long line

_____   8 which the driver hit

_____   9 an inexpensive Japanese model

_____ 10 before the rain had stopped

_____ 11 driving fifty-five miles an hour

_____ 12 which he passed easily

_____ 13 exercising every morning

_____ 14 until the summer ends

_____ 15 as soon as it is over

_____ 16 a self-correcting typewriter

_____ 17 what he did during the holidays

_____ 18 where she used to live

_____ 19 during the president's talk

_____ 20 that he had gone bankrupt

Exercise S-32

_____

Objective: To distinguish among main clauses, subordinate clauses, and phrases.

Directions: Decide whether each group of words is a **main clause (MC)**, a **subordinate clause (SC)**, or a **phrase (PHR)** and put the appropriate abbreviation in the blank.

MC   1 the water is used for irrigation

_____   2 which is used to make chewing gum

_____   3 a famous talk show host

_____   4 her hopes for the future

_____   5 the population increased greatly

_____   6 a brain infection causing jerking

_____   7 the fourth largest city of the state

_____   8 although the law was repealed

_____   9 who lived in Oregon

_____ 10 several different writing systems

_____ 11 when the radio was invented

_____ 12 the first ships were only logs

_____ 13 mollusks live in shells for protection

_____ 14 a city located near the coast

_____ 15 a boat floating down the river

_____ 16 staying busy makes the time fly

_____ 17 alligators living in Florida

_____ 18 before inflation slowed

_____ 19 because the temperature is never high

_____ 20 walking burns many calories

Exercise S-33

<u>Objective:</u> To utilize sentence structure to distinguish among main clauses, subordinate clauses, and phrases.

<u>Directions:</u> Part of each sentence is underlined. Decide whether it is a **main clause (MC)**, a **subordinate clause (SC)**, or a **phrase (PHR)**. Put the appropriate abbreviation in the blank.

SC   1 The aardvark, <u>which hunts at night</u>, feeds entirely on ants and termites.

_____   2 <u>In a group of African musicians</u>, the drummer will probably serve as the leader.

_____   3 <u>Before he entered public service in 1794</u>, John Quincy Adams was a successful Boston lawyer.

_____ 4 Former President Dwight Eisenhower considered himself a <u>Kansan</u> although he was born in Denison, Texas.

_____ 5 King Edward VIII of England abdicated his throne in 1936 <u>because the government disapproved of his marriage plans.</u>

_____ 6 In terms of population, <u>Bangkok, Thailand is quite a bit larger than Barcelona, Spain</u>.

_____ 7 Adsorption, <u>which is often confused with absorption</u>, refers to a mixing or intermingling of two substances.

_____ 8 <u>Through his use of the mobile</u>, Alexander Calder created a new definition of sculpture.

_____ 9 <u>When winter descends on North America</u>, the weather in Acapulco, Mexico is warm and pleasant.

_____ 10 <u>An accountant is a person</u> who organizes, maintains, analyzes, and interprets business records.

_____ 11 <u>An ancient Chinese medical procedure</u>, acupuncture involves the insertion of thin metal needles into various parts of the human body.

_____ 12 An adult American alligator will range in length <u>from six to twenty feet</u>.

_____ 13 Sacramento, <u>the capital of California</u>, is located about ninety miles northeast of San Francisco.

_____ 14 As the price of pocket calculators has dropped, engineering students have almost completely given up slide rules <u>which were once extremely popular</u>.

_____ 15 Although growing children need up to twelve hours of sleep in some cases, <u>many adults do well on only six hours per night</u>.

_____ 16 The tsetse fly is primarily responsible for the transmission of sleeping sickness <u>from one victim to another</u>.

_____ 17 Florida is located at about the same latitude in the northern hemisphere <u>as parts of South Africa are in the southern. hemisphere</u>.

_____ 18 <u>Born in Athens about 469 B.C.</u>, Socrates was the son of a sculptor.

_____ 19 The sextant is an instrument <u>that is used by navigators</u> to find their location on the earth's surface.

_____ 20 Saturn is the second largest planet in our solar system and <u>the sixth from the sun</u>.

Exercise S-34

Objective: To recognize whether a pronoun, such as *who* or *which*, is introducing a main clause or an adjective clause.

Directions: Indicate whether each group of words is a main clause or an adjective clause by putting the appropriate abbreviation in the blank. Remember that a **main clause (MC)**, in either statement form or question form, can function alone. An **adjective clause (ADJ)** is a subordinate clause which must always follow a noun in the main clause. Some of these clauses can function in **both ways (BOTH)**.

ADJ   1   whom the doctors treated

MC   2   whom did they visit

BOTH   3   who failed the last exam

_____   4   that one is an old photograph

_____   5   which dog bit the child

_____   6   that scientists recently discovered

_____   7   which movie did he see

_____   8   whose test had the teacher misplaced

_____   9   whom they saw at the hotel

_____   10   that the sailors threw overboard

_____   11   those people have recently moved in

_____   12   who babysits for the next-door neighbors

_____   13   whose name he had forgotten

_____   14   at what time did he leave

_____   15   for which he carefully looked

_____   16   whose cattle the veterinarian treated

_____   17   whom were you looking for

_____   18   which he put his books into

_____   19   that dog bit him

_____   20   whom officials felt had the best qualifications

Exercise S-35

Objective: To identify all the subordinate clauses within a complex sentence.

Directions: A **complex sentence** contains at least one main clause and one subordinate clause. Each of the following complex sentences contains at least one subordinate adjective clause which begins with a word such as *who, whom, which, that, where, when,* etc. Count the adjective clauses in the sentence and put the number in the blank. Put a box around the introductory words and underline the clauses.

2 1 Pottery makers ⬚who⬚ used "the metal of clay" for cooking utensils foreshadowed one of the early uses of aluminum ⬚that⬚ modern man developed.

_____ 2 Modern man struggled for many years to develop a process that he could use to separate aluminum from other elements to which it was bonded.

_____ 3 Until 1845, scientists failed to discover a process which could separate aluminum from its various alloys.

_____ 4 The particles of aluminum that were formed by early processes were no larger than the head of a pin.

_____ 5 In 1854 a Frenchman named Deville developed a process which produced lumps of aluminum that were the size of a marble.

_____ 6 His process, which represented an important advance and which founded the aluminum industry, produced pure aluminum by chemical means.

_____ 7 The cost of the new metal, which was at first considered almost priceless, was $545 per pound in 1852.

_____ 8 Napoleon's honored guests were served with forks and spoons which were made of the new metal, but his less important guests had to use tableware which was made of less expensive metals such as gold and silver.

_____ 9 The price of the metal, which had surpassed even that of gold, fell rapidly in 1859 when French plants began full production.

_____ 10 France, where the process was developed, took an early lead in aluminum production.

Exercise S-36

Objective: To identify adjective clauses that are not marked by introductory words.

Directions: Adjective clauses may be **marked** by introductory words such as *which, whom, that,* etc., or they may be **unmarked**.

marked: The people <u>that</u> we met were not foreigners.
unmarked: The people we met were not foreigners.
There are **14 unmarked adjective clauses** in these sentences. Find them and **underline** them.

1 The twenty-eight space missions <u>the United States launched in the 1960's and 1970's</u> involved very expensive spacecraft <u>NASA could use only once</u>.

2 The rocket system engineers designed launched the spacecraft successfully but burned up as it fell back to earth.

3 The capsule the astronauts rode in was also designed to be used only once.

4 The Space Transportation System (STS) program President Nixon approved in 1972 called for the development of a spacecraft NASA could reuse many times.

5 The design NASA selected for the STS program is made up of three basic parts.

6 The part the astronauts can control is the cargo-carrier.

7 The first STS flight NASA had originally scheduled for April 10 finally lifted off on Sunday, April 12, 1981.

8 The first launch was delayed because of a problem with the computer system the spacecraft used.

9 The astronaut NASA officials chose for the first STS flight had a great deal of experience because of the five other space flights he had made.

10 The STS flight NASA launched in April 1981 was intended to be the first of many shuttle flights the United States would send up in the following years.

Exercise S-37

<u>TOEFL Practice:</u> Structure and Written Expression: Time 7 minutes.

<u>Objective:</u> To recognize correct sentence completions and structure errors related to subordinate adjective clauses.

<u>Questions 1–4</u>

<u>Directions:</u> Choose the <u>one</u> word or phrase, (A), (B), (C), or (D), that best completes the sentence. Write your answer in the blank.

_____ 1 Great Britain, which is now an island, - - - - - - - - once part of the European mainland.

       (A) which   (C) with
       (B) being   (D) was

_____ 2   The province of Brittany - - - - - - - a peninsula that juts out
into the Atlantic.

(A) upon   (C) lies on
(B) lying on   (D) which is on

_____ 3   Elizabeth Barrett Browning, - - - - - - - remembered for her
love poems, published her first work at the age of twelve.

(A) is   (C) who
(B) who is   (D) being

_____ 4   The Adriatic Sea, which lies between the coasts of Italy and
Yugoslavia, - - - - - - - the Mediterranean Sea.

(A) part of   (C) an arm is
(B) belonging to   (D) is an arm of

Questions 5–10

<u>Directions</u>: Identify the <u>one</u> underlined word or phrase, (A), (B), (C), or (D),
that should be corrected or rewritten. Write your answer in the blank.

_____ 5   Bangkok, Thailand, <u>who is</u> nicknamed the "Venice of Asia", <u>has</u>
                       A   B   C
<u>many</u> canals.
  D

_____ 6   Toward the <u>front</u> of the cortex is the motor <u>area</u> sends <u>nerve</u>
             A   B   C   D
messages to the muscles.

_____ 7   Egyptians, who <u>are gathering</u> <u>their</u> clay from the Nile, used
                            A   B
<u>straw or reeds</u> <u>to strengthen</u> their bricks.
      C   D

_____ 8   The Brooklyn Bridge <u>which</u> was <u>built by</u> John Roeblings who
                              A   B
<u>perfected</u> the <u>suspension</u> bridge.
      C   D

_____ 9   <u>In 1678,</u> John Bunyan <u>who</u> published his masterpiece *Pilgrim's*
             A   B
Progress which was <u>extremely</u> popular <u>for over</u> 200 years.
                        C   D

_____ 10 Pearl Buck, <u>who</u> <u>growing</u> up in China, was <u>an American</u> <u>by birth</u>.
                         A   B   C   D

174

Exercise S-38

Objective: To identify all the adverb clauses within a complex sentence.

Here is a table of some of the words that can introduce subordinate adverb clauses, arranged in columns according to their meanings. Some introductory words can have more than one meaning. If you can think of any other introductory words, write them in the appropriate columns.

time	cause/result	condition	opposition	manner	comparison
after	because	if	although	as though	than
since	since	even if	while	as if	as
before	so (that)	unless	though		
by the time	whereas	only if	whereas		
when	in order that	once	even though		
whenever		in case (that)			
while		whether or not			
now that		in the event			
until		(that)			
once		provided (that)			
as soon as					
as/so long as					
as					

Directions: Each of these complex sentences contains one or more subordinate adverb clause. In the blank, put the number of adverb clauses the sentence contains. Put a box around each introductory word and underline the full adverb clause. Identify each adverb clause as has been done in the example.

<u> 1 </u> 1 *time* |Until| cable television was invented, many viewers could not get clear reception on their sets.

_____ 2 Applicants will be considered provided that their files are complete before the deadline.

_____ 3 Mr. Williamson will be leaving the firm soon whether or not he voluntarily turns in his resignation.

_____ 4 As water vapor cools, it changes from a gas to a liquid and finally to solid ice.

_____ 5 Because Neptune orbits the sun only once every 165 years, it has not yet completed a full revolution since it was discovered in 1946.

_____ 6 While vision is the dominant sense in sighted people, for the blind the sense of touch is the most important.

_____ 7 In the late 1800's the number of murders in the U.S. fell although the percentage of murders committed with handguns increased.

_____ 8 Unless the sewing machine is repaired by Monday, the costumes will not be ready in time for the first performance.

_____ 9 The weeds and tall grass in that yard make the house look as if it has been vacant for quite some time.

175

_____ 10 Stacy Pool will be closed for a week so that it can be repainted before the summer season begins.

_____ 11 In the event that it rains, the picnic will be postponed until the ground is dry again.

_____ 12 Even though Tunisia is a small country, it has a booming tourist industry.

_____ 13 Only if ten more students register this afternoon will another pronunciation section be opened.

_____ 14 Notify the landlord as soon as you know if you are leaving the city.

_____ 15 If individuals are awakened each time they begin a dream phase of sleep, they are likely to become irritable even though their total amount of sleep has been sufficient.

Exercise S-39

<u>TOEFL Practice:</u> Structure and Written Expression: Time 6 minutes.

<u>Objective:</u> To recognize correct sentence completions and structure errors relating to subordinate adverb clauses.

<u>Questions 1–4</u>

<u>Directions:</u> Choose the <u>one</u> word or phrase, (A), (B), (C), or (D), that best completes the sentence. Write your answer in the blank.

_____ 1 - - - - - - - James Buchanan was a bachelor, his niece served as hostess of the White House during his presidency.

    (A) It was   (C) Because of
    (B) During   (D) Since

_____ 2 Because - - - - - - - has depleted many wildlife species, game preserves are being established.

    (A) excessive hunting   (C) of hunting excessively
    (B) hunting was excessive   (D) they hunted excessively

_____ 3 The lowlands of Albania are quite fertile - - - - - - - are alluvial.

    (A) because they   (C) because of which
    (B) which is because   (D) and because

_____ 4 American Indian languages, which differ widely, - - - - - - - to group many units of meaning into multisyllabic words.

    (A) and tend   (C) to tend
    (B) tending   (D) all tend

Questions 5–10

Directions: Identify the <u>one</u> underlined word or phrase, (A), (B), (C), or (D), that should be corrected or rewritten. Write your answer in the blank.

_____ 5 <u>Although was</u> defeated for the <u>presidency</u> three times, William
            A   B
        Jennings Bryan was <u>a major</u> influence in <u>the</u> United States.
                             C   D

_____ 6 <u>Because</u> wood <u>which was</u> <u>abundant</u> in the North American
            A   B   C
        continent, it was the chief <u>building</u> material of early settlers.
                                       D

_____ 7 The Bunsen burner is <u>so</u> named because it <u>thought</u> <u>to have</u> been
                                A   B   C
        <u>invented by</u> Robert Bunsen.
            D

_____ 8 Seventy-five percent of the <u>Burmese farmers</u> although <u>only</u> ten
                                        A   B
        percent <u>of their</u> land is <u>under cultivation.</u>
                    C   D

_____ 9 Buttercups <u>are</u> avoided <u>by</u> <u>grazing</u> animals <u>because</u> their bitter
                       A   B   C   D
        juices.

_____ 10 Plastic buttons are used on <u>men's shirts</u> <u>because</u> they are <u>strength</u>
                                         A   B   C
        and can withstand many <u>washings.</u>
                                   D

Exercise S-40

Objective: To recognize noun clauses and identify their function in a sentence.

Directions: **A noun clause** is a subordinate clause that functions as a noun. Noun clauses can function as subjects, but they are more commonly used as objects of verbs of telling, feeling, and thinking. These noun clauses frequently begin with the word *that*.
    Put a box around the noun clauses and indicate whether they function as **subjects (S)** or **objects (O).** For example:

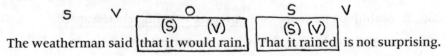

177

_____ 1 The doctor said that the man would get well quickly.

_____ 2 That it rained so much this year is fortunate for farmers.

_____ 3 Everyone hopes that the world will remain at peace.

_____ 4 The teacher feels that the students are progressing well.

_____ 5 That Fred got the best grade on the quiz surprised everyone.

_____ 6 That woman said that she was angry.

_____ 7 Charles believes that his opinions are not important.

_____ 8 That the world was flat used to be an established "fact".

_____ 9 That man feels that he is better than everyone else.

_____ 10 The advertisement states that this product stops perspiration.

_____ 11 That no one ate her special dish upset the hostess.

_____ 12 Archeologists believe that these artifacts are old.

_____ 13 The class argued that the test was unfair.

_____ 14 That the building burned down is a terrible shame.

_____ 15 Researchers believe that they have isolated an important virus.

_____ 16 The policeman claimed that the woman was speeding.

_____ 17 The experiment showed that the boiling points of the two liquids differ.

_____ 18 That the Loch Ness monster exists has not been proved.

_____ 19 The instructions state that the toy car needs two batteries.

_____ 20 The company knows that its employees will go on strike soon.

Exercise S-41

Objective: To identify unmarked noun clauses.

Directions: When a noun clause functions as an object, the word *that* is frequently omitted. Indicate whether the sentence contains an **unmarked noun clause** by putting **NC** in the blank. Underline the full noun clause and insert the word *that* at the beginning of the noun clause.

 unmarked noun clause: The boy said he felt sick.

 marked noun clause: The boy said <u>that</u> he felt sick.

If the sentence does not contain a noun clause, put an **X** in the blank.

_X_ 1 The speaker summarized the main points of his report.

_NC_ 2 Ambitious students feel/^{that} <u>hard work is ultimately rewarded.</u>

_____ 3 The pilot said his plane was in good condition.

178

_____ 4 That experiment demonstrates people have trouble recalling more than seven digits in sequence.

_____ 5 The man that caused the accident believed in his own innocence.

_____ 6 A woman that witnessed the fight said she would not testify willingly.

_____ 7 The fire inspector stated the building lacked sufficient safety equipment.

_____ 8 That encyclopedia contains 1,523 pages and 470 articles.

_____ 9 Results of the garbage study reveal fifteen percent of the city's edible food is wasted.

_____ 10 Search parties reported they had found the lost hikers.

_____ 11 Environmentalists are worried about the disappearance of many species of cacti in the Southwest.

_____ 12 The chief of police said his men have arrested a suspect.

_____ 13 The instruction booklet says the appliance should not be immersed in water.

_____ 14 The book club is designed especially for the computer professional.

_____ 15 Few believe the report is accurate.

_____ 16 That magazine is said to be useful to amateur radio operators.

_____ 17 Glass that is handblown often contains imperfections.

_____ 18 The city council believes the planning commission has been heavily influenced by developers.

_____ 19 That company reports its electric cars are virtually trouble-free.

_____ 20 The upholsterer felt the old couch was not worth recovering.

Exercise S-42

<u>Objective:</u> To recognize noun clauses beginning with question words and identify their function in a sentence.

<u>Directions:</u> Noun clauses can also begin with **question words** such as *what, why, how,* and so on. This type of noun clause can also function as a subject or as an object. Put a box around each noun clause and indicate whether it functions as a **subject (S)** or as an **object (O)**. For example:

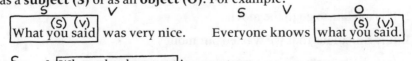

___S___ 1 Where the dog went is a mystery.

_____ 2 My father does not know how much money I spent.

179

_____ 3 What you said hurt my feelings.

_____ 4 Harry knows how he did on the test.

_____ 5 What the reporter asked was not polite.

_____ 6 The babysitter knows what the children like to eat.

_____ 7 Where we spent our vacation is not far from here.

_____ 8 The advertisement doesn't say how much the car costs.

_____ 9 Even his parents don't know why he ran away from home.

_____ 10 This class will explore how children learn.

_____ 11 I cannot explain why I didn't like the book.

_____ 12 How I spent my summer vacation is a boring topic.

_____ 13 The pamphlet explains where students can get a library card.

_____ 14 How dolphins communicate is the subject of the film.

_____ 15 The officer asked where I lived.

_____ 16 The computer program explains how irregular plurals are formed.

_____ 17 Your parole officer must know where you are at all times.

_____ 18 How he can afford such nice things is a mystery to me.

_____ 19 Few people really understand how a photocopy machine operates.

_____ 20 This map shows where the city's main tourist attractions are located.

Exercise S-43

Objective: To distinguish between noun clauses and infinitive phrases in sentences beginning with the subject *it*.

Directions: **Noun clauses (NC)** and **infinitive phrases (INF)** are often found in sentences beginning with the subject *it*. These structures explain the meaning of the subject *it*. For example:

noun clause: It is nice (that) you came. **means** That you came is nice.

infinitive phrase: It is nice to see you. **means** To see you is nice.

Indicate whether a sentence contains a **noun clause (NC)** or an **infinitive phrase (INF)** by writing the appropriate abbreviation in the blank.

_NC_ 1 It is remarkable he survived the crash.

_____ 2 It is too late to go to the movie.

_____ 3 It is ridiculous that we wasted our money.

_____ 4 It is unlikely doctors can save the man's life.

_____ 5 It is absurd to be upset over such an insignificant incident.

_____ 6 It is interesting that that man can hold his breath so long.

_____ 7 It is foolish to waste time trying to convince him.

_____ 8 It is doubtful Congress will lower taxes this year.

_____ 9 It is unfortunate that the picnic had to be cancelled.

_____ 10 It is surprising to see him volunteering to help clean up the kitchen.

_____ 11 It was in 1860 that Abraham Lincoln was elected president.

_____ 12 It is reasonable to assume that they will be late again today.

_____ 13 It is likely that it will rain this afternoon.

_____ 14 It is stupid to go out into the cold without some kind of wrap.

_____ 15 It is requested that you refrain from smoking in the halls.

_____ 16 It was in the Philippines that the Tasaday tribe was discovered.

_____ 17 It is essential that he call me tomorrow.

_____ 18 It is important for him to have the operation soon.

_____ 19 It is wise to see a dentist once a year.

_____ 20 It was during the Johnson administration that students protested against the war.

Exercise S-44

Objective: To identify both marked and unmarked noun clauses of all types.

Directions: Underline all the noun clauses. Then, in the blank, write the number of noun clauses each sentence contains.

__1__ 1 One archeologist thinks that human beings did not develop the idea of numbers until after 3100 B.C.

_____ 2 That Samuel Colt developed a practical handgun in 1836 has had a great influence on modern society.

_____ 3 Christians' belief that Jesus Christ rose from the dead is one of the bases of their religion.

_____ 4 The fact that he proved unreliable made them reluctant to employ him again.

_____ 5 Recent news articles have reported that fifty to eighty percent of all handguns are used for criminal purposes.

_____ 6 Why man sleeps has been the subject of much research.

_____ 7 There is a biologist at Boston University who believes that insects developed wings in order to collect solar heat.

_____ 8 What caused dinosaurs to disappear from the earth is still unknown.

_____ 9 The tropics are where the study of biology really begins.

_____ 10 Few people realize that there are only six landing strips in the world long enough for the space shuttle to land safely.

_____ 11 A computer program called "Eliza" acts as a personal counselor and asks "her clients" how they are feeling.

_____ 12 No one knows what a quasar is or how it produces such gigantic amounts of energy.

_____ 13 Satellite photographs can provide information on where and how much rain is falling.

_____ 14 Einstein stated that gravity was a warp in space and time caused by the presence of an object.

_____ 15 It was only recently that a professor in California discovered how wine can be made from cheese byproducts.

_____ 16 What may be the largest school of sea animals was recently seen near the coast of Antarctica.

_____ 17 Geothermal scientists believe there is enough hot water beneath the United States to fill 20 percent of its energy needs for a hundred years.

_____ 18 Astronomers have demonstrated that light bends in the gravitational field of the sun.

_____ 19 It was in 1492 that Christopher Columbus arrived in the New World.

_____ 20 Advertising specialists know how important packaging is for a new product.

Exercise S-45

Objective: To distinguish between noun clauses and adjective clauses beginning with the word *that*.

Directions: Both noun clauses and adjective clauses following special words like *fact, hope,* etc. can begin with the word *that*, but only adjective clauses can also begin with the word *which*. There is a quick way to test a clause to determine whether or not it is a noun clause: if you can insert the word *is* between the noun and its clause, you have a **noun clause (NC)**; if you cannot insert *is*, the clause is an **adjective clause (ADJ)**. For example:

    noun clause: the news *is (that)*   Austin flooded

    adjective clause: the news *— (that)*   you gave me

Indicate which one of each of the following pairs contains a **noun clause** by writing its letter, (A) or (B), in the blank and the word *is* in the appropriate space.

_B_ 1 (A) the fact _─ (that)___   the book contains (ADJ)
      (B) the fact _is (that)__   the man is very rich (NC)

_____ 2 (A) her hope _____ her friends will arrive tomorrow
      (B) her hope _____ she never revealed

_____ 3 (A) the news _____ the newspaper printed
      (B) the news _____ the war is over

_____ 4 (A) the proof _____ the drug is effective
      (B) the proof _____ the scientists offered

_____ 5 (A) her dream _____ she will win the Nobel Prize
      (B) the dream _____ he had last night

_____ 6 (A) the theory _____ the pottery is over 2,000 years old
      (B) the theory _____ the researcher explained

_____ 7 (A) the argument _____ the family had
      (B) the argument _____ the defendant is insane

_____ 8 (A) the claim _____ the newspaper prints only the truth
      (B) the claim _____ the company made about its products

Exercise S-46

<u>Objective:</u> To recognize errors related to noun clauses.

<u>Directions:</u> In each pair, both subordinate clauses begin with *which*, but one clause is a noun clause and should therefore begin with *that*. In the blank write the letter, (A) or (B), of the **incorrect** clause, the noun clause that should begin with *that* instead of *which*.

_B_ 1 (A) her feelings <u>which</u> she could never explain

      (B) her feelings <u>which</u> she would fail the test

_____ 2 (A) because of his theory <u>which</u> his method was best

      (B) because of his theory <u>which</u> he carefully explained

_____ 3 (A) their hope <u>which</u> they concealed from everyone

      (B) their hope <u>which</u> their son would succeed

_____ 4 (A) her hypothesis <u>which</u> the two groups would differ

      (B) her hypothesis <u>which</u> was clearly stated

_____ 5 (A) despite the statement <u>which</u> the president made

       (B) despite the statement <u>which</u> the airplane had been inspected

_____ 6 (A) doubted the claim <u>which</u> the garment was poorly made

       (B) doubted the claim <u>which</u> the customer made

_____ 7 (A) according to the argument <u>which</u> the speaker used

       (B) according to the argument <u>which</u> television harms children

_____ 8 (A) the idea <u>which</u> the essay contained

       (B) the idea <u>which</u> breast-feeding benefits infants

_____ 9 (A) the remark <u>which</u> I could not hear

       (B) the remark <u>which</u> it was time for lunch

_____ 10 (A) the evidence <u>which</u> the house had been robbed

       (B) the evidence <u>which</u> the police were looking for

Exercise S-47

Objective: To distinguish between noun clauses and adjective clauses on the basis of meaning.

Directions: This exercise is similar to S-46, but in this exercise you must write *that* (instead of *is*) to signal **noun clauses**. You will write *which* to signal **adjective clauses**. Each pair contains one of each type of clause.

1 (A) the news ___*that*___ Mount St. Helen erupted **(NC)**
   (B) the news ___*which*___ the magazine prints **(ADJ)**

2 (A) the fact _____ handguns are dangerous
   (B) the fact _____ the student had forgotten to mention

3 (A) the claim _____ the senator made
   (B) the claim _____ laetrile cures cancer

4 (A) the belief _____ God exists
   (B) the belief _____ the woman expressed

5 (A) the proof _____ there is life on Mars
   (B) the proof _____ the scientists were looking for

6 (A) the statement _____ the man made
   (B) the statement _____ dolphins can communicate

7 (A) the hope ＿＿＿＿＿＿ the man would survive
   (B) the hope ＿＿＿＿＿＿ the teacher expressed

8 (A) the dream ＿＿＿＿＿＿ Freud analyzed
   (B) the dream ＿＿＿＿＿＿ the world will remain at peace

9 (A) the theory ＿＿＿＿＿＿ there are black holes in the universe
   (B) the theory ＿＿＿＿＿＿ the psychologist explained

10 (A) the argument ＿＿＿＿＿＿ the man is innocent
    (B) the argument ＿＿＿＿＿＿ the lawyer used in court.

Exercise S-48

Objective: To determine whether a subordinate clause beginning with *that* is an adjective clause or a noun clause, on the basis of its function in a sentence.

Directions: Each of these sentences contains a subordinate clause beginning with *that*. If the clause is an **adjective clause**, write **ADJ** in the blank. If the clause is a **noun clause**, write **NC** in the blank.

NC   1 Newspapers reported the fact that a major earthquake had occurred in Algeria.

＿＿＿   2 The lawyer expressed his belief that his client was innocent.

＿＿＿   3 The beliefs that Moslems hold are based on the teachings of Mohammed.

＿＿＿   4 The facts that the witness concealed would have saved the defendant from being convicted.

＿＿＿   5 Searchers have given up hope that the hikers will be found before nightfall.

＿＿＿   6 The newspaper frequently misquoted the statements that the governor made.

＿＿＿   7 The jurors seemed unconvinced by the witness's statement that he had seen an armed man running from the house.

＿＿＿   8 Several people overheard the argument that the couple had.

＿＿＿   9 News that a ship had sunk off the Georgia coast reached the Coast Guard very quickly.

＿＿＿ 10 The hope that all students have is to pass their exams with flying colors.

＿＿＿ 11 That aluminum can be alloyed with a variety of metals makes it very versatile.

＿＿＿ 12 The fact that hummingbirds can fly backwards distinguishes them from other bird species.

_____ 13 That you invited them to your wedding surprises me greatly.

_____ 14 It is a well known fact that Christopher Columbus was not the first European to sail to the Americas.

_____ 15 That man has actually walked on the moon is still not believed by some people.

Exercise S-49

TOEFL Practice: Structure and Written Expression: Time 6 minutes.

Objective: To recognize correct completions for sentences containing noun clauses, among other structures.

Directions: Choose the one word or phrase, (A), (B), (C), or (D), that best completes the sentence. Write your answer in the blank.

_____ 1 A Washington researcher claims - - - - - - - he has developed a test for early symptoms of multiple sclerosis.

    (A) are that   (C) which
    (B) that   (D) are

_____ 2 - - - - - - - possible scientists will someday release the energy stored in water.

    (A) That is   (C) It is
    (B) That it is   (D) To be

_____ 3 Geologists cannot accurately predict - - - - - - - Mount St. Helens will erupt again.

    (A) when   (C) is that
    (B) which   (D) and when

_____ 4 - - - - - - - 1980 that Voyager transmitted photographs of Saturn to earth.

    (A) When it was   (C) During
    (B) That was in   (D) It was in

_____ 5 Many newspapers printed the governor's statement - - - - - - - would support a tax cut.

    (A) that he   (C) which he
    (B) was that he   (D) and it

_____ 6 - - - - - - - said under oath was disputed by several other witnesses.

    (A) It is the man   (C) That the man
    (B) What the man   (D) The man has

_____ 7 It was in 1901 - - - - - - - Theodore Roosevelt became president of the United States.

    (A) when   (C) that
    (B) and   (D) which

_____ 8 It was Albert Einstein who developed the theory - - - - - - - relativity.

    (A) of   (C) is
    (B) that   (D) and

_____ 9 It is believed - - - - - - - occur after rock strata break and before they settle into a new position.

    (A) to be earthquakes   (C) that earthquakes
    (B) earthquakes which   (D) earthquakes that

_____ 10 Why - - - - - - - at a given time is not known.

    (A) does a drought occur   (C) a drought should occur
    (B) it is a drought that   (D) a drought that occurs

Exercise S-50

Objective: To distinguish among the three types of subordinate clauses on the basis of the introductory word and the internal structure of the clause.

Directions: Each of the following items is a subordinate clause. Indicate whether the item is an **adjective clause (ADJ),** an **adverb clause (ADV),** or a **noun clause (NC)** by writing the appropriate abbreviation in the blank.

ADJ 1 whom they visited last weekend

ADV 2 because the creek flooded

_NC_ 3 what the people used to do

_____ 4 whose language the researcher studied

_____ 5 how much money the candidates spent

_____ 6 as long as it takes to learn them

_____ 7 when Europeans came to North America

_____ 8 which early settlers knew nothing about

_____ 9 who came to their rescue

_____ 10 how well he did on the last test

_____ 11 that he knew the answer to the question

_____ 12 that he talked to yesterday

_____ 13 if the students fail to do homework

_____ 14 until the deadline has passed

_____ 15 which was given to each applicant

_____ 16 how many dollars they lost gambling

_____ 17 which is situated on the Delaware River

_____ 18 that he will come to school every day

_____ 19 unless the tribe loses its land

_____ 20 since there is little fresh water

Exercise S-51

<u>TOEFL Practice:</u> Structure and Written Expression: Time 7 minutes.

<u>Objective:</u> To recognize correct completions of sentences containing subordinate clauses.

<u>Directions:</u> Choose the <u>one</u> word or phrase, (A), (B), (C), or (D), that best completes the sentence. Write your answer in the blank.

_____ 1 Christopher Columbus, a famous Italian navigator, - - - - - - - until recently considered to be the first European to sail to the New World.

    (A) has   (C) was

    (B) who has been   (D) that was

_____ 2 A lunar eclipse - - - - - - - the earth passes between the sun and the moon, causing the moon to become dark.

    (A) occurs   (C) which occurs

    (B) that occurs   (D) occurs when

_____ 3 Most early American inventions - - - - - - - important to the agricultural community.

    (A) were   •   (C) being

    (B) that were very   (D) very

_____ 4* Modern man is careless - - - - - - - of his garbage.

    (A) when disposing   (C) he disposes
    (B) disposing about   (D) disposes

_____ 5 It - - - - - - - the Titanic sank while crossing the Atlantic.

    (A) is 1912 when   (C) in 1912 that
    (B) which was in 1912   (D) was in 1912 that

_____ 6 An almanac - - - - - - - contains much information including details about the yearly movements of the sun and moon.

    (A) which   (C) a book which
    (B) is which   (D) is a book which

_____ 7 Romany is an Indic language - - - - - - - gypsies speak.

    (A) which   (C) and which
    (B) which is of   (D) is that which

_____ 8 Usually a bird species gains public recognition - - - - - - - faces the danger of extinction.

    (A) which only   (C) only when it
    (B) only when   (D) which only it

_____ 9 Dry cleaning is a wet process in which the first step - - - - - - - a garment in a cleaning solution.

    (A) involves soaking   (C) involving
    (B) that soaks   (D) which involves

_____ 10 Gulls are sometimes called "rats of the air" - - - - - - - they will eat almost anything.

    (A) which   (C) but
    (B) since   (D) that

Exercise S-52

Objective: To determine whether a sentence with a missing element contains a subordinate clause.

Directions: One or more words have been omitted from each of the following sentences so that the sentences resemble those found in Part A of the Structure and Written Expression section. Read the sentence carefully, and in the blank beside the number:

(i) write **S** if the sentence, when completed, will be a **simple sentence**, a sentence containing only one clause.

(ii) write **CX** if the sentence, when completed, will be a **complex sentence**, a sentence with at least one main clause and one subordinate clause.

S 1 Tigers - - - - - - - the largest members of the cat family.

_____ 2 Male tigers weigh as much as 420 pounds while females - - - - - - - around 300.

_____ 3 Most tigers reach a length of ten feet - - - - - - - includes a three-foot tail.

_____ 4 In the past, tigers - - - - - - - over a 6,000 mile area from Turkey to Far Eastern Asia.

_____ 5 Although most authorities recognize eight different species of tigers, - - - - - - - are now almost extinct.

_____ 6 Man cannot easily coexist with tigers - - - - - - - they attack livestock.

_____ 7 Tigers rarely attack man - - - - - - - are hungry or too sick to catch faster animals.

_____ 8 Men greatly value tiger skins - - - - - - - tawny with black stripes.

_____ 9 - - - - - - - are killed for their skins each year, the tiger population is decreasing rapidly.

_____ 10 Governments - - - - - - - pass strict laws against killing tigers can help prevent the total extinction of this beautiful animal.

_____ 11 Tigers - - - - - - - essentially solitary animals.

_____ 12 - - - - - - - tigers want to advertise their presence, they roar and leave their scent on bushes and trees.

_____ 13 When tiger cubs are born, - - - - - - - are blind and helpless.

_____ 14 The maximum life span of a tiger - - - - - - - about 20 years.

_____ 15 Tigers - - - - - - - by biting their prey through the neck or by suffocating them.

Exercise S-53

Objective: To distinguish between simple sentences and complex sentences, and to determine what element is missing.

Directions: As in the previous exercise, one or more words have been omitted from each of the sentences. **In the first blank**, write **S** if the sentence, when completed, will be a **simple sentence** containing only one main clause. Write **CX** if the completed sentence will be a **complex sentence** containing one main clause and one subordinate clause. **In the second blank**, write the **number** that tells what has been omitted from the sentence: **1 = main subject; 2 = main verb; 3 = subordinating signal; 4 = subordinate verb.**

_S_ _2_   1   Tigers - - - - - - the largest members of the cat family.

_____ _____   2   With their strong legs and claws, - - - - - - catch and hold their prey.

_____ _____   3   - - - - - - tigers can eat over 50 pounds of meat at one time, they can go without food for over a week.

_____ _____   4   Tigers eat hoofed animals which - - - - - - sheep and cattle.

_____ _____   5   - - - - - - men turn forests into fields for crops, they destroy the tiger's home.

_____ _____   6   Without large hunting areas, - - - - - - cannot catch enough food to survive.

_____ _____   7   Siberian tigers, which once existed in great numbers in the Soviet Far East, - - - - - - a current population of only 110.

_____ _____   8   Now only about twelve Javan tigers, - - - - - - used to exist in great numbers, are still alive.

_____ _____   9   Laws against trade in tiger skins - - - - - - the lives of many tigers.

_____ _____   10   The danger which tigers - - - - - - to man is much less than most people realize.

_____ _____   11   - - - - - - man's population increases, the tiger population decreases.

_____ _____   12   Men usually - - - - - - tigers by shooting or poisoning them.

_____ _____   13   Contrary to popular belief, a man rarely has to kill a tiger - - - - - - a human life is in danger.

_____ _____   14   Men may understand the true value of tigers only when the last tiger - - - - - - dead.

_____ _____   15   Zoos - - - - - - an important part in keeping tigers alive.

Exercise S-54

<u>TOEFL Practice:</u> Structure and Written Expression: Time 6 minutes.

<u>Objective:</u> To determine what element or elements are missing from simple and complex sentences.

<u>Directions:</u> Choose <u>one</u> word or phrase, (A), (B), (C), or (D), that best completes the sentence. Write your answer in the blank.

_____ 1 The articles - - - - - - - the magazine publishes are very scholarly.

  (A) which   (C) and
  (B) of   (D) in

_____ 2 Physicist J. Robert Oppenheimer - - - - - - - an important role in the birth of the atomic age.

  (A) who played   (C) ·playing
  (B) had   (D) was

_____ 3 In 1952 Lillian Hellman appeared before a House committee - - - - - - - because of it.

  (A) which suffered (C) and suffered
  (B) who suffered   (D) suffered

_____ 4 A new television series teaches handicapped children - - - - - - - can and should think about career development.

  (A) and   (C) both
  (B) that they   (D) who they

_____ 5 Some geologists believe that in the shale of the Rockies - - - - - - - more oil than in the Middle East.

  (A) with   (C) having
  (B) which have   (D) there is

_____ 6 The fact that the gorilla is becoming extinct - - - - - - - wildlife preservationists.

  (A) disturbing to (C) disturbing
  (B) disturbs   (D) disturbance of

_____ 7 Dinosaurs dominated the earth for 150 million years - - - - - - - suddenly vanished 65 million years ago.

  (A) until they   (C) until
  (B) that they   (D) because they

_____ 8 - - - - - - - the legendary lost continent of Atlantis may someday be found.

    (A) The belief   (C) Believing
    (B) It is believed   (D) That belief

_____ 9 - - - - - - - the 1980 World Cup ski competition, a Canadian almost won over the long-dominant Europeans.

    (A) In   (C) It was in
    (B) He was in   (D) His being in

_____ 10 Mari Sandoz was a Nebraskan - - - - - - - about the American West.

    (A) author who wrote   (C) author wrote
    (B) who authored   (D) whose writing

Exercise S-55

<u>Objective:</u> To identify adjective, adverb, and noun clauses on the basis of the meaning and structure of a sentence.

<u>Directions:</u> In each blank, write *which, although,* or *what* to complete the sentence. Use each word only once in each trio of sentences.

1 Everyone was surprised at the number of flowers __*which*__ the family grew in their garden.

2 _____ the family worked hard, the results were disappointing.

3 _____ they did to encourage such growth was to tend the garden with great care.

4 COBOL was chosen _____ many computer languages were available.

5 Computer experts know _____ the best language is for a specific purpose.

6 COBOL is a computer language _____ is used for business purposes.

7 _____ forecasters did not predict was rainfall heavy enough to cause flooding.

8 _____ forecasters predicted rain, no one expected serious flooding.

9 The rainfall _____ the city received was heavier than expected.

193

10 The fabric fence _____ was constructed in Marin County was 24 miles long.

11 Most ranchers understood _____ the artist was trying to do.

12 The long fence was built _____ some local residents tried to stop its construction.

13 _____ caused his insomnia was caffeine.

14 Caffeine is a stimulant _____ can cause sleeplessness in some users.

15 _____ it has little effect on some, for others caffeine inhibits sleep.

Exercise S-56

Objective: To distinguish between sentences and sentence fragments.

Directions: Some of these groups of words are sentences; mark them with a **check** (✓) in the blank. Other groups of words are not complete sentences. Mark them with an **X** in the blank.

✓ 1 When the seasons change, many small animals change their colors.

✗ 2 When winter approaches and the landscape turns white with snow.

_____ 3 Nature has given different types of creatures different types of camouflage.

_____ 4 Camouflage which refers to an animal's ability to hide itself.

_____ 5 Because many insects and small lizards have no way to protect themselves.

_____ 6 Unless a camouflaged insect is seen against a contrasting background, it may be completely invisible.

_____ 7 A small insect needs camouflage so that its enemies cannot find it.

_____ 8 Although some fish can become almost transparent.

_____ 9 Many species of fish which protect themselves through camouflage.

_____ 10 Reef fish can escape an enemy by changing their appearance to match almost any background.

_____ 11 Chameleons which may be the best known of all animals that change colors rapidly.

_____ 12 Because some animals have dark and light coloring, they are well protected in shady areas.

_____ 13 Baby deer which are born with spots on their backs which help hide them.

_____ 14 Large, strong, fast animals rarely have elaborate camouflage systems.

_____ 15 In times of war, man often borrows some techniques of camouflage from animals.

Exercise S-57

TOEFL Practice: Structure and Written Expression: Time 7 minutes.

Objective: To recognize correct completions of sentences containing all three types of subordinate clauses.

Directions: Choose the <u>one</u> word or phrase, (A), (B), (C), or (D), that best completes the sentence. Write your answer in the blank.

_____ 1 - - - - - - - , a famous Italian navigator, was until recently considered the first European to sail to the New World.

    (A) It is Columbus   (C) Columbus was
    (B) Columbus   (D) It was Columbus

_____ 2 - - - - - - - occurs when the earth passes between the sun and the moon.

    (A) An eclipse   (C) Eclipse
    (B) It is an eclipse   (D) When an eclipse

_____ 3 - - - - - - - early American inventions were important to the agricultural community.

    (A) The most   (C) Most are
    (B) The most were   (D) Most

_____ 4 - - - - - - - is careless when disposing of his garbage.

    (A) Man who is   (C) It is man
    (B) Man   (D) The man who

_____ 5 - - - - - - - in 1912 that the Titanic sank while crossing the Atlantic.

    (A) It was   (C) When was
    (B) Being   (D) When it was

_____ 6 - - - - - - - a book that contains information about the yearly movements of the sun and the moon.

    (A) An almanac is   (C) An almanac
    (B) An almanac which is (D) That an almanac is

_____ 7 - - - - - - - is an Indic language which gypsies speak.

    (A) It is Romany which   (C) Romany which

    (B) Romany   (D) That Romany

_____ 8 - - - - - - - usually gains public recognition only when it faces the danger of extinction.

    (A) A bird species   (C) A bird species which

    (B) When a bird species   (D) It is a bird species

_____ 9 - - - - - - - is a wet process in which the first step involves soaking a garment in a cleaning solution.

    (A) Dry cleaning which   (C) Dry cleaning

    (B) When dry cleaning   (D) It is dry cleaning

_____ 10 - - - - - - - are sometimes called "rats of the air" since they will eat anything.

    (A) They are called gulls   (C) Gulls which

    (B) Gulls   (D) Because gulls

Note: After checking your answers, compare your success rate on this exercise with that on Exercise S-51, a previous exercise based on the same sentences.

Objectives for Structure and Written Expression Section

Parts A and B: Sentence Completion and Error Identification

10-Point Checklist of Problem Areas

1 Check the subject and verb (both present; neither repeated).
2 Check verb agreement, tense, and form.
3 Check for full subordination.
▶ 4 Check the verbals.
5 Check pronoun form, agreement, and reference.
6 Check word form.
7 Check word order.
8 Check for parallel structure.
9 Check for unnecessary repetition.
10 Check for correct usage.

Objective 4: Check the Verbals
Exercise S-58

Objective: To review the ten important types of structure errors.

Directions: Match each sentence to a problem area from the 10-point checklist above. Write the appropriate number in the blank.

_____ a The Arabian horse was so sick that died before the veterinarian's arrival.

_____ b Peter got the best grade though he spent less hours studying than anyone else.

_____ c It is danger to transport eight people in one small car.

_____ d That dealer sells cars to many people made in Japan.

_____ e Tickets for that frightened movie are sold out.

_____ f In Holland that beautiful tulips are grown.

_____ g Dead animals should be promptly buried as soon as they are no longer alive.

_____ h Neither of the boys have arrived yet.

_____ i Everyone but the janitors has their own parking space.

_____ j During vacation, he plans to swim every day and daily evening walks.

197

Exercise S-59

Objective: To distinguish between infinitives and prepositional phrases beginning with *to*.

Directions: An **infinitive** is a verbal which is formed with *to* and the base form of the verb. Although the word *to* may be the first word of an infinitive, it also begins many prepositional phrases. Put **INF** beside **infinitives** and **PREP** beside **prepositional phrases.** For example:
   infinitives: to eat, to walk, to enjoy
   prepositional phrases: to school, to Alaska, to the dance

INF	1	to laugh	_____	11	to save
PREP	2	to town	_____	12	to drive
_____	3	to trip	_____	13	to run
_____	4	to notify	_____	14	to the drive
_____	5	to the park	_____	15	to peace
_____	6	to be angry	_____	16	to the walk
_____	7	to park	_____	17	to her laugh
_____	8	to shout	_____	18	to pieces
_____	9	to the shore	_____	19	to his shout
_____	10	to the supermarket	_____	20	to tear

Exercise S-60

Objective: To identify the subject and the verb of sentences containing infinitives.

Directions: An infinitive can function as a noun, an adverb, etc., but it cannot function as a **finite** verb in a clause. Underline and label the subject and finite verb in each of the following. Then, put parentheses ( ) around each infinitive.

1 The cats want (to eat.)

2 (To cooperate) with others is important.

3 Settlers came to Texas (to live.)

4 They are going to swim to shore.

5 Fred wanted to walk to school.

6 She tried to put her wallet into her pocket.

7 The senators intend to pass the bill.

8 She likes to entertain often.

9 Students go to school to learn.

10 To eat three times a day is healthy.

11 Smoke tends to rise to the ceiling.

12 To drink while driving is dangerous.

13 She went to the post office to mail some letters.

14 Scientists hope to find a cure for cancer.

15 We are going to have beautiful weather today.

16 She is going to break his heart.

17 They plan to move to the north.

18 To kill bugs, spray the area regularly.

19 They flew to Austin to see their friends.

20 To drive to New York is her plan.

Exercise S-61

Objective: To identify the subject and the verb in sentences containing gerunds, some of which function as subjects.

Directions: A **gerund** is a verbal which is formed by adding the suffix *-ing* to the base form of a verb. A gerund never functions as a verb in a sentence. It always functions as a **noun**. Gerunds should not be confused with *-ing* words that are part of all progressive tense verbs. Put parentheses ( ) around each gerund and underline and label the subject and verb in each sentence. Not all of the sentences contain gerunds.

   gerunds: swimming, singing, participating

   verbs: are swimming, were singing, have been participating

1 (Swimming) is good exercise.

2 He has been eating too much.

3 They go fishing every weekend.

4 Your writing is improving little by little.

5 He hates receiving anonymous notes.

6 Teachers despise cheating.

7 Backpacking is popular among college students.

8 He can't go out without drinking too much.

9 My students are turning in their papers on time this semester.

10 Rollerskating on rough pavement invites accidents.

11 No one appreciates their singing so loudly.

12 Gardening has been becoming more popular.

13 She thanked me for helping her.

14 Turning a corner quickly is frightening to pedestrians.

15 He has obviously been staying up too late.

16 The children are growing tired.

17 Expecting too much leads to frustration.

18 Having an accident can be costly.

19 She is developing good handwriting.

20 Growing up can be a difficult experience.

Exercise S-62

Objective: To review the five types of structure that can function as the subject of a sentence.

Directions: Review the types of structures listed in Exercise S-4 on page 140 that can function as the subject of a sentence. Underline and label the subject(s) and verb(s) of the **main clause** of each sentence.

1 Every baby needs protection in order to survive.

2 A kangaroo is blind and helpless at birth.

3 Its tiny size and helpless condition make it extremely vulnerable.

4 The mother kangaroo will encourage it to climb into her pouch.

5 That will be its home for about four months.

6 Using special muscles, the mother will have to pump milk into the baby.

7 Living in a pouch and being fed in this way are unusual characteristics.

8 There are only a few animals in the world with pouches.

9 To see these animals in the zoo is a treat for many children.

10 After a time, the baby can be seen peeking out of the pouch.

11 Warmth, protection, and nourishment enable the baby to survive and grow.

12 Finally, the adolescent kangaroo jumps out of the pouch for the last time.

13 A full-grown adult male will weigh around two hundred pounds.

14 To grow from five inches to over five feet is quite an accomplishment.

15 A grown kangaroo's skill at jumping enables it to leap thirty feet.

16 A native of Australia, the kangaroo is a member of the "marsupial" family.

17 "Marsupial" means "pouched".

18 There are three especially well-known animals in the marsupial family.

19 Kangaroos, koalas, and opossums are all marsupials.

20 That these species are protected is everyone's concern.

Exercise S-63

Objective: To recognize verbal adjectives, and to identify the nouns they describe.

Directions: A **verbal adjective** can be formed by reducing an adjective clause to a phrase or a word. A one-word verbal adjective goes before the noun it describes. A verbal phrase follows the noun it describes. For example:

adjective clause: Doctors couldn't save the man who was dying of cancer. →

verbal adjective phrase: Doctors couldn't save the man dying of cancer. →

one-word verbal adjective: Doctors couldn't save the (dying) man.

Put parentheses ( ) around each verbal adjective (of either type) and draw an arrow from the verbal adjective to the word it describes. You should find 20 verbal adjectives.

1 That (hanging) basket contains a rare species of bromeliad.

2 People suffering from a severe depression should seek help from a licensed psychologist.

3 A crying child is easily comforted by a few soothing words.

4 The homes destroyed by the hurricane will be demolished by one of the city's wrecking crews during the coming weeks.

5 The number of vacation days provided by the university is adequate for most people.

6 Baked potatoes are frequently served with sour cream, grated cheese, and bits of fried bacon.

7 The old movies shown late at night are frequently better than movies produced in the last five years.

8 Badly torn garments should be mended by an experienced seamstress or tailor.

9 Volunteers recruited by the sheriff searched for the lost hikers for several exhausting days.

10 People walking in poorly lighted areas at night should be extremely careful.

Exercise S-64

<u>Objective:</u> To distinguish between complete verb forms and verbal adjectives.

<u>Directions:</u> Like gerunds and infinitives, verbal adjectives are formed from verbs but do not function as finite verbs. Each verb has two basic verbal adjective forms: the present participle and the past participle.
   verb: eat   → **verbal adjectives:**   eating, eaten
   verb: interest   → **verbal adjectives:**   interesting, interested
Put **V** beside each **complete verb** form, put **V ADJ** beside each **verbal adjective** form.

__V__ 1 have been eating   (e.g. They *have been eating* dinner.)

__V ADJ__ 2 eating dinner   (e.g. The man *eating dinner* is my uncle.)

_____ 3 is walking   _____ 12 being watched

_____ 4 listening   _____ 13 having gone

_____ 5 will examine   _____ 14 eaten

_____ 6 are   _____ 15 forgotten

_____ 7 has finished   _____ 16 drank

_____ 8 looks   _____ 17 were lost

_____ 9 being   _____ 18 buying

_____ 10 having been seen   _____ 19 are reading

_____ 11 was visited   _____ 20 spoken

Exercise S-65

<u>Objective:</u> To form verbal adjectives from the main verb in the sentence.

<u>Directions:</u> A verbal adjective can take the form of either the present participle (*-ing*) or the past participle (*-d, -n, -t*). When the noun that is being described is **actively** "doing" the action, the present participle is used as the verbal adjective. But, when the noun is the receiver of the action and is **passively** having something "done" to it, the past participle is used.

                                    the <u>burning</u> sun   (active)
   The sun <u>burned</u> the hikers. <
                                    the <u>sunburned</u> hikers   (passive)

In the blanks beneath each sentence, first describe the subject and then describe the object. Use verbal adjectives derived from the main verb.

1 Horror movies frighten children.

   ___*frightening horror movies*___   ___*frightened children*___

202

2 The speech bored the audience.

_____   _____

3 The clowns amused the spectators.

_____   _____

4 The ten-mile walk exhausted the campers.

_____   _____

5 The test grades disappointed the teacher.

_____   _____

6 The gift surprised the youngster.

_____   _____

7 The three-hour class tired the students.

_____   _____

8 The math problem confused the class.

_____   _____

9 The review disgusted the artist.

_____   _____

10 The lawyer's argument convinced the jury.

_____   _____

Exercise S-66

<u>Objective:</u> To identify errors related to the form of verbal adjectives on the basis of the intended meaning of a sentence.

<u>Directions:</u> There are two underlined **verbal adjectives** in each sentence; one is in the correct form, but the other is not. In the blank, write the letter, (A) or (B), of the **incorrect** verbal adjective.

__A__ 1   The <u>excited</u> movie drew large crowds of <u>excited</u> children every
           A   B
      Saturday.

_____ 2   The family, <u>tiring</u> from the <u>exhausting</u> trip, fell asleep as soon as
                 A   B
      they went to bed.

_____ 3   After a grueling review session, some confusing students asked the
                        A   B
            teaching assistant for still more help.

_____ 4   Money spent on frivolous items is money completely wasting.
                     A   B

_____ 5   A couple needing a yard for their children rented the house
                         A
            advertising in the weekend newspaper.
                 B

_____ 6   The police keep an updating file on all people reported to be
                                  A   B
            dangerous.

_____ 7   Because she was a lively and amused person, hostesses knew Paula
                                         A
            would keep their guests entertained.
                                          B

_____ 8   The newly-elected governor impressed the reporters with her
                    A
            interested news conference.
                 B

_____ 9   Stimulated by the teacher's presentation, the class asked many
                    A
            thought-provoked questions.
                    B

_____ 10   The children, delighting by the amusing clown, laughed
                               A   B
            throughout his performance.

Exercise S-67

Objective: To identify structure errors related to the form of the verbal adjective, on the basis of the meaning of the sentence.

Directions: Some of the following sentences contain verbal adjectives that are wrong. Put a **check** (√) beside correct sentences and an **X** beside incorrect sentences. Underline the incorrect verbal adjectives.

__X__ 1 The large jar <u>filling</u> with freshly-baked cookies was quickly emptied by the hungry children.

_____ 2 Artificially-sweetened beverages are purchased by individuals trying to lose weight.

_____ 3 Television viewers boring with the reruns shown at the end of the season turn to public television for more interesting programs.

_____ 4 The verdict handed down by the jury surprised none of the lawyers involved in the case.

_____ 5 Household pets infected with fleas should be bathed weekly with a specially-prepared flea soap.

_____ 6 Publishing houses constantly receive manuscripts from aspired young writers.

_____ 7 Letters of recommendation received after the first of the month will not be reviewed by the admissions officer assigning to your file.

_____ 8 A chimney filled with soot requires the services of a qualified chimneysweep.

_____ 9 Houseplants requiring constant attention are not suitable for working couples with little spare time.

_____ 10 Steamed vegetables retain more nutrients than boiling ones.

Exercise S-68

<u>Objective:</u> To reduce subordinate adverb clauses to verbal phrases.

<u>Directions:</u> Subordinate clauses of time beginning with a word such as *after*, *while*, or *before* and **subordinate clauses** of cause/result beginning with a word such as *because*, or *since*, can be **reduced** to a **verbal phrase**. This reduction is possible only when the subject of the subordinate clause is the same as the subject of the main clause.

time: While ̶h̶e̶ was eating, the man choked on a small bone. (subordinate clause)

While eating, the man choked on a small bone. (verbal phrase)

cause: Because ̶i̶t̶ seriously injured, the dog may die. (subordinate clause)

Being seriously injured, the dog may die. (verbal phrase)

Rewrite the following sentences and reduce the subordinate clauses to verbal phrases. Keep introductory time words, but drop introductory cause/result words.

1 While she was playing outside, the child hurt herself.

   <u>While playing outside, the child hurt herself.</u>

2 Because he had broken his leg, he was taken to the emergency room.

   <u>Having broken his leg, he was taken to the emergency room.</u>

3 After he had developed a new drug, the doctor was invited to give a speech.

   _____

4 Because it has a lot of oil, Saudi Arabia is a rich country.

   _____

5 After it has arrived at the factory, raw silk is carefully washed and dried.

   _____

6 Because it is easy to mine and refine, silver was worked by early man.

   _____

7 When it is threatened, a skunk sprays an offensive liquid on its enemy.

   _____

8 Before he planted the seeds, he tilled the soil carefully.

   _____

9 After it had been installed, the new equipment was thoroughly tested.

   _____

10 Since they have a high protein content, soybeans are a popular meat
   substitute.

   _____

Exercise S-69

Objective: To determine whether the implied subject of a verbal phrase is the same as the stated subject of the main clause.

Directions: Each sentence begins with a verbal phrase with an implied but not stated subject. If the implied subject of the verbal phrase is the same as the subject of the main clause, the sentence is correct. If the two subjects are different, the sentence is wrong. In the blank, write the letter of the **correct** sentence in each pair.

wrong: Walking home, a ~~No~~ noise frightened the girl.

correct: Walking home, the ~~Yes~~ girl was frightened by a noise.

B 1 (A) When applying for a parking sticker, the campus police require students to have proper identification.

    (B) When applying for a parking sticker, students must show campus police proper identification.

_____ 2 (A) Sleeping in the corner of an old shed, the kittens were not bothered by neighborhood dogs.

    (B) Sleeping in the corner of an old shed, the neighborhood dogs did not bother the kittens.

_____ 3 (A) While using the microwave oven for the first time, the roast was burned so badly that the chef couldn't serve it to the guests.

    (B) While using the microwave oven for the first time, the chef burned the roast so badly that he couldn't serve it to the guests.

_____ 4 (A) Increasing from 2.5 billion in 1950, the late 1970's saw the world's population reach 4.25 billion.

    (B) Increasing from 2.5 billion in 1950, the population of the world reached 4.25 billion in the late 1970's.

_____ 5 (A) Hoping to save taxpayers' money, biologists are experimenting with a weed-eating fish that can clean canals.

    (B) Hoping to save taxpayers' money, a weed-eating fish that can clean canals is being studied by biologists.

_____ 6 (A) Borrowing from nature's designs, new oil tankers designed by bio-medical engineers will be stable and fuel-efficient.

    (B) Borrowing from nature's designs, engineers are designing stable and fuel-efficient oil tankers.

_____ 7 (A) When renting an apartment, a lease is signed by the tenant.

    (B) When renting an apartment, the tenant is asked to sign a lease.

_____ 8 (A) After passing through a pleasant first stage, most foreign visitors find the second stage of cultural adaptation difficult and depressing.

    (B) After passing through a pleasant first stage, the second stage of cultural adaptation is difficult and depressing for most foreign visitors.

_____ 9 (A) After twice losing Congressional campaigns, Abraham Lincoln's presidential campaign in 1860 was successful.

(B) After twice losing Congressional campaigns, Abraham Lincoln was successful in his 1860 presidential campaign.

_____ 10 (A) Challenging established hypotheses about the origin of modern man, very old Ethiopian fossils have led to new questions.

(B) Challenging established hypotheses about the origin of modern man, archeologists have begun asking new questions based on data from some very old Ethiopian fossils.

Exercise S-70

Objective: To identify structure errors related to the lack of agreement between the implied subject of a verbal phrase and the stated subject of the main clause.

Directions: Underline the verbal in the introductory phrase and the subject in the main clause. Put a **check** (√) beside correct sentences and an **X** beside sentences containing dangling verbal phrases that do not describe the subject

_√_ 1 Before <u>winning</u> the war for independence in 1965, <u>Algeria</u> lost many of its young men.

_X_ 2 <u>Awarded</u> in 1901, <u>René Sully-Prudhomme</u> received the first Nobel Prize for literature.

_____ 3 Decorated with intricate geometric designs, Moslem metal workers produce beautiful trays of copper, tin, and bronze.

_____ 4 After fleeing Mecca, the city of Medina was founded in 622 A.D. by Mohammed and his followers.

_____ 5 Located on an island in the Seine River, the Cathedral of Notre Dame is one of the most famous landmarks in Paris.

_____ 6 Although rejected as a cause of death for many years, miners' widows are now receiving compensation for black-lung disease.

_____ 7 When forced to compete with motion pictures, vaudeville variety shows lost popularity.

_____ 8 After drinking as much water as it wants, it is possible for a camel to survive without water for up to two weeks.

_____ 9 When formed with copper, aluminum alloys are quite strong.

_____ 10 Flourishing in the thirteenth century, traveling musicians, called minstrels, played an important part in the cultural life of the time.

_____ 11 When placed in direct sunlight, plants tend to wilt.

_____ 12 Although once ranging over a 6000-mile area, all species of tigers are now endangered.

_____ 13 If grabbed by an enemy, the tail of a salamander breaks off and allows the animal to escape.

_____ 14 Running home through the snow, her nose got extremely cold.

_____ 15 Living off only wild food, two weeks without a visit to the supermarket is no problem for an experienced camper.

_____ 16 Not knowing of Mount St. Helens' violent past, local residents were shocked when it erupted suddenly.

_____ 17 Riding without helmets, motorcycle accidents often result in fatal head injuries.

_____ 18 Made of small scraps of cloth, old handmade quilts are becoming very valuable to antique collectors.

_____ 19 After being isolated for thousands of years, the discovery of the Tasaday tribe has brought these people into contact with the modern world.

_____ 20 Having been Paris' central food market for over a century, the destruction of Les Halles in 1969 dismayed people all over the world.

Exercise S-71

TOEFL Practice: Structure and Written Expression: Time 6 minutes.

Objective: To recognize correct sentence completions and identify structure errors related to verbals, among other errors.

Questions 1–2

Directions: Choose the <u>one</u> word or phrase, (A), (B), (C), or (D), that best completes the sentence. Write your answer in the blank.

_____ 1 The eagle uses the same nest year after year, - - - - - - - - new material each time.

    (A) and   (C) adds
    (B) which is   (D) adding

_____ 2 - - - - - - - mainly for the invention of the telephone, Alexander Graham Bell devoted his life to helping the deaf.

    (A) He is remembered   (C) While remembering
    (B) To remember   (D) Though remembered

Questions 3–10

<u>Directions:</u> Identify the <u>one</u> underlined word or phrase, (A), (B), (C), or (D), that should be corrected or rewritten. Write your answer in the blank.

_____ 3 <u>Highly</u> <u>interesting</u> in music as a youth, young Johann Sebastian
        A   B
Bach may have damaged his eyes <u>copying</u> <u>musical</u> scores.
                             C   D

_____ 4 Located <u>between</u> <u>the</u> Tigris and the Euphrates rivers, <u>the history of</u>
           A   B   C
the city of <u>Babylon was</u> <u>long and rich.</u>
            C   D

_____ 5 <u>Baking</u> powder, <u>composed</u> of an alkali and one or more acid salts,
        A   B
<u>are used</u> <u>to make</u> cakes and biscuits light.
    C   D

_____ 6 <u>Loving</u> throughout the Western world, ballet is a <u>theatrical art that</u>
        A   B
<u>tells a story</u> through dance <u>accompanied by</u> music.
    C   D

_____ 7 When <u>filled</u> with a gas <u>more lighter</u> than air, a balloon <u>becomes</u>
            A   B   C
buoyant and <u>rises.</u>
            D

_____ 8 In 1937 <u>while approaching</u> its <u>moorings</u>, the Hindenburg <u>catch</u> fire,
                A   B   C
<u>killing</u> a third of its passengers.
    D

_____ 9 The bear, a <u>meat-eaten</u> land animal, is <u>generally</u> <u>peaceable</u> if it and
                A   B   C
its young <u>are left</u> undisturbed.
          D

_____ 10 <u>Original</u> <u>cultivated</u> in India, the banana was <u>brought</u> to the
       A   B   C
Americas by the Portuguese who <u>found</u> it in Africa.
                                   D

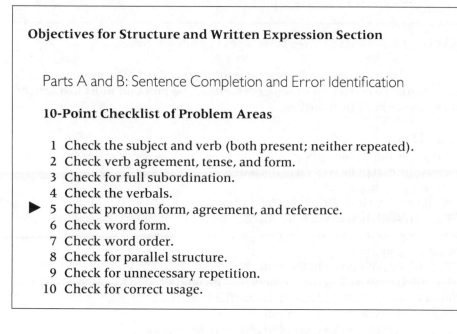

Objectives for Structure and Written Expression Section

Parts A and B: Sentence Completion and Error Identification

10-Point Checklist of Problem Areas

1 Check the subject and verb (both present; neither repeated).
2 Check verb agreement, tense, and form.
3 Check for full subordination.
4 Check the verbals.
▶ 5 Check pronoun form, agreement, and reference.
6 Check word form.
7 Check word order.
8 Check for parallel structure.
9 Check for unnecessary repetition.
10 Check for correct usage.

Objective 5: Check Pronoun Form, Agreement, and Reference
Exercise S-72

Objective: To review the ten important types of structure errors.

Directions: Match each sentence to a problem area from the 10-point checklist above. Write the appropriate number in the blank.

_____ a That television program may soon be cancelled in the near future.

_____ b After a length discussion, the entire class finally understood the sentence.

_____ c Fortunately, the child was not enough tall to reach the medicine cabinet.

_____ d In 1961 John Kennedy was being president of the United States.

_____ e He asked about the cost of the course and when it began.

_____ f It was them who tricked us.

_____ g While watching television, our telephone rang.

_____ h The speaker could not hardly be heard.

_____ i Everyone looks as if he tired.

_____ j Mediterranean fruit flies they have infested California orchards.

Exercise S-73

Objective: To understand three basic types of pronoun errors.

Directions: Each sentence contains a pronoun error. Circle the pronoun that is wrong. **Note:** To correct these sentences, either the pronoun must be changed or the sentence must be rewritten.

Pronoun Form
1 It must be him at the door.
2 Everyone except he will go to the party.
3 She is taller than him.
4 We do not like him lifting that heavy box.
5 They dressed theirselves hurriedly.

Pronoun Agreement
6 Each of the boys brought their lunch.
7 The director as well as the teachers is in their office.
8 Either you or he should have brought their watch.
9 None of the women has their purse.
10 That species of bird has lost their ability to reproduce.

Pronoun Reference
11 He is very careful which prevents many accidents.
12 He is frequently absent which his teacher doesn't like.
13 He was accepted by the university which made him very happy.
14 No one likes children which are rude and boisterous.
15 The books whom I bought were interesting.

Exercise S-74

Objective: To categorize the five forms of the personal pronouns.

Directions: A pronoun can have up to five different forms. Fill in the blanks in the following table with the correct forms of the given pronouns.

	subject (S)	object (O)	possessive		reflexive (R)
			adjective (PA)	pronoun (PP)	
1	I	me	my	mine	myself
2		you(*sing.*)			
3			his		

4	she				
5				*(none)*	itself
6	we				
7			your(*plur.*)		
8				theirs	
9		one		*(none)*	
10	who				*(none)*

Exercise S-75

<u>Objective:</u> To identify the form of the personal pronoun, on the basis of its use in a sentence.

<u>Directions:</u> One pronoun in each sentence is underlined. Identify which of the five forms the pronoun is in. Use the abbreviations from the table in Exercise S-74: **(S), (O), (PA), (PP), (R)**. These sentences are **correct**.

<u>S</u>   1 Without a doubt, it was <u>they</u> who won the game.

_____   2 This is a picture of Bryan, one of <u>his</u> friends, and me.

_____   3 <u>Whom</u> have you visited since you came to town?

_____   4 The judges will choose <u>whomever</u> they feel is best.

_____   5 Stephen hurt <u>himself</u> playing on the swing.

_____   6 She is a lot taller than <u>I</u>.

_____   7 <u>Anyone</u> who registers early will probably get first choice.

_____   8 Your daughter will soon be as tall as <u>mine</u>.

_____   9 <u>Your</u> winning a scholarship came as no surprise.

_____   10 Children can usually dress <u>themselves</u> by the age of five.

Exercise S-76

___

Objective: To improve your understanding of rules 1–3 concerning the subject form of pronouns.

Rules for Pronoun Forms: Rules for the Subject Form

1. The **subject form** is used for a subject of a main clause or of a subordinate clause.

   He left his books in the classroom. (main clause)

   John talked to the man who was standing near him. (adjective clause)

   After he left, I went to bed. (adverb clause)

   I know who broke the window. (noun clause)

2. The **subject form** is used for pronouns that follow the verb *to be*.
   It was he at the door.

   It must have been they who left the message.

3. The **subject form** is used when the subjects of two clauses are being compared.
   She is taller than he (is).

   They have more money than we (have).

Questions 1–5

Directions: Fill in the blank with the correct subject pronoun.

1 It was _____ who forgot to do our homework.

2 _____ and their friends are coming to visit tonight.

3 Unless _____ helps me, I will be mad at him.

4 The professor _____ teaches my class is very nice.

5 My little sister is angry because I get to stay out later than _____.

Questions 6–10

Directions: Put a **check** (✓) beside sentences with correct pronouns and an **X** beside sentences with one or more incorrect pronouns. **Circle** incorrect pronouns.

_____ 6 It was I whom called you last night.

_____ 7 It is true that I am taller than he.

_____ 8 It must have been he whom the police arrested.

_____ 9 If you were me, would you lend him the money?

_____ 10 My teacher thinks that I am more intelligent than him.

Exercise S-77

Objective: To improve your understanding of rules 4–6 concerning the object form of pronouns.

Rules for Pronoun Forms (continued): Rules for the Object Form

4 The **object form** is used for a pronoun that functions as the object (either direct or indirect) of a verb in a main clause or in a subordinate clause.

> That policeman is watching <u>me</u>. (direct object – main clause)
>
> The student <u>whom</u> I advised is Algerian. (direct object – adjective clause)
>
> If I send <u>him</u> a letter, he will be happy. (indirect object – adverb clause)

5 The **object form** is used for a pronoun that functions as the object of a preposition.

> Everyone <u>except her</u> took the test.
>
> <u>Between you and me</u>, I didn't like that party.
>
> Bill won't go to the party <u>without her</u>.
>
> The person <u>with whom</u> I live is my cousin.
>
> The person <u>whom</u> I live <u>with</u> is my cousin.

6 The **object form** is used when the objects of two clauses are being compared.

> The teacher likes <u>you</u> better than (she likes) <u>me</u>.
>
> The child responds <u>to her</u> more readily than (to) <u>him</u>.

Questions 1–5

Directions: Fill in the blank with the correct object pronoun.

1 Our parents worry about my brother more than about _____.

2 Mary asked us not to leave without _____.

3 The doctor _____ he visited specializes in eye diseases.

4 If I see _____ tonight, I will tell him to call you.

5 No one likes that waitress because it takes _____ so long to bring the food.

Questions 6–10

Directions: Put a **check** (✓) beside sentences with correct pronouns and an **X** beside sentences with one or more pronoun errors. **Circle** incorrect pronouns.

_____ 6 The fraternity men whom live across the street make a lot of noise.

_____ 7 No one knows what happened except you, Harry, and I.

215

_____ 8 It must have been he whom we saw at the movie.

_____ 9 This is a good picture of him.

_____ 10 I think that the teacher knows whom took these photographs.

Exercise S-78

Objective: To improve your understanding of rules 7–8 concerning the possessive adjective form of pronouns.

Rules for Pronoun Forms (continued): Rules for the Possessive Adjective Form

7 The **possessive adjective form** is used to modify a noun and indicate possession.

This is his coat.   Whose book is this?

I lost my wallet in the park.   The boy whose dog is lost is sad.

8 The **possessive adjective form** is used when a pronoun modifies a gerund.
The audience really likes his singing.

I appreciate your helping me.

Her singing will calm the baby.

The music teacher knows whose playing is the best.

Questions 1–5

Directions: Fill in the blank with the correct possessive adjective form.

1 He doesn't realize that _____ whistling annoys the class.

2 The queen greeted _____ subjects outside the palace.

3 The person _____ car I just hit is going to be very angry.

4 That gentleman seems to have lost _____ way.

5 Everyone did _____ best on the homework.

Questions 6–10

Directions: Put a **check** (√) beside sentences with correct pronouns and an **X** beside sentences with one or more pronoun errors. **Circle** incorrect pronouns.

_____ 6 You will have to go alone unless you can wait until I finish me lunch.

_____ 7 The student whom forgot his books is going to be unhappy tonight.

_____ 8 Her mother reminded her three times to do her homework.

_____ 9 Until he finds out whose car this is, he can't ask the owner to move it.

_____ 10 Our teacher doesn't like us speaking Spanish in class.

Exercise S-79

Objective: To improve your understanding of rules 9–12 concerning the possessive form of pronouns.

Rules for Pronoun Forms (continued): Rules for the Possessive Pronoun Form

9 The **possessive pronoun form** is used to replace a noun functioning as subject or object.

> Your coat is new, but mine isn't.

> I forgot my book so I borrowed hers.

> Everyone likes your singing but not theirs.

10 The **possessive pronoun form** is used with the verb *to be* to indicate possession.

> This coat is mine.

> I don't know whose that is.

11 The **possessive pronoun form** is used after the preposition *of* meaning possession.

> Marianne is a good friend of mine.

> I found an old composition of yours in the file.

> Some friends of hers are visiting Austin this week.

12 The **possessive pronoun form** is used to replace the second noun when comparing two objects of the same kind that are possessed by different people.

> His car can go faster than yours.

> Lynn's house is larger than mine.

Questions 1–5

Directions: Fill in the blank with the correct possessive pronoun.

1 Didn't you tell me that a friend of _____ is staying with you?

2 Charlotte insisted the coat was _____ .

3 I brought my car, but Phil refused to bring _____ .

4 The little boy dropped his ice-cream, so his mother gave him _____ .

5 The silver spoon had belonged to us for years, but the police refused to believe it was _____ .

Questions 6–10

Directions: Put a **check** (✓) beside sentences with correct pronouns and an **X** beside sentences containing pronoun errors. **Circle** incorrect pronouns.

_____ 6 Your cat is much larger than me.

_____ 7 The director has no idea whose car is blocking his.

_____ 8 George brought a friend of him to class yesterday.

_____ 9 Bill forgot to bring his pencil to class so he borrowed me.

_____ 10 If I can do my homework, you should certainly be able to do your.

Exercise S-80

<u>Objective:</u> To test your understanding of rules 13–15 concerning the reflexive form of pronouns.

Rules for Pronoun Forms (continued): Rules for the Reflexive Form

13 The **reflexive form** is used to emphasize the noun or pronoun it refers to.
   The president himself wrote me a letter.

   I always do the dishes myself.

14 The **reflexive form** is used as the object of the preposition *by* to mean that a person does something *alone* or *without help*.
   Young children cannot get dressed by themselves.

   After a busy day, he likes to be by himself.

15 The **reflexive form** is used when the object of the sentence or of a preposition is the same person as the subject.
   You may burn yourself with those matches.

   He is always talking to himself.

<u>Questions 1–5</u>

<u>Directions:</u> Fill in the blank with the correct reflexive pronoun form.

1 We prefer living by _____.

2 You cannot expect a baby to take care of _____.

3 One can easily injure _____ while skiing.

4 The governor _____ will speak at the university.

5 That woman has put _____ in a difficult position.

<u>Questions 6–10</u>

<u>Directions:</u> Put a **check** (√) beside sentences in which the pronouns are correct. Put an **X** beside sentences containing an incorrect pronoun. **Circle** incorrect pronouns.

_____ 6 His son often gets hisself in trouble.

_____ 7 My brother and I usually drive ourself to work.

218

_____ 8 Every teenager looks forward to taking the car out by himself.

_____ 9 The hostess invited everyone to help himself to the hors d'oeuvres.

_____ 10 Both of you can help yourself more by working than by wasting time.

Exercise S-81

Objective: To review rules 1–15 concerning the five pronouns forms.

Directions: **In the first blank**, identify the underlined pronoun form (see page 212). **In the second blank**, write the number of the rule for pronoun form which applies to the underlined pronoun, (see pages 214 through 218). All of these sentences are **correct**.

_O_ _4_ 1 His father calls <u>him</u> every week.

_S_ _2_ 2 George Washington said it was <u>he</u> who had chopped down the cherry tree.

_____ _____ 3 Bach dedicated <u>himself</u> to music.

_____ _____ 4 Each ex-president builds a library for <u>his</u> papers.

_____ _____ 5 No one except <u>me</u> has any money.

_____ _____ 6 They are staying at our house until <u>theirs</u> is finished.

_____ _____ 7 Her husband is two years younger than <u>she</u>.

_____ _____ 8 The boss gives him more responsibility than <u>her</u>.

_____ _____ 9 These magazines are not <u>ours</u>.

_____ _____ 10 It was the woman <u>who</u> made the best grade on the test.

_____ _____ 11 The man blamed <u>himself</u> for the accident.

_____ _____ 12 John is working hard to improve <u>his</u> handwriting.

_____ _____ 13 The director's ideas are very different from <u>theirs</u>.

_____ _____ 14 The mayor <u>herself</u> cut the ribbon to open the new city hospital.

_____ _____ 15 While in New York, I will stay with a friend of <u>mine</u>.

Exercise S-82

Objective: To identify the correct form for a pronoun on the basis of its function in a sentence.

Directions: Circle the correct pronoun from the two choices given in parentheses.

1 The director will hire the person ((who,) whom) has the best credentials.

2 No one except (*she, her*) brought a lunch.

3 The first ones in line were Nancy, Jim, and (*he, him*).

4 (*Who, Whom*) did you visit in Austin?

5 With (*who, whom*) is Bryan talking?

6 His shoes are much newer than (*her, hers*).

7 They offered their seats to you and (*I, me*).

8 It was (*she, her*) that asked the question.

9 No one was surprised at (*him, his*) winning the contest.

10 There should be no secrets between you and (*he, him*).

11 (*Who, Whom*) was it that asked that question?

12 Only (*he, him*) forgot about the test.

13 Beverly is a good friend of (*me, mine*).

14 She wants to know (*who, whom*) is giving the party.

15 The picnic won't be any fun without you and (*they, them*).

16 I can't figure out (*who, whom*) is on the phone.

17 John did all the homework by (*him, himself*).

18 This is a picture of Scott, his sister, and (*I, me*).

19 Everyone but (*he, him*) did well on the test.

20 If you were (*I, me*), where would you go for vacation?

Exercise S-83

<u>TOEFL Practice:</u> Structure and Written Expression: Time 6 minutes.

<u>Objective:</u> To recognize correct sentence completions and structure errors related to pronoun form, as well as other errors.

<u>Questions 1–2</u>

<u>Directions:</u> Choose <u>one</u> word or phrase, (A), (B), (C), or (D), that best completes the sentence. Write your answer in the blank.

_____ 1 Socrates spent - - - - - - - working as a sculptor.

   (A) he was young   (C) as a youth
   (B) youth   (D) his youth

_____ 2 Skiing is a sport - - - - - - - goes back 4,000 years.

   (A) and he   (C) and its
   (B) whose history (D) whose

Questions 3–10

Directions: Identify the <u>one</u> underlined word or phrase, (A), (B), (C), or (D), that should be corrected or rewritten. Write your answer in the blank.

_____ 3 Jan Sibelius, <u>a Finnish</u> <u>composer</u>, captured the spirit <u>of him</u> country
                  A   B   C

     in <u>his music</u>.
          D

_____ 4 The <u>injured</u> passengers on the airplane <u>that</u> crashed found <u>themself</u>
            A   B   C

     miles from the <u>nearest</u> hospital.
                  D

_____ 5 Sequoya, <u>whom English</u> <u>name was</u> George Guess, <u>invented a</u>
                A   B   C

     syllabary for <u>the Cherokee</u> language.
                D

_____ 6 <u>Regarding</u> as the creator of the <u>historical</u> novel, Sir Walter Scott
        A   B

     captured <u>his</u> readers' imagination <u>with his</u> stirring tales.
             C   D

_____ 7 <u>At the age</u> of twenty-six, William Shakespeare <u>married a</u> woman
        A   B

     who was eight <u>years older</u> than <u>him</u>.
                 C   D

_____ 8 The Queen of England <u>she keeps</u> <u>her</u> crown in the Tower of London
                        A   B

     <u>where</u> both tourists and English citizens can view <u>it</u>.
       C   D

_____ 9 <u>Faced with</u> the possibility of a water shortage during the summer
        A

     months, the city has asked <u>it</u> citizens to <u>limit</u> <u>their</u> use of water.
                          B   C   D

_____ 10 As the population of Africa <u>continues</u> to <u>grow</u>, animals will
                               A   B

     <u>continue</u> to <u>lose</u> theirs native habitat.
        C   D

Exercise S-84

Objective: To improve your understanding of rules 1–2 concerning pronoun agreement.

Rules for Pronoun Agreement

1   A plural pronoun is used to refer to two words joined by *both . . . and* or two or more words joined by *and.*

   Both John and Mary are returning to their class.

   John and I are returning to our class.

2   A singular pronoun is used to refer to these indefinite pronouns which are singular in form and require singular verbs. Any of the third person singular pronouns may be used (*he, his, she, it, its,* etc.) depending on the meaning of the sentence.

	-body	**-one**	**-thing**
some-	somebody	someone	something
any-	anybody	anyone	anything
no-	nobody	no one	nothing
every-	everybody	everyone	everything

   Everyone must do his homework.

   He never puts anything back in its place.

Questions 1–5

Directions: Fill in the blank with the correct pronoun.

1 Anyone who wishes can bring _____ husband to the party.

2 You can tell from the blood on the bench that someone on the football team hurt _____.

3 Both the cat and the dog spend _____ days outside.

4 Everyone should sit quietly until _____ is asked to speak.

5 Anyone who turns in a paper late will have _____ grade lowered.

Questions 6–10

Directions: Put a **check (✓)** beside correct sentences and an **X** beside incorrect sentences. **Circle** incorrect pronouns.

_____ 6 Everyone in the American literature class will receive their textbooks tomorrow.

_____ 7 Somebody put his cigarette out in the sink.

_____ 8 The queen and her daughter spend much of her free time on horseback.

_____ 9 My brother and I will spend my weekend at the lake.

_____ 10 It is surprising that no one turned in their paper on time.

Exercise S-85

Objective: To improve your understanding of rules 3–4 concerning pronoun agreement.

Rules for Pronoun Agreement (continued)

3 When two words are joined by *either . . . or . . ., neither . . . nor . . .,* or *not only . . . but also . . .,* the pronoun should agree with the part that is closer.

Either the students or the <u>teacher</u> will give you <u>his</u> book.

Neither the dog nor the <u>cats</u> have on <u>their</u> collars.

Not only the players but also the <u>coach</u> has on <u>his</u> uniform.

4 Collective nouns which represent a number of persons or things, such as *group, team,* etc., can be either singular or plural. The verb that goes with the collective noun will indicate whether the writer views the noun as singular or plural in a particular sentence.

singular: The <u>team</u> <u>is</u> preparing for <u>its</u> big game.

plural: The <u>team</u> <u>are</u> going to <u>their</u> homes now.

Questions 1–5

Directions: Fill in the blank with the correct pronoun.

1 Not only the director but also the members of the choir invited _____ friends.

2 The committee is issuing _____ report tomorrow.

3 Everyone will feel proud if the team finishes _____ season without a loss.

4 The herd of cattle has broken the fence in _____ pasture.

5 The crew has to make repairs on _____ boat.

Questions 6–10

Directions: Put a **check** (✓) beside correct sentences and an **X** beside sentences containing incorrect pronouns. **Circle** incorrect pronouns.

_____ 6 Neither of the boys has had their hair cut lately.

_____ 7 The family has sold its summer home.

_____ 8 No one realized that both Bill and Tom had visited their families recently.

_____ 9 Either Martin or Jones will give their report next.

_____ 10 The faculty has cancelled its monthly meeting.

Exercise S-86

<u>Objective:</u> To review rules 1–4 concerning pronoun agreement, (see Exercises S-84 and S-85).

<u>Directions:</u> Assume that the given word or phrase is the subject of a sentence and the referent of the missing pronouns. Fill in the blanks with the **pronoun** or **possessive adjective** that will agree with it.

subject	object	possessive adjective
1 John	him	his
2 Two women	them	their
3 Bill or Mary		
4 Many of us		
5 Some sheep		
6 Time		
7 My father		
8 His mother		
9 Many a man		
10 Neither he nor she		
11 Both of us		
12 Everyone		
13 Whoever		
14 Our photographs		
15 None of you		
16 Either of the women		
17 Each of the mice		
18 Our books		
19 A species		
20 Mathematics		

Exercise S-87

Objective: To review all rules concerning both verb and pronoun agreement.

Directions: These sentences are **wrong**. Rewrite them, correcting the errors in **verb** and **pronoun** agreement. (Review verb agreement rules, Exercises S-14 through S-22).

1 Neither the reporters nor the editor have received their paycheck.

   Neither the reporters nor the editor has received his paycheck.

2 Everyone have to use their identification number to activate the computer.

   _____

3 In the bus sit the musicians, each holding their instrument.

   _____

4 The boy's blue jeans is so old that they look like a rag.

   _____

5 Anyone who abuse their children should be punished for their actions.

   _____

6 No one are as ambitious as he who want to be rich.

   _____

7 Both London and Paris is crowded in the summer because it is so famous.

   _____

8 The list of special courses are available at the front desk because they are requested by so many students.

   _____

9 The hundred thousand dollars were found because the thief dropped them while escaping.

   _____

10 The welfare department, as well as the other social services, will have their budget cut.

   _____

Exercise S-88

Objective: To identify errors in pronoun agreement.

Directions: Two pronouns are underlined in each sentence. Write the letter of the **incorrect** pronoun in the blank.

__A__ 1 Each of the companies claims <u>their</u> products will outlast <u>its</u>

                           A   B

      competitors'.

_____ 2 The recording equipment and <u>their</u> carrying case were never put

                                      A

      back in <u>their</u> proper place.

            B

_____ 3 <u>His</u> family was shocked when James killed <u>themselves</u>.

      A   B

_____ 4 That chain of discount stores will lose customers if <u>it</u> doesn't

                                                 A

      improve <u>their</u> service department.

              B

_____ 5 *The New York Times*, renowned for <u>their</u> news coverage, recently

                                            A

      increased <u>its</u> readership.

               B

_____ 6 Neither the students nor <u>their</u> teacher was happy with <u>his</u> test

                               A   B

      grades.

_____ 7 Just offstage stood the conductor and <u>its</u> assistants with <u>their</u>

                                        A   B

      equipment.

_____ 8 The secretary put the letter back in <u>her</u> envelope and filed <u>it</u>.

                                           A   B

_____ 9 Unlike <u>his</u> predecessor, the president feels it is in <u>their</u> country's

               A   B

      best interest to reduce taxes.

_____ 10 Alaska's North Slope has found <u>itself</u> full of geologists and <u>its</u>

                                        A   B

      seismic equipment.

Exercise S-89

Objective: To recognize errors in pronoun reference related to pronouns which introduce subordinate adjective clauses.

Directions: The pronouns which begin **adjective** clauses, *who, which, etc.,* refer to the nouns that come before them. Different pronouns are used to refer to different types of nouns.

    who, whom: refer to people and household animals
    which: refers to things, collective nouns, and animals
    that, whose: refer to all types of nouns

Put a **check** (✓) when the pronoun reference is correct. Put an **X** when the pronoun reference is wrong.

X   1 ....woman which....

✓   2 ....musician whom....

_____   3 ....actress that....

_____   4 ....silver who....

_____   5 ....acrobat that....

_____   6 ....uncle which....

_____   7 ....antelope whose....

_____   8 ....disaster whom....

_____   9 ....arrival who....

_____   10 ....surgeon whom....

_____   11 The river which divides Texas and Mexico is the Rio Grande.

_____   12 A friend recommended the doctor which is treating my son.

_____   13 The beautician who does her hair is very good.

_____   14 The senator which introduced the bill was defeated in the last election.

_____   15 Tigers who live in Africa are endangered.

_____   16 The artist whose works are on display is a native Texan.

_____   17 Someone stole the forklift which had been left unlocked.

_____   18 The tape dispenser that Phyllis borrowed was mine.

_____   19 The rain whom the crops needed never came.

_____   20 The advantages of which he spoke are numerous.

Exercise S-90

<u>Objective:</u> To recognize errors that result from the use of a pronoun to refer to something other than a noun structure.

<u>Directions:</u> Pronouns which begin adjective clauses, *who, which, etc.*, can refer only to nouns, and are usually, but not always, found immediately after this noun. These pronouns cannot refer to verbs, adjectives, adverbs, etc.

  wrong: The class was <u>long which</u> no one liked.

  correct: No one liked the length of the class.

Put a **check** (✓) when the reference of the underlined pronoun is correct. Put an **X** when the reference is wrong.

  X   1   The weather was too hot <u>which</u> spoiled the picnic.

_____ 2   Everyone enjoyed the concert <u>which</u> was held in the park.

_____ 3   The staff was disorganized <u>which</u> caused administrative problems.

_____ 4   His alarm clock was broken <u>which</u> made him late to class every day.

_____ 5   The crowd cheered the singer <u>who</u> performed last.

_____ 6   The teacher was disliked <u>who</u> gave many difficult tests.

_____ 7   The line was long <u>which</u> discouraged many movie goers.

_____ 8   The army tank was extremely heavy <u>which</u> made it sink into the sand.

_____ 9   It rained heavily <u>which</u> caused the picnic to be cancelled.

_____ 10   Aluminum is very light <u>which</u> is one of its many advantages.

Exercise S-91

<u>Objective:</u> To recognize errors in pronoun reference.

<u>Directions:</u> Only one sentence in each pair is correct; the other sentence contains a problem of pronoun reference. Put the letter of the **correct** sentence in the blank.

  B   1 (A) My mother's job is new, which is not satisfying.
          (B) My mother has a new job which doesn't satisfy her.

_____ 2 (A) Your frequent absences are not good for your record.
          (B) You have been absent which is not good for your record.

_____ 3 (A) The disorganization of the picnic spoiled the day for everyone.
          (B) The picnic was disorganized which spoiled the day for everyone.

_____ 4 (A) The Cherokee alphabet was developed by one of their leaders, a man named Sequoya.

      (B) The alphabet of the Cherokees was developed by one of their leaders, a man named Sequoya.

_____ 5 (A) The president was assassinated which shocked the nation.

      (B) The assassination of the president shocked the nation.

_____ 6 (A) English teachers need to know all the grammar rules of the language.

      (B) English teachers need to know all of its grammar rules.

_____ 7 (A) My friend is a mathematics teacher, but it is a subject that I know little about.

      (B) My friend teaches mathematics, but it is a subject that I know little about.

_____ 8 (A) Once a clothes hanger is bent, they are likely to fall off easily.

      (B) Once a clothes hanger is bent, the clothes are likely to fall off easily.

_____ 9 (A) When the flea eggs hatch about seven days later, they will quickly reinfest the area.

      (B) When their eggs hatch about seven days later, the fleas will reinfest the area.

_____ 10 (A) Responsibility for small children's lives causes a person to become much more attentive to their needs.

      (B) Responsibility for the lives of small children causes a person to become much more attentive to their needs.

Exercise S-92

TOEFL Practice: Structure and Written Expression: Time 6 minutes.

Objective: To recognize correct sentence completions and all types of errors in pronoun reference, as well as other errors.

Questions 1–2

Directions: Choose the <u>one</u> word or phrase, (A), (B), (C), or (D), that best completes the sentence. Write your answer in the blank.

_____ 1 Dehydrated food doesn't spoil - - - - - - - - desirable for long-term storage.

    (A) so it is   (C) and its

    (B) which makes it   (D) that is

_____ 2 Ethics is a branch of philosophy - - - - - - - with moral
principles.

    (A) is concerned   (C) who concerns

    (B) whose concern   (D) which is concerned

Questions 3–10

Directions: Identify the one underlined word or phrase, (A), (B), (C), or (D),
that should be corrected or rewritten. Write your answer in the blank.

  B   3 Levees and dikes are walls or embankments and which are used
                       A   B
to keep the sea or a river from overflowing an area.
   C   D

_____ 4 Sassafras, who belongs to the laurel family, has bright green leaves
              A   B   C
and produces yellow flowers and dark blue berries.
     D

_____ 5 Carlsbad Caverns in New Mexico are famous for their spectacular
                          A   B
icicle-shaped formations that hang from the roof and rises from the
                      C   D
floor.

_____ 6 When butterfly eggs hatch, they eat the leaves of plants and become
                   A   B   C
a nuisance to man.
       D

_____ 7 Dramamine is an effective drug against motion sickness which
               A   B   C
produces dizziness and nausea in their victims.
                   D

_____ 8 The opening of the Suez Canal in 1869 gave ships the means
       A
by whom they could travel from Europe to the Orient
   B   C
without sailing around Africa.
     D

_____ 9 Borneo is the third largest island in the world which is exceeded in
             A   B   C   D
size only by New Guinea and Greenland.

_____ 10 Sharks are <u>catched</u> for food <u>as well as</u> for <u>their</u> livers <u>which</u> provide
                       A   B   C   D

a rich source of vitamin A.

Exercise S-93

Objective: To review all the pronoun rules and identify errors in pronoun form, agreement, and reference.

Directions: All these sentences contain pronouns, some used correctly, and some incorrectly. If a sentence is correct, put a **check** (✓) in the blank. If it is incorrect, **circle** the error and identify it by writing the appropriate letter in the blank: **F = error in pronoun form; A = error in pronoun agreement;** and **R = error in pronoun reference.**

_A___ 1 The local soccer team has a season record that will put (them) in the final competition.

_____ 2 Mary reads just as well as him.

_____ 3 Do you actually believe it is they who sent the letter?

_____ 4 The children were extremely boisterous, which annoyed their teacher.

_____ 5 When a person decides to move from the city to a farm, they should be prepared to make some mistakes.

_____ 6 The fields were muddy, which made them difficult to plow.

_____ 7 You will never be able to convince him or her.

_____ 8 Him that speaks before he thinks will get himself in trouble.

_____ 9 The last owner of this house obviously didn't enjoy working outdoors because they neglected the lawn.

_____ 10 The coach appreciated them giving him a new jacket.

_____ 11 The crowd was so large that it took us a long time to get through them.

_____ 12 One or the other of these people must give up their turn to speak.

_____ 13 The engineers studied the data carefully, but it did not seem correct.

_____ 14 I forgot my books which will force me to return home to get them.

_____ 15 There is some disagreement among they who were at the meeting.

_____ 16 The teachers made all these improvements themselves.

_____ 17 If you were I, what would you do about the problem?

_____ 18 She is very sad which makes me sad, too.

_____ 19 You cannot please both George and me.

_____ 20 Did you know it was him who started the fire in the wastebasket?

Exercise S-94

<u>TOEFL Practice:</u> Structure and Written Expression: Time 6 minutes.

<u>Objective:</u> To recognize correct sentence completions and structure errors related to pronoun form, agreement, and reference, as well as other errors.

<u>Questions 1–2</u>

<u>Directions:</u> Choose the <u>one</u> word or phrase, (A), (B), (C), or (D), that best completes the sentence. Write your answer in the blank.

_____ 1 Since there were no honeybees in North America, early European settlers - - - - - - -.

    (A) importing them   (C) imported themselves
    (B) imported them   (D) their importation

_____ 2 Beethoven did not let his deafness - - - - - - - from writing music.

    (A) his preventing   (C) prevent him
    (B) prevented him   (D) he prevented

<u>Questions 3–10</u>

<u>Directions:</u> Identify the <u>one</u> underlined word or phrase, (A), (B), (C), or (D), that should be corrected or rewritten. Write your answer in the blank.

_____ 3 Although the beaver's hind <u>feet are</u> <u>webbed</u> for swimming, <u>their</u>
                 A   B   C

front feet are small and <u>handlike.</u>
                     D

_____ 4 Esperanto <u>is</u> unique <u>among</u> languages because <u>they were</u>
            A   B   C

<u>invented by</u> a single man, Ludwig Zamenhof.
     D

_____ 5 The banyan <u>tree</u> of tropical <u>African</u> propagates <u>by sending</u> down
               A   B   C

shoots from <u>its</u> branches.
          D

_____ 6 <u>Founded</u> in the seventeenth century, Harvard University took <u>its</u>
      A   B

name from an early benefactor <u>which</u> donated <u>his</u> books to the
                             C   D

library.

_____ 7 With specially designed vaults, modern banks protects
      A   B   C
their customers' money and other valuables.
      D

_____ 8 The golden eagle, one of two species of eagles in the United States,
                             A   B
builds the nest on high, inaccessible cliffs.
      C   D

_____ 9 The boomerang, a remarkable primitive weapon, it is so
                                                  A
sophisticated in its design that it can be thrown forward and
                B
yet return to its starting point.
      C   D

_____ 10 Ducks, geese, and swans are different types of waterfowl, but
          A
because their similar in behavior and physical characteristics,
         B   C
they comprise a single bird family.
       D

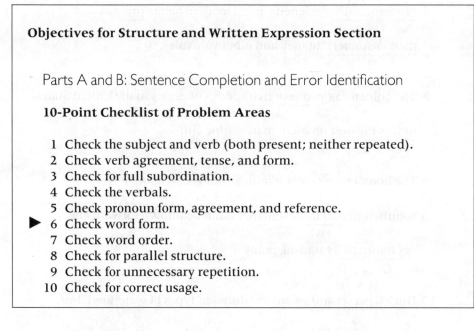

Objectives for Structure and Written Expression Section

Parts A and B: Sentence Completion and Error Identification

10-Point Checklist of Problem Areas

1 Check the subject and verb (both present; neither repeated).
2 Check verb agreement, tense, and form.
3 Check for full subordination.
4 Check the verbals.
5 Check pronoun form, agreement, and reference.
► 6 Check word form.
7 Check word order.
8 Check for parallel structure.
9 Check for unnecessary repetition.
10 Check for correct usage.

Objective 6: Check Word Form
Exercise S-95

Objective: To review the ten types of important structure errors.

Directions: Match each sentence to a problem area from the 10-point checklist above. Write the appropriate number in the blank.

_____ a Wilt Chamberlain is taller than everyone on his team.

_____ b Each of the waitresses lost their job.

_____ c If he was rich, he would probably lend us the money.

_____ d The Honda, a Japanese-made car, it is increasingly popular.

_____ e While the doctor out of the office, the patients waited.

_____ f He was tired so he stopped resting.

_____ g Why did he leave is not known.

_____ h Dogs can hear inaudible sounds to human ears.

_____ i Scientists could see little difference between the three drugs.

_____ j He has no reason to be so anger.

Exercise S-96

<u>Objective:</u> To recognize various types of errors in word form:

<u>Directions:</u> Each of these sentences contains an error in **word form**. **Circle** the error, and **write** the correct word form beside the sentence.

1. That student is majoring in (agricultural.) *agriculture.*
2. The teacher finally separationed the two noisy students.
3. The hunters never realized they were in a danger situation.
4. The children ran rapid to the swings.
5. His wife is extreme nice.
6. That erasing detracts from the appearance of the paper.
7. Red roses smell very sweetly.
8. Those paintings are the expensivest in her entire collection.
9. He earned a great deal of money from his inventing.
10. On the eye of a hurricane, the sea remained calmly.

Exercise S-97

<u>Objective:</u> To derive nouns from verbs by adding an appropriate suffix.

<u>Directions:</u> Here are some of the common **suffixes** that may be added to certain **verbs** to create **derived nouns**. Using the suffix indicated for each group of verbs, write the appropriate derived noun form in the blank. Consult a dictionary only after completing the exercise. Study these suffixes before going on to the next exercise.

1 **-ation**		2 **-ment**	
1 observe	*observation*	*1* conceal	*concealment*
2 inform		*2* move	
3 determine		*3* align	
4 form		*4* judge	
5 examine		*5* advertise	
6 oblige		*6* encourage	

3 -ence/-ance

1 depend <u>dependence</u>

2 infer _____

3 accept _____

4 exist _____

5 abhor _____

6 correspond _____

4 -al

1 survive <u>survival</u>

2 remove _____

3 approve _____

4 refuse _____

5 try _____

6 withdraw _____

5 -ure

1 disclose <u>disclosure</u>

2 press _____

3 expose _____

4 please _____

5 erase _____

6 fail _____

6 -y

1 deliver <u>delivery</u>

2 inquire _____

3 discover _____

4 perjure _____

5 recover _____

6 flatter _____

Exercise S-98

<u>Objective:</u> To identify nouns which are derived from verbs.

<u>Questions 1–30</u>

<u>Directions:</u> Put a **check** (✓) beside all the words that are nouns derived from verbs. Use your dictionary when necessary.

✓ 1 conveyance	____ 11 capable	____ 21 emission
____ 2 similar	____ 12 battery	____ 22 cardiac
✓ 3 installment	____ 13 forbearance	____ 23 ageless
____ 4 dilapidate	____ 14 aberrent	____ 24 disposal
____ 5 fusion	____ 15 aperture	____ 25 deterioration
____ 6 execution	____ 16 tungsten	____ 26 chancellor
____ 7 recovery	____ 17 manually	____ 27 procurement
____ 8 accept	____ 18 useful	____ 28 coherence
____ 9 ineptness	____ 19 play	____ 29 obstreperous
____ 10 dispersal	____ 20 urban	____ 30 morose

Questions 31–40

Directions: Read each sentence carefully. **Circle** the word that is a noun derived from a verb. **Write the verb** from which the noun was derived in the blank.

<u>__fail__</u> 31 The man was arrested because of his (failure) to pay income taxes.

_____ 32 The removal of his car was illegal.

_____ 33 His father is an art collector.

_____ 34 The paper he wrote shows his mastery of the subject.

_____ 35 We need your assistance before we can finish repairing this bicycle.

_____ 36 Eli Whitney's invention of the cotton gin brought about significant changes in plantation life.

_____ 37 The departure of the airplane was delayed by stormy weather.

_____ 38 At the conclusion of the movie, please remain seated.

_____ 39 A group of volunteers will put up the party decorations tonight.

_____ 40 His proposal was approved by the head of the company.

Exercise S-99

Objective: To distinguish between verbs for which a gerund is the only possible derived noun form, and verbs for which other derived forms are possible.

Directions: In the blank beside each verb, write a derived noun form. Write a gerund only when no other noun form is possible. You may use a dictionary as you work.

<u>_earnings_</u>	1 earn		_____	7 refuse
_____	2 prefer		_____	8 recover
_____	3 erase		_____	9 agree
_____	4 inform		_____	10 join
_____	5 surround		_____	11 learn
_____	6 decide		_____	12 excite

_____ 13	come	_____ 17	sit
_____ 14	divide	_____ 18	exist
_____ 15	withdraw	_____ 19	depart
_____ 16	imply	_____ 20	leave

Exercise S-100

<u>Objective:</u> To recognize errors resulting from the incorrect use of a gerund where another derived noun form is preferable.

<u>Directions:</u> Each sentence contains at least one gerund. If a **gerund** should be replaced by a **derived noun**, put an **X** in the blank, **underline the gerund** and **write the derived noun** at the end of the sentence. If the **gerund** cannot be replaced, write a **check (√)** in the blank.

X 1 The <u>resigning</u> of the president was a shock to many of his supporters. *resignation*

√ 2 School rules forbid leaving the building during breaks.

_____ 3 Citizens were angry at the failing of the city council to fund new parks.

_____ 4 Crossing a street in the middle of a block is called jay-walking.

_____ 5 The discovering of gold in California caused many people to travel west in hope of becoming rich.

_____ 6 Before leaving the country, all visitors must turn in their visas.

_____ 7 News of the couple's separating quickly spread through the neighborhood.

_____ 8 During the period of westward moving, pioneers suffered many hardships.

_____ 9 Although both parties were intent on reaching an agreement quickly, several days passed before a contract was signed.

_____ 10 New restrictions have been placed on the developing of areas outside the city's preferred growth corridor.

_____ 11 Learning a new language is usually easier for children than for adults.

_____ 12 The story of his upbringing is shocking to all who read it.

_____ 13 The woman's believing in God was a source of strength during her long illness.

_____ 14 The president's recommending to the board of trustees was ignored.

_____ 15 Before entering a mosque, Moslems remove their shoes.

_____ 16 The arranging of chairs permits maximum seating.

_____ 17 Repeating of a difficult lesson can help weaker students.

_____ 18 Firm pressing on a wound can prevent severe bleeding.

_____ 19 Students may not leave class without the teacher's permitting.

_____ 20 His report on school desegregating presented both sides of the issue.

Exercise S-101

<u>Objective:</u> To recognize the suffixes used to produce derived noun forms that refer to people.

<u>Directions:</u> Here are ten pairs of nouns that are randomly arranged. One of each pair is an **abstract noun**, while the other is a **noun that refers to a person**. Using the suffixes as a guide, **write** each noun in the proper column. The first pair has been done. **Underline** the suffixes that refer to people. Then, study this list of suffixes that refer to people.

✓ employee	alcoholic	authorship	carpenter
service	racket	servant	✓ employment
carpentry	geology	youth	geologist
racketeer	innovator	sociability	alcoholism
socialite	youngster	authoress	innovation

abstract nouns	nouns referring to people
employment	employ<u>ee</u>

239

Exercise S-102

Objective: To recognize some of the suffixes used to derive adjectives from nouns.

Directions: Here are fifteen pairs of words that are randomly arranged. One word in each pair functions as **a noun** while the other functions as **an adjective.** Using the adjective suffixes as a guide, write each word in the proper column. **Underline** the fifteen adjective suffixes. The first two pairs have been done.

✓ease	heroic	✓fame	foolish	care
✓famous	traditional	Texas	troublesome	supplement
truth	statue	comfortable	death	wooden
active	✓easy	heroism	tradition	statuesque
supplementary	careless	trouble	action	comfort
deathly	fool	wood	Texan	truthful

nouns	adjectives
ease	easy
fame	famous

Note: Study the suffixes that form adjectives from nouns before doing the next exercise.

Exercise S-103

___

Objective: To identify and use adjectives derived from nouns.

Questions 1–10

Directions: Read each sentence carefully. Then, select the appropriate adjective from the list and write it in the blank.

rocky	penniless	eventful	yearly	babyish
silklike	careless	musical	metallic	stormy

1 The __yearly__ cost of the insurance is $452.

2 Polyester is a _____ material.

3 Saturday was certainly an _____ day.

4 The car was badly damaged on the _____ road.

5 Sheila made some _____ mistakes on her income tax.

6 She liked silver and other _____ colors.

7 The _____ old man lived alone in his big house.

8 The piano is his favorite _____ instrument.

9 That seven-year-old boy still behaves in a _____ manner.

10 The _____ sky showed how near the hurricane was.

Questions 11–30

Directions: Put a **check** (✓) beside each word which is an adjective derived from a noun.

✓ 11 guileless		_____ 21 exemplar
_____ 12 basalt		_____ 22 demonic
_____ 13 impish		_____ 23 simplest
_____ 14 starry		_____ 24 moronic
_____ 15 fibrous		_____ 25 daily
_____ 16 pal		_____ 26 carillon
_____ 17 supplementary		_____ 27 fulfill
_____ 18 sadness		_____ 28 vengeful
_____ 19 marvelous		_____ 29 still life
_____ 20 swish		_____ 30 caress

Exercise S-104

Objective: To distinguish between *-ly* adjectives derived from nouns and *-ly* adverbs derived from adjectives.

Directions: The suffix *-ly* can be added to words to form both **adjectives** and **adverbs**. An *-ly* **adjective** is formed by adding *-ly* to a **noun**. An *-ly* **adverb** is formed by adding the suffix *-ly* to an **adjective**. By examining the base to which the *-ly* has been added, indicate the function of each word by writing it in the correct column. The first two have been done. There are ten of each.

√ worldly	nervously	neighborly	foolishly
√ beautifully	friendly	seriously	costly
womanly	easily	ghostly	universally
carelessly	yearly	enjoyably	cowardly
shapely	stately	finally	passively

adjectives ending with *-ly*	adverbs ending with *-ly*
worldly	*beautifully*

Exercise S-105

<u>Objective:</u> To create word families by deriving four word forms from a single base word.

<u>Directions:</u> Complete the following table by writing words that fit each category. Do **not** use any **verbals** (gerunds, infinitives, present participles, or past participles). There may be more than one possibility for some categories.

	verb	noun	adjective	adverb
1		energy		
2			quick	
3				basically
4	succeed			
5		electricity		
6			exclusive	
7	economize			
8		sensation		
9				categorically
10	repeat			

Exercise S-106

_____

Objective: To identify derived forms, their grammatical functions, and the base words from which they were derived.

Questions 1–5

Directions: **Circle** the derived form in each sentence. **In the first blank**, write the part of speech of the derived form. **In the second blank**, write the root or base form of the word. Check your dictionary if necessary.

1 The (radicalism) of those students is demonstrated in their speeches.

_____ noun _____   _____ radical _____

2 In order to get what you want, you often have to be assertive.

_____   _____

3 The new president of the research institute is a quiet person.

_____   _____

4 His sister's ability to fix things is astonishing.

_____   _____

5 People in the north have to winterize their homes to reduce heat loss.

_____   _____

Questions 6–10

Directions: Choose the correct **root or base word** from the list and add the **suffix** given under the blank. Write the **derived word** in the blank. Check your dictionary if necessary.

change	instruct	lonely	summary	national

6 The orientation session about hospitals was *instructive*.
                                                    (-ive)

7 On the application, please include your name and _____.
                                                                (-ity)

8 The weather in Austin, Texas is very _____.
                                                    (-able)

9 Could you please _____ this information in your report?
                                    (-ize)

10 Since his mother died, he has been overwhelmed by _____.
                                                          (-ness)

Exercise S-107

<u>Objective:</u> To identify structure errors arising from the use of a word whose form is incorrect according to its function in a sentence.

<u>Directions:</u> Decide which underlined word has the correct word form for its use in the sentence. Put the letter of the **incorrect** word form in the blank beside the sentence.

<u>B</u> 1 <u>Useful</u> prizes will be awarded to students writing the most
           A
        <u>imagination</u> essays.
           B

_____ 2 Those who answer the questions <u>successfully</u> will be moved into a
                                          A
        more <u>rapidly</u> class.
              B

_____ 3 The defendant was acquitted <u>primarily</u> because of his lawyer's
                                        A
        <u>persuasion</u> argument.
           B

_____ 4 Courses in <u>comparison</u> linguistics are <u>frequently</u> offered at the
                       A   B
        university.

_____ 5 After several years of <u>unhappiness</u>, the couple finally <u>separation</u>.
                                  A   B

_____ 6 The firemen's <u>decision</u> action averted total <u>destruction</u> of the
                         A   B
        building.

_____ 7 The family reported the <u>mystery</u> <u>disappearance</u> of their child to the
                                   A   B
        police immediately.

245

_____ 8 The university bestowed an <u>honor</u> degree on an <u>outstanding</u>

$\qquad\qquad\qquad$ A $\qquad\qquad\qquad$ B

community leader last week at the graduation ceremony.

_____ 9 All <u>poisonous</u> wastes from the <u>chemicals</u> plant were disposed of

$\qquad\qquad$ A $\qquad\qquad\qquad$ B

safely.

_____ 10 The builder's last house is a <u>repetitive</u> of his first one.

$\qquad\qquad\quad$ A $\qquad\qquad\qquad$ B

_____ 11 The <u>agriculture</u> <u>development</u> of a country is a good measure of its

$\qquad\qquad$ A $\qquad$ B

progress.

_____ 12 Fortunately, the mayor has <u>comparative</u> few friends in the business

$\qquad$ A $\qquad\qquad\qquad$ B

community.

_____ 13 The author of this book is also a <u>well-respected</u> <u>lecture</u>.

$\qquad\qquad\qquad\qquad$ A $\qquad$ B

_____ 14 The troupe gave <u>satisfactorily</u> performances of some <u>classic</u> plays.

$\qquad\qquad$ A $\qquad\qquad\qquad$ B

_____ 15 The head of the <u>departmental</u> is waging a war on <u>mediocrity</u>.

$\qquad\qquad$ A $\qquad\qquad\qquad$ B

Exercise S-108

Objective: To distinguish between verbs that are followed by adjectives and those followed by adverbs.

Directions: **Adverbs** are used with all verbs **except** those which fall into three special categories. These special verbs are almost always followed by **adjectives:**
   (i) Verbs used as **linking verbs:** be, seem, appear, become, grow, remain, get, go, prove, turn.
   (ii) Verbs used as **sense verbs:** look, sound, smell, taste, feel.
   (iii) **Special combinations:** hold tight, stand still, keep quiet, open wide, etc.
Choose the correct word form from the two choices in parentheses.

1 At the height of the season, the roses smelled (*sweet*, *sweetly*).

2 The child grew (*silent, silently*) when his father entered the room.

3 The water flowed (*rapid, rapidly*) over the falls.

246

4 When his team fumbled the ball, the coach shouted at them (*angry, angrily*).

5 After a rigorous training program, the boy could lift the weights (*easy, easily*).

6 At the mention of a test, the child turned (*pale, palely*).

7 The police checked out the man's story, and it proved (*false, falsely*).

8 Aluminum can be (*easy, easily*) bent.

9 Going (*crazy, crazily*) in their tiny apartment, the couple decided to move.

10 That bubbling soup smells very (*good, well*).

11 The small puppy couldn't remain (*quiet, quietly*) for very long.

12 No one suspected her of being the thief because she looked so (*honest, honestly*).

13 A waiter should be able to add up a bill (*swift, swiftly*).

14 Closing the door (*slow, slowly*), the nurse tried not to awaken the patient.

15 The music sounded (*beautiful, beautifully*) to her ears.

16 The class felt (*sad, sadly*) when they heard of their teacher's accident.

17 The horses broke (*loose, loosely*) and trampled the garden.

18 That woman laughs (*nervous, nervously*) when she is embarrassed.

19 The couple strolled (*lazy, lazily*) through the park.

20 The children giggled (*uncontrollable, uncontrollably*) at the clown's antics.

Exercise S-109

Objective: To determine on the basis of sentence meaning whether a verb is being used as a sense verb, and hence whether it should be followed by an adverb or an adjective.

Directions: Think about the meaning of each of the following sentences and decide whether the verbs are being used as **sense verbs** or as **action verbs**. Then choose the correct word form from the two choices in parentheses. For example:

sense verb (description of noun):   The <u>girl</u> felt <u>nervous</u> before the big test.

action verb (description of verb):   The girl <u>felt</u> <u>nervously</u> in her purse for her keys.

1 The woman got the job because the boss thought she looked (*careful*, *carefully*).

2 The secretary looked (*careful, carefully*) on the floor for her earring.

3 The cook looked (*sad, sadly*) at the burned food.

247

4 The cook looked (*sad, sadly*) when he saw the food was burned.

5 After digging in the garbage, the dog didn't smell (*good, well*).

6 After injuring his nose, the dog couldn't smell (*good, well*).

7 Not wanting to burn his tongue, he tasted the soup (*cautious, cautiously*).

8 To a hungry person, even dry bread can taste (*delicious, deliciously*).

9 Flames had engulfed the building before the alarm was (*final, finally*) sounded.

10 Trying to avoid further disagreement, the teacher made her decision sound (*final, finally*).

Exercise S-110

<u>Objective:</u> To determine whether a word is an adjective or an adverb by identifying the word it modifies.

<u>Directions:</u> **Adjectives modify nouns**, and **adverbs modify verbs. In the first blank**, write **ADJ** if the underlined word is an adjective or **ADV** if it is an **adverb. In the second blank**, write the word that the underlined word modifies. These sentences are **correct.**

1 The pilot flew <u>higher</u> to get above the storm clouds.

_____ADV_____   _____Flew_____

2 The singer strained his voice when he attempted <u>high</u> notes.

_____   _____

3 All of these applicants have been <u>highly</u> recommended.

_____   _____

4 The defendant thought that the judge looked <u>friendly</u>.

_____   _____

5 The small plane flew <u>low</u> and frightened the livestock.

_____   _____

6 A person in his <u>lowly</u> position should not criticize the boss.

_____   _____

7 A row of <u>stately</u> trees lined the road leading to the house.

_____   _____

8 The woman looked <u>carefully</u> for her lost contact lens.

_____   _____

9 Often a <u>stern</u> look can quiet a noisy child.

_____   _____

10 Everyone admired the <u>costly</u> jewelry, but no one bought any.

_____   _____

Exercise S-111

<u>Objective:</u> To distinguish words modified by adjectives from those modified by adverbs.

<u>Directions:</u> Although adjectives can modify only nouns (and some verbs), adverbs can modify **adjectives** and **other adverbs** as well as **verbs**. Many adverbs are used to intensify the meaning of an adjective or another adverb. These **intensifiers** have approximately the same meaning as *very: extremely, really, highly, quite, considerably,* etc. For example:

ADV → ADJ → N   V ← ADV → ADV
extremely interesting person;   walked really slowly

Fill in the blank with the appropriate adjective or adverb.

real/really

1 a ___*real*___ story

2 _____ frightened

3 smelled _____ good

4 _____ quickly

5 _____ diamonds

6 appeared _____

7 _____ original poem

8 appeared _____ sad

9 shouted _____ loudly

10 with _____ sincerity

extreme/extremely

11 ___*extremely*___ long

12 _____ heat

13 was _____ depressed

14 in an _____ way

15 was _____

16 _____ amusing

17 in an _____ loud voice

18 became _____ quiet

19 _____ well-known

20 with _____ pleasure

Exercise S-112

TOEFL Practice: Structure and Written Expression: Time 6 minutes.

Objective: To recognize correct sentence completions and structure errors related to the use of the wrong word form, on the basis of a word's function in a sentence, as well as other errors.

Questions 1-2

Directions: Choose the <u>one</u> word or phrase, (A), (B), (C), or (D), that best completes the sentence. Write your answer in the blank.

_____ 1 The history of ancient Egypt has been revealed only through - - - - - - - remains.

(A) archeological
(B) archeologically
(C) archeologist
(D) archeology

_____ 2 - - - - - - - is surpassed only by that of monkeys and apes.

(A) The intelligent dog
(B) The dogs have intelligence
(C) The dogs whose intelligence
(D) The intelligence of dogs

Questions 3–10

Directions: Identify the <u>one</u> underlined word or phrase, (A), (B), (C), or (D), that should be corrected or rewritten. Write your answer in the blank.

_____ 3 Because they were <u>sacred</u> places and believed to be <u>safety from</u>
                                A   B
robbers, temples <u>in ancient</u> Greece served as bank vaults.
                      C   D

_____ 4 Earthworms <u>make</u> their path through <u>heavily</u> soil by eating <u>it</u> and
                              A   B   C
then eliminating it behind <u>them.</u>
                                      D

_____ 5 Thunder is the sound <u>produced</u> by the <u>rapid</u> <u>expanding</u> of air
                                          A   B   C
heated by <u>lightning.</u>
                  D

250

_____ 6 When the dogwood trees <u>bloom</u> <u>in</u> East Texas, the number
                                    A B
     of <u>tourism</u> increases <u>dramatically</u>.
          C   D

_____ 7 Contrary to <u>popular belief</u>, bananas <u>grown</u> on the soft stalk of a
                    A   B
     <u>leafy</u> plant and not on trees with <u>woody</u> trunks.
      C   D

_____ 8 <u>As early as</u> 1784, balloonists <u>took</u> instruments <u>with them</u> to
       A   B   C
     measure the pressure, temperature, and <u>moist</u> of air at different
                                            D
     altitudes.

_____ 9 Wyatt Earp gained <u>his</u> reputation as the <u>toughest</u> <u>gunfight</u> in the
                         A   B   C
     country while he was <u>serving</u> as marshal of Wichita, Kansas.
                        D

_____ 10 Elasticity refers to an <u>object's</u> ability to return to <u>it's</u> <u>original</u> shape
                         A   B C
     after being deformed by <u>external</u> pressure.
                          D

Exercise S-113

<u>Objective:</u> To form the comparative and superlative forms of adjectives correctly.

<u>Directions:</u> Most adjectives have three forms: absolute, comparative, superlative. The **comparative** is used to describe a difference between **two** people or things. The **superlative** is used when **three or more** persons or things are involved. The **general** rules for the formation of comparative and superlative forms of adjectives are as follows:

	one syllable	**two syllables with** -*y*	**two or more syllables**
absolute	tall	busy	beautiful
comparative	tall<u>er</u> (than)	bus<u>ier</u> (than)	<u>more</u> beautiful (than)
superlative	(the) tall<u>est</u>	(the) bus<u>iest</u>	(the) <u>most</u> beautiful

Fill in the blanks with the correct comparative and superlative forms.

		comparative	superlative
1	old	*older (than)*	*(the) oldest*
2	happy		
3	foolish		
4	thin		
5	enthusiastic		
6	strange		
7	crazy		
8	interesting		
9	energetic		
10	funny		
11	slow		
12	regular		
13	messy		
14	common		
15	wise		

16 threatened   _____   _____

17 clever   _____   _____

18 noisy   _____   _____

19 distressing   _____   _____

20 amorous   _____   _____

Exercise S-114

Objective: To identify adjectives for which no comparative or superlative form is possible.

Directions: Some adjectives are non-comparable; they have no comparative or superlative forms because they have an absolute meaning. Assuming all the following are adjectives, put an **X** in the blanks beside the ten which are **non-comparable.**

1 __X__ perfect   11 _____ total

2 _____ restless   12 _____ futile

3 _____ unique   13 _____ breakable

4 _____ dead   14 _____ main

5 _____ active   15 _____ new

6 _____ lonely   16 _____ principal

7 _____ serious   17 _____ right ´

8 _____ complete   18 _____ sound

9 _____ helpful   19 _____ effective

10 _____ wrong   20 _____ well

Exercise S-115

<u>Objective:</u> To recognize structure errors related to the use and form of adjectives and adverbs.

<u>Directions:</u> Some of these sentences are correct, while others contain an incorrect adjective or adverb. Put a **check** (✓) beside correct sentences and an **X** beside incorrect ones. **Circle** the incorrect forms.

___✓___ 1 The carpet layers worked so hard they were absolutely exhausted.

___X___ 2 A late paper is (more better) than none at all.

_____ 3 Since it is reusable, the space shuttle is least expensive than other spacecraft.

_____ 4 At the end of the performance, the crowd left quick.

_____ 5 The bride was real polite to her new in-laws.

_____ 6 Although the camera is costly, it is the best on the market today.

_____ 7 The audience laughed throughout the extremely humorous movie.

_____ 8 He went home because he felt extremely bad.

_____ 9 Some mothers of twins dress their children exactly the same.

_____ 10 During adolescence, girls are generally taller than boys of the same age.

_____ 11 It was difficult to choose a cologne because they all smelled sweetly.

_____ 12 The acrobats performed skillful, dangerous leaps without a net.

_____ 13 After a considerable long wait, teachers were granted a pay increase.

_____ 14 Parents should keep their children out of school until they are completely sure they are well.

_____ 15 Elephants will probable become extinct unless governments change existing laws.

_____ 16 After some careful thinking, the judge decided to place the children in a foster home.

_____ 17 The use of solar heat can be helpfully in reducing utility bills.

_____ 18 The use of a bilingual dictionary is extreme common among beginning students.

_____ 19 Believing herself to be homely, the girl was timid about making friends.

_____ 20 After extensive research, the doctoral candidate presented an extremely useful dissertation.

Exercise S-116

Objective: To choose between comparative and superlative forms on the basis of overall sentence meaning and structure.

Directions: Choose the correct absolute, comparative, or superlative form from the two choices in parentheses.

1. Of the two papers, the one on non-verbal communication is the (_better_, _best_).

2. Wilt Chamberlain used to be one of the (_taller_, _tallest_) professional basketball players in the United States.

3. He is earning (_less_, _fewer_) money than he was ten years ago.

4. The (_longer_, _longest_) suspension bridge in North America is the Verrazano-Narrows Bridge in New York City.

5. The Woolworth Building has as (_many_, _much_) floors as One Chase Manhattan Plaza.

6. The gazelle can run much (_quicklier_, _more quickly_) than the zebra.

7. Kanmon Bridge in Japan is as long (_than_, _as_) Angostura Bridge in Venezuela.

8. Some feel that silver is inherently (_attractiver_, _more attractive_) than gold.

9. Compared (_to_, _with_) children her own age, Jane is quite tall.

10. It is unlikely that he will do his (_better_, _best_) on the exam since he is sick.

11. Of all the children in the kindergarten, Charles is (_more_, _the most_) active.

12. The harder a person studies, the (_more_, _most_) he learns.

13. This test was much (_less_, _least_) difficult than the first one.

14. Of her two kicks, the second was definitely the (_better_, _best_).

15. The (_faster_, _fastest_) he ran, the more difficult it was for him to breathe.

16. The higher he climbed, the (_less_, _least_) oxygen there was to breathe.

17. History is (_more easy_, _easier_) for him than chemistry.

18. Her test score is superior (_than_, _to_) his.

19. The more she scolded the child, the (_wilder_, _wildest_) he became.

20. Taking calculus was the (_worse_, _worst_) experience in his life.

Exercise S-117

<u>TOEFL Practice:</u> Structure and Written Expression: Time 6 minutes.

<u>Objective:</u> To recognize correct sentence completions and structure errors related to the use of comparative and superlative word forms, as well as other errors.

<u>Questions 1–2</u>

<u>Directions:</u> Choose the <u>one</u> word or phrase, (A), (B), (C), or (D), that best completes the sentence. Write your answer in the blank.

_____ 1 One survey indicated each American household averaged
- - - - - - - - of daily television usage in 1979 than in 1978.

    (A) more than sixteen minutes
    (B) more minutes than sixteen
    (C) as many as sixteen minutes
    (D) sixteen more minutes

_____ 2 - - - - - - - - people in the United States saw the King
Tutankhamen exhibit.

    (A) Of the more than eight million
    (B) Eight million more than
    (C) More than eight million
    (D) Eight million of the most

<u>Questions 3–10</u>

<u>Directions:</u> Identify the <u>one</u> underlined word or phrase, (A), (B), (C), or (D), that should be corrected or rewritten. Write your answer in the blank.

_____ 3 The more famous skyscraper in the world is the Empire State
         A   B   C
Building, located in the heart of New York City.
         D

_____ 4 Although neither animal can outrun the cheetah, both the gazelle
               A   B
or the impala run faster than fifty miles per hour.
  C   D

_____ 5 Rogunsky Dam in Russia may be the tallest dam in the world, but it
                                   A   B
provides the least reservoir capacity than the Daniel Johnson Dam
  C   D
in Canada.

_____ 6 The most Americans were killed in World War II than in any other
         A   B   C
war since the birth of the nation.
    D

_____ 7 The World Trade Center, the tallest skyscraper in New York City,
                                  A   B
has eight floors taller than the Empire State Building.
C   D

_____ 8 Although Pluto is not the most large planet in the solar system, it
                              A   B
is the most distant from the sun.
    C   D

_____ 9 One decibel, which is a unit of relative loud, is the smallest amount
                                               A   B   C
of change detectable by the human ear.
                     D

_____ 10 Life on earth originated about 2,000 million years ago, but the
             A
older good fossil remains are merely 550 million years old.
B   C   D

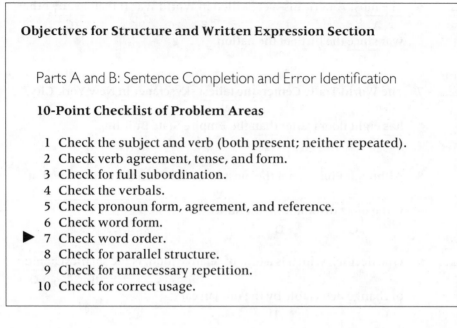

Objectives for Structure and Written Expression Section

Parts A and B: Sentence Completion and Error Identification

10-Point Checklist of Problem Areas

1 Check the subject and verb (both present; neither repeated).
2 Check verb agreement, tense, and form.
3 Check for full subordination.
4 Check the verbals.
5 Check pronoun form, agreement, and reference.
6 Check word form.
► 7 Check word order.
8 Check for parallel structure.
9 Check for unnecessary repetition.
10 Check for correct usage.

Objective 7: Check Word Order
Exercise S-118

Objective: To review the ten important types of structure error.

Directions: Match each sentence to a problem area from the 10-point checklist above. Write the appropriate number in the blank.

_____ a Sioux Indians lived in South Dakota before it becomes a state.

_____ b Three youngsters hurt himself on the playground.

_____ c The discover of gold brought many new settlers to California.

_____ d Sports such as soccer and tennis they are popular in Texas.

_____ e His chief and principal reason for working was money.

_____ f Because very frightened, the woman called the police.

_____ g The tiring boy fell asleep immediately.

_____ h The teacher arrived latter than the students.

_____ i Benjamin Franklin was a writer, a scientist, and he liked politics.

_____ j The faculty wanted to know when would they get a pay raise.

Exersise S-119

Objective: To recognize a variety of errors caused by incorrect word order.

Directions: Each of these sentences contains an error in word order. Underline that part of the sentence which is wrong.

1 He asked where <u>did I live.</u>

2 Only once he has visited Texas.

3 It is not yet enough hot to swim.

4 Never she had seen so much rain in such a short time.

5 During the holidays, they plan to do new something every day.

6 At the age of six, my father taught me how to ride a horse.

7 At parties, she tells always such humorous stories.

8 None of the sandwiches on the dish made of cheese were eaten.

9 She purchased a sweater at the department store made of wool.

10 Questions about how was he doing in school always bothered him.

Exercise S-120

Objective: To understand eight basic rules for word order.

Directions: Read through the following grammar notes carefully, and then go on to Exercises S-121 through S-129 concerning word order.

Rules for Word Order: Inversion of Subject and Verb

The **most common word order** of the core parts of a sentence in English is **subject + verb + object (S + V + O)**. The subject comes before the verb in all but a few special situations. In these situations the word order of the core parts is **inverted** and the verb is placed before the subject: just as it is in all direct questions. (Note that the TOEFL rarely presents direct questions in the **Structure and Written Expression** Section.)

Inverted order is needed:
1 When a sentence begins with *there*.
   There <u>is</u> no <u>basis</u> for this complaint.

   There <u>are</u> few <u>excuses</u> that teachers will accept.

2 When a sentence begins with a prepositional phrase, has an intransitive verb as a main verb, and states a location.
   On the corner <u>stood</u> a police <u>officer</u>.

   In the box <u>were</u> several old <u>photographs</u>.

259

3 In conditional sentences (of types 2 and 3) without *if* or *unless*.
(If he asked her, she would surely help him.) →

Were he to ask her, she would surely help him.

Should he ask her, she would surely help him.

(If he had known, he would have come.) →

Had he known, he would have come.

4 When a sentence begins with a "negative" word or expression such as *never, hardly, seldom, rarely, barely, scarcely, not only, at no time, nowhere,* etc.

Not only did they go but they also stayed until the end.

Never has the world faced so many problems.

At no time were the passengers in any danger.

5 When a sentence begins with *only* and a time expression, the subject and verb of the main clause are inverted.

Only once was John late to class.

Only after her mother died, did she know loneliness.

6 When an adverb such as *down, in , out, up* is placed at the beginning of the sentence, the verb is placed before the subject if the subject is a noun.

Down came the rain.

In walked the doctor with his bag in hand.

7 When a sentence begins with *few, such, so, little* unless this word modifies a noun.

Little did she know that she had won the grand prize.

So great was her love for her children that she sacrificed everything for them.

8 When a passive verb is split and the main verb begins the sentence.

Held as hostages were several reporters.

Discovered at the bottom of the well were two small children.

Note: Although inverted word order is required in the situations listed above, normal word order (**S + V + 0**) is required in **indirect questions**. No inversion is possible.

The man asked where the bus station was.

The reporters want to know when the president will give his address.

Exercise S-121

<u>Objective:</u> To distinguish between direct and indirect questions, on the basis of the order of the subject and the verb.

<u>Directions:</u> The word order used in a direct question is different from that used in an indirect question. In a **direct question**, the auxiliary verb comes before the subject (**AUX + S + V**). In an **indirect question**, which is a subordinate noun clause, the subject comes before the verb (**S + V**).

   direct question: Where <u>did he go</u>?   (**AUX + S + V**)
   indirect question: I know where <u>he went</u>. (**S + V**)

Indicate whether each item is a **direct question (D)** or an **indirect question (IND)** by putting the appropriate abbreviation in the blank.

_D_	1 what did John see	_____	11 whom Marianne teaches
_____	2 what we saw yesterday	_____	12 whom will they visit
_____	3 where James spent the night	_____	13 which car he bought
_____	4 how did the cat get out	_____	14 which movie Frank has seen
_____	5 when the rain stopped	_____	15 how long the class lasted
_____	6 why Ricky never came home	_____	16 where the bread is kept
_____	7 where will you go	_____	17 how much money can I borrow
_____	8 when he should leave	_____	18 where was the wallet found
_____	9 how you are feeling	_____	19 how long he stayed angry
_____	10 why is Annie laughing	_____	20 how far did the dog wander

Exercise S-122

<u>Objective:</u> To recognize indirect questions that must be rewritten so that the order of the subject and verb is correct.

<u>Directions:</u> Each sentence contains an indirect question but the word order of the subject and verb is **wrong**. Underline the full subordinate noun clause and correct the word order and any consequently incorrect verb forms.

1 No one knows <u>why was the teacher absent yesterday</u>.

   No one knows why the teacher was absent yesterday.

2 The instruction booklet explains what kind of batteries does the toy need.

3 Scientists cannot predict when will the next earthquake occur.

_____

4 The professor informed the class when would the test be given.

_____

5 She is old enough to go wherever does she want to go.

_____

6 The reporters asked what time would the president arrive.

_____

7 Sister Mystic can tell from the lines on your palm what will your future be.

_____

8 The policeman asked him where was he going and why was he speeding.

_____

9 The newspaper story doesn't state where did the accident take place.

_____

10 Zoo officials are puzzled about how did the tiger get out of its cage.

_____

Exercise S-123

Objective: To recognize structure errors related to the incorrect order of the subject and verb in indirect questions.

Directions: When a **yes/no question** functions as a subordinate noun clause, the subject and verb come after *if, whether,* or *whether or not.*

   direct yes/no question: Has the dog been fed? (**AUX + S + V**)
  indirect yes/no question: My brother asked if the dog had been fed.
                       (*if* + **S + V**)

Every sentence in this exercise contains at least one indirect yes/no question, but in some cases the word order of the subject and verb is wrong. Put a **check** (✓) beside correct indirect questions and an **X** beside those with incorrect word order. **Underline** the indirect questions.

  ✓   1 The chauffeur wondered whether or not the limousine would start.

  _____ 2 The receptionist inquired whether I wanted a magazine to read
          while I waited.

_____ 3 The babysitter asked if could he watch television during the evening.

_____ 4 The dentist asked the boy if he brushed his teeth regularly.

_____ 5 Everyone wanted to know if had the test been graded.

_____ 6 The hostess wondered if her guests were having a good time.

_____ 7 The secretary wondered if the boss would give her a raise or not.

_____ 8 The shopper inquired whether was the dress washable.

_____ 9 The lawyer wanted to know if the will had been found.

_____ 10 There is no way to know if will she arrive before dark.

Exercise S-124

Objective: To recognize errors in the word order of the subject and verb in sentences beginning with certain "negative" expressions.

Directions: When a sentence **begins** with a "**negative**" **word**, or *only* and a **time expression**, the verb and the subject are **inverted**. If the verb has more than one part, only the first part is moved. The inversion of a clause containing any verb in a simple tense, except a form of the verb *to be*, requires the addition of an auxiliary verb.

   negatives: *never, hardly, seldom, rarely, not only, at no time, nowhere,* etc. For example:

   The world has never faced so many problems. → Never has the world faced so many problems.

   only + **time:** *only once, only at night, only after,* etc. For example:

   Bats leave the cave only at night. → Only at night do bats leave the cave.

In each of the following sentences, the word order of the subject and verb in the **main clause** is **wrong**. Correct the sentence by rewriting it and inverting the verb and the noun or noun phrase that functions as the subject. The subject and verb have been underlined in questions 1–5: do the same for questions 6–10.

1 Not only they went, but they stayed until the end.

   Not only did they go, but they stayed until the end.

2 Only after her mother died she knew real loneliness.

   _____

3 At no time the passengers were in any danger.

   _____

4 Only once John was late to class.

   _____

5 Never <u>air pollution has been as</u> bad as it is now.

_____

6 Seldom his family has seen him this angry.

_____

7 Only after you have taken the placement test, we can tell you your level.

_____

8 Scarcely they had sat down for dinner when the telephone rang.

_____

9 Nowhere in the world the weather is so changeable as it is in Texas.

_____

10 Only after it rains the cacti in the desert bloom.

_____

Exercise S-125

<u>Objective:</u> To rewrite conditional sentences by omitting the introductory word and inverting the subject and verb of the subordinate clause.

<u>Directions:</u> Subject-verb inversion is required in subordinate clauses of condition (types 2 and 3) when the introductory *if* or *unless* is omitted.
   Type 2: If he asked her, she would surely help him.
            <u>Were he to ask</u> her, she would surely help him.

            <u>Should he ask</u> her, she would surely help him.

         If he were rich, he would have an expensive car.
         <u>Were he</u> rich, he would have an expensive car.

   Type 3: If he had known, he would have come.
            <u>Had he known</u>, he would have come.

The following sentences are **correct. Rewrite** them by dropping *if* or *unless* and inverting the subject and verb in the subordinate clause.

  1 If the truth were known, that man would go to jail.

     Were the truth known, that men would go to jail.

  2 If she had passed the test, she would be smiling.

_____

3 If he had gone to the doctor right away, he might have been alive today.

_____

4 If the old woman were to get sick, she would not be able to call a doctor.

_____

5 If you should see Fred, tell him to telephone me.

_____

6 Unless he were very sick, he would not be in the hospital.

Were he not very sick, he would not be in the hospital.

7 Unless it were important, my friend would not have asked me that favor.

_____

8 Unless he had gotten a raise, he would have resigned from the company.

_____

9 Unless they had borrowed some money, they could not have bought a new house.

_____

10 Unless he had been tired, he wouldn't have missed the party.

_____

Exercise S-126

Objective: To recognize structure errors arising from incorrect word order.

Directions: When a sentence **begins** with *little, such, so, few,* the subject and verb of the main clause are inverted. The inversion of a verb in a simple tense, except a form of the verb *to be*, requires the addition of an auxiliary verb.

       V   S
Little did she know that she had won first prize.

       V   S
Such was her desire to win that she practiced night and day.

          V   S
So great was her surprise that she almost fainted.

        V   S
Few were her words of praise for her son.

However, if one of these words modifies a noun which follows it, the inversion does not take place.

       S   V

Such a desire to win is not healthy.

      S   V

Few words of praise are meaningful.

Put a **check** (√) beside sentences with correct word order and an **X** beside sentences with incorrect word order and **underline** the part that is wrong.

√   1 Such behavior is not permitted in this classroom.

X   2 So tired <u>the boy was</u> that he fell asleep almost immediately.

_____   3 Little do teenagers realize how much they have to learn.

_____   4 Few and far between the gas stations are on this stretch of road.

_____   5 So old the book was that its pages had turned yellow.

_____   6 Little the boy realizes how sick he is.

_____   7 So perfect was the foreigner's accent that everyone thought he was a native speaker.

_____   8 Few were the nights that he went to bed before midnight.

_____   9 Such crimes are punished by death in that country.

_____ 10 So great her love was that she sacrificed everything for her children.

Exercise S-127

<u>Objective:</u> To recognize and correct errors in subject-verb word order.

<u>Questions 1–15</u>

<u>Directions:</u> Part of each sentence is underlined because it is **wrong. Rewrite** this part by changing the word order and, if necessary, adding or dropping an auxiliary verb.

1 In the corner of the room <u>a television set is</u>.

   In the corner of the room is a television set.

2 <u>Not only the police arrived</u>, but the firemen came too.

_____

3 <u>Scarcely the injured man had arrived</u> at the hospital when he was rushed into the operating room.

_____

4 <u>Nowhere children have</u> as much fun as at Disneyland.

_____

5 <u>So few the woman's possessions were</u> that she could carry them in a single suitcase.

_____

6 Only after elephants have become extinct, <u>many people will realize</u> their true value.

_____

7 <u>Were seen leaving the convenience store</u> two masked hold-up men.

_____

8 The newspaper carried several articles on <u>how much money was each candidate spending</u> on his campaign.

_____

9 <u>Never foreign students have come</u> to the United States in such numbers.

_____

10 Few people realize <u>how quickly are many species of cacti becoming extinct.</u>

_____

11 <u>Came up the flowers</u> after the heavy rain.

_____

12 <u>Little they realize</u> the importance of wearing seat belts while driving.

_____

13 There are few details on <u>how did Howard Hughes spend his final years.</u>

_____

14 <u>Were lying beside the road</u> hundreds of pieces of litter.

_____

15 <u>There several reasons were</u> for the committee's decision.

_____

Questions 16–25

Directions: Because of word order, some of the following sentences are incorrect. Put an **X** in the blank beside each of them. Put a **check** (√) beside all correct sentences.

_____ 16 Out of the catcher's mitt flew the ball.

_____ 17 Only at dusk on warm summer nights fireflies appear.

_____ 18 Were an international student to work without proper papers, he would be in violation of his visa.

_____ 19 On the beach were large globs of oil lying.

_____ 20 Seldom children under the age of sixteen are permitted to register for classes at this institute.

_____ 21 Nowhere else in the U.S. can bird watchers see as many different species as at Aransas Pass Wildlife Refuge.

_____ 22 Had the motorist been stopped by the police, he would surely have received a stiff fine.

_____ 23 Through the deserted halls walked a security guard on his nightly rounds.

_____ 24 Was at the end of the tunnel a ray of sunshine seen.

_____ 25 Only once this dog has been taken to a veterinarian's office.

Exercise S-128

Objective: To recognize word order errors that relate to the placement of an adjective in the sentence.

Questions 1–5

Directions: Unless it is used predicatively or in an interrogative sentence, an adjective is usually placed before the word it describes. However, adjectives follow words that end with *-one, -body,* and *-thing*. For example:

Something terrible must have happened to him.

We didn't learn anything useful in that class.

Put a **check** (√) beside sentences with correct word order and an **X** beside sentences with incorrect word order.

_____ 1 The company has not developed anything new in a long time.

_____ 2 Next semester everyone will have different someone for a teacher.

_____ 3 Frieda's smile told everyone that wonderful something had happened to her.

_____ 4 The apartment looked lovely with all the new things the couple had bought.

_____ 5 It is unlikely that you will meet interesting anyone at that party.

Questions 6–10

Directions: The word *enough* follows adjectives, adverbs, and verbs, but comes before nouns. For example:

    adverb: She sings <u>well enough</u> to be a soloist.

    noun: She doesn't have <u>enough time</u> to study.

Put a **check (✓)** beside sentences with correct word order and an **X** beside sentences with incorrect word order.

_____ 6 That girl doesn't read enough fast to finish the book before the exam.

_____ 7 The child was barely enough tall to open the refrigerator door.

_____ 8 That man doesn't have enough nerve to ask for a raise.

_____ 9 Some teachers always have time enough to answer their students' questions.

_____ 10 The right wing didn't kick the ball low enough to make a goal.

Exercise S-129

TOEFL Practice: Structure and Written Expression: Time 6 minutes.

Objective: To recognize correct sentence completions and errors related to the word order of the subject and verb, as well as other errors.

Questions 1–5

Directions: Choose the <u>one</u> word or phrase, (A), (B), (C), or (D), that best completes the sentence. Write your answer in the blank.

_____ 1 Not until a baby kangaroo is four months old - - - - - - - to live outside its mother's pouch.

    (A) it begins   (C) beginning
    (B) and begins   (D) does it begin

_____ 2 Public acceptance of rabbit as an economical source of protein depends on - - - - - - - .

    (A) how aggressively do producers market it
    (B) if is marketed aggressively
    (C) how aggressively producers market it
    (D) whether or not aggressive marketing

_____ 3   - - - - - - - the hobo's belongings that he carried them in a
           bundle slung over his shoulder.

   (A) Were so few
   (B) Few were so
   (C) So few were
   (D) They were so few

_____ 4   Only after a baby seal is pushed into the sea by its mother
           - - - - - - - to swim.

   (A) how will it learn
   (B) will it learn how
   (C) it will learn how
   (D) and it learns how

_____ 5   Proponents of solar energy wonder - - - - - - - funded so few
           research projects.

   (A) why the government has
   (B) has the government
   (C) why has the government
   (D) about the government

Questions 6–10

Directions: Identify the one underlined word or phrase, (A), (B), (C), or (D),
that should be corrected or rewritten. Write your answer in the blank.

_____ 6   Little do scientists know about conditions on Uranus and Neptune,
                 A   B   C
           two giant planet in the solar system.
               D

_____ 7   Only after local residents became sick and publicly voiced their
                       A   B
           displeasure the chemical company began to clean up its dump sites.
                        C   D

_____ 8   So far is Pluto from the sun that it has not completed a full revolve
                  A   B   C
           around it since being discovered in 1930.
                         D

_____ 9   Few inventors have to their credit as much useful inventions as
                     A   B   C   D
           Thomas Alva Edison.

_____ 10   Not until recent has interest in synthetic fuels been revived.
                     A   B   C   D

270

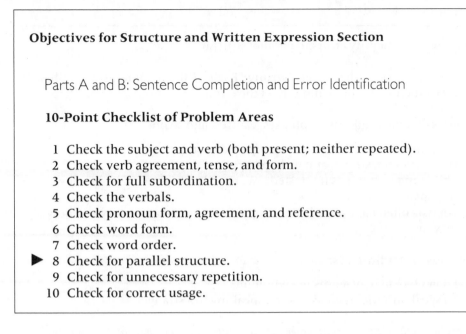

Objectives for Structure and Written Expression Section

Parts A and B: Sentence Completion and Error Identification

10-Point Checklist of Problem Areas

1 Check the subject and verb (both present; neither repeated).
2 Check verb agreement, tense, and form.
3 Check for full subordination.
4 Check the verbals.
5 Check pronoun form, agreement, and reference.
6 Check word form.
7 Check word order.
▶ 8 Check for parallel structure.
9 Check for unnecessary repetition.
10 Check for correct usage.

Objective 8: Check for Parallel Structure

Exercise S-130

Objective: To review the ten important types of structure errors.

Directions: Match each sentence to a problem area from the 10-point checklist above. Write the appropriate number in the blank.

_____ a Pine trees are trees that grow in East Texas.

_____ b Everyone is capable in doing this exercise.

_____ c After dining, dancing, and three hours in the restaurant, they went home.

_____ d Some people felt that there was more nothing they could learn.

_____ e The woman felt sadly when her husband died.

_____ f Everyone brought their books to class every day.

_____ g James never got good grades although was a serious student.

_____ h The burned sun causes mirages in the desert.

_____ i Cacti, according to a recent survey, they are quickly becoming extinct.

_____ j Fifty pounds of sand are not enough for this project.

Exercise S-131

Objective: To identify errors in parallel structure.

Directions These sentences are **wrong**. Each of them contains a problem in parallel structure. Identify and correct the errors.

A series of nouns, adjectives, phrases, clauses, and so on:

1 They offered their time, their money, and energy.
2 He was young, strong, and feeling happy.
3 The young doctor was interested, aware of, but frightened by her new responsibilities.
4 Tourists often have trouble deciding where to go in a new city and how they can get there.

Gerunds and infinitives:

5 I don't like to play tennis or swimming.
6 To speak to a friend is easier than speaking to a stranger.

Correlatives: *both . . . and; either . . . or; neither . . . nor; not only . . . but also; whether . . . or*

7 She was not only pretty but also knew how to dress well.
8 We haven't decided whether we'll go or stay home.

Comparisons:

9 I like John's car better than Fred.
10 He runs as fast but not faster than his brother.

Exercise S-132

Objective: To identify and categorize series of words with correct parallel structure.

Directions: Many sentences present a **series** of ideas about one person or object. All parts of a series must have the same grammatical structure. A sentence might have a series of adjectives, verbs, or nouns.

series of adjectives:	He is tall, blond, and handsome.
series of verbs:	He sings, dances, and plays the guitar.
series of adverbs:	He does his work quickly, carefully, and efficiently.

When all the parts of a series in a sentence have the same grammatical structure, the sentence has **good parallel structure**. A series may have two, three, four, or more parts, but all parts must be parallel. Each of the following sentences contains a series. **Underline** and **count** the number of parts in the series and put your answer **in the first blank**. Then, indicate what type of series the sentence contains by putting the correct abbreviation **in the second blank: nouns (N), verbs (V), adjectives (ADJ), adverbs (ADV)**.

   _3_   _V_   1 In the summer, John <u>swims</u>, <u>jogs</u>, and <u>plays</u> tennis.
                                           1   2   3

____ ____ 2 The director, the teachers, and the students are watching the film.

____ ____ 3 That girl is certainly tall and slim.

____ ____ 4 Slowly and cautiously, the rescue workers pulled the boy to safety.

____ ____ 5 Without a doubt, he is the most ambitious and energetic person here.

____ ____ 6 That amazing woman can speak English, French, Spanish, Arabic, and Berber.

____ ____ 7 John Glenn has served his country as a pilot, an astronaut, and a senator.

____ ____ 8 During the trip, the children were noisy and restless.

____ ____ · 9 That lazy student always takes a nap or watches television in the afternoon.

____ ____ 10 At the banquet, guests were served roast beef, mashed potatoes, green beans, and a tossed salad.

Exercise S-133

<u>Objective:</u> To identify and correct errors in parallel structure arising from the use of an incorrect word form.

<u>Directions:</u> Each sentence contains a series consisting of three parts. Two of the three parts have the same grammatical structure, but one is different. **Circle** the part that is **different**. In the blank, write the correct form of the "different" part.

a politician   1 Benjamin Franklin was a writer, a scientist, and (politics).

_____ 2 Pele was a quick, skillful, and accuracy soccer player.

_____ 3 Among his vices are cigarettes, alcoholic, and drugs.

_____ 4 After a day at the lake, the children came home tired, sunburned, and hunger.

_____ 5 After dinner, Maria usually has a cup of coffee, a cup of tea, or wine.

_____ 6 This anthology of American literature contains poetic, short stories, and a novel.

_____ 7 A sentence can contain a series of two, third, or four items.

_____ 8 The motto of the French revolution was liberty, equal, and fraternity.

_____ 9 A good writer edits his work slowly, careful, and regularly.

_____ 10 On the TOEFL, you should check each verb for agree, tense, and form.

Exercise S-134

<u>Objective:</u> To recognize errors in parallel structure arising from the use of a mixture of infinitives and gerunds in a single sentence.

<u>Directions:</u> It is important to watch for **gerunds** and **infinitives** when checking the parallel structure of a sentence. Although both gerunds and infinitives can function as nouns and can be used interchangeably in many places, it is not good to change from one type of verbal noun to another in the same sentence.

wrong: She likes to swim, to jog, and <u>playing</u> tennis.

correct: She likes swimming, jogging, and playing tennis.
correct: She likes to swim, to jog, and to play tennis.

Check the gerunds and infinitives in each sentence. If a sentence has good parallel structure, put a **check** (√) in the blank. If the sentence contains a problem in parallel structure, put an **X** in the blank. **Underline** gerunds and infinitives.

__X__ 1 <u>To tell</u> a problem to a stranger is sometimes easier than <u>explaining</u> it to a friend.

_____ 2 Two solutions for controlling the seagull population are to kill the birds or limiting their food supply.

_____ 3 The purpose of this paper is to describe how people spend their vacations and explaining where they go.

_____ 4 The 10-point Checklist tells you to check the subject and the verb, to check the subordination, and to check the pronouns.

_____ 5 It is better to give than receiving.

_____ 6 Walking briskly for thirty minutes will burn as many calories as to run for fifteen minutes.

_____ 7 All elementary school children learn to read, to write and to do simple arithmetic problems.

_____ 8 Washing dishes, vacuuming the carpet, and to take out the garbage are tedious tasks.

_____ 9 Most visitors in New York City spend their time attending Broadway plays, to visit some of the museums, and going shopping.

_____ 10 During the fall semester, he plans to work full time, to take one course at the university, and to do some consulting work.

Exercise S-135

Objective: To recognize errors in parallel structure caused by an incorrect shift from clauses to phrases.

Directions: Within a sentence, phrases must be parallel with phrases, and clauses must be parallel with other clauses. It is not good to express one of two similar ideas in the form of a phrase and the other in the form of a clause. For example:

clauses:	<u>because</u> she works hard	<u>because</u> she is intelligent
phrases:	<u>because of</u> her hard work	<u>because of</u> her intelligence
wrong:	She has succeeded <u>because</u> she works hard and <u>because of</u> her intelligence.	
correct:	She has succeeded <u>because</u> she works hard and <u>because</u> she is intelligent.	
correct:	She has succeeded <u>because of</u> her hard work and <u>because of</u> her intelligence.	

Indicate whether a sentence contains **two subordinate clauses (SC)** or **two subordinate phrases (PHR)** by writing the correct abbreviation in the blank.

_SC_ 1 The library was popular with students because it had a good collection of books and because it offered comfortable surroundings.

_____ 2 Despite the threat of lawsuits and despite the benefits of pollution control, the chemical company continues its unsafe practices.

_____ 3 Plastic buttons are commonly used on men's shirts because they are inexpensive and because they can withstand many washings.

_____ 4 Although much of their land is poor and although only ten percent of the land can be cultivated, over ninety percent of the population are agricultural workers.

_____ 5 No one really knows what a quasar is or how it produces so much energy.

_____ 6 The lawyer's collapse was due to overwork and to lack of proper rest.

_____ 7 Provided that we can reserve the park on that day and that the weather clears up, we will have our annual school picnic on August 5.

_____ 8 With five new teachers and with over 100 students, that supervisor is quite overworked this semester.

_____ 9 Usually a bird species is publicized only when it has experienced a population explosion or when it is in danger of extinction.

_____ 10 What he said was exactly what no one wanted to hear.

Exercise S-136

Objective: To recognize errors in parallel structure related to the placement of pairs of correlative conjunctions.

Directions: Attention to parallel structure is very important when a sentence contains any of the pairs of **correlative conjunctions:** *either . . . or, neither . . . nor, not only . . . but also, both . . . and.* The correlatives must be correctly placed so that the structures which follow them have the same grammatical structure.

                      V   prep

wrong: Water (both) flows over (and) through porous soil.

                             prep   prep

correct: Water flows (both) over (and) through porous soil.

Put the letter of the **correct** sentence in the blank.

_B_ 1 (A) A stream either can erode or deposit material as it flows.
        (B) A stream can either erode or deposit material as it flows.

_____ 2 (A) Lichen both carries on photosynthesis and respiration.
        (B) Lichen carries on both photosynthesis and respiration.

_____ 3 (A) Climate influences soil formation not only through moisture and temperature but also through the vegetation it permits.
        (B) Climate influences soil formation through not only moisture and temperature but also through the vegetation it permits.

_____ 4 (A) Computer languages are classified as either high-level or as low-level.
        (B) Computer languages are classified either as high-level or as low-level.

_____ 5 (A) Erosion can occur either through the action of water or the action of wind.
        (B) Erosion can occur through the action of either water or wind.

_____ 6 (A) Edmund Haley not only published the first map of the winds but also contributed to knowledge of weather by relating winds to heat.
        (B) Edmund Haley published not only the first map of the winds but also contributed to knowledge of weather by relating winds to heat.

_____ 7 (A) Computer languages can be further classified as either problem-oriented or procedure-oriented.

     (B) Computer languages can be further classified either as problem-oriented or procedure-oriented.

_____ 8 (A) Lunar craters may have originated from either the collapse of volcanoes or from the impact of large meteorites.

     (B) Lunar craters may have originated either from the collapse of volcanoes or from the impact of large meteorites.

_____ 9 (A) Science can neither explain the effect of the moon on rainfall cycles nor accurately predict the motion of the earth's atmosphere.

     (B) Science can explain neither the effect of the moon on rainfall cycles nor accurately predict the motion of the earth's atmosphere.

_____ 10 (A) Solar energy is reflected back to space by not only cloud cover but also by water surfaces, sand, soil, vegetation and snow fields.

     (B) Solar energy is reflected back to space not only by cloud cover but also by water surfaces, sand, soil, vegetation, and snow fields.

Exercise S-137

Objective: To identify errors in parallel structure related to incomplete comparisons.

Directions: Good parallel structure demands that only those things that are alike can actually be compared.

$$x \text{ of } y \qquad > \qquad z$$
wrong: The area of Alaska is greater than $\lambda\lambda$ Texas.
correct: The area of Alaska is greater than that of Texas.
$$x \text{ of } y \qquad > \qquad x \text{ of } z$$

It is possible to compare the **area of Alaska** to the **area of Texas**, but it is not possible to compare the **area of Alaska** to **Texas**. Examine each pair of sentences and place the letter of the **correct** sentence in the blank.

__B__ 1 (A) The books on the top shelves are older than the bottom shelves.

     (B) The books on the top shelves are older than those on the bottom shelves.

_____ 2 (A) The damage caused by the first flood was greater than that caused by the second flood.

     (B) The damage caused by the first flood was greater than the second flood.

_____ 3 (A) The paintings of Van Gogh are perhaps better known than Cézanne.

(B) The paintings of Van Gogh are perhaps better known than those of Cézanne.

_____ 4 (A) Oil reserves in Texas are not as great as those in Alaska.

(B) Oil reserves in Texas are not as great as Alaska.

_____ 5 (A) A secretary's pay is less than an administrator.

(B) A secretary's pay is less than an administrator's.

_____ 6 (A) You will find that the customs in the United States are different from your country.

(B) You will find that the customs in the United States are different from those in your country.

_____ 7 (A) The rent for an efficiency apartment is much less than that for a one-bedroom apartment.

(B) The rent for an efficiency apartment is much less than a one-bedroom apartment.

_____ 8 (A) In our institution, morning classes are far more popular than the afternoon.

(B) In our institution, morning classes are far more popular than afternoon ones.

_____ 9 (A) According to recent surveys, the CBS news programs have bigger audiences than NBC.

(B) According to recent surveys, the CBS news programs have bigger audiences than those of NBC.

_____ 10 (A) The mean gain scores for students in the experimental group were greater than students in the control group.

(B) The mean gain scores for students in the experimental group were greater than those for students in the control group.

Exercise S-138

Objective: To identify errors in parallel structure arising from incomplete comparisons.

Directions: When one member of a group is compared to the other members of the group, it is necessary to exclude that member from the group by using the words *any other* or *anyone else*.

wrong: Alaska is larger than any state. *(Alaska is larger than Alaska???)*
correct: Alaska is larger than any other state.

wrong: John is taller than anyone in his class. *(John is taller than John???)*
correct: John is taller than anyone else in his class.

Write the letter of the correct sentence in the blank.

_B_ 1 (A) The university's administration building is taller than any building on the campus.

        (B) The university's administration building is taller than any other building on the campus.

_____ 2 (A) Monkeys and apes are more intelligent than any animals except man.

        (B) Monkeys and apes are more intelligent than any other animals except man.

_____ 3 (A) More skyscrapers are located in New York City than in any city in the United States.

        (B) More skyscrapers are located in New York City than in any other city in the United States.

_____ 4 (A) Wilbur and Orville Wright are more famous in the history of U.S. aviation than anyone.

        (B) Wilbur and Orville Wright are more famous in the history of U.S. aviation than anyone else.

_____ 5 (A) Ms. Gilman has taught English in that program for more years than anyone else.

        (B) Ms. Gilman has taught English in that program for more years than anyone.

Exercise S-139

Objective: To identify errors in parallel structure in sentences containing double comparisons.

Directions: In some sentences, two persons or things are compared in two ways. When two comparisons are combined, all parts of both comparisons must be retained. For example:

comparison 1: Mary is <u>as tall as</u> John.

comparison 2: Mary may be <u>taller than</u> John.

Combined comparisons:

wrong: Mary is <u>as tall</u> ⁄ , if not <u>taller than</u>, John.

correct: Mary is <u>as tall as</u>, if not <u>taller than</u>, John.

Write the letter of the correct sentence in the blank.

_A_ 1 (A) Latex paint is as good as, if not better than, oil-based paint.

        (B) Latex paint is as good, if not better than, oil-based paint.

_____ 2 (A) Rebuilding that worn-out carburetor will be as expensive, if not more expensive than, buying a new one.
(B) Rebuilding that worn-out carburetor will be as expensive as, if not more expensive than, buying a new one.

_____ 3 (A) Her skill as a typist is equal or exceeds that of her predecessor.
(B) Her skill as a typist is equal to or exceeds that of her predecessor.

_____ 4 (A) John Phillips received grades that were as high as, if not higher than, those of any other person in his class.
(B) John Phillips received grades that were as high, if not higher than, those of any other person in his class.

_____ 5 (A) Track lighting is one of the most popular types, if not most popular type, of lighting on the market today.
(B) Track lighting is one of the most popular types, if not the most popular type, of lighting on the market today.

_____ 6 (A) Even if they are on sale, these refrigerators are equal in price to, if not more expensive than, the ones at the other store.
(B) Even if they are on sale, these refrigerators are equal in price, if not more expensive than, the ones at the other store.

_____ 7 (A) Low tar cigarettes are as dangerous as, if not more dangerous than, regular cigarettes.
(B) Low tar cigarettes are as dangerous, if not more dangerous than, regular cicarettes.

_____ 8 (A) The warranty on the radial tires is as good if not better than that on the four-ply tires.
(B) The warranty on the radial tires is as good as if not better than that on the four-ply tires.

_____ 9 (A) His science-fiction novels formed one of the best collections, if not best collection, I had ever seen.
(B) His science-fiction novels formed one of the best collections, if not the best collection, I had ever seen.

_____ 10 (A) The weather this winter was as bad as, if not worse than, last year's.
(B) The weather this winter was as bad, if not worse than, last year's.

Exercise S-140

Objective: To recognize all types of errors in parallel structure.

Directions: If a sentence contains good parallel structure, put a **check** (√) in the blank. If it has faulty parallel structure, put an **X** in the blank.

__X__ 1 Tourists in our city usually visit the Capitol, spend some time in the presidential library, and walking around the university campus.

_____ 2 Even though that car is used, it is clean, economical and new paint.

_____ 3 If you wish to change your level, you should talk either to your teacher or your level supervisor.

_____ 4 His shoes are much newer than you.

_____ 5 That new student is friendly, talkative, and everyone likes him.

_____ 6 That is the store where I used to work and where my sister works now.

_____ 7 If a tenant fails to pay his rent, the landlord either can change the lock on the door or enter the apartment and seize luxury items.

_____ 8 The public broadcasting station is asking people to donate goods to the auction or to give money.

_____ 9 Heat the soup for ten minutes and then you should remove it from the stove.

_____ 10 The contest winner not only receives ten free records but also dinner in his favorite restaurant.

_____ 11 The Housing Office will provide information on how to rent an apartment and how to give notice about leaving.

_____ 12 It is much easier to adopt a pet than getting rid of one.

_____ 13 The foreman of the jury rose to his feet, turned toward the judge, and addresses him quietly.

_____ 14 The students asked to speak either to the director or to his assistant.

_____ 15 This filing cabinet contains not only the records of all former students but also the minutes of all the staff meetings.

_____ 16 That tree is as tall if not taller than the tree in the park.

_____ 17 Many species of African wildlife are in danger despite new laws and more people know about the problem.

_____ 18 The city map lists streets, parks, and what the tourists like to see.

_____ 19 All employees must buy either a parking sticker or leave their cars at home.

_____ 20 The population of Asia is larger than Europe.

Exercise S-141

<u>TOEFL Practice:</u> Structure and Written Expression: Time 6 minutes.

<u>Objective:</u> To recognize correct sentence completions and structure errors related to parallel structure, as well as other errors.

Questions 1–4

<u>Directions:</u> Choose the <u>one</u> word or phrase, (A), (B), (C), or (D), that best completes the sentence. Write your answer in the blank.

_____ 1   Gravity not only causes bodies to fall - - - - - - - increases their speed.

(A) and to
(B) and also
(C) but also
(D) and so

_____ 2   Because sheep - - - - - - - meat and wool, they are valued in many countries.

(A) both produce
(B) having both
(C) both
(D) produce both

_____ 3   Fainting can result from either a lack of oxygen - - - - - - - a loss of blood.

(A) or
(B) and from
(C) or from
(D) and

_____ 4   - - - - - - - oats and rye can endure severe winter weather.

(A) Either
(B) They are
(C) Both
(D) Both of

Questions 5–10

<u>Directions:</u> Identify the <u>one</u> underlined word or phrase, (A), (B), (C), or (D), that should be corrected or rewritten. Write your answer in the blank.

_____ 5   Methods of flood <u>control focus on</u> preventing rivers from <u>rising</u> and
               A   B   C
<u>to keep</u> them within their banks.
   D

_____ 6   Painters of the expressionist school <u>concentrated on</u> <u>themes of</u>
         A   B   C
horror, fear, and <u>violent</u>.
                   D

_____ 7   The discovery of gold hastened the settlement of California <u>as much,</u>
                                                                                                    A

if <u>not more</u> than, the <u>reports of</u> the fertile land and <u>the good</u> climate.
     B   C   D

_____ 8   The Gadsden Purchase <u>came</u> <u>about</u> because of a <u>boundary dispute</u>
                                              A   B   C

and because <u>a railway was proposed.</u>
                              D

_____ 9   Cave explorers are <u>called either</u> spelunkers or <u>speleology</u>
                                            A   B

depending <u>on whether</u> they enter caves <u>for sport</u> or science.
                     C   D

_____ 10 Success <u>in fencing</u> requires not only skill <u>and balance</u> but also
                          A   B

<u>mental alertness</u> and <u>concentrate.</u>
           C   D

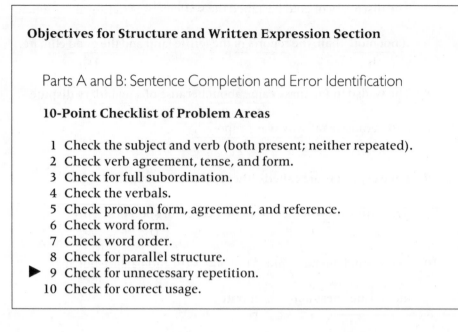

Objectives for Structure and Written Expression Section

Parts A and B: Sentence Completion and Error Identification

10-Point Checklist of Problem Areas

1 Check the subject and verb (both present; neither repeated).
2 Check verb agreement, tense, and form.
3 Check for full subordination.
4 Check the verbals.
5 Check pronoun form, agreement, and reference.
6 Check word form.
7 Check word order.
8 Check for parallel structure.
▶ 9 Check for unnecessary repetition.
10 Check for correct usage.

Objective 9: Check for Unnecessary Repetition

Exercise S-142

Objective: To review the ten important types of structure errors.

Directions: Match each sentence to a problem area from the 10-point checklist above. Write the appropriate number in the blank.

_____ a Yuri Gagarin made a name for hisself by being the first man in space.

_____ b Neither the dog nor the cat belong to me.

_____ c What did the speaker say was quite interesting.

_____ d Dogs wear identification tags are quickly returned to their owners.

_____ e The area of Alaska is bigger than Texas.

_____ f After waiting an hour, she was anger.

_____ g Light beer has less calories than regular beer.

_____ h Students in that class they are learning more quickly than the others.

_____ i Walking home, a noise frightened the little girl.

_____ j Motorcyclists are no longer required by law to wear helmets on their heads.

Exercise S-143

Objective: To match words that have the same meaning.

Directions: A phrase that contains two or more adjectives or adverbs that express the same meaning is not acceptable in formal English. To find these repetitive phrases, you need to recognize words that can have the same meaning. Beside each word in **Column A**, **write the numbers** of the words in **Column B** that can have the same meaning.

Column A

___3, 6__ (A) fast

_____ (B) important

_____ (C) very

_____ (D) short

_____ (E) correct

_____ (F) simple

_____ (G) main

_____ (H) complete

_____ (I) strong

_____ (J) difficult

Column B

1 significant	11 easy
2 extremely	12 principal
3 rapid	13 powerful
4 accurate	14 total
5 exceedingly	15 hard
6 quick	16 plain
7 concise	17 comprehensive
8 vital	18 mighty
9 right	19 central
10 brief	20 full

Exercise S-144

Objective: To categorize verbs on the basis of whether they have an **implied meaning** of *more* or *less*.

Directions: Many verbs express the general idea of *more* or *less* within their specific meaning. If a verb implies the idea of *more*, it is unnecessary to repeat this idea by adding the word *more* to the sentence.

   wrong: The store <u>raised</u> the cost by ten dollars <u>more</u>.

   correct: The store <u>raised</u> the cost by ten dollars.

Half of the following verbs imply *more* while the other half imply *less*. Write each verb in the correct column according to its meaning.

✓ exceed	deflate	improve	diminish
✓ decrease	outweigh	expand	ascend
decline	augment	regress	shrink
enlarge	reduce	relapse	accelerate
inflate	lower	deplete	increase
surpass	devalue	overrate	undervalue

implication of *more*	**implication of** *less*
exceed	*decrease*

Exercise S-145

Objective: To identify phrases which contain unnecessary repetition.

Directions: Some of these phrases contain unnecessary repetition because both verbs have the same meaning. Put an **X** beside such phrases.

X   1 perished and died suddenly

_____   2 divided and conquered the enemy

_____   3 will sterilize and disinfect the wound

_____   4 dampened and moistened the soil

_____   5 examined and selected the coin

_____   6 initiated and terminated the discussion

_____   7 joined and connected the wires

_____   8 read and considered the report

_____   9 guess and speculate about the results

_____   10 discovered and explored the island

_____   11 cultivated and marketed the flowers

_____   12 sheds and discards its skin

_____ 13 fled and escaped the prison

_____ 14 tilted and folded the layers

_____ 15 surprised and impressed the audience

_____ 16 followed and pursued the thief

_____ 17 resuscitate and revive the patient

_____ 18 reduced and decreased the flow

_____ 19 designed and constructed the building

_____ 20 injure or wound the animal

Exercise S-146

Objective: To eliminate unnecessary repetition by identifying unnecessary words.

Directions: Each of these sentences contains unnecessary repetition because each contains words that repeat the meaning of other words. Find these unnecessary words and cross them out.

1 The Kentucky rifle played an important ~~and~~ signi~~f~~icant part in helping early settlers get food.

2 The distant thunder was audible to the ear.

3 A shrub called the Nandini is a popular shrub which was introduced into America from the Orient.

4 A room that is pink in color can soothe and calm even the most violent, aggressive prisoner.

5 Beginning with an initial investment of only ten thousand dollars, both of the two partners have increased their money by twenty thousand more.

6 Extensive use of pesticides can kill pelicans and cause the birds to die.

7 Despite the repeal of the helmet law, not each and every motorcyclist has given up wearing a helmet on his head.

8 Almost simultaneously at the same time, residents in several parts of the city were experiencing severe flooding.

9 In the 1960's, students all over the whole country were discussing the war and they were protesting against it.

10 Although the brief, short report was well written and documented, it failed to convince the committee to vote against the project.

11 There are several vital and important reasons for the nation to invest money in renewable energy sources.

12 The only fast, quick way to rid a yard of fleas is to spray thoroughly all vegetation in a very complete manner.

13 Since squashbugs can rapidly kill young plants almost overnight, it is extremely, very important to check and investigate the garden daily.

14 The city is quite fortunate to have two daily newspapers that provide both local and national coverage every day.

15 It is possible that a male tiger may outweigh a female tiger by seventy to one hundred pounds more.

16 A student is less likely to fail an examination if he knows exactly and specifically what topics will be tested.

17 The reason why one should always read every day is to improve one's speed and comprehension.

18 The dog was purchased to guard and protect the house and yard while the owners were away.

19 The issues that divided and separated the States and brought about the Civil War were not easily resolved.

20 A hot iron can scorch and discolor delicate, fragile fabrics quickly.

Exercise S-147

TOEFL Practice: Structure and Written Expression: Time 6 minutes.

Objective: To recognize correct sentence completions and structure errors caused by unnecessary repetition, as well as other errors.

Questions 1–2

Directions: Choose the one word or phrase, (A), (B), (C), or (D), that best completes the sentence. Write your answer in the blank.

_____ 1 Water vapor changing to liquid - - - - - - - heat.

      (A) releases   (C) it releases
      (B) its   (D) the

_____ 2 Yeasts are tiny - - - - - - - plants.

      (A) and small   (C) small single-celled
      (B) single-celled   (D) small one-celled

Questions 3–10

Directions: Identify the <u>one</u> underlined word or phrase, (A), (B), (C), or (D), that should be corrected or rewritten. Write your answer in the blank.

_____ 3 Expressionism is characterized <u>by both</u> the simplification <u>of form</u>
             A   B   C
   and the use <u>and utilization</u> of certain colors.
         D

_____ 4 Both the <u>rising</u> of bread dough and the changing of grapejuice
        A
   <u>to wine</u> are <u>famous</u>, well-known examples of <u>fermentation</u>.
    B   C   D

_____ 5 Sand dunes <u>are formed</u> where the wind <u>loses</u> energy <u>and drops</u>
          A   B   C
   <u>their</u> load of particles.
    D

_____ 6 Fatigue is a <u>feeling</u> of weariness and <u>exhaustion</u> <u>which</u> is remedied
          A   B   C
   <u>by</u> eating or sleeping.
   D

_____ 7 Sheep <u>can live</u> and <u>thrive</u> on semiarid, mountainous, <u>hilly</u> lands
      A   B   C
   <u>where cattle</u> cannot exist.
    D

_____ 8 Ferdinand and Isabella, who <u>ruled in</u> the <u>fifteen</u> and sixteenth
               A   B
   centuries, <u>helped create</u> the boundaries of <u>modern-day</u> Spain.
         C   D

_____ 9 The flamingo is a graceful, <u>aquatic</u> bird that is pink <u>in color</u> and has
              A   B
   a <u>long neck</u> <u>and slender</u> legs.
     C   D

_____ 10 A coma is a <u>deep state</u> of unconsciousness <u>from which</u> a patient
         A   B
   cannot <u>be roused</u> by ordinary, <u>common</u> means.
      C   D

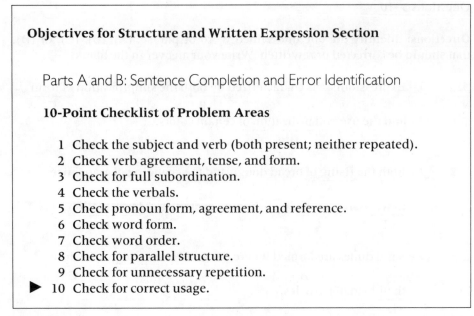

Objectives for Structure and Written Expression Section

Parts A and B: Sentence Completion and Error Identification

10-Point Checklist of Problem Areas

1 Check the subject and verb (both present; neither repeated).
2 Check verb agreement, tense, and form.
3 Check for full subordination.
4 Check the verbals.
5 Check pronoun form, agreement, and reference.
6 Check word form.
7 Check word order.
8 Check for parallel structure.
9 Check for unnecessary repetition.
▶ 10 Check for correct usage.

Objective 10: Check for Correct Usage
Exercise S-148

Objective: To review the ten important types of structure errors.

Directions: Match each sentence to a problem area from the 10-point checklist above. Write the appropriate number in the blank.

_____ a Aluminum is plentiful, versatile, and does not cost much.

_____ b No one except he knew the answer to the last question.

_____ c In the final analyze, there were at least three causes of the Civil War.

_____ d Neither John or his sister came to the party.

_____ e Only once Harry has arrived on time.

_____ f If you out some words, your sentence will be difficult to understand.

_____ g All of my time have been profitably spent.

_____ h Insulation, despite its initial cost, it will lower utility bills.

_____ i It will cost about twelve dollars to replace the breaking window.

_____ j Fred obviously outweighs Steve by twenty pounds more.

Exercise S-149

Objective: To categorize words on the basis of whether they are used in conjunction with two things or three or more things.

Directions: Some words can be used only in reference to two persons, things, or groups. Other words can be used only in reference to three or more persons, things, or groups. Write each word in the proper column according to its usage.

✓ either	largest	former	best
✓ most	neither	among	between
both	least	worst	latter
less	superior	more	worse
inferior	better	none	all

refers to two	refers to three or more
either	*most*

Exercise S-150

Objective: To recognize errors in usage related to words that refer to two things and words that refer to three or more things.

Directions: Write the letter of the incorrect word or phrase in the blank.

__A__ 1 Both of the three girls were among the contestants who were
      A   B
    selected for the final competition.

_____ 2 None of the tires on the motorcycle looks any better than the other.
        A   B

_____ 3 The third city on the tour had the worse weather but the most
                                                            A   B

        interesting sights.

_____ 4 Arabic and Berber are spoken in Algeria, but the former is used
                                                                     A

        most.
        B

_____ 5 Neither of the angles of an equilateral triangle ever has more or less
          A   B

        than sixty degrees.

_____ 6 Between the teachers, students, and administrators, there is a sharp
        A

        disagreement over the parking situation, but the students have the

        least chance of winning.
        B

_____ 7 Of the three options presented, the latter seems the best.
                                              A   B

_____ 8 Although he claims to be bilingual, his Spanish is no better, if not
                                                                                      A

        worst, than mine.
        B

_____ 9 Either of the four best essays may appear in today's newspaper.
          A   B

_____ 10 Of all the apartments in this building, mine is in the worse
         A   B
        condition.

Exercise S-151

Objective: To form and use correctly the various forms of *sit/set, rise/raise,* and *lie/lay.*

Directions: There are six verbs that cause problems in correct usage because their meanings are similar and some of their forms are irregular. The base form of each verb is listed below. Look it up in a dictionary if you are unsure of its meaning. Then, fill in the blanks with the other principal parts.

base	simple past	past participle	present participle
1 sit	*sat*	*sat*	*sitting*
2 set			
3 lie			
4 lay			
5 rise			
6 raise			

Three of these verbs (*sit, lie,* and *rise*) are never followed by a direct object and are never in the passive form. The other three verbs (*set, lay,* and *raise*) are followed by direct objects and can be passive in form. Choose the correct verb in each sentence from the two choices in parentheses.

7 The flag was (*risen, raised*) to the top of the pole.

8 The campers got up as soon as the sun had (*risen, raised*).

9 The defendant (*rose, raised*) and faced the jury.

10 The old man has (*sat, set*) on the park bench all afternoon.

11 The pastry chef (*sat, set*) the pies on the counter to cool.

12 The pies had been (*sat, set*) out on the counter to cool.

13 The old tools had (*lain, laid*) in the basement for years.

14 The tools were (*lain, laid*) away in the basement.

15 As soon as the child (*lay, laid*) his head on the pillow, he fell asleep.

16 (*Lying, Laying*) in the driveway was a bicycle.

Exercise S-152

Objective: To categorize verbs as active or passive in order to identify errors in usage of *sit/set, lie/lay,* and *rise/raise.*

Directions: **In the first blank,** put **A** if the underlined verb is **active** and **P** if it is **passive. In the second blank,** put a **check (√)** if the verb is correct and an **X** if it is wrong. Then, write the **correct** form of each incorrect verb in the **third blank.**

_A_ _X_ 1 Birds begin one of the most active periods of their day soon after the sun has ra~~i~~sed.

risen

——— ——— 2 The motorist ran over a child's toy that was <u>lying</u> in the street.

———————

——— ——— 3 The old box that had <u>laid</u> in the attic for ten years was covered with dust and cobwebs.

———————

——— ——— 4 After <u>sitting</u> the plants outside, the housekeeper was able to clean.

———————

——— ——— 5 The flag was <u>raised</u> to half-mast to honor the dead soldier.

———————

——— ——— 6 The bathmat <u>lying</u> on the floor is over ten years old.

———————

——— ——— 7 Prices of citrus fruits were <u>risen</u> because of the severe freeze.

———————

——— ——— 8 Metal tools which <u>lie</u> outside in the rain will eventually rust.

———————

——— ——— 9 No sooner had the moon <u>risen</u> than a cloud obscured it from view.

———————

——— ——— 10 The seedlings should not be <u>set</u> out until after the last frost.

———————

——— ——— 11 His fear of a relapse was <u>lain</u> to rest by the doctor's words.

———————

——— ——— 12 Presuming the price of silver would soon <u>raise</u>, investors bought large quantities of the metal.

———————

——— ——— 13 By <u>lying</u> motionless, an animal can more easily camouflage itself.

———————

____ ____ 14 Clocks should be <u>sit</u> forward one hour when daylight saving time ends.

_____

____ ____ 15 <u>Setting</u> in the hot sun for a long time can be dangerous to fair-skinned individuals.

_____

____ ____ 16 Although the rent was <u>raised</u> twice, it is still lower than one might expect.

_____

____ ____ 17 These bricks were obviously <u>laid</u> by a very careless worker.

_____

____ ____ 18 Having been <u>risen</u> in a small town, the writer was at his best when describing scenes of rural America.

_____

____ ____ 19 Kittens which are not <u>raised</u> around humans are difficult to tame completely.

_____

____ ____ 20 The letter which <u>laid</u> on the desk for so long has disappeared.

_____

Exercise S-153

<u>TOEFL Practice:</u> Structure and Written Expression: Time 6 minutes.

<u>Objective:</u> To recognize structure errors related to verb usage, as well as other errors.

<u>Directions:</u> Identify the <u>one</u> underlined word or phrase, (A), (B), (C), or (D), that should be corrected or rewritten. Write your answer in the blank.

_____ 1 Chesapeake Bay was <u>formed</u> when a <u>retreating</u> glacier <u>leaves</u> a
                       A   B   C

trough over one hundred and fifty miles long where the

Susquehanna River used <u>to enter</u> the Atlantic Ocean.
                       D

_____ 2 Since a pet may go into shock after a serious injury, it is important
                      A   B

    to take preventive action before this condition sits in.
       C   D

_____ 3 The cliff dwellings of Mesa Verde, Colorado were build over 800
               A   B

    years ago by Indians who found safety in caves in the canyon walls.
                  C   D

_____ 4 Many commuters have recently began to choose ride-sharing over
                        A   B   C

    independent travel because of the friendships that they can make.
               D

_____ 5 The Black Hills of South Dakota which raise above the inhospitable
                                  A   B

    desert are an interesting tourist attraction.
        C   D

_____ 6 The exotic lotus plant can be successfully raised at home by lying
                               A   B

    the tuber horizontally in a container full of fresh potting soil.
          C   D

_____ 7 Since even the gentlest pet may bit when it is in pain, it is wise to
                        A   B

    muzzle an injured animal by wrapping a soft cloth around its
                    C   D

    jaws.

_____ 8 With temperatures and energy costs rising, attic fans which draw
                            A   B

    fresh air through open windows they are becoming popular again.
                     C   D

_____ 9 From 1923 until 1929, Calvin Coolidge, known as a man
             A   B

    of few words, was being president of the United States.
         C   D

_____ 10 Because recent studies have shown that obesity can cause some
                A   B

    types of diabetes, doctors usually put his diabetic patients on a
                           C   D

    special diet.

Exercise S-154

Objective: To review the use of *take, make,* and *do.*

Directions: The verbs *take, make,* and *do* cause special problems in correct usage. The choice of which verb to use depends on the direct object that follows rather than on the dictionary meaning of the verb. Check your understanding of the correct usage of these verbs by writing each direct object in the appropriate column under the correct verb. In some cases, more than one verb may be correct, depending on the meaning of the expression.

✓ a mistake	an experiment	a trip	a promise
✓ housework	your best	a speech	a chance
✓ your time	an appointment	an effort	progress
a comparison	a good job	medicine	a turn
a suggestion	homework	money	a deposit
arrangements	exercises	an airplane	a recommendation
a favor	friends	a bet	a reservation
a proposal	advances	a project	research

take	make	do
your time	*a mistake*	*housework*

Exercise S-155

Objective: To recognize errors in usage.

Directions: Write the letter of the incorrect word or phrase in the blank.

_____ 1 The committee has done several recommendations about
A   B

arrangements for the annual picnic.

_____ 2 Unless a patient takes his medicine regularly, he is unlikely to do
A   B

fast progress toward full recovery.

_____ 3 The president have not yet made several key appointments in the
A   B

judiciary branch.

_____ 4 The handicapped have done advances in changing public opinion
A

about their value as employees.
B

_____ 5 Individuals who take time to do some type of daily exercise are
A

likely to be healthy and energetically.
B

_____ 6 Sleep scientists are still making research on various types of sleep
A

disorders.
B

_____ 7 Candidates for high-level political office are likely to do promises
A   B

which they cannot keep.

_____ 8 Carnivals and gambling establishments attract people

whom enjoy taking chances and making bets.
A   B

_____ 9 Several proposals have been done concerning designs for the new
A   B

civic center.

_____ 10 The fact that the space shuttle is reusable shows the progress that
A

has been done in space technology.
B

Exercise S-156

Objective: To distinguish words preceded by *a* from those preceded by *an*, on the basis of pronunciation.

Directions: The indefinite articles, *a* and *an*, create some usage problems. *A* is used before consonant **sounds**, and *an* is used before vowel **sounds**. It is easy to determine which article to use except when a word begins with *h, u,* or *o.* It is necessary to choose the appropriate article based on the **pronunciation** of the word which follows.

   consonant sounds: a human being/a utility bill/a one-piece bathing suit
   vowel sounds: an honor student/an uncle/an orange dress

According to the pronunciation of the following words, put them in the appropriate column.

✓ university	hurricane	honor
✓ orange	honest person	umbrella
✓ hour	umpire	once-familiar face
union	one-story house	herb
home	unit	only child
uniform	honorary degree	owner

a + consonant sound	*an* + vowel sound
a university	*an orange* *an hour*

Exercise S-157

Objective: To determine whether to use *a* or *an* on the basis of sound.

Directions: Fill in the blanks with *a* or *an* according to the first sound of the following word.

1 _____ union leader

2 _____ only child

3 _____ ape

4 _____ baseball uniform

5 only _____ dollar bill

6 _____ honorary degree

7 _____ homely face   14 _____ urge to kill

8 _____ hourly wage   15 _____ one-legged man

9 _____ metric unit   16 after _____ hour

10 _____ umbrella stand   17 _____ horn

11 once _____ property owner   18 _____ honest person

12 _____ herb garden   19 _____ energetic individual

13 _____ homemade pie   20 _____ shiny apple

Exercise S-158

Objective: To distinguish between count and non-count nouns.

Directions: Nouns can be divided into two categories: **count nouns** and **non-count nouns**. Write each of the following nouns in the proper column. Make each countable noun plural.

√ companionship	decision	electricity	organism
√ acid	exhaustion	moisture	age
√ arrival	evaporation	challenge	architecture
information	withdrawal	electron	wave
technique	oxygen	lumber	accounting
furniture	aluminum	substance	enthusiast

count nouns	non-count nouns
acids *arrivals*	*companionship*

Exercise S-159

_____

<u>Objective:</u> To distinguish among words that may be used with count nouns, non-count nouns, or both.

<u>Directions:</u> Many words or phrases can be used only with nouns that are **countable** while other words can be used only with nouns that are **non-countable**. There are some words that can be used with **both countable and non-countable nouns**. Put each word or phrase in the appropriate column according to its correct usage.

✓ few	some	less
✓ any	amount	much
✓ little	both of	neither of/either of
several	each/every	quantity
a/an	many	all
the	one/two/three etc.	fewer

used with count nouns	used with both	used with non-count nouns
few	*any*	*little*

Exercise S-160

_____

<u>Objective:</u> To recognize errors in usage related to count and non-count nouns.

<u>Directions:</u> Write the letter of the incorrect word or phrase in the blank beside the sentence.

___B___ 1 All of the water that falls on the land eventually <u>return</u> to the
            A   B
oceans.

_____ 2 <u>Much</u> changes that the earth undergoes <u>are</u> so slow that they are
        A   B
            hardly noticed.

_____ 3 Some rocks have <u>much</u> of the <u>characteristics</u> of sand and mud found
                    A   B
            in and near bodies of water.

_____ 4 Work is a measure of the <u>quantity</u> of energy, or force, needed to
                                A
            move <u>an</u> object.
                  B

_____ 5 <u>Fewer</u> rain falls in the coastal desert of Peru than along <u>the</u>
        A   B
            California coast.

_____ 6 In <u>over 200</u> years there have been <u>little</u> changes in Isaac Newton's
            A   B
            theories about motion and gravity.

_____ 7 Modern <u>geologist</u> use <u>many</u> complex instruments to find
                 A   B
            underground deposits of metals.

_____ 8 All <u>substance</u> are composed of <u>small</u> particles called atoms.
               A   B

_____ 9 <u>A</u> water below <u>the</u> earth's surface is called ground water.
         A   B

_____ 10 The <u>amount</u> of moisture in the atmosphere is less important to us
            A
            than the <u>quantity</u> of water that falls to earth.
                  B

Exercise S-161

<u>Objective:</u> To recognize errors in usage.

<u>Directions:</u> In each sentence a word or phrase is underlined. If the word or phrase is used correctly, put a **check** (✓) in the blank. If it is used incorrectly, put an **X** in the blank.

__X__ 1 A Ford is <u>different than</u> a Cadillac in more than price.

_____ 2 We are <u>all ready</u> to see the movie.

_____ 3 The <u>former</u> of the three items was placed on sale only yesterday.

_____ 4 Most readers enjoy <u>these kind</u> of books.

_____ 5 As he was <u>sitting</u> the table for dinner, he broke a crystal goblet.

_____ 6 Many of our items <u>like</u> sheets, towels, and bedspreads will go on sale soon.

_____ 7 There were <u>less</u> people in attendance than the management expected.

_____ 8 The foreman of the jury <u>rose</u> to his feet and addressed the judge.

_____ 9 As far as the audience knew, the movie would last no longer <u>as</u> two hours.

_____ 10 There <u>maybe</u> more reasons for his erratic behavior than his parents realize.

_____ 11 Sometimes nothing <u>accept</u> crying will completely relieve stress.

_____ 12 The doctor stated that he <u>had rather</u> treat the woman on an out-patient basis.

_____ 13 <u>Besides</u> the watch lay three heavy gold chains.

_____ 14 The committee's <u>principle</u> objection to the book is the obscene language it contains.

_____ 15 The Better Business Bureau can provide sound <u>advise</u> on choosing a reputable contractor.

_____ 16 Even lifelong residents of the city were astonished by the <u>amount</u> of businesses inundated by the flood waters.

_____ 17 Tough environmental laws have been <u>passed</u> in many states because many chemical plants have not adopted safe disposal practices of their own.

_____ 18 Money from federal grants will be divided <u>between</u> all the agencies according to guidelines set up by the governor.

_____ 19 <u>Farther</u> information will be issued by the weather bureau as the situation develops.

_____ 20 A reduction in the posted speed limit should have some <u>affect</u> on the number of accidents on this road.

Exercise S-162

Objective: To study basic rules for correct usage.

Directions: Read through the following brief glossary carefully. If you made many errors on Exercises S-149 through S-161, do them again after you have read the following rules.

Brief Glossary of Correct Usage
(For key to abbreviations, see page 309.)

1 A, AN (art)   Before consonant sounds, use *a*; before vowel sounds, use *an*.
They left an hour ago.

I will attend a university next semester.

2 ACCEPT (v), EXCEPT (prep)
They accepted my invitation.

Everyone except me attended the meeting.

3 ADVICE (n), ADVISE (v)
His advice was very useful.

I advised him to buy a car.

4 AFFECT (v), EFFECT (n, v)   The verb *affect* means *to influence;* the verb *effect* means *to cause to happen,* and the noun *effect* means *the result.*
Pollution affects everyone.

Arbitrators have effected a settlement of the dispute.

The effect of the drug is well known.

5 ALMOST (adv), MOST (adj, pron)   The adverb *almost* is used with verbs, adjectives, and other adverbs to mean *nearly but not completely. Most* means *the majority or greatest part.*
Almost all students work very hard.

Most students work very hard.

6 ALREADY (adv), ALL READY (adj)   *Already* means *before the time specified; all ready* means *completely prepared.*
The movie had already begun by the time we arrived.

The president was all ready to go on vacation.

7 AMOUNT, NUMBER (n)   *Amount* refers to non-count items; *number* refers to countable items.
The amount of money you have is not enough.

The number of students in the program is increasing.

8 BARELY, HARDLY, SCARCELY (adv)   These words have a negative connotation and cannot be used with other negative words.
I could barely see him.

Scarcely had the picnic begun when the rain started.

9 **BESIDE, BESIDES (prep)**   *Beside* means *next to; besides* means *in addition to*.

He sat beside the pretty girl.

He has a bicycle besides a car.

10 **BETWEEN, AMONG (prep)**   *Between* refers to only **two** persons or things; *among* refers to **three or more** persons or things.

There is little difference between the two ideas.

There is little difference among the three ideas.

11 **CAPITAL, CAPITOL (n, adj)**   *Capital* can mean either *a person's wealth* or *the city which houses the government. Capitol* refers to the specific building that is the center of the government.

He invested a lot of his capital in the project.

The capitol building is near the downtown shopping area.

12 **CLOTHES (n), CLOTHE (v), CLOSE (adj, prep, v)**

The man was wearing old, dirty clothes.

She lives close to the university.

The lawyer clothed his arguments in pompous phraseology.

The store closes at midnight.

13 **COMPARED (v, adj)**   *Compared with* is used to indicate differences, while *compared to* is used to point out similarities.

He compared the crowd with the larger crowds of previous years.

He compared the crowd to a swarm of angry bees.

14 **COMPLEMENT, COMPLIMENT (v, n)**   A *complement* is something that completes something else. A *compliment* is a statement of approval or congratulations. The related verbs have the same sense.

A subject complement follows the verb "to be".

She got many compliments on her new ring.

The brown walls complement the generally dark effect of the room.

She complimented him on his cooking.

15 **COSTUME, CUSTOM, CUSTOMS (n)**   *Costume* refers to clothing; *custom* refers to a traditional practice or habit; *customs* means the agency for collecting duties imposed by a country on imports or exports.

She wore a beautiful costume to the party.

Customs differ from country to country.

You must pass through customs when you enter a country.

16 **COUNCIL (n), COUNSEL (v, n)**   A *council* is an official group. *Counsel* means to *give advice*. The noun *counsel* means *advice*.

The city council meets every week.

His doctor counseled him to stop smoking.

His counsel was useful to us.

17 DESERT (n, v), DESSERT (n)

It is very hot and dry in the <u>desert</u>.

The camp was <u>deserted</u>

Her favorite <u>dessert</u> is chocolate ice cream.

18 DIFFER (v), DIFFERENT (adj) Both words are followed by *from* and not *than*.

My current teacher <u>differs</u> in method <u>from</u> my last one.

The ending of the book was <u>different from</u> what I expected.

19 FARTHER, FURTHER (adj, adj/adv) *Farther/further* refers to distance; only *further* is used to mean more time, degree, or quantity.

Chicago is <u>farther/further</u> north than Austin.

I will give you <u>further</u> information later.

20 FEWER, LESS (adj, pron) *Fewer* is used with countable items; *less* is used with non-count items.

He spent <u>fewer hours</u> studying for the exam.

He spent <u>less time</u> studying for the exam.

21 FORMER, FIRST (n, adj) *Former* refers to the first of **two** persons or things named. *First* refers to the first of **three or more** persons or things named.

Both Mary and Jane were invited, but only the <u>former</u> came.

Ann, Jane, and Amy are sisters, but the <u>first</u> was adopted.

22 FORMERLY, FORMALLY (adv) *Formerly* means *previously or earlier*; *formally* means *in a formal manner*.

Elizabeth was <u>formerly</u> called Betty.

You are too <u>formally</u> dressed for an outdoor picnic.

23 FORTH (adv), FOURTH (adj) *Forth* means *in a forward direction*; *fourth* refers to the place in numerical order coming after third.

She rocked the baby back and <u>forth</u> until he fell asleep.

You are the <u>fourth</u> person to ask that question.

24 HAD BETTER, WOULD RATHER (v) *Had better* expresses advisability; *would rather* expresses preference.

I <u>had better</u> study tonight.

I <u>would rather</u> watch television than study.

25 ITS (adj), IT'S (pron + v)

The snake is shedding <u>its</u> skin.

<u>It's</u> time to go home.

26 KIND, SORT, TYPE (n) These words may be singular or plural. When the word is singular, it is modified by *this* or *that*; when it is plural, it is modified by *these* or *those*.

I like <u>this kind</u> of cookie.	I like <u>these kinds</u> of cookies.
He always buys <u>that sort</u> of shoe.	He always buys <u>those sorts</u> of shoes.
They enjoy reading <u>that type</u> of book.	They enjoy <u>those types</u> of books.

27 **LATER (adj, adv), LATTER (pron, adj), LAST (adj)**   *Later* is the comparative form of late; *latter* refers to the second of **two** persons or things named; *last* refers to the **final** person or thing.

The movie began later than we expected.

Both Frank and Philip are likeable, but the latter is the more intelligent.

December is the last month of the year.

28 **LAY, LIE (v)**   The verb *lay*, which means *to put* or *place*, can be active or passive and take an object. The verb *lie*, when it means *to repose*, is never passive and never followed by an object.

Lay (laid, laid, laying)   He laid the book aside.

Lie (lay, lain, lying)   He lay down on the bed.

29 **LIE, LIE (v)**   The verb *lie* meaning *to repose* has different principal parts from the verb *lie* which means *not to tell the truth*.

Lie (lay, lain, lying)   He lies in bed until noon.

Lie (lied, lied, lying)   He lies, cheats, and steals.

30 **LIKE (prep), SUCH AS (prep), AS IF (conj)**   *Like*, which is followed by an object, means *resembling*; *such as* means *for example*; *as if* means *as though* and introduces an adverb clause of manner.

He looks like his father. (resemblance = *like* + noun)

Fruits such as oranges and grapefruit grow in Texas. (example = *such as* + noun)

He looks as if he is tired. (manner = *as if* + clause)

31 **LOOSE (adj), LOSE (v), LOSS (n), LOOSEN (v)**

I need a screwdriver to tighten the loose screws.

He is losing weight very quickly.

She was saddened by the loss of her wedding ring.

I am loosening the screws.

32 **MAYBE (adv), MAY BE (v)**   *Maybe* means *possibly or perhaps*; *may be* is a verb form indicating that a possibility exists.

Maybe you will find the wallet you lost.

She may be late.

33 **PASSED (v), PAST (adj, prep)**

The car passed the house very slowly.

The boy ran past the house.

34 **PEACE, PIECE (n)**   *Peace* means the opposite of *war or other conflict*; *piece* means *a part of a whole*.

Peace came after long years of war.

He sold a piece of his land.

35 **PERSONAL (adj), PERSONNEL (n)**   *Personal* means *private*; *personnel* refers to the workers or staff of a business.

It is difficult to discuss personal problems.

All personnel must attend the meeting.

36 PRECEDE, PROCEED (v) *Precede* means *to come before something else*; *proceed* means to *go forward or continue*.

The subject usually precedes the verb.

After a brief interruption, we proceeded with class.

37 PRINCIPAL (n, adj), PRINCIPLE (n) *Principal* means *primary or very important* and is also the title given to the director of a school; *principle* means a *belief or doctrine*.

The principal side effect of the drug is drowsiness.

He has been principal of that high school for many years.

The experiment demonstrated a basic scientific principle.

38 QUIET (adj), QUITE (adv) *Quiet* is the opposite of *noisy*; *quite* can mean *completely* or *fairly*.

After the children left, the house was quiet.

She is quite beautiful.

The film was quite good.

39 RAISE, RISE (v) *Raise*, which means *to lift*, takes an object and can be either active or passive; *rise*, which means *to ascend or increase*, is never passive and never takes an object.

raise (raised, raised, raising) They raised the flag.

rise (rose, risen, rising) Prices have risen sharply.

40 SET, SIT (v) *Set*, which means *to put or place*, takes an object and can be either active or passive; *sit*, which means *to seat oneself*, is never passive and never takes an object.

set (set, set, setting) She set the flowers on the table.

sit (sat, sat, sitting) They were sitting on the porch.

41 STATIONARY (adj), STATIONERY (n) *Stationary* means *permanent, not changing places*; *stationery* refers to paper for writing letters.

After remaining stationary for two days, the cold front finally moved west.

She wrote the letter on university stationery.

42 SUPERIOR (adj) *Superior* is always used to compare two persons or things and is followed by *to* and **not** *than*. It cannot be qualified by the words *more* or *most*.

Her score is superior to his.

43 THEIR (adj), THEY'RE (pron + v), THERE (adv)

They left their books at home.

Please put your books over there.

They're studying for the examination.

44 THOROUGH (adj), THROUGH (prep)

The report was very thorough.

He walked through the room.

45 TO (prep), TOO (adv), TWO (adj)

The children walk <u>to</u> school every day.

You are working <u>too</u> slowly.

I lost <u>two</u> books yesterday.

46 WEATHER (n), WHETHER (conj)

The <u>weather</u> is warm in the spring.

He hasn't decided <u>whether or not</u> to go.

47 WHO'S (pron + v), WHOSE (adj)

<u>Who's</u> giving the party?

No one knows <u>whose</u> coat this is.

Key to abbreviations	
adj	*adjective*
adv	*adverb*
art	*article*
conj	*conjunction*
n	*noun*
prep	*preposition*
pron	*pronoun*
v	*verb*

Exercise S-163

<u>TOEFL Practice:</u> Structure and Written Expression: Time 6 minutes.

<u>Objective:</u> To identify the ten important types of structure errors.

<u>Questions 1–5</u>

<u>Directions:</u> Choose the <u>one</u> word or phrase, (A), (B), (C), or (D), that best completes the sentence. Write your answer in the blank.

_____ 1 The U.S. space missions of the 1960's and 1970's - - - - - - - expendable equipment.

    (A) that used

    (B) used

    (C) using

    (D) which used

_____ 2 - - - - - - -, the North Country Trail will be the world's longest hiking system.

    (A) It stretches 3,246 miles over seven states

    (B) That it stretches 3,246 miles over seven states

    (C) Stretching 3,246 miles over seven states

    (D) Because stretching 3,246 miles over seven states

309

_____ 3   - - - - - - - - conventional photography, holography produces
three-dimensional images.

(A) Unlike
(B) Unlikely
(C) It is unlike
(D) It is unlikely

_____ 4   Success in convincing the public to accept rabbit as part of its diet
depends on - - - - - - -.

(A) how well information and recipes are distributed by the media
(B) the media distributes information and recipes
(C) how well are information and recipes distributed by the media
(D) information and recipes are distributed by the media

_____ 5   - - - - - - - - jet lag and insomnia result from disturbances of an
individual's biological clock.

(A) Alike
(B) Neither
(C) Both of
(D) Both

Questions 6–10

<u>Directions:</u> Identify the <u>one</u> underlined word or phrase, (A), (B), (C), or (D),
that should be corrected or rewritten. Write your answer in the blank.

_____ 6   Gardening, <u>according to</u> recent surveys, <u>it is</u> the <u>eighth</u> most

                A   B   C

popular American <u>leisure-time</u> activity.

                      D

_____ 7   The place of solar energy among <u>more popular</u> energy sources <u>are</u>

                                     A   B

still <u>being</u> <u>debated</u> in scientific circles.

       C   D

_____ 8   <u>Because of</u> advances in <u>medical</u> technology, doctors can now

       A   B

administer drugs at a time when <u>the body</u> can make optimum use

                                       C

<u>of it</u>.

  D

_____ 9 From only 10,000 in 1900, gulls have increased to about 1.25
         A   B

million more.
  C   D

_____ 10 Many a man faced with seemingly insurmountable problems
                  A   B

have considered suicide as an escape.
     C   D

Section 3: Reading Comprehension and Vocabulary

Introduction

The last of the three sections of the TOEFL is called Reading Comprehension and Vocabulary. It contains **sixty items**, which are divided into **two parts. Forty-five minutes** is allowed to complete both parts.

It is extremely important for you to budget your time carefully on the Reading Comprehension and Vocabulary Section. You may begin working on either Part A or Part B first. It is probably better to begin with Part A. Regardless of where you begin, you must remember to complete the vocabulary items very quickly in order to save as much time as possible for the passages and restatements. Extra time spent on Part B is very useful. By reading the passages several times, you may find new clues that are helpful in answering the questions. On the vocabulary items, however, re-reading does not help. Generally either you know the answer immediately or you do not know it at all.

Part A: Vocabulary: Part A contains thirty items which test your knowledge of vocabulary. Each item consists of one sentence in which a word or phrase is underlined. Below the sentence, there are four other words or phrases. You must choose the answer which is closest in meaning to the underlined word or phrase in the original sentence. You should take only about **twenty seconds** to answer each item (i.e. ten to twelve minutes for the whole of Section A).

Part B: Reading Comprehension: Part B also contains thirty items of two different types: **comprehension of passages** and **recognition of restatements**.

(i) Passages There are four to six short readings in each test. These passages might be as long as two hundred words or as short as twenty-five words. The number of questions following each passage varies. There might be as few as two questions on one passage, and as many as ten questions on another. There are a total of twenty-six to thirty questions on passages in Part B. The passages vary in subject matter, length, and purpose. They may be historical essays, announcements, reports of progress in a specific field, etc., but they do not vary essentially in style. The reading passages are in formal English. It should also be noted that even if you know something about the topic of a passage, it is still necessary to read the text in order to answer the questions which follow it. Conversely, if you know nothing about the subject matter, do not be worried. All the information required for answering the questions is contained in the passage. The exercises which you find in this book have been written to reflect the type of language, subject matter, and questions that you will find on the TOEFL.

(ii) Restatements At the end of Part B, you will usually find two to four restatement items. The task you are required to perform is very similar to that in Part A of the Listening Comprehension Section, except that these restatements are in written form and test your understanding of formal written English. You are asked to read one sentence and choose, from four possible answers, the closest restatement of the original sentence.

To be successful in Part A, you must be familiar with words found in formal written English. In Part B, you must be able to read carefully and interpret information accurately. You can prepare for both Part A and Part B by reading articles and essays in books, magazines, and news-papers. You should choose material in formal English and cover a wide range of topics. Read about what you know, as well as what you are unfamiliar with. Your extensive reading will familiarize you with the kind of vocabulary as well as the kinds of sentences and paragraph types that you will find in this section of the test.

In the following pages, the Reading Comprehension and Vocabulary Section is approached through ten objectives, which should help you focus your attention on important strategies for completing this section of the TOEFL successfully.

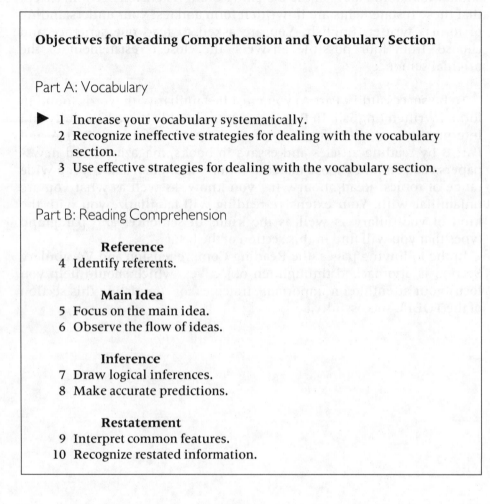

Objectives for Reading Comprehension and Vocabulary Section

Part A: Vocabulary

▶ 1 Increase your vocabulary systematically.
2 Recognize ineffective strategies for dealing with the vocabulary section.
3 Use effective strategies for dealing with the vocabulary section.

Part B: Reading Comprehension

Reference
4 Identify referents.

Main Idea
5 Focus on the main idea.
6 Observe the flow of ideas.

Inference
7 Draw logical inferences.
8 Make accurate predictions.

Restatement
9 Interpret common features.
10 Recognize restated information.

Objective 1: Increase Your Vocabulary Systematically

To prepare for the vocabulary questions in Part A of the Reading Comprehension and Vocabulary Section, you should follow certain guidelines **before** taking the TOEFL. These guidelines will help you build your vocabulary and will also help you learn to read more carefully. Careful reading is the most important requirement for success in Part B questions. **Note:** An extensive vocabulary and careful reading are essential for success on every section of the TOEFL, not just on the vocabulary questions.

1 **Look for contextual clues to the meaning of unknown words as you read.**

> The research team spent years investigating whales, dolphins,
> - - - - - - -, and other marine mammals.

From the information in the sentence, you can deduce that the missing word must be another example of a marine mammal. Being able to determine the meaning of unknown words from contextual clues can be used to expand your vocabulary efficiently as you read. You save time by not looking up every new word in a dictionary, and you see how and when the word is used as well as understanding its meaning.

2 **Notice the grammatical function of words as you read.**
Recognizing the relationship in meaning and the difference in grammatical function among *attraction:* **noun,** *attract:* **verb,** *attractive:* **adjective,** and *attractively:* **adverb,** will help you expand your vocabulary quickly. If you know that *persuasion* is a **noun,** when you are reading, you should be able to guess that *persuade* is a **verb,** *persuasive* is an **adjective,** and *persuasively* is an **adverb.** Also, you should learn the **three principal parts of verbs:** the **simple form,** the **past form,** and the **past participle form.**

3 **Learn the meaning of common Latin and Greek stems and affixes.**
Words derived from Latin and Greek stems and affixes appear very frequently in formal written English. Knowledge of these stems and affixes will enable you to decipher many of the new words that you find in your reading. Compared to the vocabulary of spoken English, the vocabulary items on the TOEFL are somewhat biased towards words derived from Latin and, to a lesser extent, words derived from Greek. This bias appears both in the underlined words and in the possible answers. It is understandable since there is also a very high percentage of such words in the type of formal written English involved in university studies. You can find lists of Latin and Greek stems, prefixes, and suffixes, with definitions and sample words in sample sentences, in some dictionaries and in most books written specifically for vocabulary study.

4 **Look up words you do not understand in a college dictionary.**
It is essential that you become familiar with and use regularly an American-English dictionary. Although bilingual dictionaries are useful, especially to students with only beginning proficiency in English, they are not suitable for students who are planning to take the TOEFL and enter an American university. If you cannot buy or borrow a good college dictionary, you can find such a dictionary in the library.

5 **Develop a vocabulary study system, and attempt to use new words.**
Each individual has a preferred learning style. You must find the best way for **you** to review and practice new vocabulary. In the following exercises, you will experiment with several different study systems. As long as it is **you** who decides, from your extensive reading, what new words you wish to add to your active vocabulary, any study system will do. You should not, however, rely on

someone else's list of words or definitions. Develop your own lists and your own systems. Attempt to use the new words that you choose in both speaking and writing, thus expanding your active English vocabulary. Remember, however, that the average English native speaker has a **passive vocabulary** (words he can **recognize** the meaning of, even if he rarely or never uses them) that is about seventeen times as large as his **active vocabulary**. Even if you do not find opportunities to use many of the new words you encounter, intelligent extensive reading will help develop your passive vocabulary as well as, or even more than, your active vocabulary.

Exercise R-1

Objective: To learn how to make vocabulary cards.

Directions: (i) Cut stiff paper into small pieces about 2 × 3 inches and fold the pieces in half. (Your cards should be pocket-sized so that you can carry them with you.)

 (ii) Write one new word on each card.

 (iii) Using a good college dictionary, fill in the card with other useful information as shown in the example below.

 (iv) Study your words. As you study, divide the words into two groups: words that are easy and those that are difficult for you to remember. Then, study the words that are difficult for you. Later, divide the words in that group into easy and difficult words again. Continue this process until all of the words are in the easy category. Then mix the words well and review all of them.

Example:

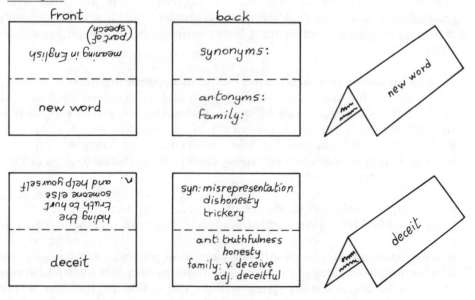

Exercise R-2

Objective: To learn new words by finding their synonyms and antonyms.

Directions: Use a good college dictionary to find at least one synonym and one antonym for each underlined word in the paragraph. Write the base form of each key word.

Moving up professionally usually means an <u>increasing</u> amount of business
1

travel. This can present some <u>special</u> problems for you if you are a woman. For
2

one thing, families and friends do not like being left behind. Also, you may be

<u>concerned</u> about <u>coping with</u> novel situations on your own in strange places
    3   4

and often at strange hours of the day or night. Eating alone may not be a

<u>pleasant</u> prospect. But, despite the <u>penalties</u> of travel, the <u>benefits</u> can be
   5   6   7

<u>substantial</u>.
   8

key word	synonyms	antonyms
1 increase	mount expand	decrease lessen
2		
3		
4		
5		
6		
7		
8		

Note: Make vocabulary cards (shown in Exercise R-1) for any of these words that you wish to add to your active vocabulary. Continue this list on another page and add new words as you encounter them.

Exercise R-3

_____

<u>Objective:</u> To increase vocabulary by making lists of related words.

<u>Directions:</u> Fill in the blanks in the following chart. Use a dictionary to help you. Sometimes the same word is used for more than one category.

general name of animals	name for male	name for female	name for young
1 cattle	*bull*	cow	*calf*
2	rooster		
3		mare	
4			puppy
5 geese			
6	buck		
7		bear	
8			duckling
9 lions			
10	tom cat		

Note: Continue this list on another page by adding any other animals that you already know and any that you find in your extensive reading.

Exercise R-4

<u>Objective:</u> To increase vocabulary by making lists of related words.

<u>Directions:</u> Put the following objects in the appropriate columns on the basis of where they are most likely to be found.

✓ dresser	swivel chair	ottoman
✓ tub	buffet	night stand
chest of drawers	filing cabinet	lawn chair
medicine cabinet	recliner	toilet
hammock	china cabinet	stove
dining table	couch	refrigerator
chopping block	desk	barbecue grill

kitchen	bedroom	bathroom	living room	dining room	patio	office
	dresser	tub				

Note: Add to this list any other words that you can think of now and any new words that you encounter later. Make any other categories that you find useful.

Exercise R-5

<u>Objective:</u> To increase vocabulary by making lists of related words.

<u>Directions:</u> Look over the possibilities listed below. Add at least three ideas of your own to this list. Then, choose three of the possibilities, and begin word lists to which you can add as you pursue your extensive reading program.

1 Make a list of geometric shapes. *example: trapezoid*
2 Make a list of vehicles used for land, sea, and air travel. *example: van*
3 Make a list of scientific fields. *example: microbiology*
4 Make a list of countries and points of geographical interest within them. *examples: the United States, the Appalachians*
5 Make a list of mathematical terms. *example: logarithm*
6 Make a list of various equipment used in photography. *example: tripod*
7 Make a list of fruits and vegetables. *example: zucchini*
8 Make a list of emotional feelings. *example: bewilderment*
9 Make a list of colors, tastes, and smells. *example: mauve*
10 Make a list of sounds. *example: whir*
11 Make a list of adjectives which describe the texture of objects. *example: mushy*
12 Make a list of terms describing family relationships. *example: brother-in-law*
13 Make a list of kitchen utensils. *example: whisk*
14 Make a list of articles of clothing and their parts. *example: culottes*
15 Make a list of tools. *example: wrench*
16 Make a list of parts of the body. *example: trachea*
17 Make a list of verbs that describe non-verbal communication. *example: shrug*
18 _____
19 _____
20 _____

Objectives for Reading Comprehension and Vocabulary Section

Part A: Vocabulary

1 Increase your vocabulary systematically.
▶ 2 Recognize ineffective strategies for dealing with the vocabulary section.
3 Use effective strategies for dealing with the vocabulary section.

Part B: Reading Comprehension

Reference
4 Identify referents.

Main Idea
5 Focus on the main idea.
6 Observe the flow of ideas.

Inference
7 Draw logical inferences.
8 Make accurate predictions.

Restatement
9 Interpret common features.
10 Recognize restated information.

Objective 2: Recognize Ineffective Strategies for Dealing with the Vocabulary Section

When you are actually answering the vocabulary items in Part A of the Reading Comprehension and Vocabulary Section, **none** of the strategies discussed in Objective 1 (page 315) will help you. In the vocabulary items, there are **no** contextual clues, **no** grammar clues, **no** stem clues, and **no** visual clues. The only reason for reading the whole sentence is that it gives an indication of **which sense** of the underlined word is being used, in cases where such words have more than one meaning.

1 Do not look for contextual clues to the meaning of the underlined words.

The sentences in Part A, Vocabulary, are contextually neutral. Almost always, the four words or phrases given can replace the underlined item, and the result will be an acceptable English sentence.

> During the initiation ceremony, <u>incisions</u> are made on the young men's foreheads.

(A) patterns   (C) tattoos

(B) cuts   (D) scars

Any of the four possible answers could replace *incision* in the sentence and result in an acceptable sentence.

(A) During the initiation ceremony, <u>patterns</u> are made on the young men's foreheads.

(B) During the initiation ceremony, <u>cuts</u> are made on the young men's foreheads.

(C) During the initiation ceremony, <u>tattoos</u> are made on the young men's foreheads.

(D) During the initiation ceremony, <u>scars</u> are made on the young men's foreheads.

But *incisions* means *cuts,* and therefore, the correct answer is (B). You <u>cannot</u> deduce that the answer is (B) from the information in the sentence. You must simply know that *incisions* means *cuts*, and does not mean *patterns, tattoos,* or *scars.*

2 Do not try to eliminate possible answers on the basis of grammar.

The four possible answers are always the appropriate part of speech to replace the underlined word or phrase. Thus, if the underlined item is a singular noun, all four possible answers will also be singular nouns or noun phrases. Notice that in the previous example, the distractors cannot be eliminated on the basis of grammar. The four possible answers can replace the word and result in a sentence that is meaningful and grammatically correct.

Only very occasionally can some of the possible answers not be used in conjunction with other parts of the original sentence.

> They <u>derived</u> their conclusions from a statistically insignificant sample.

(A) investigated   (C) drew

(B) selected   (D) based

Investigated and *based* cannot be followed by the preposition *from.* But it is possible for the word *from* to follow *selected* and *drew.* The correct answer, however, is (C) because *drew* has the same meaning as *derived.* Even in such rare cases, however, three answers are wrong in any event, solely on the basis of meaning. Therefore, do not waste time trying to eliminate answers on a purely grammatical basis.

3 Do not attempt to divide unknown words into parts in order to work out their meanings.

There are two reasons that analyzing the stems and affixes of unknown words is a bad idea. First, you do not have enough time to analyze individual words.

You should spend only about twenty seconds on each vocabulary item. Second, studying the parts of a word can often be misleading if you do not have any other clues to its meaning.

The policeman presented <u>a report</u> of the incident to the captain.

(A) an account   (C) a caricature
(B) a re-enactment   (D) an overview

Analyzing the constituent parts of the word *report* would bring up the ideas of *again* for the prefix *re-*, and *carry* for the stem *port*. By concentrating on *again*, you might be led to choose *re-enactment* because of *re*, or *overview* because of *over*, which can also mean *again*. Alternatively, by focusing on *carry*, you might choose *caricature* because of its sound similarity if you were unaware of its meaning. The correct answer, *account*, has nothing to do with either *again* or *carry*. The main idea of this explanation is that too much reliance should not be placed on an etymological analysis. It requires too much time and is not helpful.

4 Do not be confused by the appearance of the possible answers.
In Objective 6, (Word Form), of the Structure and Written Expression Section, you learn that the formation of words by adding suffixes is not a standardized process in English. Certain suffixes can be used to derive more than one part of speech.

It was <u>subsequently</u> discovered that several errors had been made.

(A) duly   (C) consequently
(B) finally   (D) later

Subsequently is an adverb and looks like one because it ends in *-ly*. *Duly, finally*, and *consequently* are also adverbs ending in *-ly*. *Later* does not end in *-ly*, but, as indicated above in point number 2, you can be confident that *later* is also an adverb. In fact, *later* is the correct answer.

5 Do not waste time trying to figure out the answer if you have no idea about the meaning of the underlined word or phrase.
You should spend ten to twelve minutes **at the most** on the thirty vocabulary items in Part A in order to save sufficient time to answer the reading questions in Part B. In the reading passages the correct answers can be deduced from the information given. They are there if you can only recognize them. The opposite is true with regard to the vocabulary items; there are virtually no clues to the correct answers. Reading slowly and thinking carefully will not help you very much. When you look at a vocabulary item, either you know the answer or you do not; therefore, you must use as much time as possible on the reading items, where careful thinking can make a big difference.

6 Be aware that Part A, Vocabulary, immediately follows Structure and Written Expression, Part B, Error Identification.
In the Structure section you are required to identify mistakes in sentences. It is therefore of the utmost importance to realize that you must change your attitude completely between the last structure item and the first vocabulary item. Different strategies are important in the two sections of the test.

Objectives for Reading Comprehension and Vocabulary Section

Part A: Vocabulary

    1 Increase your vocabulary systematically.
    2 Recognize ineffective strategies for dealing with the vocabulary
       section.
▶ 3 Use effective strategies for dealing with the vocabulary section.

Part B: Reading Comprehension

       Reference
    4 Identify referents.

       Main Idea
    5 Focus on the main idea.
    6 Observe the flow of ideas.

       Inference
    7 Draw logical inferences.
    8 Make accurate predictions.

       Restatement
    9 Interpret common features.
   10 Recognize restated information.

Objective 3: Use Effective Strategies for Dealing with the Vocabulary Section

If you have worked systematically to expand your vocabulary during the months preceding your TOEFL, you should approach Part A vocabulary items with confidence. It is extremely doubtful, however, that you will know the meaning of all the words you encounter. Lack of familiarity with some of the words is to be expected. Keep calm, and use these strategies to approach the TOEFL vocabulary items intelligently.

1 Focus on the underlined word(s) and the four possible answers.
It is unimportant that you may not know all the words in the sentences. Only the underlined word or phrase is important. Therefore, you should not allow yourself to be distracted by other unknown words. Because the sentences are devoid of contextual clues, you will not gain anything by working out the meanings of words which are not underlined.

2 Look for the most exact synonym.
Sometimes you will know the underlined word and all four possible answers. Keep in mind that some of the answers differ only in their degree of meaning. You must choose the answer that is closest in meaning to the underlined word. Therefore, even if answer (A) seems promising, read all the other answers before making a final choice.

3 Remember the tricks that TOEFL writers might employ.
Before the day of your TOEFL, review the points made in Objective 2: Ineffective strategies. The TOEFL writers expect that you may try to use some of these ineffective strategies and have prepared some items that will trick you, if you are not wary.

4 Guess if you are not sure of an answer.
Never leave an answer blank. Always guess immediately when you do not know the answer. You are not penalized for guessing. Some students like to choose one letter as their "guessing letter". For example, you might choose the letter (B) and use this letter to answer any items for which you cannot make even an intelligent guess. If, however, you have even the smallest "hunch" about the correct answer, you should **not** use your "guessing letter" but rather mark your "hunch" as the answer on the answer sheet.

5 Work quickly and budget your time wisely.
When you do the practice tests, you should keep one eye on a clock or watch. Practice completing the vocabulary part in ten minutes, spending an average of only twenty seconds on each of the thirty items. Be as careful as you can, but watch the clock and budget your time wisely.

Exercise R-6

<u>TOEFL Practice:</u> Vocabulary: Time 3 minutes 20 seconds.

<u>Objective:</u> To practice budgeting your time wisely on vocabulary items.

<u>Directions:</u> Use a clock to time your work. Allow yourself **exactly** three minutes and twenty seconds. By working neither too quickly nor too slowly, try to finish this exercise **exactly** when the time is up.

　Choose the one word or phrase which would <u>best keep the meaning</u> of the original sentence if it were substituted for the underlined word. Write your answer in the blank.

_____ 1 Without a sufficient amount of <u>evidence</u>, no justifiable conclusions can be drawn.

(A) time   (C) data
(B) money   (D) funds

_____ 2 The complexities of modern life make the services of a lawyer a necessity all too often.

    (A) an accountant   (C) an attorney
    (B) a psychiatrist   (D) a technician

_____ 3 The sun's rays irritate certain skin types, but new lotions on the market can screen out most of the harmful effects.
    (A) inflame   (C) darken
    (B) infect   (D) scar

_____ 4 The feeling of competition in the classroom was noticeable to everyone.

    (A) discord   (C) rivalry
    (B) discovery   (D) cooperation

_____ 5 The fact that economists are able to distinguish virtually all of the causes of recessions does not mean they can accurately predict them.

    (A) prevent   (C) promote
    (B) discern   (D) define

_____ 6 The country is plagued by turmoil.

    (A) constant change   (C) utter confusion
    (B) bad weather   (D) fuel shortages

_____ 7 The land was allocated on a first-come, first-served basis.

    (A) apportioned   (C) auctioned
    (B) fertilized   (D) used

_____ 8 After seeing the performance, the audience felt that they had been shortchanged.

    (A) entertained   (C) surprised
    (B) bored   (D) swindled

_____ 9 The impact of what happened influenced events all over the western world.

    (A) concealment   (C) knowledge
    (B) effect   (D) discovery

_____ 10 Several factors led to the workers' experiencing stress in their jobs.

    (A) boredom   (C) excitement
    (B) strain   (D) success

Exercise R-7

<u>TOEFL Practice:</u> Vocabulary: Time 3 minutes 20 seconds.

<u>Objective and Directions:</u> see Exercise R-6.

_____ 1 In some parts of the country a surprising number of goods are still transported by <u>barges</u>.

    (A) pack animals   (C) wagons
    (B) flat boats   (D) wheelbarrows

_____ 2 The museum has recently purchased an early <u>draft</u> of the author's poems.

    (A) version   (C) edition
    (B) collection   (D) critique

_____ 3 The space shuttle program <u>entails</u> the use of sophisticated technology.

    (A) enhances   (C) develops
    (B) creates   (D) involves

_____ 4 In the nineteenth century, it was almost a tradition for promising young artists not to receive the attention they <u>deserved</u>.

    (A) expected   (C) merited
    (B) craved   (D) demanded

_____ 5 From the <u>rubble</u> came the glitter of gold.

    (A) debris   (C) hole
    (B) vault   (D) chest

_____ 6 The Irish setter is well-known for its <u>keen</u> sense of smell.

    (A) pungent   (C) dull
    (B) sensitive   (D) sharp

_____ 7 Recent population shifts have <u>fundamentally</u> drawn people away from the old industrial centers towards sunnier climates and more spacious environments.

    (A) originally   (C) clearly
    (B) basically   (D) gradually

_____ 8 Network employees and employees of <u>associated</u> companies are not allowed to participate in TV quiz games.

    (A) subsidiary   (C) connected
    (B) social   (D) member

_____ 9 As the minute hand approaches the hour, hordes of employees throughout the financial district <u>rush</u> towards elevators.

(A) move   (C) hurry
(B) scatter   (D) ascend

_____ 10 Von Stroheim's behavior was often considered <u>strange</u>, even by his friends.

(A) unusual   (C) cold
(B) foreign   (D) unknown

Exercise R-8

<u>TOEFL Practice:</u> Vocabulary: Time 3 minutes 20 seconds.

<u>Objective and Directions:</u> see Exercise R-6.

_____ 1 The course provides <u>a comprehensive</u> overview of nineteenth century American literature.

(A) an understandable   (C) a contemporary
(B) a wide-ranging   (D) a simple

_____ 2 Early settlers usually moved their <u>belongings</u> west in wagon trains.

(A) relations   (C) livestock
(B) supplies   (D) possessions

_____ 3 Clara Barton founded the American Red Cross fundamentally to deal with the <u>wounded</u> during the Civil War.

(A) injured   (C) dying
(B) poverty-stricken   (D) diseased

_____ 4 Due to unfavorable conditions, the launch has been postponed <u>for the time being</u>.

(A) temporarily   (C) as a result of the late hour
(B) because of the weather   (D) irreparably

_____ 5 The President proposed several tax reform measures which Congress <u>subsequently turned down</u>.

(A) reduced   (C) revised
(B) rejected   (D) reviewed

_____ 6 Expectations that the drug would offer a miracle cure for cancer turned out to be <u>illusory</u>.

(A) ingenuous   (C) false
(B) exaggerated   (D) hopeful

_____ 7   Innovative approaches to manufacturing, <u>coupled with</u> the tremendous size of the domestic market, led to the emergence of the United States as an industrial giant.

(A) followed by   (C) deriving from
(B) combined with   (D) mixed with

_____ 8   As they approached Cincinnati, it was <u>nearly</u> midnight and they decided to pull into a motel to sleep.

(A) just past   (C) around
(B) already   (D) almost

_____ 9   Young Spanish imperial eagles <u>disperse</u> before they are fully mature.

(A) fly   (C) split up
(B) hide out   (D) mate

_____ 10 At the end of the year, lands throughout the state were <u>parched</u>.

(A) bone-dry   (C) repaired
(B) turned into parks   (D) sectioned off

Part B: Reading Comprehension

Objectives for Reading Comprehension and Vocabulary Section

Part A: Vocabulary

1 Increase your vocabulary systematically.
2 Recognize ineffective strategies for dealing with the vocabulary section.
3 Use effective strategies for dealing with the vocabulary section.

Part B: Reading Comprehension

Reference
► 4 Identify referents.

Main Idea
5 Focus on the main idea.
6 Observe the flow of ideas.

Inference
7 Draw logical inferences.
8 Make accurate predictions.

Restatement
9 Interpret common features.
10 Recognize restated information.

Objective 4: Identify Referents

In English, as in other languages, it would be clumsy and boring to have to repeat the same word or phrase every time you used it.

American and Mexican biologists have found that diephenodione, a man-made anticoagulant, is a lethal weapon against vampire bats. American and Mexican biologists have devised a method of using the blood of the victims as the means of getting the drug into the bats.

Instead of repeating the same word or phrase several times, after it has been used, we can usually refer to it rather than repeat it. For this purpose, we use **reference words**:

American and Mexican biologists have found that diephenodione, a man-made anticoagulant, is a lethal weapon against vampire bats. They have devised a method of using the blood of the victims as the means of getting the drug into the bats.

Recognizing reference words and being able to identify the words or phrases to which they refer will help you understand the reading passages in Part B.

Students of English might learn many rules for the use of reference words and yet be confused about what a particular word refers to in a sentence. For example, students might learn that *it* can refer to an animal or an object. Then they might run across the following sentence:

> When a bat feeds on a treated cow, it picks up the anticoagulant, and within a few days it dies from internal bleeding.

Because *it* can refer to an animal, the reader might be confused about whether this *it* refers to *a bat* or to *a treated cow*. Where there is this type of possible confusion, however, the structure of the sentence and/or the meaning of the sentence should make the reference clear. In this sentence, *it* refers to *a bat*.

Reference words are often, but not always, pronouns. They may refer to a single noun or to a noun phrase made up of several words.

> Cases abound of poor rural families from Mexico to Argentina losing their cows to the deadly effect of rabies.

Their refers to *poor rural families from Mexico to Argentina*. It is important to consider all the words in a phrase when determining what a pronoun refers to.

It is also important to note that words may refer **forwards** as well as backwards, especially in formal written English.

> For the first time that they can remember, farmers in Latin America are relieved of the constant fear of vampire bats.

The word *they* refers forwards to *farmers in Latin America*.

As you may have noticed in the examples, reference words are usually short and are very frequently pronouns, such as *it, she, this, those, their,* and so forth. These words may appear unimportant, but understanding them is crucial. Reference words help you comprehend how the elements in a sentence or a paragraph hold together. Even though the TOEFL rarely contains questions that specifically ask you to identify referents, you must be able to identify them in order to answer the questions that do appear.

In this group of exercises, you will be asked to identify **reference words** (such as pronouns) and their **referents** (the words to which they refer). Being one hundred percent sure which words the pronouns refer to is the first step in interpreting an entire reading passage and its parts accurately.

Exercise R-9

Objective: To identify the referents (the word or words referred to) of *it, she, he,* and *they.*

Directions: **Underline** the referent of the word in *italics*. (**Note:** Reference words may refer to a single word or to several words.)

> Example: In a news conference this afternoon, the university announced that *it* intends to make several important changes in next year's budget.

1 The administration has decided to give more financial support to the average student. This week *it* indicated its intention to increase the number of scholarships based on need by 35 percent in the next year.

2 Although Professor Elkins has recently been challenged by Associate Professor Talbott and Professor Thayer, *she* received the Golden Apple Award for outstanding teaching for the fifth year in a row.

3 *She* has often been compared to her mother, Judy Garland, but Liza Minelli has proven herself to be a star in her own right.

4 Although a woman in the lifeboat shouted to her to jump, the woman standing at the rail of the ship appeared to realize *she* would not have any chance of being rescued.

5 One thing that Duran did prove about Leonard in their first fight was that *he* was capable of taking a great deal of punishment.

6 A spokesman for the film company discussed the failure of the firm's latest western epic with reporters. *He* stated that the company would probably lose more than the 15 million dollars it had cost to make the film.

7 Michael Cimino, director of **Heaven's Gate,** which stars Kris Kristofferson, recently reported that *he* will begin work on another film before the end of the year.

8 Even though *they* have been in a more difficult position in recent years, small bankers continue to be able to influence the direction of development in their communities.

9 The committee has made the suggestion to all foreign investors that *they* should study all applicable laws before buying property.

10 The basketball team never lacked vociferous supporters, but *they* rarely responded to this show of enthusiasm.

Exercise R-10

Objective: To identify the referents of *him, her,* and *them.*

Directions: **Underline** the referent of the word in *italics.*

Example: As the bullets struck *them,* the police cars rocked dangerously from side to side.

1 Scott Fitzgerald, who first introduced *him* to a publisher, was one of the few contemporary writers that Hemingway did not turn against.

2 Catching sight of *him* in a supermarket one day, Archer followed the man with the limp to an apartment in a run-down neighborhood.

3 The award was presented to the playwright by the Chairman of the Committee, who said of *him* that he brought pleasure to literally millions of theatergoers and television viewers.

4 While Jane was persuading Mary to ask *her* for the keys to the car, Mrs. Jones happened to be listening at the door and quickly went downstairs and out of the house.

5 Looking at *her* closely for the first time in months, Elizabeth realized sadly that the woman was indeed beginning to grow old.

6 Violet pushed past the general's daughter, strode to the door of the drawing room, and turned to throw *her* a look of withering scorn before slamming the door with grim satisfaction.

7 Knowing *them* well, the Hammonds realized that the Shepherds were unlikely to be on time to meet their guests.

8 Doctors treating patients with diet pills usually warn *them* of the dangers of addiction.

9 Though it is not usually difficult to understand *them*, stutterers often cause parents a lot of worries.

10 Intrigued by insects of all kinds, the youngsters spent hours trapping and studying *them*.

Exercise R-11

Objective: To identify referents of *its, her, his, their*.

Directions: **Underline** the referent of the word in *italics*.

Example: The main lobby of the hotel, with *its* antique brass chandeliers and wall sconces is highlighted by a magnificent marble staircase.

1 In 1977, the former home of John D. Spreckels acquired the status of Historical Landmark. *Its* history goes back to 1908, when it was built by Mr. Spreckels.

2 Many people visit San Diego every year because of the mild year-round climate, the beaches, and Sea World. But *its* most famous attraction is probably the exceptionally fine San Diego Zoo.

3 *Its* usefulness was a thing of the past, but his first bicycle continued to stand in the corner in his bedroom.

4 The music teacher reported that *her* newest pupil, Donna Winter, had the greatest potential of any student she had ever had.

5 In an account based on *her* years sharing an apartment with economist Barbara Ward, Elizabeth Monroe described her as an early-morning writer of extraordinary facility.

6 *His* business began to grow when Sterne joined forces with a young lawyer from his hometown.

7 With *his* sixty acres of land covered with five hundred varieties of lilacs, it is easy to understand why Ken Berdeen of Kennebunk, Maine is known as "The Lilac Man".

8 *Their* neighbors, the Bantu, have begun to have some effect on the way the Bushmen live.

9 As it is the ideas and above all the ways these are expressed, rather than *their* plots, that interest us about Shakespeare's plays, it is a pleasure to see them over and over again.

10 The defendants insisted on addressing the members of the jury, thus disregarding the advice of *their* lawyers.

Exercise R-12

<u>Objective:</u> To identify the referents of *hers, his,* and *theirs.*

<u>Directions:</u> **Underline** the referent of the word in *italics.*

<u>Example:</u> Although <u>most economists</u> accept the fact that their colleagues' <u>models</u> may be useful, they are rarely willing to admit that *theirs* may not be the best.

1 Jean, along with her sisters Doris and May, baked cakes for the annual contest at the county fair. Jean was sorry *hers* lost, but happy that Doris won a ribbon for her entry.
2 In her article about teaching dance, Carolyn describes the methods of Marion Rice and points out that *hers,* more than those of any other local dance teacher, have influenced the aspiring dancers in the neighborhood.
3 The critic hardly referred to *hers* at all, but when Sally heard what he had to say about Mary's paintings, she felt relieved rather than disappointed.
4 Van Cliburn has given advice and encouragement to many young pianists just beginning their concert careers. *His* took off in 1958 when he took top honors at Moscow's first Tchaikovsky Competition.
5 Pierre Cardin has expanded his interests and become a restaurant owner. *His* is the famous Maxim's of Paris, founded in 1893.
6 After Bill had read Tom Burns' article, he was sure it would win the prize as *his* dealt with the same subject in a much more superficial manner.
7 Since *theirs* was the float which evoked most response from the crowd, the members of the boys' club were disappointed when it placed only second.
8 David and Roxanna thought that Rose and Charlie's apartment was very luxuriously decorated, but that *theirs* had a better view.
9 The English surprisingly beat the French at the battle of Agincourt in 1415 because *theirs* were the more disciplined archers.
10 John had entered recipes in so many local contests without success that he was astonished that *his* was the winning entry in a national competition.

Exercise R-13

<u>Objective:</u> To identify the referents of *this, that, these,* and *those.*

<u>Directions:</u> **Underline** the referent of the word in *italics.*

<u>Example:</u> High on his list of priorities was <u>becoming independent of his</u> <u>father.</u> *That,* however, was easier said than done.

1 The Smith and Philips Research Institute was designated as the recipient of a grant of two million dollars by the Taylor Foundation. *This* is to be used for the continuation of a study of the cause of warts.
2 A group of horticulturalists in New Jersey has been working on a new project. *This* involves the development of a completely different type of rose.

3 A daily exercise program results in the need for less sleep for most people. *This* is partly attributable to the fact that exercisers sleep more soundly than do people who do not exercise regularly.

4 He blamed his failure in business on drink. *That* was also why he ended up in the hospital with cirrhosis of the liver.

5 Many people connect alcohol intake with drunkenness, but *that* is by no means the only consequence of drinking too much.

6 He insisted on going to the Bahamas for their honeymoon. Fortunately, *that* was exactly where she wanted to go.

7 Many overweight people blame their condition on physical disorders such as thyroid trouble, but doctors claim that *these* are seldom the cause of obesity.

8 After winning the lottery in Pennsylvania, she bought a Mercedes and a condominium. *These* were the first two large purchases she had ever been able to pay for in cash.

9 The opportunity to sample several possible majors as well as greater career flexibility after graduation are two reasons why students choose a liberal arts college; *these* are not the only ones, however.

10 Drinking fine wines and eating Italian food were his favorite pastimes as a young man. Later in his life, *these* led to his investing all his money in a small Italian restaurant.

11 Faulty equipment is sometimes responsible for rollerskating accidents, but problems with balance are *those* which cause the most falls.

12 The first things the new settlers tried to decide on were a flag and a national anthem, *those* being the most striking symbols of national identity.

13 Fuchsia and mauve were fashionable that year, but *those* are by no means the most flattering colors for everyone.

14 Lyndon Johnson was president from 1963 to 1968; *those* were the years in which the Vietnam War first came to the attention of the American public.

15 Signs of aging are unavoidable, but *those* that can be disguised are of particular interest to cosmetic companies.

Exercise R-14

Objective: To identify the referents of specified items.

Directions: **Underline** the referent of the words in *italics*.

Example: In her most famous book, Barbara Tuchman deals with the fourteenth century. *This work* takes the life of one individual, the Comte de Coucy, as its basis.

1 In 1954, Roger Bannister became the first man to run the mile in four minutes. *This time* seems incredibly slow by modern-day standards.

2 Eventually the two scientists opted to follow their original line. *This choice* proved to be the right one, and ten years later they were awarded the Nobel Prize for Chemistry.

3 The conductor was presented with a gold watch at the banquet in his honor. *This gift* was to commemorate his fifty years of service with the railroad.

4 Many educators now believe that students remember information that they learn on their own better than that presented formally by a teacher. *This fact* has led to methodological changes in many classrooms.

5 The doctor decided to take out the boy's appendix. *This operation* was made much more difficult by the circumstances on the island.

6 The Thunderbird was the most popular American sports car in the fifties. *That particular make* has changed so greatly, however, that it is no longer considered a sports car by most people.

7 Somewhat reluctantly, Isabel and Ferdinand agreed to fund Columbus' voyage in search of the Indies. *That decision* led to perhaps the most important discovery of the last thousand years.

8 Albert Einstein was slow to read and write as a child. *That surprising fact* has lent credence to the idea that not all children should be expected to learn the same things at the same age.

9 Wellington defeated Napoleon at Waterloo in 1815. *That battle* marked the end of one era and the beginning of another.

10 John F. Kennedy was fatally shot on November 22, 1963. *That tragedy* ended what has been described by some as the Camelot era.

11 The treasurer of the company was convicted of embezzlement. *That fact* did not prevent the company from re-hiring him upon his release from prison.

12 Caesar salad owes its distinctive taste to raw egg yolk and anchovies. *These ingredients* can be bought in most supermarkets.

13 She refused to continue to go out with him because he had wrecked three cars in less than six months. For her, *these accidents* reflected a lack of control that she refused to tolerate.

14 He covered his eyes and moaned softly at the sight of insects. Even though he knew *these reactions* were not rational, he could not control them.

15 Our local library receives as many as ten best-sellers each month. *These books* can be found on a special rack near the entrance.

16 The map of the new shopping mall shows five restaurants. *Those facilities*, which are marked in red, are available for business meetings and private banquets.

17 In addition to completing all the requirements for a degree in international finance, the future ambassador also took several Spanish courses. *Those language classes* eventually proved to be of great value to him in his diplomatic career.

18 Several months previously, the steelworkers had petitioned the company for a 25 percent wage increase and enforcement of stricter safety regulations. In view of the company's failure to act on *those requests*, a strike was called.

19 He drank and ate to excess, and *those problems* eventually prevented his becoming a vice-president of the firm.

20 As a child, he had taken lessons in tennis and swimming, spent summers at a sports camp, and played Little League Baseball. As a professional athlete, he pointed to *those experiences* as being responsible for his disciplined attitude.

Exercise R-15

Objective: To identify the referents of specified items.

Directions: **Underline** the referent of the words in *italics*.

Example: On a table by the entrance, were <u>glasses of champagne</u> on silver trays, and Frederick took *one* as he walked in.

1 There were clocks of every description in every corner of the shop, but John eventually chose the *one* he had noticed first.
2 The visitors saw a number of shows during the days they were in New York, but only *one* of them was really exciting.
3 The proposals were discussed at length by the members of the committee, with only *one* of them emerging intact.
4 Lithographs by Grant, Simkins, and several other well-known artists were on display at the opening, but the only *ones* to attract favorable comment from the critics were by a relatively unknown artist.
5 Note that the instructions preceding the questions encourage students to concentrate only on the *ones* they feel they understand.
6 After eliminating the *ones* which were obviously of no interest, the members of the board passed around the remaining applications for further consideration.
7 American and European tourists visit Yucatan for its archeological sites and for its seaside resorts, *the former* being among the most varied and most attractive in the world.
8 Both graduate and undergraduate students should be interested in the two alternatives, but if *the latter* is selected it must be completed within two semesters following the end of the course.
9 Los Angeles and Minneapolis offer the visitor both a range of major-league sporting attractions and a variety of cultural attractions, but the climate of *the former* exerts year-round appeal.
10 The NASA scientists and astronauts were equally excited by Al Shepherd's first sub-orbital flight and by John Glenn's orbital journey, but it was *the latter* which most caught the attention of the American public.
11 Both the government and the private sector fund basic and applied research, but grants for *the former* tend to be relatively restricted in times of economic difficulties.
12 The Chinese "opera" actually consisted largely of a series of astonishing performances and tricks by jugglers and acrobats, *the latter* showing amazing agility.

Exercise R-16

<u>Objective:</u> To select reference words on the basis of their referents in continuous prose.

<u>Directions:</u> Choose the appropriate word from those in *italics* to fill each blank. Use each of the words only once in the paragraph.

<u>Example:</u> *they   them   it   its*

Since _____*its*_____ foundation, the North American Soccer League has grown considerably in size. One of the most important moves _____*it*_____ has made is to attract big-name stars from Europe and Latin America by offering _____*them*_____ much larger salaries than _____*they*_____ could earn at home.

1 *this   those   that   these*

The thing I want you to remember above all is _____:

                                                                   1

_____ ideas we are talking about are top secret. _____ we

         2   3

discussed at our last meeting have already been made public. This time

there must be no leaks! _____ is an order.

                                    4

2 *them   they   its   it*

Though _____ did not recognize _____ at the time, the

             1   2

disease the doctors encountered was dengue. This delay in diagnosis

was hardly surprising since _____ symptoms were so unfamiliar to

                                          3

_____.

      4

3 *its   those   she   her   these   hers*

Discipline and consistency, ladies! _____ are the qualities you

                                                    1

must cultivate. A casual attitude is all right for _____ people who

                                                                 2

do not aspire to becoming champions. But the woman who wants the world

to be _____ must discipline _____ body and mind;

            3   4

_____ must make sacrifices and suffer boredom and pain. The

      5

championship is a great prize, but such glory has _____ price!

                                                                    6

4 *their*   *theirs*   *his*   *it*   *him*   *he*

   When _____ looked at _____ face in the mirror the next
                1   2

morning, Peter Thompson hardly recognized _____. The men who
                                                    3

had attacked _____ the night before had certainly left _____
                    4   5

mark. All the same, he had not been gentle himself, and he was pleased

with the thought that _____ must look almost as disfigured as his
                              6

own.

5 *the former's*   *his*   *one*   *the latter's*   *he*   *ones*

   There are a number of great baseball players in the game today.

_____ is Pete Rose, a player who, by dedication and enthusiasm,
       1

has made such use of _____ quite limited natural talent that
                              2

_____ must be compared with the great _____ of the past,
       3   4

such as Ty Cobb of the American League and Stan Musial of the National

League. Indeed, Rose has already surpassed _____ National
                                                       5

League hit record, while _____ major league record of 4,109
                                  6

appears to be just within his reach.

6 *theirs*   *that*   *its*   *him*   *his*   *this*   *them*

   It was clear to both Robert Jackson and Don Turner that _____
                                                                    1

was no easy task. Jackson was to take _____ men south around the
                                               2

back of the hill and lead _____ up _____ most difficult
                                  3   4

slope. Meanwhile, Turner's men were expected to follow _____
                                                               5

northwards in the pitch darkness for more than three hundred yards

through a swamp up to the main entrance. It was true that _____
                                                                  6

was what the two leaders had been trained for, but _____ had
                                                            7

seemed like playing games. Now it was the real thing.

7 *she   her   hers   theirs   they   them   their*

In _____ most famous film, *The Wizard of Oz*, Judy Garland, as
            1

Dorothy, is transported from Kansas to the fantastic Land of Oz. On the way

to find the Great Wizard, _____ meets a scarecrow, a tin man, and a
                            2

cowardly lion. The four join forces and, of course, many adventures

befall _____ on _____ journey. By capturing a witch's
        3   4

broom for the wizard, _____ each win the right to a single wish.
                        5

First, Dorothy's companions have _____ granted and then the film
                                    6

ends with Dorothy having _____ come true as she wakes up back
                            7

home in Kansas.

8 *these   they   it   this   their*

Though _____ have as yet failed to exert _____ full effect,
            1   2

the measures taken by the government to reduce the rate of unemployment

have kept _____ within acceptable limits. _____ in itself
            3   4

represents considerable progress, but the government has promised both

full employment and an end to inflation and _____ will be
                                                5

achieved only if there is a sharp upturn in world trade.

9 *those   his   her   hers   this   these*

_____, then, are some of the features which must be borne in
    1

mind: the man's tasks are clearly distinguished from the woman's.

_____ frequently involve building and fighting, where necessary,
    2

while _____ include not only _____ related to
        3   4

childbearing and the home, but also backbreaking agricultural chores such

as weeding. _____ division of labor means that the man
                5

commonly has more free time for social recreation while the woman is

likely to find _____ social contacts severely limited.
                6

340

10 *this   them   the former   ones   one   the latter*

There are a number of differences between American English and

British English. _____, and _____ is perhaps the most

‎ ‎1 ‎ ‎ ‎ ‎ ‎ ‎ ‎ ‎ ‎ ‎ ‎ ‎ ‎ ‎ ‎ ‎ ‎ 2

obvious, is accent. Although both types naturally embrace a wide variety of

local speech patterns, there is, nevertheless, a clear broad distinction

between _____. Spelling and vocabulary variations constitute other

‎ ‎ ‎ ‎ ‎ ‎ ‎ ‎ ‎ ‎ ‎ ‎ ‎ ‎ ‎ ‎ 3

differences, but _____ are relatively slight ("o" for "ou" in many

‎ ‎ ‎ ‎ ‎ ‎ ‎ ‎ ‎ ‎ ‎ ‎ ‎ ‎ ‎ ‎ ‎ ‎ ‎ 4

American words, or single instead of double consonants), while

_____ tend to be exaggerated simply because certain _____

‎ ‎ ‎ 5 ‎ 6

are so familiar (elevator/lift, apartment/flat, for example).

Exercise R-17

Objective: To select reference and content words on the basis of referents and sentence meaning, respectively.

Directions: Choose the appropriate word from those in *italics* to fill each blank. Use each of the words only once in the paragraph.

Example: *generations   they   the latter's   people   this*

In the recent past, a grade-school education was usually typical for members of the older generation, but today, more than half of all Americans thirty to forty years old have completed at least high school. Studies show that _people_ with more education live longer. _They_ get better jobs, suffer less economic stress, and tend to be more active and more receptive to new ideas. Another difference between the older and younger _generation_ is _the latter's_ concern for physical fitness. _This_ is reflected in a drop in per capita consumption of tobacco since 1966, significant life-style changes among twenty-five to forty year olds, and increased participation in exercise programs.

1 *it   they   them   miles   streams   woods*

There are several little _____ a few miles from the college.

‎ 1

_____ flow through pastureland and _____, then some of

‎ ‎ ‎ 2 ‎ 3

_____ pass through town and become one big stream, which flows

‎ ‎ ‎ 4

on for some twenty _____ before _____ empties into Lake

‎ 5 ‎ ‎ ‎ ‎ ‎ ‎ ‎ ‎ ‎ ‎ ‎ ‎ ‎ ‎ ‎ ‎ ‎ ‎ 6

Erie.

2 *their   it   there   these   the authors'   operetta   performance*

When _____ was first produced, the _____ *The Pirates*
          1   2

of Penzance enjoyed tremendous success. It comes as a surprise to learn that

the first _____, in 1879, was given in New York, but this was
          3

precisely because _____ earlier hit, *HMS Pinafore*, had been
               4

produced _____ in no less than eight "pirated" versions.
         5

_____ unauthorized adaptations had made Gilbert and Sullivan
  6

more popular but had not helped _____ finances.
              7

3 *those   they   these   deaths   thousand   million   injuries*

Automobile accidents in the United States have been called a national

tragedy, for _____ kill fifty _____ people and injure more
         1   2

than five _____ every year. Many of _____ _____
        3   4   5

and severe _____ are due to human error, which will never be
        6

completely eliminated, but something is being done about _____
       7

which are attributable to unsafe automotive design.

4 *these   it   this   abundance   rates   prejudices   advantages*

Though we have developed many _____ against coal,
           1

_____ nevertheless has a number of _____. Of
  2   3

_____, the most obvious is its _____. There are over two
  4   5

hundred billion tons of economically recoverable coal in the

United States. _____ would be a sufficient amount to last for three
         6

hundred years at present _____ of consumption.
             7

5 *he   his   this   them   novelist   physicist   discovery   novel   physics   Gell-Mann's*

When _____ Murray Gell-Mann identified the smallest units of
        1

matter, _____ decided to call _____ "quarks". _____
        2   3   4

strange name was taken from the Irish _____, James Joyce. In
                    5

_____ extraordinary _____ *Finnegan's Wake* (the source
  6   7

of _____ borrowing), Joyce adopts a triadic approach, which is
    8

342

reflected in Gell-Mann's _____ of the quark's threefold nature, a
                              9
discovery for which he received the Nobel Prize for _____ in 1969.
                                                        10

6 *they   these   which   300   86.3   country   state   flowers   value*

San Diego County's leading agricultural product is flowers. Last year

_____ accounted for a total _____ of _____ million
     1   2   3
dollars _____ is equal to 10 percent of production in the whole
            4
_____, while the _____ as a whole produced more than
     5   6
one-third of the nation's _____ with a total worth of over
                               7
_____ million dollars. _____ figures graphically demonstrate
     8   9
that California is easily the leading flower power in the nation.

7 *this   their   it   fresh water   planet's   ice   earth   oceans*

Although _____ is the driest continent on _____,
              1   2
Antarctica is 98 percent covered by _____, and _____
                                        3   4
contains 90 percent of our _____ _____. The West Antarctic
                                5   6
ice-sheet accounts for only about 10 percent of this fresh water, but

if it were to melt and pour into the _____, _____
                                          7   8
level would rise by a catastrophic twenty feet.

8 *one   river   this   these   waters   dams*
  its   their   inhabitants   people   it   irrigation projects

More than 1.5 million _____ of three countries who depend
                           1
for _____ livelihood on the _____ of the River Senegal will
       2   3
benefit from one of the world's most ambitious _____.
                                                    4
_____ involves the construction of two _____, _____
     5   6   7
on the _____ delta and the other five hundred miles upstream,
            8
in Mali. However, some _____ believe that, though the project
                           9
will benefit Mali, _____ will also cause the country problems since
                       10
_____ inhabitants depend heavily on fish and _____ will
     11   12
be adversely affected.

343

9 *he   their   understandings   behavior   life   human beings*

While Clifford Geertz emphasizes the common _____ held about
                                                    1

the different particulars of social _____ and individual
                                              2

_____ which _____ refers to as "shared meanings",
         3   4

sociologist Daniel Bell views culture as "an effort to provide a coherent set

of answers to the existentialist situations that confront _____ in
                                                                  5

the passage of _____ lives."
                     6

10 *it   that   this   those*
    suburbs   prices   house   rates
    fashionable part residences 150,000   1,000,000

Soaring _____ and high interest _____ have made it very
                1   2

difficult for young middle-class families to buy property in West Los

Angeles. Prices now average around $_____ for an ordinary
                                            3

_____ in the less fashionable west side _____ ,while the cost
       4   5

of four-bedroom _____ in the _____ now averages over
                        6   7

$_____. _____ has been the case since about 1976, and
      8   9

_____ will probably continue to be a problem for _____ who
      10   11

were not fortunate enough to buy before _____ time.
                                                12

Exercise R-18

<u>Objective:</u> To identify referents of specified items in short paragraphs.

<u>Directions:</u> Read the paragraph, and then write what each *italicized* item refers to in the corresponding blanks below the paragraph.

Example:

A small group of scientists do not believe that dinosaurs became

extinct because *they* were big, clumsy beasts. Through *their* painstaking
                1   2

studies, *these researchers* are trying to prove what really happened to
            3

those giants of yesteryear on the basis of a theory that will astonish many:
            4

they think the cause of *their* demise came from outer space.
 5   6

1 They: **dinosaurs**

2 their: **these researchers**

3 these researchers: **a small group of scientists**

4 those giants of yesteryear: **dinosaurs**

5 they: **these researchers**

6 their: **dinosaurs**

1   The pyramids on the west bank of the Nile were built by the pharaohs

as royal tombs. *They* date from 3000 B.C. The most celebrated are *those* at
                    1   2

Giza, built during the fourth dynasty, of which the largest is *the one* that
                                                3

housed the pharaoh Khufu, better known as Cheops. *This* is now called the
                                                      4

Great Pyramid.

1 they: _____

2 those: _____

3 the one: _____

4 This: _____

2   In 1337 King Edward III did something special for his eldest son, Prince

Edward: *he* created the title of Duke of Cornwall and a duchy to go with *it*.
        1   2

For most of the next 644 years, the duchy has provided a generous income

for the Duke. Prince Charles is the twenty-fourth heir to the throne to hold

this title.
        3

1 *he:* _____

2 *it:* _____

3 *this title:* _____

3   The streets of Manhattan are a frontier, a no man's land. In the business

districts, *they* interrupt the flow of civilized behavior, contrasting with the
                        1

seeming orderliness of the buildings that border *them*. If there are laws
                                                                            2

regulating New York City traffic, *they* are barely enforced. There are
                                                                3

approximately six hundred bicycle messengers working in

Manhattan. *They* are fast and contemptuous of whatever traffic rules there
                        4

are. *They* intimidate pedestrians and alarm the drivers of other vehicles
        5

competing with *them* for space on the road.
                                    6

1 *they:* _____

2 *them:* _____

3 *they:* _____

4 *They:* _____

5 *They:* _____

6 *them:* _____

4   The Voyager 2 spacecraft provided astronomers with new information

concerning Saturn's rings. Instead of being concentric circles, a few of *them*
                                                                                                            1

seem more like the spiraling grooves of a phonograph record. The ring

spirals may come from forces similar to *those* that pushed the Milky Way
                                                                2

galaxy into two spiral arms. If an outer moon pushed and pulled a spinning

sheet of particles, *it* would eventually become denser at certain spots in
3
its orbit. *This clump* would then tug on nearby particles, herding *them* into
4   5   6
a dense ring whirling around the planet. Voyager 2 detected traits that look

like such spiral density waves in Saturn's A ring. *It* also returned pictures
7
showing that some of the rings are not perfect circles.

1 *them:* _____

2 *those:* _____

3 *it:* _____

4 *its:* _____

5 *This clump:* _____

6 *them:* _____

7 *It:* _____

5   One oil company has a computer center on one of *its* research vessels. *It* is
1   2
the only ship in the industry that has complete data processing right on

board. The typical oil exploration ship is equipped only to record raw data

from whatever equipment *it* has on board to detect oil deposits under the
3
ocean floor. Usually *it* has seismic sounding gear, occasionally
4
magnetometers and gravity meters. The raw data are sent to onshore

computer centers, and by the time *they* are analyzed, the ship could be a
5
thousand miles away. Having computer equipment on the vessel permits

the crew to make preliminary analyses immediately, and if advisable, *they*
6
can return to the location for a closer look; *this procedure* can save significant
7
exploration time. The challenge is to find that invisible spot under the

seabed that is likely to produce oil, and vessels with computer equipment

seem to provide one of the best ways of finding *it.*
8
1 *its:* _____

2 *It:* _____

3 *it:* _____

4 *it:* _____

5 *they:* _____

6 *they:* _____

7 *this procedure:* _____

8 *it:* _____

6   Altogether, the engineers made over one hundred refinements and

improvements in *their* latest model. The most impressive thing about
                    1
it, however, is what *they* did not change. And *that* is *its* classic
2   3   4   5
exterior design. If you want an automobile with a look that will never

become outmoded, you should consider *this one.*
                                      6

1 *their:* _____

2 *it:* _____

3 *they:* _____

4 *that:* _____

5 *its:* _____

6 *this one:* _____

7   The American Museum of Natural History spent four years arranging *its*
                                                                       1
extraordinary exhibition of more than 500 pieces of ancient gold from

Colombia. But *those few years* are a brief time when compared with the
              2
decades archeologists have spent digging for and studying gold artifacts.

And *all that time* is short when compared with the many centuries
    3
prehistoric Indians practiced *their* craftsmanship and artistry to create
                              4
these treasures.
5

1 *its:* _____

2 *those few years:* _____

3 *all that time:* _____

4 *their:* _____

5 *these treasures:* _____

8   In *its* winding course to the Mississippi, the Wisconsin powers plants,
       1

factories, and mills, making *it* one of America's hardest working rivers. And
               2

through *that same course, it* also proves *itself* to be one of the most beautiful
          3   4   5

rivers in the world. Like *their* river, Wisconsinites see no contradiction
              6

between hard work and natural beauty. *Their* fertile farmlands are an ode to
                 7

natural beauty and productive enough to make *them* the nation's leading
                 8

producer of milk, butter, and cheese.

1 its: _____

2 it: _____

3 that same course: _____

4 it: _____

5 itself: _____

6 their: _____

7 Their: _____

8 them: _____

9   *It* happens early in the night, usually during the first two or three hours of
     1

sleep. The person sits up in bed suddenly, talks incoherently, and may get

up and move around wildly. *He* appears to be terrified of something unseen,
               2

and *his* pulse and respiratory rates may have doubled. But no external
      3

danger is present. Until recently, *this episode* would have been classified as a
                4

nightmare. Today, *it* would be recognized as representing one of two
         5

distinct phenomena. *One* is the familiar nightmare, a bad dream that occurs
         6

rather late at night and ends in a sudden awakening. *The other* (described
          7

above) is more correctly called a night terror.

1 It: _____

2 He: _____

3 his: _____

4 this episode: _____

5 it: _____

6 One: _____

7 The other: _____

10   Finally, there is stalking followed by an "all out" chase. *This* is the fourth
hunting technique used by red foxes in these northern forests. Typically,
when hunting a hare, the fox keeps close to the ground while slowly
stalking *its* prey and staring fixedly at *it.* Becoming aware of the fox, the hare
suddenly flees into cover with the fox pursuing. When *it* closes in on the
hare, the fox tries to bite *it* in the leg. At *this point,* the hare often shoots off in
another direction. By zigzagging, *it* seeks to widen the gap between *it* and
the fox. In the end, either the hare escapes into undergrowth so dense that
the fox cannot follow, or the predator gets a hold on *its* quarry. If *the latter*
happens, the fox quickly pulls the hare off *its* feet and both collapse. The fox
then leaps upon *its* victim and pins *it* to the ground.

1 This: _____

2 its: _____

3 it: _____

4 it: _____

5 it: _____

6 this point: _____

7 it: _____

8 it: _____

9 its: _____

10 the latter: _____

11 its: _____

12 its: _____

13 it: _____

Exercise R-19

TOEFL Practice: Reading Comprehension (Reference): Time 8 minutes.

Objective: To practice answering questions which are similar to the reference type questions on the TOEFL.

Directions: Read the passage and then choose the one best answer, (A), (B), (C), or (D), to each question. Write your answer in the blank. Answer all questions following a passage on the basis of what is stated or implied in that passage.

A relatively new feature of radio broadcasts in the United States is the call-in therapy shows, in which callers get the opportunity to air problems, however intimate, while the hosts offer them free, and immediate, advice. They started, like so many other self-help psychology ideas, in California in the early 1970's,
5   but now they have spread to many other parts of the country and enjoy considerable popularity. This phenomenon certainly does not please all psychologists and the shows have become a matter of some concern to their professional association, the APA.
     Present APA guidelines merely prohibit psychologists from diagnosing
10   problems, or from offering psychotherapy on the radio, while the earlier ones had prohibited all giving of advice outside the traditional therapist-patient relationship. This prohibition fails to satisfy many psychologists. Some consider all giving of psychological advice over the radio totally unacceptable, but there are others who believe there should be even more of it.
15   The former are typified by a Hastings Center psychiatrist, who describes the activity as "disgusting". On one occasion, he backed up his view by walking out of a radio program when the host insisted he answer listeners' calls. But radio therapy hosts, who are mostly attractive, youngish and qualified women, are fully capable of backing up theirs, and do so charmingly and effectively, as
20   might be expected from professionals combining psychological expertise with entertainment know-how.

_____ 1   *them* (line 3) refers to

   (A) problems
   (B) call-in therapy shows
   (C) callers
   (D) hosts

_____ 2   *they* (line 3) refers to

   (A) problems
   (B) call-in therapy shows
   (C) callers
   (D) hosts

_____ 3   *this phenomenon* (line 6) refers to

   (A) the fact that the shows started in California
   (B) the fact that callers air intimate problems
   (C) the fact that the shows started in the early 1970's
   (D) the fact that the shows enjoy considerable popularity

351

_____ 4   *their* (line 7) refers to

   (A) therapy shows
   (B) self-help psychology ideas
   (C) the hosts
   (D) psychologists

_____ 5   *ones* (line 10) refers to

   (A) APA guidelines
   (B) psychologists
   (C) problems
   (D) the shows

_____ 6   *this prohibition* (line 12) refers to

   (A) that no advice be given outside the traditional therapist-patient
        relationship
   (B) that psychologists do not diagnose problems or offer
        psychotherapy on the radio
   (C) that not all psychologists are pleased
   (D) that it is a matter of some concern to the APA

_____ 7   *it* (line 14) refers to

   (A) this prohibition
   (B) the traditional therapist-patient relationship
   (C) giving of psychological advice over the radio
   (D) psychological advice

_____ 8   *the former* (line 15) refers to

   (A) psychologists who object to call-in therapy shows
   (B) psychologists who advocate more advice-giving over the radio
   (C) the APA's present prohibitions
   (D) dispensing psychological advice

_____ 9   *he* (line 16) refers to

   (A) a Hastings Center psychiatrist
   (B) the host
   (C) a listener
   (D) the former

_____ 10   *theirs* (line 19) refers to

   (A) activity
   (B) radio-therapy programs
   (C) listeners
   (D) views

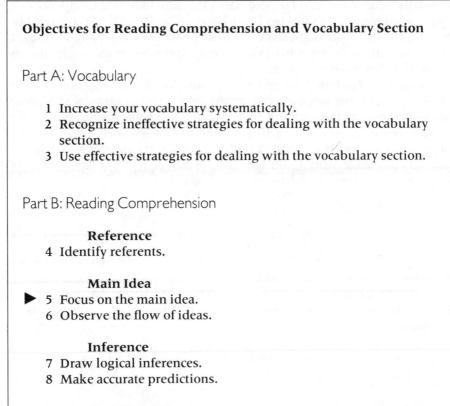

Objectives for Reading Comprehension and Vocabulary Section

Part A: Vocabulary

1 Increase your vocabulary systematically.
2 Recognize ineffective strategies for dealing with the vocabulary section.
3 Use effective strategies for dealing with the vocabulary section.

Part B: Reading Comprehension

Reference
4 Identify referents.

Main Idea
▶ 5 Focus on the main idea.
6 Observe the flow of ideas.

Inference
7 Draw logical inferences.
8 Make accurate predictions.

Restatement
9 Interpret common features.
10 Recognize restated information.

Objective 5: Focus on the Main Idea

Reading is concerned with meaning to a greater extent than it is with form, although the two are interdependent. We read for the ideas contained in the reading. Not all the ideas, however, are of equal importance. Efficient readers understand not only the ideas but also their relative significance, as expressed by the author; in other words, that some of the ideas are superordinate while others are subordinate.

Speakers and writers have a number of ways of indicating the relative importance that should be attached to the ideas they express. In speaking, such ways include stress, tone of voice, and body language. These means, however, are not available to writers. Of particular note among the means at writers' disposal are where to position one idea or another and whether to put an idea in a main or subordinate clause.

The whole issue of main and subordinate ideas provides strong evidence that word-by-word reading in a foreign language is just as worthless as it would be in the reader's native language. In fact, students who read in a foreign language must discriminate between what matters more and what matters less, just as they would in their own language.

Part B of the Reading Comprehension and Vocabulary Section always includes questions that focus directly on the issue of main idea. Most of these questions concern the main idea of a passage, but some may focus on the main idea of a given paragraph or of a single, complicated sentence. Even where a question is not explicitly concerned with main idea, the question of discrimination remains an essential concern of all efficient readers. This group of exercises provides practice in determining the main idea.

Exercise R-20

Objective: To distinguish degrees of generality among individual words or expressions.

Directions: Choose the most general word or phrase in each set. Write your answer in the blank.

Example: __C__ (A) chemist
              (B) physicist
              (C) scientist
              (D) biologist

_____ 1 (A) company
      (B) organization
      (C) partnership
      (D) government agency

_____ 5 (A) secretary
      (B) employee
      (C) teacher
      (D) policeman

_____ 2 (A) animal
      (B) mammal
      (C) amphibian
      (D) reptile

_____ 6 (A) anger
      (B) revulsion
      (C) emotion
      (D) fear

_____ 3 (A) dolphin
      (B) man
      (C) elephant
      (D) mammal

_____ 7 (A) brochure
      (B) novel
      (C) reading matter
      (D) magazine

_____ 4 (A) addition
      (B) calculation
      (C) subtraction
      (D) multiplication

_____ 8 (A) cartoonist
      (B) artist
      (C) painter
      (D) sculptor

_____ 9 (A) dolphin
        (B) sea anemone
        (C) sea lion
        (D) sea creature

_____ 15 (A) glider
        (B) jet plane
        (C) airliner
        (D) aircraft

_____ 10 (A) increase
        (B) affect
        (C) reduce
        (D) darken

_____ 16 (A) widen
        (B) lengthen
        (C) increase
        (D) multiply

_____ 11 (A) cardiologist
        (B) doctor
        (C) pediatrician
        (D) intern

_____ 17 (A) Head of State
        (B) King
        (C) Monarch
        (D) Emperor

_____ 12 (A) knife
        (B) scalpel
        (C) cutting implement
        (D) tool

_____ 18 (A) whisky
        (B) alcoholic beverage
        (C) brandy
        (D) drink

_____ 13 (A) fuel
        (B) fuel-oil
        (C) oil
        (D) gas

_____ 19 (A) vessel
        (B) fishing vessel
        (C) oil-tanker
        (D) ocean liner

_____ 14 (A) living matter
        (B) grass
        (C) vegetation
        (D) tree

_____ 20 (A) crimson
        (B) scarlet
        (C) red
        (D) brick-red

Exercise R-21

Objective: To distinguish degrees of generality among phrases.

Directions: Choose the most general phrase in each set. Write your answer in the blank.

Example: _D_ (A) going dancing at a disco
            (B) reading a good book
            (C) having a picnic in the country
            (D) spending free time

_____ 1 (A) repairing dilapidated woodwork
       (B) planning the order of renovations
       (C) restoring an old house
       (D) purchasing fixtures and materials

_____ 2 (A) haircuts to suit the contours of the face
      (B) permanent waves
      (C) manicures and pedicures
      (D) beauty-salon services

_____ 3 (A) investigating original sources
      (B) carrying out research
      (C) reading background material
      (D) testing hypotheses

_____ 4 (A) reduction in T-lymphocytes
      (B) secretion of hormones leading to increased heart rate
      (C) stress-induced changes in the body's immune system
      (D) alterations in the hypothalamus

_____ 5 (A) writing a term paper
      (B) completing a course in your major
      (C) deciding on an outline
      (D) choosing a topic according to guidelines provided

_____ 6 (A) working as an actor
      (B) attending rehearsals
      (C) learning lines
      (D) forging a career

_____ 7 (A) looking after a motor vehicle
      (B) following the service guide
      (C) maintaining the engine
      (D) caring for the bodywork

_____ 8 (A) studying the physical conditions of pandas in remote areas
      (B) concentrating undernourished pandas in collection areas
      (C) foraging for umbrella bamboo, the staple diet of pandas
      (D) ensuring the survival of the Great Panda

_____ 9 (A) reducing income-tax rates
      (B) reducing budget deficits
      (C) expanding the money supply
      (D) running a country's economy

_____ 10 (A) being in the Navy
      (B) serving one's country
      (C) being a member of the armed services
      (D) serving as an ambassador

Exercise R-22

Objective: To distinguish degrees of generality among sentences.

Directions: Choose the most general sentence in each set. Write your answer in the blank.

Example: __B__ (A) The hotel offers complimentary coffee from 7 to 10 a.m. daily.
   (B) There are many reasons why guests feel at home at the Glorietta Bay Inn.
   (C) The coin-operated laundry room has an ironing board, and an iron is available for the use of guests.
   (D) There are a number of extra services at the Glorietta Bay Inn including baby-sitting.

_____ 1 (A) Recently, reports on Glenn Campbell, Phyllis George, and Governor Hugh Carey have all appeared.
   (B) *People* magazine contains articles on people in the news, unusual happenings, and the latest entertainment events.
   (C) Typical of the unusual was an article on recipes for and the benefits of earthworms.
   (D) The reviews are entertainingly written and sometimes highly critical though they are shorter than in some older, established magazines.

_____ 2 (A) The speaker related a number of amusing anecdotes, which were well-told as well as intrinsically comical.
   (B) The talk covered every aspect of the subject and included examples from other, related fields.
   (C) All of those attending the lecture felt that they learned something new and interesting from the speaker.
   (D) The lecture was wide-ranging, amusing, and informative.

_____ 3 (A) The orbit of Uranus does not follow the orbit calculated for it because it is being pulled slightly off course by the gravitational attraction of another, unknown planet.
   (B) The tiny planet Pluto is too small to account for the distortion in Uranus' orbit.
   (C) The planetoid Chiron, discovered in 1977, is too small to cause the irregularity exhibited in Uranus' orbit.
   (D) Planetary observations show why astronomers believe a tenth planet may exist.

_____ 4 (A) When rib roasts are on sale, you should ask your butcher to cut one into steaks for you.

(B) If you debone whole chicken breasts yourself, you can save more than a dollar per pound on chicken cutlets.

(C) By following our special cost-cutting meat guide you can reduce your family's meat bill by as much as 50 percent.

(D) When buying a whole shell of beef to be cut into steaks, you should keep in mind that there can be as many as five pounds of waste per twenty pounds.

_____ 5 (A) In short, science-fiction writing offers the reader the entire universe and all of the past, present, and future.

(B) One thing that all good science-fiction stories have in common is that they deal with the idea of change.

(C) The middle range of stories often deals with the frontiers of modern knowledge and the ethics involved in scientific decisions.

(D) Modern science fiction covers a wide range of topics, from stories about robots and high technology to fantasies about enchanted kingdoms in outer space.

_____ 6 (A) Stray animals usually do not trust people.

(B) Stray animals almost never make good pets.

(C) Most stray animals have received little or no training.

(D) Stray animals are frequently the victims of poor nutrition and a lack of medical treatment.

_____ 7 (A) Undoubtedly, the most important decision was the one concerning the rebuilding of the Otter Creek bridge.

(B) There was some opposition to the proposal to increase the budget for law enforcement, but it eventually passed.

(C) At their last meeting this year, the town council made a number of long-awaited decisions.

(D) A few members wanted to earmark extra funds for next year's town festival, but a majority felt that the limited resources available should be used for other, more pressing needs.

_____ 8 (A) Newborn babies sob seemingly in sympathy when they hear the cries of other babies.

(B) A calm baby does not cry if it hears a recording of its own cries.

(C) The crying of a baby chimpanzee has no effect on newborn human babies.

(D) Newborn babies can distinguish among their own cries, the cries of other babies, and the cries of non-human babies.

_____ 9 (A) Microwave ovens have eliminated many of the inconveniences previously associated with the preparation of meals.

(B) Many foods can go directly from the freezer to the microwave oven without being defrosted.

    (C) Many microwave ovens can be pre-set to cook your food while you are away from the kitchen.

    (D) The microwave oven has greatly reduced the amount of time it takes to cook a meal.

_____ 10 (A) Many people think social anthropologists spend their time measuring the size of people's heads or other parts of their bodies.

    (B) Perhaps because it is a relatively new discipline, social anthropology causes a great deal of confusion among laymen.

    (C) Some misunderstandings undoubtedly derive from the fact that many social anthropologists work in areas where archaeologists are seeking, or have sought, clues to man's past.

    (D) It is a popular misconception that social anthropology focuses exclusively on pyramids, old temple sites, and other archaeological remains.

Exercise R-23

Objectives: (i) To determine the point of view expressed in a sentence or passage by identifying the main idea.

    (ii) To recognize in which part of the sentence evidence (apparently) favoring a particular point of view is likely to be put forward.

Directions: (i) **Check** (✓) (A) or (B) in response to the question at the head of each pair of items.

    (ii) **Underline** the part of the item you have **checked** (✓, (A) or (B), **favoring** the point of view mentioned in the question.

    (iii) Then, notice that the other sentence or passage also contains information **favorable** to the particular point of view asked about, even though an opposite point of view is expressed. **Underline** the part of this item that seems to support the point of view you are looking for. **Note:** No key has been provided for this, but the example gives a model for focusing your ideas in this way.

Example:

Which of the following statements was written by a <u>baseball fan</u>?

✓(A) Although American football is a game of great appeal, it fails to match the <u>extraordinary individual skills</u> or <u>the season-long build up of excitement that professional baseball</u> <u>provides.</u>

  (B) <u>Professional baseball used to be a wonderful game, the nation's favorite</u>; but times have changed and baseball has fallen behind the times, its place in the country's heart having been taken by professional football.

1 Which of the following statements was written by <u>a supporter of gun-control laws</u>?

(A) It is not our desire to curtail individual freedoms, but we cannot allow the purchasing of small arms to spread unchecked.

(B) Much as we appreciate the fear that widespread ownership of small arms leads to increased bloodshed, we insist on the fundamental right of American citizens to freely defend themselves and their families.

2 Which of the following statements was written by <u>a person who likes Cleveland</u>?

(A) For all its boosters' claims that Cleveland has again become a city to be proud of, there's a great deal to be said for the jokes you hear about it on radio and television.

(B) Despite the jokes about Cleveland you hear on radio and television, thanks to recent municipal efforts, it has once again become a city to be proud of.

3 Which of the following statements was written by <u>someone who prefers large cars to small ones</u>?

(A) Their excellent gas mileage and even their improved interior design notwithstanding, today's compact cars simply fail to provide the feel a traditional motorist yearns for.

(B) They lack some of the size and even the character of the full-sized autos we were accustomed to, but today's compacts more than make up for this with their excellent gas mileage.

4 Which of the following statements was written by <u>an opponent of bullfighting</u>?

(A) Though bullfighting may have its detractors, those are usually people who either have never been to a bull-ring or are quite unable to appreciate the bravery and the art involved.

(B) Hemingway and his ilk may write all they want about the drama of the bullfight, or the matador's "grace under pressure", but that does nothing to mitigate the suffering of the innocent bull.

5 Which of the following statements was written by <u>a proponent of the view that live theater is dying</u>?

(A) In this modern age, with its freely available entertainment, accessible at the turn of a switch, the live theater is merely a peripheral activity, however much it might have been a vehicle for cultural progress in the past.

(B) Of course the theater has suffered from competition that takes advantage of modern technology. All the same, there is a qualitative difference in being present at an actual performance which, though it may be a luxury, will never be replaced by second-hand audience participation.

6 Which of the following statements was written by <u>a vegetarian</u>?

(A) The argument is sometimes put forward that man is not naturally a vegetarian since he was originally omnivorous. While such a claim may contain a grain of truth, it nevertheless ignores the obvious fact that there are many aspects of the original human condition that we have seen fit to improve.

(B) In spite of the insistence of those who exclude meat and fish from their diet that such a course is both spiritually and physically beneficial, there is no evidence that fighting is less prevalent or exceptional longevity more likely in areas where vegetarianism is the rule.

7 Which of the following statements was written by <u>a detractor of the President</u>?

(A) The President has certainly achieved a number of minor improvements and there is no denying that thus far, the country has not quite gone to rack and ruin under his leadership. Nevertheless, one searches in vain for the great attitudinal and economic breakthroughs we were so lavishly promised during the course of his campaign.

(B) Though the great breakthroughs the President has promised obviously take some time to engineer, he can nonetheless already point to significant improvements in the nation's standard of living, which are portents of the exciting changes soon to be implemented.

8 Which of the following statements was written by <u>a person in favor of small-town life</u>?

(A) Possibly there are those who derive pleasure from turning back the clock and seeking out the virtues we fondly imagine to have been associated with life in small towns in bygone days. Yet the most superficial perusal of contemporary accounts dealing with such an existence makes it quite clear that sterile deprivation of life's true pleasures would be a much more accurate assessment.

(B) It is true that city-dwellers and suburbanites have access to certain facilities that may be denied to the inhabitants of small towns. What they miss, however, far outweighs such advantages, which, in any case, the vast majority rarely has the time or energy to take advantage of.

9 Which of the following statements was written by <u>someone who opposes a particular job applicant</u>?

(A) Smith certainly has a number of qualities that would appeal to my colleagues on the selection panel. However, it should be noted that he has a history of flitting from one job to another that is hardly consistent with this company's management approach.

(B) Although Smith has shown a perhaps regrettable tendency in the past to move rather quickly from one job to another, he is clearly the best-qualified candidate and would undoubtedly respond to our own brand of company loyalty.

10 Which of the following statements was written by <u>a tour operator</u>?

   (A) The cost of the tour is admittedly high. Against this, though, consideration must be given to the fact that it offers a unique opportunity to visit one of the world's most extraordinary tourist attractions in the company of congenial fellow-explorers and expert guides.

   (B) However unusual the opportunity or expert the accompanying personnel, these can hardly be a justification for charging an amount that appears to fall not far short of the Gross National Product in some of the world's less developed nations, including that which is the destination of this "extraordinary" tour.

Exercise R-24

<u>Objective:</u> To predict a writer's point of view on the basis of partial sentences.

<u>Directions:</u> Mark the following sentences **F (for)** or **A (against)**, according to whether you think the writer will favor or oppose the matter (or person) in question.

Part A

  __F__   1 In spite of the difficulties associated with . . . .

  _____   2 While it cannot be denied that problems will need to be overcome . . . .

  _____   3 In view of the objections raised . . . .

  _____   4 Thanks to his hard work, dedication, and unstinting loyalty . . . .

  _____   5 Given the generally disappointing reaction to the plan . . . .

  _____   6 Because of the controversy surrounding this recommendation . . . .

  _____   7 For all his obvious weaknesses . . . .

  _____   8 He may well have certain habits we would all disapprove of . . . .

  _____   9 Of course, everyone appreciated the excitement generated by the team . . . .

  _____   10 As a result of the overwhelmingly enthusiastic response to this idea . . . .

Part B

  __A__   1 . . . . his undoubted talents notwithstanding.

362

_____ 2 . . . . he is, nevertheless, the sort of man we are looking for.

_____ 3 . . . . however enthusiastically he may be recommended.

_____ 4 . . . . despite the expense involved.

_____ 5 . . . . all the same, there are strong reservations in some quarters.

_____ 6 . . . . whereas this candidate is one of doubtful ability.

_____ 7 . . . . nonetheless, we should take advantage of this unusual opportunity.

_____ 8 . . . . much as I respect her excellent reputation as a judge.

_____ 9 . . . . yet this should not prejudice our opinion of him.

_____ 10 . . . . even though I think he is an excellent statistician.

Exercise R-25

Objective: To choose the best title for an article on the basis of three main ideas from the article.

Directions: Read the three topic sentences from three paragraphs of an article. Choose the best title for the article. Write your answer in the blank.

Example: __C__ The water smoker is part Chinese smoker and part sub-urban-American barbecue grill.

— — — — — — — —

To cook, for example, a venison ham, you build a charcoal fire in the bottom pan.

— — — — — — — —

You should follow the instruction book very carefully until you learn enough to begin experimenting with your water smoker.

— — — — — — — —

(A) *The Best Recipes for Cooking Venison*
(B) *Organizing a Backyard Barbecue*
(C) *Joy of Cooking with Smoke*

_____ 1 Some interesting research is now being done on liquid injection molded (LIM) tires.

— — — — — — — —

LIM tires are built in three stages.

— — — — — — — —

Because these tires have no carcass, the part of the tire that leaves the road reverts to its normal shape almost immediately.

— — — — — — — —

(A) *Tires for the Future*

(B) *The Revolutionary LIM Tires*

(C) *New Ideas for Your Next Automobile*

_____ 2 The Venezuelan capital has many large shopping centers called "centros comerciales".

\- \- \- \- \- \- \- \- \-

A lifetime could be spent sampling the many cuisines of Caracas' restaurants.

\- \- \- \- \- \- \- \- \-

The Spanish flavor of the city is reflected in the popular Flamenco clubs.

\- \- \- \- \- \- \- \- \-

(A) *Sights and Sounds of Venezuela*

(B) *The Spanish Influence in Venezuela*

(C) *Caracas Cornucopia*

_____ 3 Researchers believe that MAO (Monoamine oxidase) in the brain has an effect on behavior by breaking down the chemical neurotransmitters that carry messages between neurons.

\- \- \- \- \- \- \- \- \-

Scientists have found a connection between levels of MAO and adult behavior.

\- \- \- \- \- \- \- \- \-

One study found approximately the same range of MAO levels in infants and adults.

\- \- \- \- \- \- \- \- \-

(A) *MAO and Behavior Patterns*

(B) *What is MAO?*

(C) *MAO's Effect on Adult Behavior*

_____ 4 "No one knows the ways of the wind and the caribou", says an old Chipewyan Indian proverb.

\- \- \- \- \- \- \- \- \-

The migratory habits and the numbers of the caribou were unknown to man until this century.

\- \- \- \- \- \- \- \- \-

Much of the mystery of caribou movement and numbers began to disappear when biologists were able to survey and census the animals from the air.

\- \- \- \- \- \- \- \- \-

(A) *Migratory Habits of the Caribou*

(B) *Collecting Information on the Caribou*

(C) *Chipewyan Dependence on the Caribou*

_____ 5   A mounting body of evidence suggests that fighting violence with violence rarely deters a crime in progress and greatly increases the chances of changing a robbery into a violent attack on the victim.

— — — — — — — —

One report shows that at least 100 thousand handguns are stolen from private owners each year, the vast majority during burglaries.

— — — — — — — —

Moreover, a study of robberies in eight American cities states that in less than 4 percent of the crimes did the victim have the opportunity to use a weapon.

— — — — — — — —

(A) *What Happens to the Victims of Crime?*

(B) *Is Your Family Safe?*

(C) *Should You Arm Yourself against Crime?*

_____ 6   Proponents of father-attended childbirth assert that the father's experience encourages him to develop a closer bond with his child.

— — — — — — — —

As a father of three teenagers from a previous marriage, one man compared his past experience as a new father to being in the delivery room during the birth of his newborn daughter.

— — — — — — — —

Women report that they are much less anxious and more aware of what is going on when their husbands are with them when they give birth.

— — — — — — — —

(A) *The Father-Daughter Relationship*

(B) *Baby's First View of Life*

(C) *Dad in the Delivery Room*

_____ 7   In contrast to classical music, which is restricted by form and by tradition, jazz is spontaneous and free-form.

— — — — — — — —

Jazz is a native American music which was developed by American Negroes in the South.

— — — — — — — —

The influences of West African music, spirituals, and the blues are evident in jazz.

— — — — — — — —

(A) *The Origins of American Music*

(B) *The Story of Jazz*

(C) *The Future of Jazz in America*

_____ 8   To lose weight permanently, a dieter needs a nutritionally balanced eating plan that reduces caloric intake by cutting down on certain foods without eliminating them completely.

— — — — — — — —

To lose weight that is fat instead of water, a dieter must lose weight gradually.

— — — — — — — —

Dieters should also have occasional treats to avoid the feeling of permanent deprivation, which can lead to food binges when the resolve to diet weakens.

— — — — — — — —

(A) *Fad Diets*
(B) *Dieting Tips*
(C) *Recipes for Dieters*

_____ 9 The notion that exercising parental power is bad developed out of early psychoanalytic theory, which suggested many neuroses are caused by the repression of a child's natural impulses.

— — — — — — — —

Today, child psychologists insist that children actually like to be disciplined and that set rules which are consistently enforced make a child feel protected and loved.

— — — — — — — —

The necessity for a balance between love and discipline in raising good kids is not just a hunch or theory.

— — — — — — — —

(A) *The Family as a Disciplined Democracy*
(B) *Disciplined Parents and Free Children*
(C) *Discipline: An Old Theory Gains New Ground*

_____ 10 Even at the molecular level, change is not spontaneous.

— — — — — — — —

Resistance to change obviously occurs in the biological realm.

— — — — — — — —

Nature has special rewards for living systems which seek improvement.

— — — — — — — —

(A) *Change: The Special Rewards in Nature*
(B) *Change: Nature Resists but Rewards*
(C) *Change: A Problem of Molecular Biology*

Exercise R-26

Objective: To evaluate alternative titles for short passages.

Directions: In the blanks provided, **check** (√) the best title for the passage. Mark the other possibilities **A, B or C** to explain why they are not suitable titles.

A: too broad   **B: too narrow**   **C: insignificant detail**

Example:

When tobacco leaves are a ripe, yellowish green, they are picked and the curing process is begun. The leaves are first hung in sheds to dry to a rich golden color, a process artificially encouraged in nontropical regions by charcoal fires or gas burners. The leaves are then piled up to form huge "bulks" weighing thousands of pounds each. The pressure of the leaves on each other and the temperatures of up to 100 degrees that are generated set up a fermentation process that develops the natural aroma and flavor of the leaf.

Next, the leaves are packed into bales and go through a second fermentation under controlled atmospheric conditions. The stacked bales are rotated and the leaves are checked regularly until they are fully cured. The entire process from harvesting through aging takes from six months to three or more years, depending on the area where the tobacco is grown, on the curing techniques, and on the quality of the leaf.

   A   *1 The Tobacco Industry*

   ✓   *2 Curing Tobacco*

   C   *3 Tobacco "Bulks"*

   B   *4 Effects of Fermentation on Tobacco Curing*

1   Asteroids, even small ones, can be devastating if they hit the earth. The Grand Canyon, which is almost a mile wide, might have been created by an asteroid only 150 feet in diameter. Experts estimate that if an object 500 feet in diameter were to hit the earth, it could set fire to trees within a radius of 30 miles, knock down houses within one of 100 miles, and change weather patterns worldwide for as long as a year because of the dust it would throw up.

In the near future, it may be possible to prevent such disasters. A scanning system may soon be able to provide information on the brightness and position of objects in space. The system would be able to indicate changes in the position of these celestial objects and tell us if there is an asteroid headed for earth. A bomb could then be carried to the asteroid by a spacecraft and fired by a radio signal from earth. The explosion would cause a small change in the asteroid's orbit, but if done early enough, a very slight change would be enough to cause the asteroid to miss the earth.

   _____   *1 Asteroid Risk Resolved?*

   _____   *2 The Destructiveness of Asteroids*

   _____   *3 Asteroids – Past, Present, and Future*

   _____   *4 Asteroid Responsible for Grand Canyon?*

2   As urban apartments have come to constitute the background against which the lives of more and more poeple are lived out and as actual citiscapes have come to seem less and less attractive to many, so the

designing and decoration of such apartments have come to respond increasingly to a search for interior harmony. It is no longer so much the outward view from windows, garden, or terrace which is of most concern to the architect, but rather the creation of interior views by means of spatial sculpturing.

In this regard, clean lines and the absence of clutter are seen as particularly conducive to achieving the desired effect and this means, among other things, concealing mechanical and electronic equipment in cabinet work or behind paneling.

This whole refocusing inward has given rise to controversy since some claim that it lessens the sense of living in a community, while others insist that it protects the apartment-dwellers from a sense of alienation. This is not the place to express a view one way or the other, but one thing that can be said is that the "interior-view" approach is here to stay – for the moment.

_____ *1 Cabinetwork and Paneling: Their Function in Modern Apartment Design*

_____ *2 Living in an Urban Apartment*

_____ *3 Clean Lines: The Secret to Urban Apartment Design*

_____ *4 Urban Apartment Design: An Inward Look*

3   Physical growth among the Quechua of Peru is notably slower than among people in the United States, as is evidenced by a number of developmental characteristics, including a delay of the adolescent growth spurt until the early twenties or even later. Such retardation is, naturally, one of the effects of an insufficient intake of calories or proteins, but it also provides an excellent example of adaptation. Indeed, it is estimated that retarded growth, between the ages of fifteen and twenty, saves on the average Quechua's caloric intake requirement by more than 44,000 calories each year. While this may not seem greatly significant by American standards, such adaptation means that some 100 square yards less cropland needs to be planted each year for every Quechua who remains physically immature.

_____ *1 Causes of Growth Retardation among the Quechuan Indians*

_____ *2 Growth Differences between Quechua and Young People of the United States*

_____ *3 Effective Adaptation in the Quechuan Maturation Process*

_____ *4 Patterns of Quechuan Development*

4   The caterpillar larva of *Glaucopsyche Lygdamus*, a small butterfly found in the western part of the United States, has virtually no independent means of protecting itself from the attacks of predatory flies and wasps. If successful, such attacks result in the eggs of the predators being laid in the caterpillar and the latter's eventual death at the hands of the young it has been host to. Without outside help, it would not be long before *Glaucopsyche Lygdamus* disappeared altogether.

As a means of ensuring its survival, the caterpillar has developed an interesting symbiotic relationship with ants of the *Formica* genus. The caterpillar provides sugar-water, which it secretes by means of a gland specifically adapted to the purpose, for these ants and, in exchange, the ants offer what can best be described as a bodyguard service. What they do, in fact, is surround the caterpillar and squirt an irritant at marauding flies and wasps.

The arrangement works well for both sides: the ants enjoy a ready supply of sugar-water, while the butterfly has a much higher chance of survival.

_____ 1 *Symbiosis: Nature's Way of Living Together*

_____ 2 *Glaucopsyche Lygdamus and Formica ants: An Example of Symbiosis*

_____ 3 *Glaucopsyche Lygdamus: The Larval Stage*

_____ 4 *Predatory Flies and Wasps*

5   Violent thunderstorms are impressive phenomena wherever they occur. There are, however, certain characteristics of thunderstorms in the Great Plains region of the United States which result in an effect which is extraordinarily different from that caused by such storms in cities or hill country.

The first difference is that a storm can be seen approaching from miles away. This approach gives the spectator an unusual perspective and allows him to see the complete storm as if it were a moving entity with defined borders. Even before the storm comes into sight, however, its approach can be both heard as rolling thunder and sensed as a sharp temperature drop.

As the storm advances, like some unstoppable giant, it blacks out the daylight and thus heightens the effect of the flashes of lightning with their almost simultaneous accompanying peals of deafening thunder.

The final difference is the commonness with which hail is a feature of Great Plains thunderstorms. This hail is not just common or garden hail with pea-sized hailstones. Indeed, Spaniards in the sixteenth century spoke of hail the size of bowls, and Plains Indians also reported hail of extraordinary dimensions. Doubtless, the size lost nothing in the telling, but, even today, the hailstones in Great Plains thunderstorms are often described as being the size of large marbles or golfballs.

_____ 1 *The Great Plains in the Sixteenth Century*

_____ 2 *Hail in the Great Plains: Truth and Legend*

_____ 3 *Weather in the Great Plains*

_____ 4 *Thunderstorms in the Great Plains*

Objectives for Reading Comprehension and Vocabulary Section

Part A: Vocabulary

1 Increase your vocabulary systematically.
2 Recognize ineffective strategies for dealing with the vocabulary section.
3 Use effective strategies for dealing with the vocabulary section.

Part B: Reading Comprehension

Reference
4 Identify referents.

Main Idea
5 Focus on the main idea.
▶ 6 Observe the flow of ideas.

Inference
7 Draw logical inferences.
8 Make accurate predictions.

Restatement
9 Interpret common features.
10 Recognize restated information.

Objective 6: Observe the Flow of Ideas

You will have noticed that all the items in the Reading Comprehension and Vocabulary Section, Part A, consist of a single sentence. The majority of the passages in Part B, on the other hand, consist of several **related** sentences. These sentences are connected in meaning to each other. The writer does not expect the reader to read the third sentence before the first and second sentences and so on. There is a flow of ideas.

The exercises in this section require you to build up original passages from their constituent sentences. You are **not** asked to do this in any part of the TOEFL, but practicing doing so will help you recognize the devices used by writers to achieve coherence, and this, in turn, will make you a more efficient reader.

Among the clues you will use are a number of devices focused on earlier in this book, for example, **subordination** (Section 2, Structure and Written Expression, Objective 3, pages 165–96) and **reference words** (Section 3, Reading Comprehension and Vocabulary, Objective 4, pages 330–52) , as well as the focus of the previous Objective (**main idea**).

Let us take the first sentence in Exercise R-27, page 372, as an example. The subjects of the ten sentences are (in the order the sentences appear): *The newlyweds; His father; The Second World War; the boy; They; Frank and Lynn; He; Frank Talbott; Frank and Lynn; His widowed mother.* Of these, *his father, they, he, his widowed mother* can be eliminated as being the first sentence in the passage, since the pronouns (*they, he*) and the possessive adjectives (*his, his*) clearly refer to a person or persons already mentioned.

The newlyweds, Frank and Lynn and *Frank and Lynn* **might** start the first sentence. However, *the newlyweds* suggests that the writer already expects the reader to know who he is talking about, while the *Frank* in *Frank and Lynn* would be expected to come **after** *Frank Talbott* (the more complete version of the man's name) not **before** it. In addition, of course, the flow of ideas make it clear that this is, in fact, true.

This leaves three possibilities: *The Second World War, the boy* and *Frank Talbott.* In the first case we have "The Second World War interrupted *his* budding acting career . . ." so again the writer assumes we know whom *his* refers to. Similarly, in the second case we have "To compensate for *this* low opinion *his* mother had of *him*, the boy . . ." Clearly *this* refers to something already mentioned, and *his* and *him* refer to a person already mentioned. Only the sentence beginning *Frank Talbott* remains as a possible opening.

Although this logical explanation sounds laborious when written out, the mind is capable of processing these and all sorts of other clues very efficiently while paying attention to the overall flow of ideas. It is not just *Frank Talbott* compared with the other subjects of sentences that will help you. It is the whole meaning of the sentence: "Frank Talbott's childhood in Pittsburgh did not leave happy memories", which makes it a good candidate for beginning the passage. Biographies, after all, not uncommonly begin somewhere near the beginning!

Exercise R-27

Objective: To order a series of sentences into a coherent passage on the basis of a logical sequence of ideas and expressions.

Directions: Arrange the following sentences by numbering them in the order in which they would appear in a text. Write the numbers in the blanks provided.

_____ A   The newlyweds lived in a one-room flat and scraped by with Frank trying to make it in show business.

_____ B   His father, a shoe repairman, died when Frank was still young.

_____ C   The Second World War interrupted his budding acting career for two years when he served in the United States Navy.

_____ D   To compensate for this low opinion his mother had of him, the boy went to the movies regularly and eventually joined the children's workshop of the Pittsburgh Playhouse.

_____ E   They splurged two dollars on a marriage license one day in 1952 and were wed in City Hall.

_____ F   After a few small successes in New York, Frank and Lynn moved to Hollywood and for the next twenty years Frank never stopped working.

_____ G   He was back in Pittsburgh in 1947 when he met his future wife, Lynn.

__1__ H   Frank Talbott's childhood in Pittsburgh did not leave happy memories.

_____ I   Frank and Lynn were formally engaged two months after their first date.

_____ J   His widowed mother, embittered by her husband's death, convinced him that he could not do anything right.

Exercise R-28

Objective and Directions: see Exercise R-27.

_____ A   From there, the young doctor moved to Paris to study under Pierre Budin the problems of prematurely born babies.

_____ B   Toward the end of his career, Martin A. Couney could boast that out of 8,000 premature babies placed under his care, 6,500 had survived.

_____ C   Couney finally stopped traveling and found a permanent home for his combination side show and hospital on Coney Island in 1903.

__1__ D   Martin Couney was born either in Alsace or Breslau in 1870.

_____ E   For the next forty years on that rambunctious, dirty, noisy stretch of beach, Couney ran an elegant little clinic which offered the best,

most specialized treatment for premature babies in America at that
time.

_____ F   At Budin's request, Couney supervised a display of premature
babies in incubators at the 1896 World Fair in Berlin.

_____ G   After the turn of the century, Couney traveled with his show to the
Pan-American Exposition in Buffalo, New York and was received
enthusiastically by audiences who had paid a quarter each to see his
tiny patients.

_____ H   In the summer of 1898, the young doctor appeared at the Trans-
Mississippi Exposition in Omaha, Nebraska with another successful
showing of "preemies" in incubators.

_____ I   The "child hatchery" was a great success, and Couney found himself
with enough money to begin thinking about moving to America.

_____ J   According to one of his biographers, he completed a medical degree
in Leipzig.

Exercise R-29

Objective and Directions: see Exercise R-27.

_____ A   The mixture was allowed to ferment for twelve hours.

_____ B   Into the syrup went a quarter-pound each of sarsaparilla root,
bruised sassafras bark, and birch bark.

_____ C   The last step was to pour the root beer into sealed containers which
allowed it to build up its fizz through secondary fermentation.

_____ D   The process of making this colonial drink began with the making of
a syrup.

_____ E   After this half-day fermentation, the root beer was drawn off and
strained.

_____ F   People boiled molasses and water, approximately one and a half
gallons of molasses to five gallons of water, and then let the resulting
syrup cool for three hours.

_____ G   Finally, the brewer added a cup of yeast and enough water to fill the
fermentation vessel.

__1__ H   Traditional root beer was genuine beer, in the sense that its bubbles
rose naturally as a byproduct of yeast fermentation.

Exercise R-30

<u>Objective and Directions:</u> see Exercise R-27.

_____ **A** One case of using this type of conditioning involved a bear with a broken canine tooth.

_____ **B** This sort of operant conditioning, by no means limited to bears with toothaches, is not only a valuable addition to animal-management practices, but also a rewarding experience for staff and animals alike.

_____ **C** To spare the bear this risky and potentially even fatal procedure, the keepers trained the bear to stick its nose out through the slot in the door and allow its lip to be lifted.

_____ **D** This called for veterinary attention, since a broken tooth can get infected.

__1__ **E** Some zoo keepers have learned that operant conditioning can solve behavioral problems of zoo animals and make the animals both easier to care for and happier.

_____ **F** Once the bear was fully trained, one of the keepers could signal the bear to poke its nose out, and the vet could work on its tooth.

_____ **G** Customarily, the veterinarian would have had to shoot the bear with a very strong tranquilizer since he would certainly not have wanted the polar bear to wake up while having its teeth examined.

_____ **H** This behavior was quickly shaped through positive-reinforcement training by rewarding the bear with raisins each time it completed the task.

Exercise R-31

<u>Objective and Directions:</u> see Exercise R-27.

_____ **A** Therefore, if you spend very much time outdoors, you are likely to be "hit" by several cosmic particles a week.

_____ **B** Finding meteorites elsewhere on earth is an extraordinarily rare experience.

_____ **C** All the same, with fall speeds of a centimeter per second and masses of a billionth of a gram, the meteorites produce imperceptible impacts.

__1__ **D** About the only place on earth where meteorites can ever be found is on the Antarctic blue-ice fields.

_____ E   Although invisible without special equipment, small cosmic particles as fine as dust are actually very common everywhere in our environment.

_____ F   Altogether only about a dozen newly fallen meteorites are found each year whether in the Antarctic or elsewhere.

_____ G   Each year more than 10,000 tons of these minute particles enter the atmosphere and fall to the surface of the earth.

_____ H   This apparent scarcity, however, applies only to those extraterrestrial materials large enough to be seen with the naked eye.

Exercise R-32

<u>Objective and Directions:</u> see Exercise R-27.

_____ A   At this point, Mr. Brewster called in Dr. A. J. Prime to supervise the excavation.

_____ B   Further digging revealed a large elephant-like skull and tusks.

_____ C   Once the skeleton was mounted, it was taken on a tour of New England and New York towns where it drew crowds of fascinated spectators.

__1__ D   One of the most famous mastodon skeletons in the United States is the Warren Mastodon, named after John Warren, a professor of anatomy at Harvard who bought the skeleton in 1846.

_____ E   Because the severe weather had dried up one of his ponds, Nathaniel Brewster had hired workmen to remove the peat and marl from its bottom to use as fertilizer for his fields.

_____ F   Not only was the skeleton complete, it was also only slightly stained instead of having turned black the way most bones of this type do after a certain length of time.

_____ G   The men had dug about three feet into the bog when they struck something hard.

_____ H   The discoverers were thrilled with their find and Dr. Prime immediately began his careful reconstruction of the skeleton.

_____ I   Under his direction, the workmen uncovered the beautifully preserved skeleton of a mastodon, standing as upright as when it had sunk into the muddy ground thousands of years before.

_____ J   The skeleton was discovered on a farm in Orange County, New York in 1845 during a very hot, dry summer.

Exercise R-33

<u>Objective and Directions:</u> see Exercise R-27.

_____ A   As a result, mothers are able to rejoin their herd almost immediately after giving birth

_____ B   In contrast, wild boars, from which domestic pigs developed, may weigh up to 500 pounds.

_____ C   Pigs give birth to large litters of small, relatively helpless young; mothers spend much time alone caring for their young in a nest or den; and there are no permanent social groups.

_____ D   Second, the coats of peccaries are composed entirely of large, coarse bristles.

__1__ E   Peccaries and pigs differ in many ways.

_____ F   Finally, the two groups differ with respect to litter size and social organization.

_____ G   Those of pigs vary, but in general, pigs' coats have hair as well as bristles, the latter being more scattered, shorter, and less robust than the bristles of peccaries.

_____ H   Collared peccaries are about three feet in length, stand about a foot and a half at the shoulder, and weigh about fifty pounds.

_____ I   Peccaries, on the other hand, do have permanent social groups and females bear litters of only two young, which are able to walk soon after birth.

_____ J   To begin with, the former are quite small.

Exercise R-34

<u>Objective and Directions:</u> see Exercise R-27.

_____ A   One method they used for cooking the salmon was to boil it.

_____ B   Then hot stones from a campfire were added to the water.

_____ C   This whole roasting process continues to be practiced unchanged in many parts of the Pacific Northwest even today.

_____ D   Split salmon were placed flat on roasting tongs or skewered on crossed sticks.

__1__ E   Northwest Coast Indians had approximately 9,000 years in which to perfect salmon cookery.

_____ F   Boxes and baskets were filled with water.

_____ G   One side of the fish was completely roasted, and then the sticks were turned so that the other side could be cooked.

_____ H   A simpler method was to roast the fish over a wood fire.

_____ I   After the stones caused the water to boil, in went pieces of salmon in an openwork basket.

_____ J   These tongs and sticks had sharp ends so that they could be stuck in the ground at the edge of the fire.

Exercise R-35

Objective and Directions: see Exercise R-27.

_____ A   Because of their identification marks, the dominant shrimps in a specific area engage in fewer potentially damaging fights, and the subordinate shrimps avoid fights they would probably lose.

__1__ B   Mantis shrimps, which diverged from other major groups of crustacea some 400 million years ago, have certain features that make them of interest to animal behaviorists.

_____ C   In addition to functioning as a threat, the eyespots on mantis shrimps also convey information on species identity.

_____ D   All mantis shrimps have an indentation on the inside of each raptorial claw.

_____ E   In one of their most conspicuous threat displays, these "ferocious" species lower and spread their claws, exposing the eyespots and, at the same time, rearing back their heads and extending the antennae and the antennal scales to the side.

_____ F   In the most aggressive species, this indentation is marked with a brilliantly colored "eyespot", which can be orange, vermillion, royal purple, powder blue, yellow, rose pink, or magenta, and which is used for defense.

_____ G   Such information is significant since several species of these shrimps with similar form and structure often live in the same local habitat.

_____ H   This display, used with interlopers, potential predators, and prospective mates, serves both to surprise with the show of the eyespot and to increase the apparent size of the shrimp.

Exercise R-36

<u>Objective and Directions:</u> see Exercise R-27.

_____ A   Women for instance wear full-length woolen jumpers, called chubas, over their full-length underclothing.

_____ B   Then, at the very coldest time of the year, the men often wear thick sheepskin coats while herding or doing other work in the open.

_____ C   In addition to the boots, the costumes of both the men and the women include fur-lined hats for the winter months.

_____ D   A broad cummerbund is worn to hold brightly colored aprons over the front of the skirts of the chubas and, when the weather becomes colder, a heavy piece of fabric is draped around the back of the skirt.

__1__ E   During the winter months when the temperature is low throughout the day, the Sherpas have traditionally worn heavy clothing made from yak or sheep wool.

_____ F   Women also wear several blouses: the underblouses are made of a soft cotton and the outer blouses of a coarser, heavier material.

_____ G   As the weather becomes colder, the men might add a bakhu which is a knee-length woolen coat with long sleeves that can be worn in several different ways.

_____ H   Children who are four years and older wear smaller versions of these adult costumes.

_____ I   Like the women, Sherpa men also wear several layers of clothing, including heavy woolen pants, layers of shirts, and possibly a vest and a sweater.

_____ J   Before the introduction of Western shoes, both sexes wore leather-soled boots which were well-insulated with matted wool.

Exercise R-37

TOEFL Practice: Reading Comprehension (Main Idea): Time 6 minutes.

Objective: To practice answering questions which are similar to the main idea type questions on the TOEFL.

Directions: Read the passage and then choose the <u>one</u> best answer, (A), (B), (C), or (D), to each question. Write your answer in the blank. Answer all questions following a passage on the basis of what is <u>stated</u> or <u>implied</u> in that passage.

Procrastinators are people who have a chronic habit of putting things off, usually until the last minute and sometimes until it is too late altogether. The most common reason that procrastinators themselves give for their habit, which they are usually quite willing to talk about even if not willing to change, is that they are lazy. Other typical excuses are that they are undisciplined, brilliant but disorganized, or very poor at organizing their time.

Some procrastinators, however, almost against their very nature, actually get as far as trying to do something about their problem and seek help. Recent research with such people seems to suggest that their difficulties are much more complex than the procrastinators themselves think. The general conclusions are that such people have a vulnerable sense of self-worth, are particularly fearful of failure, and deliberately put things off precisely so that they never leave themselves time to produce their best work. The reason for their delaying tactics is that, since they do everything at the last moment and under pressure, the procrastinators can retain their illusion of brilliance without ever having to put it to the test.

_____ 1 The main idea in the first paragraph is

    (A) the nature of procrastination
    (B) The undisciplined character of procrastinators
    (C) that disorganization is the procrastinator's main problem
    (D) the reasons procrastinators give for their behavior

_____ 2 the main idea in the second paragraph is

    (A) how procrastinators have an illusion of brilliance
    (B) how procrastinators seek help
    (C) research findings regarding procrastinators
    (D) that procrastinators always leave everything until the last moment

_____ 3 A suitable title for this passage might be

    (A) The Chronic Habit of Procrastination
    (B) Procrastination: Excuses and Reality
    (C) Disorganization, the True Cause of Procrastination
    (D) Procrastination: Never Do Today What You Can Put off until Tomorrow

_____ 4 With which of the following would the author be most likely to agree?

    (A) Procrastinators are usually unaware of the true causes of their predicament.

    (B) Laziness, lack of discipline, and poor organization of time are the major causes of procrastination.

    (C) One thing most procrastinators do is seek help for their problem.

    (D) A procrastinator would automatically fail any real test of his brilliance.

_____ 5 All of the following ideas appear in the passage. Which do you think the author attributes most importance to?

    (A) Some procrastinators seek help for their problem.

    (B) Procrastinators, in general, put off things deliberately so as to avoid a real test.

    (C) Procrastinators usually think that they are very bad at organizing their time.

    (D) Procrastinators sometimes put off things until it is too late.

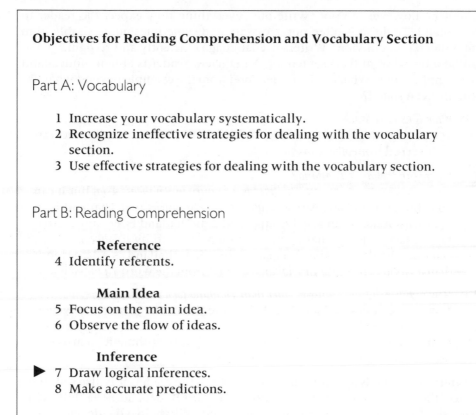

Objectives for Reading Comprehension and Vocabulary Section

Part A: Vocabulary

1 Increase your vocabulary systematically.
2 Recognize ineffective strategies for dealing with the vocabulary section.
3 Use effective strategies for dealing with the vocabulary section.

Part B: Reading Comprehension

Reference
4 Identify referents.

Main Idea
5 Focus on the main idea.
6 Observe the flow of ideas.

Inference
▶ 7 Draw logical inferences.
8 Make accurate predictions.

Restatement
9 Interpret common features.
10 Recognize restated information.

Objective 7: Draw Logical Inferences

There is no point in reading unless there is understanding. The first things that must be understood are those which are actually stated. This fact is perhaps more obvious to us when it is a question of reading in a foreign language. For example, in the sentence:

> Of the seven men taking part in the experiment two were from Chiang Mai, two from other cities in Thailand, and the remainder from neighboring Southeast Asian countries.

. . . what is actually stated is not difficult to understand:

– There were seven men taking part in the experiment.
– Two of the men were from Chiang Mai.
– Two of the men were from other cities in Thailand.
– The remainder were from neighboring Southeast Asian countries.

Writers, however, do not "write out" everything they expect the reader to understand. To do so is often not necessary and sometimes not desirable from the writer's point of view. Writers use language efficiently and recognize what can be inferred from their sentences. An efficient reader is able to understand these implications. What can be understood from the example beyond what has actually been stated?

(i) *What is Chiang Mai?*
The passage does **not** say *Chaing Mai is a city in Thailand*, but this fact can be **inferred** from *other cities in Thailand*.

(ii) *Where (and what) is Thailand?*
The passage does not say *Thailand is a country in Southeast Asia*, but it can be **inferred** from *neighboring Southeast Asian countries* that Thailand is in Southeast Asia. It can also be supposed that Thailand is a country, from (a) the fact that an equal relationship is suggested by *neighboring . . . . countries*, (b) the fact that it is suggested that Thailand is a larger unit than a city by *other cities in Thailand*, and (c) from the word *Thailand* itself.

(iii) *How many men from countries other than Thailand took part in the experiment?*
The passage does not say that there were three. The answer, however, can be inferred from *of the seven . . . . two were . . . . two from . . . . and the* **remainder** *. . . . .* It is a matter of some simple arithmetic to arrive at the correct answer.

Inference, then, is a skill which is expected of the reader. It is also a skill on which the answers to many questions in Part B depend. The following exercises focus on this aspect of reading and will help you develop your proficiency in drawing logical inferences.

Exercise R-38

Objective: To infer on the basis of logical sequence of ideas which of a number of alternative descriptions best indicates what must logically have preceded a given sentence.

Directions: Choose the item, (A), (B), (C), or (D), which best describes what came immediately before the given sentence. For each question, read the sentence marked * first. Write your answer in the blank.

Example: __C__ (A) Something about Nigeria.
(B) Something about veils.
(C) Something about purdah.
(D) Something about the absence of women in the market and streets.
* In Nigeria, purdah is represented not so much by the wearing of the veil but by the mud-brick walls surrounding every house or compound and by the absence of women in the markets and the streets.

_____ 1 (A) Something about Binta's responsibilities.
   (B) Something about Binta being typical for a girl of her age in Kano.
   (C) Something about Nigeria.
   (D) Something about life in Kano.

   * Binta's many responsibilities are typical for a girl her age in Kano, Nigeria.

_____ 2 (A) An account of why Stratford is famous.
   (B) An account of Shakespeare's works.
   (C) An account of Shakespeare's death, with reference to his birth.
   (D) An account of Shakespeare's daily routine.

   * Thus did Shakespeare begin and end his days in Stratford.

_____ 3 (A) A description of centralization at some time in the past.
   (B) A description of modern urban growth.
   (C) A description of present-day centralization.
   (D) An enumeration of the causes of urban growth.

   * Such centralization had long since vanished in the wake of urban growth.

_____ 4 (A) A description of the behavior of those without means.
   (B) An explanation of how balance-sheets work.
   (C) An account of class mobility.
   (D) A description of the consumption habits of the upper and mercantile classes.

   * But, if the upper classes consumed conspicuously and the mercantile classes with balance-sheet moderation, many in this period lacked any means at all.

_____ 5 (A) A mention of references to ornithologists.
   (B) A mention of references to something other than birds.
   (C) A mention of the reasons why ornithologists often become drowsy.
   (D) A mention of why bird references are infrequent.

   * Bird references, while less numerous, occur often enough to keep a drowsy ornithologist awake.

_____ 6 (A) Why the position is hazardous.
   (B) How to make necessary repairs.
   (C) In what circumstances staying in the car might be a good idea.
   (D) In what circumstances getting out of the car is recommended.

   * In most cases, however, it is best to get out of the car and make necessary repairs quickly so that you can move away from your hazardous position.

_____ 7 (A) Something about where the festivities are held.
   (B) Something about the festivities themselves.
   (C) Something about the men and women preparing chili.
   (D) Something about the way chili is prepared.

   * Meanwhile, at the edge of the festivities, a motley collection of
     men and women devote themselves with solemnity to the
     preparation of chili.

_____ 8 (A) A description of former, more enlightened days.
   (B) An account of the creationists' theories.
   (C) An account of the creationists' attempts to change teaching in
       the schools.
   (D) A description of the contents of the book in question.

   * In the present dark days, when impassioned creationists across
     the country are attempting to force schools to teach anti-
     evolutionary theories, a book like this is of enormous value.

_____ 9 (A) A scholarly but uninformative comment on the house.
   (B) A scholarly treatise on the creaking of doors.
   (C) An informative, academic comment on the house.
   (D) An academic account of the workings of French clocks.

   * On a less scholarly but no less informative note, the guide
     remarked that the door to the tapestry rooms creaks and that all
     the French clocks in the house work.

_____ 10 (A) The organs which have greater plasticity than the brain.
   (B) What was previously believed about the brain's relative lack of
       plasticity.
   (C) An account of the functions of the brain.
   (D) Where functions normally carried out in the hemispheres were
       previously thought to be relocated.

   * It appears, however, that the brain has greater plasticity, and
     that functions normally carried out in the hemispheres may be
     relocated elsewhere in the brain.

Exercise R-39

Objective: To determine which of a number of alternative inferences can be
drawn from a given sentence.

Directions: Choose the statements, (A), (B), (C), or (D), which can definitely
be inferred from each of the sentences below. Write your answers in the blank.
   Note: The number of inferences that can be drawn will vary from item to
item, and you may want to discuss your answers with your classmates.

Example: A, B Krill, which are the main diet of whales, have been cited as one of the world's biggest unexploited food resources.

    (A) Whales eat more krill than anything else.
    (B) The world has a number of unexploited food resources.
    (C) Whales are one of the world's biggest unexploited food resources.
    (D) The writer believes that krill constitute one of the world's biggest unexploited food resources.

_____ 1 The maps are accompanied by essays that describe what they illustrate but also go far beyond them.

    (A) It is more probable that the publication is an atlas than a collection of essays.
    (B) It is more probable that the publication is a collection of essays than an atlas.
    (C) The maps tell more than the essays.
    (D) The essays tell more than the maps.

_____ 2 Chayefsky then moved into television writing and burst on the scene with the acclaimed *Marty*; when the show was turned into a movie, it won Chayefsky his first Academy Award.

    (A) *Marty* became a television show after its success as a film.
    (B) Chayefsky won more than one Academy Award.
    (C) Chayefsky began his career as a television writer.
    (D) Chayefsky was not known as a television writer before *Marty*.

_____ 3 Buying the right tires and keeping them properly inflated can add considerable mileage to the life of your car; underinflation not only causes tires to wear out faster, but may also waste gasoline and undercut performance.

    (A) Underinflating tires always shortens their lives.
    (B) Underinflating tires always wastes gasoline.
    (C) There may be as many as four separate benefits from keeping tires properly inflated.
    (D) The writer assumes that the most obvious effects of underinflation are gasoline waste and inferior performance.

_____ 4 Like other assessments of the situation, Burke's predictably, and sensibly, forecasts a rise in unemployment among the young.

    (A) The writer agrees with Burke's forecast.
    (B) Burke expects overall unemployment to rise.
    (C) A number of predictions have been made with regard to the situation.
    (D) Other forecasters agree with Burke about unemployment among the young.

_____ 5 The Sahara and Arabian deserts together cover an area almost three times the size of Europe.

(A) Every European country is smaller than the Sahara or the Arabian desert.
(B) Europe is slightly less than one-third the size of the two deserts combined.
(C) Alone, either the Sahara or the Arabian desert is larger than Europe.
(D) Europe is slightly more than one-third the size of the deserts combined.

_____ 6 Apart from the obvious fact that rioters tend to come from the less well-off section of the community, there is no evidence that economic circumstances have any causal relationship with street violence.

(A) There is some evidence for relating economic circumstances to street violence.
(B) Not all the people in the community referred to are poor.
(C) There is no evidence that economic circumstances result from street violence.
(D) All rioters come from the poorer section of the community.

_____ 7 Even those qualities from genes that are easy to splice into a plant cell, such as salt-resistance, higher protein yield, and tolerance for heavy metals, may not be generally advertised in seed catalogues for years to come.

(A) There are just three qualities from genes which are easy to splice into a plant cell.
(B) Scientists are already capable of splicing certain qualities from genes into a plant cell.
(C) There are at least three qualities from genes which can be spliced into a plant cell.
(D) It will probably be a long time before qualities from genes, other than those mentioned, will be generally advertised in seed catalogues.

_____ 8 Very occasionally a neutrino will collide with a neutron in a chloride nucleus, thus turning it into a proton and simultaneously converting the chlorine atom into radioactive argon.

(A) Neutrinos are rare.
(B) Collisions between neutrinos and neutrons in chloride nuclei are rare.
(C) Such collisions always result in the formation of protons.
(D) Chlorine atoms are commonly transformed into argon.

_____ 9 In this work the author takes on an analytical task which his style of writing appears less well adapted to than it was to the narrative theme of his earlier book.

(A) The author appears to be capable of adapting his writing style to his subject.
(B) The author writes about different kinds of subjects.
(C) The author has written two books in total.
(D) The author is a better analyst than story-teller.

_____ 10 With the cadmium ban only months away, the largest chemical corporation in Sweden has already been experimenting with tin as a stabilizer in plastics, with results that are promising but, so far, inconclusive.

(A) A Swedish company was the first to experiment with cadmium as a stabilizer in plastics.
(B) Cadmium has been successfully used as a stabilizer in plastics.
(C) The experiments with tin as a stabilizer are continuing.
(D) The largest existing chemical company is in Sweden.

Exercise R-40

Objective: To determine which of a number of alternative inferences can be drawn from a given passage.

Directions: Choose the statements, (A), (B), (C), or (D), which can definitely be inferred from the given passage. Write your answers in the blank.

Note: The number of inferences that can be drawn will vary from item to item, and you may want to discuss your answers with your classmates.

Example: _C,D_ Families in which there are a mother and a father working almost always have a higher income than families with only a mother working. The reason is that women make on the average only 59 cents for every dollar men make, so that the two-career family has a household income of $1.59 for every 59 cents a single mother takes home. All other things being equal, the household income of the employed single mother is, in other words, about 37 percent of that of the working married couple.

(A) The average man makes $1.59 for every $1.00 a woman makes.
(B) Other things being equal, the household income of an employed single mother is 63 cents less than each $1.59 earned by a working married couple.
(C) Other things being equal, the household income of an employed single father is about 63 percent of that of a working married couple.
(D) Of every $1.59 earned by an average "two-career" family, the man makes $1.00.

_____ 1 In 1975, a federal court ruled that affirmative action hiring for police forces be extended to women. For every white male fired or promoted, a female would have to be hired or promoted. From 1975 on, Detroit actively recruited women into law enforcement. By the spring of 1980, 12 percent of the Detroit police force was female.

(A) There was affirmative action in police-force hiring before 1975.

(B) Before 1975, Detroit did not have women in law enforcement.

(C) In 1975, the Detroit police department changed its policy towards hiring women.

(D) In 1980, the proportion of women in the Detroit police department reflected their proportion in the population as a whole.

_____ 2 Back trouble is one of the most common causes of doctor visits in the United States and the leading cause of long-term disability and absenteeism from work. In fact, 80 percent of the populace will have a severe backache sometime during their lives. Yet almost all of this discomfort and inconvenience is avoidable.

(A) No other cause accounts for as many doctor visits in the United States as back trouble.

(B) No other cause accounts for as much absenteeism from work as back trouble.

(C) Eighty percent of all back trouble is avoidable.

(D) If everyone took the proper precautions, fewer than half of the populace would ever suffer from severe backache.

_____ 3 If you have a blowout, keep both hands on the wheel and steer straight ahead. If it is a front tire, the car will veer in the direction of the blowout. A rear tire may cause swerving from side to side. Ease off the accelerator, then touch brakes lightly. As you pull off the road, look for a level paved surface. On soft ground a tire jack will sink without raising the vehicle.

(A) In a front-tire blowout, drivers will have to turn the steering wheel in basically one direction in order to steer straight ahead.

(B) In a front-tire blowout, the direction in which the car moves indicates which tire has had a puncture.

(C) In a rear-tire blowout, the direction in which the car moves usually indicates which tire has been punctured.

(D) A car with a blowout sinks on soft ground.

_____ 4 M. F. K. Fisher, author of fourteen books, states that she does not usually like to read what she has written, but that she does like her own *A Cordial Water*. This book about folk medicine is a collection of odd, old recipes for medicines for people as well as animals. It has long been out of print, but a paperback edition is being considered.

(A) M. F. K. Fisher's books were out of print when this paragraph was written.

(B) *A Cordial Water* has not appeared in a paperback edition.

(C) Generally speaking, Fisher does not like reading.

(D) Fisher's books are about folk medicine.

_____ 5 Perhaps the biggest difference between young adults of the eighties and those of the seventies is their attitude toward parents and grandparents. According to surveys of high school seniors by a federal agency, the proportion of seniors who consider living close to parents and relatives very important has nearly doubled, rising from 8 percent in 1972 to 14 percent in 1980. Similarly, increases are displayed in another survey, in which 71 percent of the high school students said they agreed with their parents about what they should do with their lives, and 75 percent agreed with their parents' values.

(A) According to the federal agency study, most high school seniors now consider living close to parents and relatives very important.

(B) According to one of the studies mentioned, more students agree with their parents' values than with their parents' views about what they should do with their lives.

(C) The 75 percent mentioned is higher than the corresponding figure for the seventies.

(D) According to a study, 86 percent of high school seniors consider living close to parents and relatives unimportant.

_____ 6 In 1980, Canada announced strict additional limits on ownership of energy companies by foreign institutions and individuals. Since these may no longer own more than 50 percent of such companies, sources of capital for these corporations are now sharply restricted.

(A) Before 1980, foreigners were allowed to own a majority of shares in Canadian energy companies.

(B) Canada's 1980 limitations on energy-company ownership have caused some problems for these enterprises.

(C) Foreigners may not own a majority share in a Canadian company.

(D) Before 1980, there were no limitations on foreign individuals owning Canadian energy companies.

_____ 7 Young children in certain societies call their mother and their aunts by the same name, properly ignoring the differences and noticing the similarities. In all societies, when there is trouble in the family, an aunt may temporarily take the mother's role, for which children thus rescued extend lifetime thanks.

(A) According to the writer, aunts play a valuable role in all societies.

(B) There are more similarities than differences between mothers and aunts in some societies.

(C) The author approves of the practice of young children in certain societies calling the mother and aunt by the same name.

(D) Young children in all societies adopt the same practices towards their aunts.

389

_____ 8 There are presently six operators running only oar-powered trips, twelve offering both oar and motor, and four only motor trips on the Colorado River run. Motor trips range from three to eleven days; oar trips from three to twenty-two. Some longer trips include one or more side-canyon hikes and overnights away from the river.

(A) Oar trips may last longer than motor trips.
(B) Motor trips may last longer than oar trips.
(C) There are twenty-two companies operating trips of the kinds mentioned on the Colorado River run.
(D) Two-week motor trips may include side-canyon hikes.

_____ 9 From the limited perspective of today's high school and college students, the masses of people just ahead of them have clouded the future. Never has the United States had to absorb so many births as in the baby-boom years, 1946 through 1964. Some 76 million Americans born in those nineteen years are dominating the consumer market, imprinting their tastes and values on the culture, swamping the labor force, and generally overwhelming the economy.

(A) There are fewer people in American high schools today than there were a few years ago.
(B) Babies from the "baby-boom" period are 19 years old now.
(C) Between 1946 and 1964 an average of 4 million Americans were born every year.
(D) Both American culture and the American economy have been affected by the unusual number of babies born between 1946 and 1964.

_____ 10 When the cold, fastidious Mississippian rose to speak, a hush fell over the Senate Chamber. It was January 21, 1861 and Jefferson Davis and four other senators from the Deep South were there that day to announce their resignations, contending that Abraham Lincoln's election as president doomed their way of life.

(A) Jefferson Davis was a senator from Mississippi.
(B) Jefferson Davis was opposed to Abraham Lincoln.
(C) Lincoln had already been inaugurated as president on January 21, 1861.
(D) Abraham Lincoln's election doomed the way of life in the Deep South.

Exercise R-41

Objective: To infer on the basis of a logical sequence of ideas the endings of a series of paragraphs forming a single passage.

Directions: Choose the most appropriate ending, (A), (B), or (C), for each incomplete paragraph. Write your choice in the space provided.

1   Corporations are starting to reach the conclusion that desk-bound jobs constitute occupational hazards. So they are spending large sums of money on facilities to keep their employees physically and mentally healthy and productive. In ten years' time such programs will be so commonplace that people will not accept a job in companies without one.

2   Informed sources argue that this trend is not just a temporary one, and business health expert James Shepherd, of the Business Health Advisory Commission, emphasizes that "fitness programs are the wave of the future and in ten years there will be very few large companies that won't have become involved." Some major corporations have already set up elaborate fitness operations, costing millions of dollars to build and to keep up, *as a means of both recruiting employees and refurbishing their image.*

(A) so they no longer have the necessary funds to invest in advertising.
(B) as a means of both recruiting employees and refurbishing their image.
(C) however, other large companies have not seen the need for such expenditures.

3   However, this drive for business fitness involves much more than mere recruitment. Industry in this country suffers annual losses estimated at $25 billion a year as a result of employees' dying before their time, and loses billions more through diminished productivity because of ill health and disability. Indeed, it has been officially estimated that backaches alone cost industry no less than one billion dollars annually in production and the like, and $225 million more in employees' compensation. _____

(A) In addition, an increase in the number of highway accidents which cause permanent back damage to those involved has been officially reported.
(B) The cause and cure of backaches are not always easy to pinpoint, even though thousands of people are afflicted with back ailments.
(C) Such statistics have shaken large corporations into a realization that drastic measures need to be taken to get desk-bound employees out of their seats.

4   Even though there is as yet no hard evidence to show the benefits of in-house fitness programs, corporate physical fitness is becoming something of an industry in its own right. According to one member of the President's Council, more than five hundred companies across the country have fitness programs managed by fulltime directors. Even more noteworthy is national membership of the American Association of Fitness Directors in Business and Industry. When the organization was formed in 1974, there were twenty-five members. _____

(A) Today, their number exceeds 1,800.
(B) Members receive the latest information about the importance of fitness on the job.
(C) The association analyzes the results of company fitness programs for its members.

5   Corporate fitness is no longer the joke it once was. Physical fitness is being practiced by all sizes and shapes of corporate executives with the same kind of seriousness and determination they used to show only in the board room. At Chase Manhattan Bank, there is a five-month wait to join the company's cardiovascular fitness program, _____

(A) although participation in the program is restricted to Chase Manhattan employees.
(B) in spite of the fact that participants who fail to attend regularly lose their program membership.
(C) and at least a three-month wait to join the existing car pool.

6   What, though, are the benefits that may realistically be expected from all this physical effort? Several studies that have been carried out so far suggest that they are of considerable value. An early experiment begun in 1970 provided a regular exercise program for almost three hundred men aged thirty-five to fifty-five. After a year those taking part were given thorough medical examinations and asked to answer a number of questions. Over 90 percent of the regular participants reported that they felt better, _____

(A) and at least half said that they were now looking for employment elsewhere.
(B) and over half said that they had a more positive attitude toward work and had improved their performance on the job.
(C) but the experiment was discontinued because some participants reported that they were dissatisfied with the program.

7   There is no doubt that at the present time American companies that have instituted fitness programs are convinced of their benefits in terms of productivity, but, all the same, they have not been scientifically confirmed. The Business Health Advisory Commission has invited seventeen firms with fitness programs to cooperate in the development of standardized tests to judge _____

   (A) whether corporate programs relating to physical fitness, giving up smoking, losing weight, and reducing hyper-tension are worthwhile.
   (B) what type of employee is best suited for a particular job.
   (C) whether or not the company's rules and regulations are fair to workers at every level in the corporation.

8   All the same, even if its value cannot be proved scientifically, the fitness movement is not likely to run out of steam in the foreseeable future. Some experts are of the opinion that physical fitness could well become a required condition of employment. In the future, it is probable that employees whose ambition it is to move up the corporate ladder _____

   (A) may have to present a detailed plan of their picture of the corporation for at least five years.
   (B) may have to proceed one step at a time.
   (C) may have to show their superiors that they are not only mentally but also physically fit.

9   A further future development may involve companies' checking out the physical health of prospective employees before hiring them. Legal problems could result if this were interpreted as discriminatory, but with companies' paying for so much of their employees' health-care costs, _____

   (A) many of them consider that they have a right to be concerned, even to the extent of altering an employee's life style.
   (B) employees will have to accept lower salaries.
   (C) they assume that an employee will be loyal, possibly working for only one company in his lifetime.

10   It will not be surprising to most people to hear that employers have been having more of a say in the lives of their workers. In the field of health care, for example, what started out some years ago as rudimentary plans have since developed into full medical coverage for the worker and his whole family. Dental and optometric plans are now being included. And along with physical fitness comes the other new corporate trend: employee assistance programs for persons fighting personal problems such as

alcoholism, unhappy marriages, or overeating. Under these arrangements, employees are offered professional counseling services at company expense.

(A) Few employees need or take advantage of these services.
(B) Counselors must be highly qualified experts in their particular fields.
(C) Millions of workers in the private and public sectors are now eligible for these benefits.

Exercise R-42

Objective: To determine which of a number of alternative inferences can be drawn from a given paragraph.

Directions: Use the text in Exercise R-41. Choose the statement, (A), (B), or (C), that can be inferred about each paragraph. Write your answer in the blank.

__A__ 1 According to the information in paragraph 1, it can be inferred that

(A) companies believe that money invested in their employees' well-being will pay off in employee productivity.
(B) corporations are doing away with desks and swivel chairs and replacing them with luxurious, modern office furnishings.
(C) in the next decade, people will agree to work only for those companies which have eliminated occupational hazards.

_____ 2 According to the information in paragraph 2, it can be inferred that

(A) the image of a corporation is built around its maintenance of its operating equipment.
(B) corporations invest large amounts of money every year to stay active in the Fortune 500 group.
(C) a major reason for a company to invest in expensive fitness operations is that they are helpful in attracting employees.

_____ 3 According to the information in paragraph 3, it can be inferred that

(A) backaches are the most serious type of corporate disability.
(B) company executives are battling with office employees over wages and benefits.
(C) if an employee dies at age fifty, the company will lose money.

_____ 4 According to the information in paragraph 4, it can be inferred that

(A) eventually, fitness programs will be large enough to become independent companies separate from the original corporation.
(B) promising career options for young people are those in the health and physical fitness areas.
(C) the government is now encouraging all corporations to join the American Association of Fitness Directors in Business and Industry.

_____ 5   According to the information in paragraph 5, it can be inferred that

    (A) executives at Chase Manhattan Bank trust that the cardiovascular fitness program is beneficial to them.

    (B) having a good time is one of the chief motives behind executives' attending fitness programs regularly.

    (C) to join a fitness program, participants must be within a certain height and weight range.

_____ 6   According to the information in paragraph 6, it can be inferred that

    (A) fewer than half the workers who began the experiment in 1970 dropped out of the program after a year.

    (B) regular exercise can make workers happier on the job.

    (C) almost 10 percent of the workers studied preferred to organize their own fitness program.

_____ 7   According to the information in paragraph 7, it can be inferred that

    (A) a group of seventeen corporations is developing a set of exercise apparatus that can be used by any company wishing to begin a fitness program.

    (B) companies are promoting employees who are physically fit, those who stop smoking, and those who get their weight down.

    (C) companies install fitness programs because they believe that the effects of such programs on employees will positively affect profits.

_____ 8   According to the information in paragraph 8, it can be inferred that

    (A) most corporations will build their fitness operations as soon as statistics prove that such programs are valuable.

    (B) in the future, a person who is 50 pounds overweight will be an unlikely candidate for promotion.

    (C) future corporate executives will be required to study physical fitness as well as business.

_____ 9   According to the information in paragraph 9, it can be inferred that

    (A) companies may someday prescribe their employees' eating and drinking habits.

    (B) new employees will have to begin at the bottom of the corporate ladder and work their way up.

    (C) prospective employees will be required to be interviewed by the company's lawyers.

_____ 10   According to the information in paragraph 10, it can be inferred that

    (A) companies will soon have private, in-house dental and optometric clinics for their workers and their families.

    (B) many employers are very angry about the high proportion of employees who allow personal problems to interfere with their work.

    (C) current trends indicate that if a father needs help in dealing with his teenage son, he may get that help from his employer.

Objectives for Reading Comprehension and Vocabulary Section

Part A: Vocabulary

1 Increase your vocabulary systematically.
2 Recognize ineffective strategies for dealing with the vocabulary section.
3 Use effective strategies for dealing with the vocabulary section.

Part B: Reading Comprehension

Reference
4 Identify referents.

Main Idea
5 Focus on the main idea.
6 Observe the flow of ideas.

Inference
7 Draw logical inferences.
▶ 8 Make accurate predictions.

Restatement
9 Interpret common features.
10 Recognize restated information.

Objective 8: Make Accurate Predictions

In addition to being able to "read between the lines," an efficient reader is able to predict the general drift of what will come next in a passage. The ability to make accurate predictions is a type of inferential skill. Predictions can be made by correctly interpreting the indications a writer gives. The writer may give such indications through his choice of both function words and content words. For example, the following might be the start of a sentence:

Though progress on the subway has not actually stopped. . . .

If the sentence is part of an article about *the subway*, the efficient reader knows that something is wrong with progress on the subway. He also knows from the words *not actually stopped* that progress on the subway has **almost** stopped, and he knows these things **before** he reads the next part of the sentence.

This ability to predict puts the reader in a better position to understand quickly any details he may find in the next part of the sentence. The next part may be, for instance:

> *. . . . strikes have severely hampered the project.*
>
> **or**
>
> *. . . . it has certainly slowed beyond expectations.*
>
> **or**
>
> *. . . . it may well do so before the month is out.*

But, it will **not** be:

> *. . . . everyone is optimistic about the project.*
>
> **or**
>
> *. . . . the project will be completed ahead of time.*
>
> **or**
>
> *. . . . the subway will soon be opened.*

On the other hand, if the passage is about transport in general in a particular city, the reader may expect:

> *. . . . work on the new freeway has been at a standstill for months.*

Prediction depends on awareness of the topic of the passage as well as attention to the clues within the individual sentences. The skill of making accurate predictions is necessary in Part B of the Reading Comprehension and Vocabulary Section not only because some questions may require you to predict what might follow a specific passage but also because the use of this skill will make you a more efficient reader. This group of exercises will give you practice in making accurate predictions.

Exercise R-43

<u>Objective:</u> To predict on the basis of logical sequence of ideas which of a number of alternative sentences will immediately follow a given sentence.

<u>Directions:</u> Choose the sentence, (A), (B), or (C), which best follows the sentence given. Write your answer in the blank.

<u>Example:</u>   **B**   Shiva, the Hindu Lord of Existence, embodies the energy and paradox of life.

> (A) Shiva is represented in temple sculpture and in fine examples of Indian painting.
> (B) Shiva is motion and calm, male and female, light and dark, everything and its opposite.
> (C) Together with Vishnu and the goddess Devi, Shiva has a great cult following among Hindus.

_____ 1 A new breed of giant land and sea vehicle is solving major problems for the energy industry.

   (A) The Titan hauler rolls on 10 tires, each 12 feet in diameter and weighing 4 tons.

   (B) Some observers believe supertechnology causes a triple crisis: loss of individuality, an assault on the environment, and exhaustion of finite resources such as oil.

   (C) "Big Muskie", the world's largest dragline excavator, removes sandstone, clay, shale, and dirt to reveal buried seams of coal.

_____ 2 For a steady, controlled pace in the release of drugs, scientists recommend implants under the skin over pills, capsules, or liquids.

   (A) Unlike swallowed or injected drugs which release an immediate high concentration which tapers off until the next dose, implants deliver the drug at regular intervals.

   (B) A new kind of pill which releases its contents by osmosis may also soon be on the market.

   (C) The manufacturers of one such unit expect approval for some uses by the Food and Drug Administration this year.

_____ 3 The first true human being we know of lived about two million years ago and is called "homo habilis", meaning "handy man".

   (A) The closest we will ever come to seeing our earliest ancestors is through paintings and sculptures created by artists who work with anthropologists.

   (B) Bipedalism was already fully developed in the earliest undisputed hominids, called "Australopithecus afarensis".

   (C) The reason for his name is simple: he appears to have been the first hominid to make and use stone tools.

_____ 4 A human baby is not a finished product.

   (A) Several studies show that early deprivation of maternal care leads, in many animals, to failure of both individual and social development.

   (B) At birth, the brain of an average seven-pound infant weighs roughly 380 grams, but by the end of the infant's first year, its brain will weigh about 825 grams.

   (C) Human mothers are equipped to give sustenance and shelter outside as well as inside the womb at least as efficiently as the marsupial mother.

_____ 5 The elaborate headgear that moose, caribou, and other members of the deer family carry with them is not just for show.

   (A) Antlers can reach seven feet in width and a weight of more than forty-five pounds.

    (B) Antlers, which are made of bone and discarded annually, are unique to deer.

    (C) Antlers are very functional tools, serving their bearers not only as weapons, but also as snow shovels in winter and as air conditioners in summer.

_____ 6 By 1990, hundreds of men and women each year will be commuting to work in space aboard a space shuttle.

    (A) Life aboard the space shuttle will require the mastery of a whole range of new skills, from star identification to food preparation.

    (B) Only about one hundred men and women traveled in space during the entire twenty-year history of manned space flight before 1980.

    (C) Astronauts begin training for their jobs by learning basics such as escape from the spacecraft and survival on land and water.

_____ 7 The Giant Panda is the only bear-like animal with a thumb.

    (A) Darwin believed that the evolution of an animal as different as the panda required millions of years.

    (B) Naturalists cannot agree on whether the Giant Panda belongs to the bear family or the raccoon family or whether it is a panda-like bear or a bear-like panda.

    (C) The mitten-shaped paw that allows a panda to peel bamboo is a good example of convergent evolution.

_____ 8 Human beings have mapped the ocean floors and charted the farthest reaches of the Milky Way.

    (A) Our solar system is located in the Milky Way which is often visible as a luminous band in the night sky.

    (B) Still largely unknown, however, are the pathways by which neurons in the human brain communicate with one another.

    (C) The ocean may provide the world's growing population with its greatest source of edible protein.

_____ 9 Valium and related drugs have recently been suspected of causing cancer or speeding the growth of existing tumors.

    (A) Approximately 42 percent of American women have used valium since it came on the market in 1963.

    (B) Cyclamate is one of the many drugs already banned because of a possible link with cancer.

    (C) A recent Canadian study showed that breast tumors in experimental rats treated with valium were about three times larger than those found in untreated rats.

_____ 10 First and foremost among America's nineteenth century composers of popular music was Stephen Foster.

(A) Another famous nineteenth century American composer was William Shakespeare Hays.

(B) In the mid 1800's, everyone sang or played Foster's music, which is still well-known because of its soothing quality and true folk air.

(C) Foster ended his days in New York's tough Bowery district, where he died in poverty, a drunkard at the age of thirty-eight.

Exercise R-44

Objective: To predict on the basis of a logical sequence of ideas which of a number of alternative descriptions best indicates what will immediately follow a given sentence.

Directions: Choose the item, (A), (B), (C), or (D), which best describes what will follow the sentence given. Write your answer in the blank.

Example: __A__ Even though most Americans are upset by the rising cost of fossil fuels, few are willing to make adjustments in their life styles to make them less necessary.

(A) A description of adjustments which might be made.

(B) An explanation of why prices of fossil fuels are rising.

(C) An explanation of what it is that Americans are upset about.

(D) An account of why fossil fuels are necessary.

_____ 1 Since the bamboo plants on which the Giant Panda in its Chinese habitat depends for survival flower only once every eighty to one hundred years, it is remarkable that the creature continues to exist.

(A) Something more about the survival of the Giant Panda.

(B) Something more about the flowering cycle of the bamboo.

(C) Something about other animals native to China.

(D) Something about the way some other species are finding it difficult to survive.

_____ 2 Although several producers have been interested in backing a movie based on Hitler's last days, the necessary documentation to make such a film has not been found.

(A) A list of the interested producers.

(B) An account of Hitler's last days.

(C) More about film-making.

(D) More about the necessary documentation.

_____ 3 The invention of the cotton gin meant more than just a way to get the green seeds off the cotton without damaging the fiber.

(A) An account of how the cotton gin worked.
(B) An account of other effects the invention gave rise to.
(C) An account of how cotton was processed before the cotton gin was invented.
(D) An account of the importance of cotton to the world economy.

_____ 4 Something happens to men and women who are accepted in the astronaut program, something beyond mere improved physical fitness and increased technical competence.

(A) An explanation of the qualities required for acceptance into the astronaut program.
(B) An explanation of why improved physical fitness and increased technical competence occur.
(C) An explanation of other ways in which those accepted change.
(D) An explanation of the significance of the astronaut program in improving physical fitness and technical competence.

_____ 5 Thirty years before, it had taken him four days to make the trip from Munich to Kaufbeuren.

(A) A description of Munich thirty years later.
(B) An explanation of the number of times he had made the trip over a thirty-year period.
(C) A description of modern Kaufbeuren.
(D) A contrast involving the time taken for the trip thirty years later.

_____ 6 The student was confused, not because of the content of the lecture, but because of the speaker's style of delivery.

(A) A description of the lecturer's way of speaking.
(B) A summary of what the speaker said.
(C) A description of the course.
(D) An explanation of why the content was confusing.

_____ 7 The study of function, rather than form, produces a different scheme.

(A) How the study of form is different from that of function.
(B) How the study of function is different from that of form.
(C) Something about the study of function.
(D) Something about the study of form.

_____ 8 So fixed was the idea of the earth's being the center of the universe for people in the Middle Ages that they were reluctant to reconsider it in light of new discoveries and theories.

(A) Something about people in the Middle Ages.
(B) Something about the nature of fixed ideas.
(C) Something about the new discoveries and theories.
(D) Something about the earth's being the center of the universe.

_____ 9   Until recently, the only way different segments of a population could come to know about each other was through direct contact.

(A) Why direct contact is significant today.
(B) The difference in the situation today.
(C) Other ways in which different segments of a population could know about each other in the past.
(D) More about different segments of the population.

_____ 10   For this auto manufactuer however, there is a lot more at stake than next year's model.

(A) What is at stake for other auto manufacturers.
(B) The characteristics of next year's model.
(C) The position of this auto manufacturer in relation to the others.
(D) What else is at stake for this auto manufacturer.

_____ 11   Even at Westlake High School, where there are fully-equipped classrooms and a competent staff, there are many students who fail to pass the college entrance exams.

(A) A explanation of the kind of equipment in the school's classrooms.
(B) More details about the staff of Westlake High School.
(C) A comparison of results at Westlake High School and those at other schools.
(D) An account of how Westlake High School students do at college.

_____ 12   Perhaps we have to think in terms of bringing down unemployment levels rather than in terms of combating inflation at all costs.

(A) The importance of combating inflation.
(B) The importance of terms.
(C) The importance of costs.
(D) The importance of bringing down unemployment levels.

_____ 13   The chairman of the company had wanted to say, in his speech to the shareholders in Chicago, that future pay increases should be kept to under 5 percent.

(A) The reasons why earlier pay increases had been above 5 percent.
(B) The reasons for keeping future pay increases under 5 percent.
(C) An account of what the chairman actually said.
(D) An explanation of why the meeting had been held in Chicago.

_____ 14   While the concept of the tourist as a pilgrim who is searching for more than pleasure might be easy to understand, the notion that tourism and pilgrimage bear more than a superficial resemblance to each other is not.

(A) The difference between tourists and pilgrims.
(B) The deeper relationship between tourists and pilgrims.
(C) The superficial resemblance between tourists and pilgrims.
(D) The pleasures of being a tourist.

_____ 15 So fixed is the equation of tourism with escape and holiday-making that we are reluctant to consider it in the same light as a pilgrimage.

(A) Considerations before beginning a pilgrimage.
(B) Suggestions for unusual vacations.
(C) Distinctions between tourism and a pilgrimage.
(D) Similarities between tourism and a pilgrimage.

_____ 16 Both sacred places and sacred people may acquire great reputations, but it is to a famous holy teacher, or guru, that most people seeking some kind of specific assurance make a pilgrimage.

(A) Why it is sacred places rather than sacred people that attract most pilgrims.
(B) Why it is sacred people rather than sacred places that attract most pilgrims.
(C) A description of a pilgrimage.
(D) Why sacred places acquire great reputations.

_____ 17 Pilgrims can be met on almost any train, bus, or mountain trail in India, yet we might not recognize them as pilgrims.

(A) Statistics on the number of pilgrims in India.
(B) Something about traveling by train or bus in India.
(C) Why the pilgrims might not be recognizable as such.
(D) Other places where pilgrims might be met.

_____ 18 Most pilgrim rest houses are open to all, regardless of class or caste, but in the larger and less remote centers there may be open discrimination, both regional and religious.

(A) More about discrimination.
(B) More about class or caste.
(C) More about the remote centers.
(D) More about most pilgrim rest houses.

_____ 19 This denial of danger cannot be put down to religious fervor alone, although that plays a part.

(A) Why religious fervor is responsible for the denial of danger.
(B) Other reasons for the denial of danger.
(C) What the dangers are.
(D) How religious fervor can be repressed.

_____ 20   Some find the sacred in the company of others; some have to be alone; but most need a temple or cathedral to mediate between the sacred and themselves.

    (A)   A description of a cathedral.
    (B)   More about the sacredness in the company of others.
    (C)   Details about those described as needing to be alone.
    (D)   Details about the situation of the majority referred to.

Exercise R-45

<u>Objective:</u> To predict on the basis of a logical sequence of ideas which of a number of alternative endings will best complete the given first part of a sentence.

<u>Directions:</u> Choose the best completion, (A), (B), (C), or (D), for each item. Write your answer in the blank.

Example: _A_   The sight of an animal and its young evokes deep feelings in many of us, yet . . . .

    (A)   we seldom respond to plants in the same way.
    (B)   plants always evoke similar feelings.
    (C)   many of us feel very moved.
    (D)   this is a quite natural response.

_____ 1   The instinct for survival means that all mothers divide nourishment and protection among their offspring in such a way as to . . . .

    (A)   ensure equal shares for all.
    (B)   provide protection and nourishment for their young.
    (C)   leave as many descendants as possible.
    (D)   counteract this instinct.

_____ 2   Each embryo will try to maximize its own success, regardless of . . . .

    (A)   its concern for other embryos.
    (B)   the advantages it has.
    (C)   aid from the parent.
    (D)   the fate of its kin.

_____ 3   Beavers have evolved a variety of techniques for coping with the difficulties and dangers of long winters. In particular . . . .

    (A)   they enjoy frolicking with their young in a carefree manner.
    (B)   other animals, such as otters, have evolved different techniques.

    (C) by constructing dams and storing food, they are able to deal with hard winter conditions.

    (D) there are other techniques required to cope with dangers in summer.

_____   4 The camel, in the past, in the present, and almost certainly in the future, will be the only means by which humans can exploit the desert. Indeed, ...

    (A) camels are now virtually extinct.

    (B) the desert is a place which human beings have always been able to exploit to the utmost.

    (C) without camels the scarce desert resources are almost completely beyond human utilization.

    (D) humans find that camels are the only means by which they can exploit the desert.

_____   5 This book is expertly written and concentrates on developing the central issues involved rather than on . . . .

    (A) focusing on other issues.

    (B) being badly written.

    (C) being written by an amateur.

    (D) dealing with irrelevant peripheral complexities.

_____   6 In fact it is simple changes that can make the nomad's life a little easier and richer; for example, improvements to existing wells would insure a better supply of clean water, whereas . . . .

    (A) complex resource projects that alter the fabric of the nomad's life are actually destructive.

    (B) there are many other equally good proposals.

    (C) there are a number of more complex improvements which can also be made.

    (D) the sinking of ambitious new wells would be much better.

_____   7 While dozens of popular authors claimed to be experts on the subject of terrorism . . . .

    (A) they were not experts on other subjects.

    (B) none had studied it in a systematic and objective way.

    (C) there were many other such authors.

    (D) some of the authors were not really very popular.

_____   8 Despite extensive searches for these most distant objects . . . .

    (A) fewer than 2,000 quasars have been found.

    (B) there may be others even farther away than quasars.

    (C) quasars are not the only objects these searches have identified.

    (D) nearly 1,900 quasars have been identified.

_____ 9 What is remarkable is not so much young Valenzuela's records themselves . . . .

    (A) as the fact that he is paid so little.

    (B) but rather the reaction of crowds to his screwball.

    (C) and the records are quite astonishing in the circumstances.

    (D) but rather the equanimity with which he has reacted to them.

_____ 10 Even crude techniques used in the 1970's . . . .

    (A) failed to reveal DNA rearrangements in malignant cells.

    (B) were less sophisticated than those subsequently developed to identify DNA rearrangements.

    (C) revealed that malignant cells have specific DNA rearrangements on some of their chromosomes.

    (D) were hardly less successful than their predecessors in revealing that malignant cells have specific DNA rearrangements in some of their chromosomes.

Exercise R-46

Objective: To predict on the basis of a logical sequence of ideas which of a number of alternative descriptions best indicates how the given first part of a sentence will be completed.

Directions: Choose the item, (A), (B), or (C), which best describes what the remainder of the sentence will be about. Write your answer in the blank.

    Example: _A_ Given John's understanding of the problem . . . .

        (A) John.

        (B) The problem.

        (C) John's understanding.

_____ 1 Even though the Prime Minister's lead in the polls has recently been cut . . . .

    (A) Something bad about the Prime Minister's election chances.

    (B) Something good about the Prime Minister's election chances.

    (C) Something good about the polls.

_____ 2 While the first group of climbers reached the summit in only three days . . . .

    (A) Something about how long it took the group to descend.

    (B) Something about the second group.

    (C) Something about what the second group was doing meanwhile.

_____ 3 In addition to fine beaches and hotels . . . .

    (A) Something further positive about the hotels.

(B) Something further about the beaches.

(C) Something else about the place where the beaches and hotels are located.

_____ 4 Not only are the beach hotels overpriced . . . .

(A) Something negative about the beaches.

(B) Something negative about the hotels.

(C) Something positive about the hotels.

_____ 5 The members of the mission were well-treated by their hosts, were allowed to visit the prisoners and, moreover, ...

(A) Something more about the members of the mission.

(B) Something more about the prisons.

(C) Something more about the hosts.

_____ 6 Freda had plenty of time to get ready for the visit to the theater. Nevertheless, ...

(A) Something about Freda's being ready on time.

(B) Something about Freda's not enjoying the theater performance.

(C) Something about Freda's being late for the theater.

_____ 7 Novelist Anthony Powell is best known for the twelve-volume saga entitled *A Dance to the Music of Time*, but . . . .

(A) Other things Powell has written.

(B) Other things about the twelve-volume saga.

(C) Other things Powell has done apart from writing.

_____ 8 Von Humboldt was a scientist, geographer, explorer, writer, in short, ...

(A) A general descriptive term for Von Humboldt.

(B) A general description of what Von Humboldt wrote.

(C) Other things Von Humboldt did.

_____ 9 Perkins, apart from his role in Hitchcock's classic thriller, *Psycho*, ...

(A) More about Hitchcock.

(B) More about Perkins.

(C) More about *Psycho*.

_____ 10 However frustrating Rubik's Cube may appear to many, ...

(A) Something about those who fail to solve the puzzle.

(B) Something about the length of time it takes most people to solve the puzzle.

(C) Something about those who can solve the puzzle very quickly.

Exercise R-47

TOEFL Practice: Reading Comprehension (Inference): Time 6 minutes.

Objective: To practice answering questions which are similar to the inference type questions on the TOEFL.

Directions: Read the passage and then choose the one best answer, (A), (B), (C), or (D), to each question. Write your answer in the blank. Answer all questions following a passage on the basis of what is stated or implied in the passage.

   Dr. Trounson has gone one step further than the "test-tube" fertilization technique, first employed successfully in 1978 and since emulated in such places as the United States, South Africa, Britain itself, and Australia, by setting up an "embryo bank" to keep a supply of frozen, fertilized eggs available indefinitely. In case the first fertilized egg failed to lead to pregnancy when transplanted back into the mother, or possibly into another woman, another of the stored eggs, which had been taken from the mother and fertilized by the father at the same time as the first, could be withdrawn from the "bank" for a second attempt.
   The pioneers of successful "test-tube" births, Steptoe and Edwards, had been the first to come up with this storage idea, but they had been forced to withdraw their plan because of the controversy it aroused. The problem in both countries was, of course, one of morality, although that should not be taken to imply that there is necessarily more morality in Great Britain than in Australia. The concern has been that the embryo bank might be exploited by the unscrupulous, or that conception might precede birth by nine or even ninety years, rather than by nine months. As happened some years ago with heart transplants, and as will doubtless happen again, the present situation as far as embryo banks are concerned appears to be that "the technology has outrun the morality."

_____ 1   The paragraph preceding this extract probably dealt with

   (A) the intended recipient
   (B) Dr. Trounson
   (C) embryo banks
   (D) Steptoe and Edwards

_____ 2   The passage implies that the first "test-tube" fertilization

   (A) occurred in the United States
   (B) was carried out by Dr. Trounson
   (C) took place in Australia
   (D) was carried out by Steptoe and Edwards

_____ 3   It can be inferred from the passage that Dr. Trounson works in

   (A) Australia
   (B) South Africa
   (C) the United States
   (D) England

_____ 4   Which of the following can **not** be inferred from the passage?

   (A) The intended recipient of a fertilized egg from the embryo bank
        is the original producer of the egg.
   (B) There are at least two types of moral issue associated with
        embryo banks.
   (C) New moral attitudes develop more quickly than new
        technology.
   (D) There are similarities in the moral dilemmas surrounding heart
        transplants and embryo banks.

_____ 5   Where did this passage most probably appear?

   (A) In a specialized periodical for doctors.
   (B) On the front page of a daily newspaper.
   (C) In a weekly news magazine with a general readership.
   (D) In a specialized periodical for moral philosophers.

Objectives for Reading Comprehension and Vocabulary Section

Part A: Vocabulary

1 Increase your vocabulary systematically.
2 Recognize ineffective strategies for dealing with the vocabulary section.
3 Use effective strategies for dealing with the vocabulary section.

Part B: Reading Comprehension

Reference
4 Identify referents.

Main Idea
5 Focus on the main idea.
6 Observe the flow of ideas.

Inference
7 Draw logical inferences.
8 Make accurate predictions.

Restatement
▶ 9 Interpret common features.
10 Recognize restated information.

Objective 9: Interpret Common Features

Almost invariably, the last few questions of the Reading Comprehension and Vocabulary Section of the TOEFL ask you to choose which of four possibilities best restates the meaning of a given sentence. These final items are easily identified as restatement questions. In addition, however, a number of the questions about the reading passages involve recognizing restated information even though you might not immediately realize they are restatement questions. Whether the restatement requirement is overt or not, all such questions test your ability to analyze the **relationship of ideas** within single sentences.

In this section we look at the **four most common ways** in which such relationships are defined: **linkers, comparisons, time expressions, and cause and effect.**

In the TOEFL itself, questions of the types in the following exercises do **not** appear (though occasionally the vocabulary section has questions involving linkers). However, these exercises can familiarize you with the elements which are often crucial to your decisions on items involving restatement, whether overt or not.

Exercise R-48

Objective: To recognize the logical connecting link between two parts of a sentence.

Directions: In the blank, write the answer, (A), (B), (C), or (D), offering the best link in the sentence.

Example: __C__ The icy conditions made road travel dangerous so
- - - - - - - going by car we took the subway.

    (A) therefore   (C) instead of
    (B) as well as   (D) in spite of

_____ 1   - - - - - - - the many hardships they had to face, the balloonists managed to reach their destination.

    (A) Despite   (C) In accordance with
    (B) Because of   (D) In addition to

_____ 2   The candidate has complied with all the requirements set by the university; this institution, - - - - - - -, awards her the degree of Master of Arts.

    (A) moreover   (C) therefore
    (B) however   (D) nevertheless

_____ 3   At first glance the idea appears to be attractive; - - - - - - - there are a lot of details to be cleared up.

    (A) and   (C) furthermore,
    (B) however,   (D) in addition,

_____ 4   The problem is that, - - - - - - - children who are given cow's milk from birth benefit greatly from it, those who have never drunk it by a certain age are not able to tolerate it.

    (A) because   (C) whereas
    (B) in view of the fact that   (D) since

_____ 5   It is true that other Europeans visited the new world before the fifteenth century, - - - - - - - Columbus is rightly credited with its discovery because of the ultimate consequences of his voyages.

    (A) so   (C) but
    (B) therefore,   (D) and

411

_____ 6 - - - - - - - it must be admitted that the NASA space program has been extremely costly, there has been a considerable spin-off in terms of new commercially viable applications of space technology.

    (A) Because   (C) In addition,

    (B) Since   (D) Although

_____ 7 - - - - - - - the extraordinarily good results, it was decided to try the same approach next year.

    (A) In spite of   (C) However

    (B) In view of   (D) Despite

_____ 8 - - - - - - - no mutually acceptable agenda could be arrived at, the talks were eventually called off.

    (A) Because   (C) So

    (B) Although   (D) Instead

_____ 9 Sleep researchers have been looking for over a decade for a specific enzyme that needs to be restored at night following daily depletion, - - - - - - - it is surprising that no signs of such a substance have been encountered, if one actually exists.

    (A) so   (C) moreover

    (B) but   (D) in addition

_____ 10 The evidence for the connection includes the fact that the narwahl's tusk bears a striking resemblance to the unicorn's mythical horn and - - - - - - - the fact that northern European fishermen sold narwahl tusks reputed to have magical properties to apothecaries in the fifteenth century.

    (A) in view of   (C) therefore,

    (B) thus   (D) in addition

Exercise R-49

Objective: To recognize logical sentence completions on the basis of the relationship between sentence openings and linking words.

Directions: In the blank, write the answer, (A), (B), (C), or (D), offering the best completion for the sentence.

Example: _D_ We all thought the performance was wonderful, although

        (A) it really was wonderful.

        (B) the pianist himself appeared delighted with it.

        (C) no one disagreed with our opinion.

        (D) the pianist appeared rather nervous at first.

_____ 1 The links in the chain, instead of being amino acids, are a type of chemical called nucleic acids (or DNA). There are twenty amino acids, whereas

(A) there are twenty nucleic acids.
(B) these are combined into "amino-acid words".
(C) these same amino acids are used throughout nature.
(D) there are only four kinds of DNA.

_____ 2 The project faced a whole series of difficulties, ranging from inadequate funding to unsuitable working premises. Regardless of these problems,

(A) the organizers decided to abandon their plan.
(B) the organizers realized they were very important.
(C) the organizers decided to go on with its implementation.
(D) the organizers solved them.

_____ 3 The project faced a whole series of difficulties, ranging from inadequate funding to unsuitable working premises. Yet, despite all of this,

(A) the organizers decided to abandon their plan.
(B) it proved to be a great success.
(C) it was a failure.
(D) the difficulties proved impossible to overcome.

_____ 4 It is important that this venture be adequately capitalized and that strict accounting procedures be applied. Otherwise,

(A) its success will be assured.
(B) there is little hope that it will succeed.
(C) there are a number of further measures which should be taken.
(D) nothing will go wrong.

_____ 5 It is important that this venture be adequately capitalized and that strict accounting procedures be applied from the beginning. Then

(A) its success will be assured.
(B) there is little hope that it will succeed.
(C) a number of other difficulties will arise.
(D) it will be too late.

_____ 6 Swimmers are advised that they should observe all safety precautions, particularly when

(A) there is no lifeguard on duty.
(B) they are necessary.
(C) they are for their own safety.
(D) this advice is written in easily understood language.

413

_____ 7   Guests are advised that swimming is not allowed in the pool except when

    (A) there is no lifeguard on duty.
    (B) the pool is being repaired.
    (C) there is a lifeguard on duty.
    (D) the pool is empty.

_____ 8   The prevailing view is that man sleeps for restorative rather than adaptive reasons; nevertheless,

    (A) it is likely that those holding the restorative view will continue to dominate.
    (B) those who hold to the adaptive theory are in a minority.
    (C) this writer is a firm supporter of the restorative standpoint.
    (D) all involved agree that no proof has yet been found to support either contention.

_____ 9   The prevailing view is that man sleeps for restorative rather than adaptive reasons; moreover,

    (A) this view has retained its popularity over time and against considerable criticism.
    (B) this opinion is based largely on mere intuition rather than proof.
    (C) some people still hold to the adaptive view.
    (D) supporters of the adaptive view claim more accurate predictions regarding sleeping habits can be made with their approach.

_____ 10 Recently, publishers have looked more and more toward coming up with a few huge bestsellers from big names rather than supporting large numbers of potentially successful young writers; for all that,

    (A) many unpublished authors still devote themselves to full-time writing.
    (B) there are fewer unknown authors getting a break.
    (C) the whole nature of book publishing has recently changed.
    (D) some big-name authors are doing better than ever.

Exercise R-50

Objective: To recognize logical sentence completions on the basis of the relationship between sentence parts and linking words.

Directions: Match the sentence parts in Column A with the appropriate completions in Column B. Write the corresponding letters in the blanks provided.

Column A	Column B
(A) While the great majority of Australians live in the south-eastern part of the country	_____ 1 . . . . quite large amounts are produced there.

(B) Australia is not noted abroad for its wines; nevertheless, ...

____ 2 . . . . the country's reputation as a nation of beer-drinkers.

(C) Some excellent wines are produced in Australia despite . . . .

____ 3 . . . . in spite of its relatively small population.

(D) The large cities are mostly clustered together on the coast . . . .

_A_ 4 . . . . many of the natural resources are located elsewhere.

(E) Australia has produced a large number of world-champion sportsmen . . . .

____ 5 . . . . although this is by no means where most of the natural resources are located.

(F) The population numbers only some 13 million; . . . .

____ 6 . . . . however, this small nation has a world-wide reputation in sports.

Exercise R-51

Objective and Directions: see Exercise R-50.

Column A	Column B
(A) Because there has recently been a great influx of funds into genetic research	____ 1 . . . . the engineering difficulties in scaling up from the laboratory to large production facilities.
(B) Even though plenty of money is now available	____ 2 . . . . there are likely to be a number of industrial applications, too.
(C) Problems are posed by the number of gene combinations involved; in addition	____ 3 . . . . several recently-formed companies in the field are already valued at hundreds of millions of dollars on the New York Stock Exchange.
(D) Medicine is almost certain to benefit greatly from the new discoveries and, moreover, ...	____ 4 . . . . many new and probably surprising developments in medicine may be expected.
(E) At this stage, biological engineering on a commercial scale is a highly risky venture; for all that, ...	____ 5 . . . . there are engineering difficulties to be overcome.
(F) There are biological complexities involved, which make such research risky as a commercial venture, not counting	____ 6 . . . . enormous problems must still be overcome.

Exercise R-52

<u>Objective and Directions:</u> see Exercise R-50.

Column A	Column B
(A) Computers can now not only crunch numbers	_____ 1 . . . . it is only recently that these systems have come on the open market.
(B) The highly complex programs require extremely powerful computers	_____ 2 . . . . previously they were very skeptical about their economic feasibility.
(C) The highly complex programs required by expert systems were devised in laboratories quite some time ago, yet	_____ 3 . . . . the combination of experience and common sense the human expert brings to problems.
(D) Businessmen are now willing to finance the heavy investment required by expert systems, whereas	_____ 4 . . . . but also be taught to think along the same lines as the doctors, for example, they are helping.
(E) A number of expert systems are already available to help doctors diagnose diseases, and their advice tends to be followed without question	_____ 5 . . . . so they have only become practical propositions following recent reductions in the price of such equipment.
(F) Expert systems are highly sophisticated within a narrow range, but it is only expertise they possess, rather than	_____ 6 . . . . except when there is some overriding reason for not doing so.

Exercise R-53

<u>Objective:</u> To recognize where different words and expressions can be used in a paragraph on the basis of meaning and grammatical function.

<u>Directions:</u> Fill in each blank with a word from the box. Use each word only once.

despite	*furthermore*	*because of*	*if*
however	*unless*	*since*	*although*

___Although___ it is clear that every effort has been made to clarify the
1
test's instructions, many students still fail to understand them. So,

_____ the relative simplicity of the test itself, many students fail.
2
_____ the high failure rate, an even simpler test is being devised.
3
_____ that does not work, perhaps we should give up testing in
4
the present way altogether. _____ we find some way of testing the
5
students satisfactorily, _____, complete chaos will ensue.
6
_____ the lack of an adequate test would probably lead to loss of
7
funds. _____ we cannot afford to lose these, we must absolutely
8
ensure that the new test is effective.

Exercise R-54

Objective and Directions: see Exercise R-53.

for all that	otherwise	in addition	unless	while
so that	because	consequently	because of	nevertheless

Most people are horrified by the idea of laboratory animals being used in

experiments. _____, scientists insist that drug testing using only
1
laboratory cultures is incapable of fully replicating carcinogenic effects on

humans and that _____ live animals must be used.
2
_____ potentially very harmful substances may not be detected
3
until it is too late. The scientists point out that, _____ cell cultures
4
do reveal certain effects, other effects cannot be identified _____
5
fully-functioning animals are utilized. Therefore, they suggest that cell cultures

be used first in testing any new chemical, _____ any chemicals
6
showing carcinogenic effects at that stage need never be tested on live animals.

417

These test animals, usually inbred mice, are very remarkable beasts. They are like identical twins, and, _____, they retain specific

7
characteristics generation after generation. Strangely enough, the first scientists who tried to produce such mice were ridiculed by their colleagues _____ the prevailing view was that inbreeding would merely

8
result in poor-quality animals. _____, the pioneers

9
continued with their efforts. Now scientists would find it impossible to do research without such inbred strains, and many people are alive today only _____ the existence of these peculiar mice.

10

Exercise R-55

Objective and Directions: see Exercise R-53.

matter	in spite of	even though	the bicycle
moreover	in fact	its	so
whereas	no matter how	by contrast	it

_____ bicycling was an extremely popular sport back in the nine-

1
teenth century, many Americans these days seem to think that _____

2
was invented at about the same time as the transistor radio. They seem to imagine, _____, that _____ itself appeared fully-fledged, with

3   4
ten speeds, pneumatic tires, and all _____ other present-day

5
appurtenances, _____ the truth of the _____ is that

6   7
these features were the result of a considerable period of experimentation.

Most people who have discovered bicycling recently see it as bringing an almost revolutionary freedom from the slavery imposed by the automobile. But, _____ revolutionary the bicycle may seem today, it is not as

8
liberating as it was for women in the 1890's. In the 1970's and 1980's there must be few freedoms that American men enjoy that American women do not. In the 1890's, _____, women were severely restricted in what they

9
could do and where they could go. _____, they were usually

10

expected to remain at home. This is how they were taught to behave when they were very young, but _____ this training, many women, especially

11
young ones, rebelled against it and _____ they welcomed with

12
open arms the sport of bicycling, which, surprisingly, was considered acceptable. "To the woman, bicycling is deliverance, revolution, and salvation," wrote one enthusiast in 1895, and she had certainly never even heard of a ten-speed bike.

Exercise R-56

<u>Objective and Directions:</u> see Exercise R-53.

however	*and*	*but*	*since*
wheat production	*scientists*	*wild relatives*	*wheat's*
food	*it*	*their*	*them*

World wheat production has increased rapidly over the past few decades, but _____ will have to be raised even higher if our growing

1
population's demands for _____ are to be met. _____

2 3
there is little possibility of new croplands becoming available on a sufficient scale, _____ energy-intensive agricultural aids such as fertilizers

4
are becoming prohibitively expensive, the only solution is to increase productivity.

The problem here, _____, is that most of the genetic material in

5
cultivated wheats has already been fully exploited. Scientists have attempted to increase variability by inducing mutations, _____ so far

6
_____ efforts have met with little success. Probably the most

7
promising avenue will prove to be the incorporation of characteristics from _____ wild relatives, though much information remains to be

8
gathered about _____.

9

In any case, _____ must somehow be expanded and

10
_____ working on the problem must have the research funds they

11
need. Wheat's _____ must be tamed, and soon, if the show is to

12
go on!

419

Exercise R-57

<u>Objective and Directions:</u> see Exercise R-53.

dreams	*the dreams*	*their*	*then*	*sleep*
the sleep	*them*	*because*	*cats*	*the cats*
brain cells	*the brain cells*	*these*	*however*	*those*

Experiments with _____ have been carried out at Harvard
                          1
Medical School to find out what happens to individual brain cells during
sleep. _____ were first made sleepy, and _____ a
                2   3
microelectrode was attached to a particular cell in _____ heads.
                                                                    4

Results show that _____ the scientists were looking at
                                5
(_____ responsible for visual processing) tend to behave quite
         6
differently during _____ from in the waking state
                                    7
_____ their response to visual stimuli is much reduced.
      8
_____, the scientists were surprised to discover that
      9
_____, even when limited to the specific type they were studying,
      10
do not all behave in the same way.

_____ results are all related to "slow-wave" sleep, which is not
         11
_____ in which dreams occur. _____, or nightmares,
      12   13
produce a quite different effect on the visual-processing brain cells, more as if
the dreamer were awake. _____ of human beings have, of course,
                                    14
long been a source of interest to psychologists, and scientists have studied
some of their physical effects on eye movements. We know that human beings
have dreams and, by comparing their physical effects, scientists have shown
that animals probably have _____, too.
                                    15

Exercise R-58

<u>Objective:</u> To recognize the use of different time expressions on the basis of
meaning.

<u>Directions:</u> Choose the appropriate phrase from the box and complete each
sentence. Use each phrase only once.

on about July 4, 1976		from 1976 on
and by July 4, 1976	through 1976	throughout 1976

1 Preparations for the town's bicentennial pageant started months before the big day _**and by July 4, 1976**_ everyone was ready for the great event.

2 For three years, 1974 _____, the town's Bicentenary Committee had met at least once a week to ensure that everything would go smoothly.

3 In fact, there was a whole series of festivities, with celebrations beginning on January first and continuing _____.

4 The town itself was fifty years old _____, having been founded sometime in July 1926.

5 The celebrations attracted many visitors, and _____ the town has increased its population by at least 5 percent every year.

Exercise R-59

Objective and Directions: see Exercise R-58.

over four years		for over four years
during the four years	in the latter four years	until four years ago

1 Though later proved innocent, Rogers remained in prison _____ (January 1972 – May 1976).

2 Aaron hit 163 home runs _____ (1969–1972), an average of more than 40 per year.

3 Dwight D. Eisenhower served two terms as President of the United States (1952–1956 and 1956–1960); _____, he enjoyed even greater popularity than during his first term.

4 A number of significant changes occurred _____ of the Carter presidency (1976–1980).

5 _____ the speed limit had always been 70 m.p.h.; the change made at that time has greatly reduced the number of fatal highway accidents.

421

Exercise R-60

Objective and Directions: see Exercise R-58.

> *for the last ten years*
>
> *in the last ten years of the nineteenth century*
>
> *over the last ten years of this century*
>
> *ten years ago today*
>
> *in ten years' time*

1 They will meet again to commemorate this occasion _____.

2 They plan to meet once every year _____.

3 They have seen each other almost daily _____.

4 They saw each other almost daily _____.

5 They met for the first time _____.

Exercise R-61

Objective and Directions: see Exercise R-58.

> *until six months ago*   *six months ago*
>
> *over the coming six months*   *since six months ago*   *not until six months later*

1 The scientists completed the project _____.

2 _____ did they realize the dangers they had unleashed.

3 The scientists have worked continuously on the project _____.

4 The project will be re-examined very carefully _____.

5 _____ the project had been kept secret.

Exercise R-62

<u>Objective:</u> To recognize the use of different time expressions on the basis of meaning.

<u>Directions:</u> In the blank, write the letter, (A), (B), or (C), which corresponds to the correct answer.

A   1   Jack arrived at 3:49 and Sarah was delighted, since she had told us he would arrive - - - - - - - 3:45.

       (A)   at about
       (B)   by
       (C)   at

_____   2   Jack arrived at 3:42 and Sarah was furious, since she had told him to arrive - - - - - - - 3:45.

       (A)   about
       (B)   by
       (C)   at

_____   3   Jack arrived at 3:49 and Sarah was furious, since she had told him to arrive - - - - - - - 3:45.

       (A)   about
       (B)   by
       (C)   after

_____   4   She told him to be here at 3:30, but he never arrives - - - - - - -.

       (A)   on time
       (B)   in time
       (C)   at times

_____   5   Jack was worried we would miss the plane, but it was delayed, so we were still - - - - - - -.

       (A)   on time
       (B)   in time
       (C)   at times

_____   6   Sarah complains that Jack is always late, but Jack claims that he's only late - - - - - - -.

       (A)   on time
       (B)   in time
       (C)   at times

_____ 7 He completed the building - - - - - - -.

    (A) in three months
    (B) in three months' time
    (C) for three months

_____ 8 They worked very hard - - - - - - -.

    (A) in three months
    (B) for three months
    (C) in three months' time

_____ 9 We'll have another cup of coffee together - - - - - - -.

    (A) in three months' time
    (B) for three months
    (C) until three months ago

_____ 10 I had never seen him - - - - - - -.

    (A) for three months
    (B) until three months ago
    (C) in three months' time

Exercise R-63

<u>Objective:</u> To identify the important elements of a comparative sentence.

<u>Directions:</u> In each of the following sentences two items are being compared. In the blank, mark the sentence + if the underlined item has more of the quality on which the comparison is based, and − if it has less.

   <u>Example:</u> _+_ Jim's new apartment is less spacious than <u>his old one</u>.

_____ 1 Jets travel faster than <u>helicopters</u>.

_____ 2 The <u>Bay Bridge</u> is longer than the Golden Gate Bridge.

_____ 3 The <u>Amazon</u> is not quite as long as the Nile.

_____ 4 Andy isn't as old as <u>Elizabeth</u>.

_____ 5 <u>Martha</u> is much younger than Ruth.

_____ 6 Horses aren't nearly as tall as <u>giraffes</u>.

_____ 7 Platinum is much more expensive than <u>silver</u>.

_____ 8 Centipedes have more legs than <u>ants</u>.

_____ 9 Law school doesn't take as many years as medical school.

_____ 10 Cadillacs cost much more than Fiats.

Exercise R-64

Objectives: (i) To identify the important elements of a comparative sentence.
(ii) To reverse the comparison while keeping the meaning the same.

Directions: (i) See Exercise R-63.
(ii) **Rewrite** the sentence using the words given while keeping the meaning the same.

Example: _____ The average American eats much less fish than the average Japanese.
The average Japanese _eats much more fish than the average American._

_____ 1 High-heeled shoes are much less comfortable than sandals.

Sandals _____

_____ 2 Women's bodies don't have nearly as much muscle as men's.

Men's bodies _____

_____ 3 Soda water has fewer calories than fruit juice.

Fruit juice _____

_____ 4 Delacroix is not nearly as famous as Rembrandt.

Rembrandt _____

_____ 5 Caruso didn't sing nearly as sweetly as Gigli.

Gigli _____

_____ 6 Williams played the part less spectacularly than Polenz.

Polenz _____

_____ 7 Football offers less continuous action than soccer.

Soccer _____

_____ 8 Checkers does not require as much concentration as chess.

Chess _____

_____ 9 <u>Most Mexican state capitals</u> have far fewer Mexican inhabitants than Los Angeles.

Los Angeles _____

_____ 10 Other languages do not derive from nearly as many different roots as <u>English</u>.

English _____

Exercise R-65

<u>Objective:</u> To identify the important elements of a comparative sentence.

<u>Directions:</u> In the blank:
   (i) mark the sentence + if it favors electric cars.
   (ii) mark the sentence − if it does not favor electric cars.
   (iii) mark the sentence = if the comparison is equally balanced for both types of cars mentioned.

<u>Example:</u> _+_ Gasoline-powered cars are noisier than cars powered by electricity.

_____ 1 Although they are more likely the forerunners of tomorrow's cars, electric cars cannot compete in today's market.

_____ 2 Gasoline-powered cars, though noisier, have a far greater cruising range than the quieter electric vehicles.

_____ 3 For motorists who detest waiting in service station lines, electric cars which will recharge overnight are the better choice.

_____ 4 On-the-road service tests prove that electric vehicles are as efficient and reliable as cars powered by gasoline after long-term use.

_____ 5 Since the vital components of electric vehicles are copper, they are resistant to the types of corrosion that plague aluminum and steel parts in gasoline-powered cars.

_____ 6 The cars used by most people today produce more air pollution than electric cars.

_____ 7 Unlike gasoline-powered autos, electric cars do not require antifreeze or motor oil.

_____ 8 For city driving, electric cars both enjoy advantages and suffer from disadvantages when compared with gasoline-powered vehicles.

_____ 9 The superior design of petroleum-powered vehicles reflects the research and development of many years by top automotive experts.

_____ 10 The greatest advantage of cars powered by electricity over gasoline-powered cars is their use of energy from all sources.

Exercise R-66

Objective: To identify the cause in a sentence expressing a cause and result.

Directions: For each sentence, underline the **cause**.

Example: <u>Most of the children in the class were so tired</u> that their teacher decided to dismiss the group early.

1 Due to the sudden increase in demand, prices rose sharply.
2 Many school programs underrate children's intelligence and consequently have students spend too much time on overly simple tasks.
3 He was written about in all the papers after receiving a large advance for a book about newspaper corruption.
4 The success of the campaign for animal rights derived from an increased understanding of the nature of animal suffering by the community.
5 The ability to get along with fewer than seven or eight hours of sleep per night is usually brought about by very specific demands on the person's time.
6 Thanks to his new-found popularity, he was invited to everything going on in the city.
7 Young children engage in imitative, representational activity for no other reason than the sheer enjoyment they get from the activity itself.
8 Not so much diversification *per se*, as over-enthusiastic diversification was responsible for the company having to go outside the immediate family of the owners for the first time in search of a chief operating executive.
9 The post office's concern at its declining reputation for reliability was the cause of its introducing a new and expensive computer-originated mail system.
10 A yearning for higher soccer scores has led to the increased popularity of the indoor soccer league in the United States.
11 The relative popularity of leading network newscasters is determined by such apparently marginal features as the type of clothes they wear.
12 The very last thing she wanted to do was become a doctor precisely because both her parents had been doctors.
13 The senator was forced to retire from public office because of his family's precarious financial state and his wife's failing health.
14 Continued research into the relative mathematical abilities of boys and girls is attributable to the dissatisfaction of many women's organizations with earlier findings.
15 Not until Cable News Network proved the existence of a surprisingly large 2 to 5 a.m. television audience did a major network consider a news program in this time slot.

Exercise R-67

Objective: To identify the sentence which expresses the result.

Directions: In the blank, write the letter, (A) or (B), which corresponds to the **result** for each item.

Example: __B__   (A)   The man stopped and began to search through his pockets as if he were missing something.
(B)   A number of people nearby approached the man with offers of help.

—— 1   (A)   The professor always peers when he looks at people.
(B)   The professor has been short-sighted since childhood.

—— 2   (A)   Mabel was an inexperienced cook.
(B)   The potatoes were overcooked and the meat almost burned.

—— 3   (A)   There were heavy snowfalls in the mountains last winter.
(B)   The rivers all flooded unusually badly.

—— 4   (A)   Even though I was twenty minutes late, I caught the boat.
(B)   Because of engine trouble, the boat left half an hour late.

—— 5   (A)   The newspaper's investigative reporting has led to a considerable increase in circulation.
(B)   The newspaper has been successful at seeking advertising at higher rates.

—— 6   (A)   There is a particularly vivid, first-hand quality to the author's writing on China.
(B)   The author has spent much of his life since the Second World War in China.

—— 7   (A)   Some 75 percent of liver transplant recipients can expect to live for more than a year after the operation.
(B)   There have been a number of breakthroughs recently in research dealing with liver transplants.

—— 8   (A)   A diamond rush, not unlike the 1849 California gold rush, is taking place off the Namaqualand coast.
(B)   New life has been injected into the decaying fishing town of Port Nolloth in Namaqualand.

—— 9   (A)   Journalists have written a great deal about people who have attempted to commit suicide at Christmas time.
(B)   There is a widespread, but apparently erroneous, belief that people are more likely to commit suicide in December than in any other month.

_____ 10 (A) Theater costs soared and audiences dwindled.
(B) Inflation hit theaters and their public alike.

_____ 11 (A) Athletes, especially long-distance runners, are constantly searching for something that will reduce the weight they need to carry on their feet.
(B) Footwear companies put a great deal of money into research on the design of athletic shoes.

_____ 12 (A) This outstanding athlete cannot play on the university team this semester.
(B) This outstanding athlete failed one of his history courses.

_____ 13 (A) Conception rates for women between twenty and thirty are notably higher than those for women over thirty-five.
(B) Women are biologically programmed to have children before the age of thirty-five.

_____ 14 (A) Asbestos has been definitely linked to lung disease.
(B) Many former asbestos workers are suing their erstwhile employers.

_____ 15 (A) There is a strong belief among users of marijuana that the drug is not harmful in small amounts.
(B) Marijuana is probably the most widely-used illegal substance in the United States.

Objectives for Reading Comprehension and Vocabulary Section

Part A: Vocabulary

1 Increase your vocabulary systematically.
2 Recognize ineffective strategies for dealing with the vocabulary section.
3 Use effective strategies for dealing with the vocabulary section.

Part B: Reading Comprehension

Reference
4 Identify referents.

Main Idea
5 Focus on the main idea.
6 Observe the flow of ideas.

Inference
7 Draw logical inferences.
8 Make accurate predictions.

Restatement
9 Interpret common features.
► 10 Recognize restated information.

Objective 10: Recognize Restated Information

As we saw in Objective 9: Interpret common features, the final questions in the Reading Comprehension and Vocabulary section of the TOEFL almost invariably require you to recognize which of four possibilities best restates the meaning of a given sentence. It was also mentioned that a number of the questions following the passages in fact require you to identify restated information. This generally involves recognizing the **relationships** expressed in the original statement(s), and may well require you to make deductions or inferences from the information given (see, particularly, Objective 7: Draw logical inferences).

While Objective 9: Interpret common features, focused on some of the specific devices and specific relationships which commonly appear in the TOEFL, the following exercises focus on the use of meaning alone as a means of recognizing restatements. Their purpose is to focus your attention on the kinds of operation you will need to carry out in the TOEFL restatement-type questions, whether these are overt or not.

Exercise R-68

<u>Objective:</u> To recognize sentence-form restatements of information provided in non-sentence form.

<u>Directions:</u> Read the following announcement and then mark the statements which follow it **T** for **true** or **F** for **false**. Write your answer in the blank.

SPANISH CLASSES BEGINNING SOON!!!!
Three-week Courses

INTENSIVE	SEMI-INTENSIVE
* $150	* $90
* Monday–Friday	* Monday–Friday
* 10:30 AM–1:30 PM or 6:00 PM–9:00 PM	* 9:00 AM– 10:30 AM

Registration and Testing: August 18–21; 8:00 AM–5:00 PM
Classes begin: August 22

__F__   1 Semi-intensive classes meet only on Monday and Friday.

_____   2 Intensive classes cost less per hour than semi-intensive ones.

_____   3 The last day one can enroll for Spanish classes is August 21.

_____   4 Semi-intensive classes meet in the evening.

_____   5 Intensive classes meet twice as many hours per week as semi-intensive ones.

_____   6 Placement exams are given on four consecutive days.

_____   7 Semi-intensive classes for three weeks cost less than the intensive ones.

_____   8 Intensive classes begin earlier each morning than the semi-intensive ones.

_____   9 Semi-intensive classes begin three weeks before the intensive program.

_____ 10 A student who needs to learn Spanish quickly would be more likely to take the $150 course.

Exercise R-69

<u>Objective:</u> see Exercise R-68.

<u>Directions:</u> Refer to the announcement in Exercise R-68. For each question
 (i) In the blanks, mark the statements, (A), (B), (C), and (D), **T** for **true** or **F** for **false.**
(ii) Answer the question by writing the letter of the one false statement in the remaining blank.

_____ 1 All of the following statements are true **except**:

    _____ (A) Semi-intensive classes meet only on Monday and Friday.

    _____ (B) Intensive classes meet twice as many hours per week as semi-intensive ones.

    _____ (C) Semi-intensive classes for three weeks cost less than intensive ones.

    _____ (D) A student who needs to learn Spanish quickly would be more likely to take the $150 course.

_____ 2 All of the following statements are true **except**:

    _____ (A) Intensive classes cost less per hour than semi-intensive ones.

    _____ (B) Placement exams are given on four consecutive days.

    _____ (C) The last day one can enroll for Spanish classes is August 21.

    _____ (D) Semi-intensive classes begin three weeks before intensive ones.

_____ 3 All of the following statements are true **except**:

    _____ (A) Intensive classes meet more times per week than semi-intensive classes.

    _____ (B) The evening intensive classes are the same length as the morning ones.

    _____ (C) Only intensive classes are offered in the evening.

    _____ (D) Both types of classes meet the same number of days per week.

Exercise R-70

Objective: To recognize sentences which have the same meaning.

Directions: (i) Find three sentences with the same meaning as sentence (A) and write the numbers of those sentences in the following blanks:

    _____ _____ _____

    (ii) Find two sentences with the same meaning as sentence (B) and write the numbers of those sentences in the following blanks: _____ _____

(iii) Find one sentence with the same meaning as sentence (C) and write its number in the following blank: _____

(iv) Which sentence has no restatement? Write its number in the following blank: _____

(A) Synthetic dairy products aren't as expensive as real dairy products.
(B) Dairy producers say that synthetic products are not as wholesome as real milk products.
(C) The producers of artificial dairy products have been much more aggressive in marketing their products than real milk processors.

1 Natural milk products are reputed by dairy producers to be safer for human beings than synthetically produced products.
2 Real milk products are not as economical as artificial dairy products.
3 Processors of natural milk have not been nearly as assertive in promoting their products as producers of synthetic dairy products.
4 Imitation dairy products are cheaper than natural products.
5 According to dairy producers, man-made dairy products create greater health hazards than the real products do.
6 Synthetic dairy products have been growing faster in terms of variety than natural ones.
7 The cost of real dairy products is greater than that of imitation products.

Exercise R-71

Objective: To recognize whether or not restated information agrees with information in a passage.

Directions: The following passage provides information about places or things which an advertising agency wants to publicize.
(i) Read the passage and, in the blank, write **T** if the statement is **true** and **F** if it is **false** according to the information in the passage.
(ii) After answering the questions, **rewrite** the **false** statements to make them true according to the passage.

The Great Nockitoff Diet

For anyone who wants to shed a few pounds in a sensible but speedy manner, the Great Nockitoff Diet offers the perfect solution. It is guaranteed to work if you follow these important guidelines.

The first thing to emphasize is that, regardless of how much or how little food you eat, you must drink two quarts of water daily.

The two slices of whole wheat bread allowed each day will provide you with a sufficient amount of carbohydrates. Therefore, though vegetables, even potatoes, are recommended, these may only be eaten raw or steamed and without butter or sauces. All alcoholic beverages should be avoided, iced tea, without sugar, or soda water, with lime or lemon, being recommended as substitutes.

Two eggs are allowed per day, so long as these are boiled, poached or eaten raw, and you may have as much cottage cheese as you like, although no other cheeses are permitted. Similarly, all sauces, except for tomato catsup which has no added sugar, should be avoided. All uncooked fruits may be eaten, but a maximum amount per day is listed in Appendix B. When preparing meat, fish, or poultry, remove all fat and skin.

Like most diets, the Great Nockitoff Diet cuts out all sweets; on the other hand, it differs from most in including more than twenty-five suggestions for healthy, low-fat, tasty desserts.

According to the above information

_____ 1 the dieter's intake of water must be regulated.

_____ 2 bread may only be eaten in combination with vegetables.

_____ 3 liquor may be consumed occasionally, but should often be replaced by tea or club soda.

_____ 4 potatoes should be served with every meal.

_____ 5 there is no restriction on the amount of cottage cheese which the dieter may eat.

_____ 6 eggs in such styles as easy-over, sunny-side-up, omelettes, and eggs benedict, are not allowed.

_____ 7 tomato catsup is the first sauce which a dieter should cross off the menu.

_____ 8 meat, fish, and poultry have a place in this diet, but the dieter must not eat all parts of these foods.

_____ 9 a certain amount of raw fruit is recommended.

_____ 10 the suggested desserts are sugarless.

Exercise R-72

Objective and Directions: see Exercise R-71.

New Shopping Mall

East End Mall has fewer large department stores than most malls but, instead, features more than 200 small specialty shops, while the few remaining vacant stores will be filled as soon as the mall's owners find proprietors who fit the mall's image.

One factor which contributed to the immediate popularity of East End Mall was that all of the stores remain open from 9 a.m. until 10 p.m., Monday through Friday. This favorable start has certainly been capitalized on thanks to such features as its being the only shopping center in the area to provide free baby-sitting for children from two to ten years old and its offering restaurants to suit every pocket, with the possible exception of the highly budget-conscious. Furthermore, as far as movie entertainment is concerned, East End Mall tops Westgate Mall, which looked very impressive when it opened last year, with four separate cinemas.

Add to all this the fact that the air-conditioning system guarantees a comfortable inside temperature of 70° F no matter what the weather is like outside, and the fact that, in addition to its three beautiful fountains, the mall has a quiet garden area with comfortable benches and chairs for the weary shopper, and one might well ask whether any criticisms at all should be leveled at this exciting project.

One that is sometimes voiced is that East End Mall is located outside of the city limits. However, even this disadvantage is offset by the regular, inexpensive bus service between the mall and the central bus terminal, Monday through Saturday. A further complaint might be that, although the mall is surrounded by trees and shrubbery to merge it into the landscape, it will be several years before these effectively camouflage the main buildings and the vast parking lot.

According to the above information

_____ 1 the vacancies at East End Mall will probably be filled by large department stores.

_____ 2 the character of the mall has been established by stores which are more specialized than the usual big stores.

_____ 3 East End Mall's popularity was hard won.

_____ 4 East End Mall is one of a small group of shopping centers which provide free child-care.

_____ 5 you can have a very expensive dinner at East End Mall.

_____ 6 East End Mall has not equaled Westgate in terms of availability of movie entertainment.

_____ 7 the temperature inside the mall is not affected by climatic variations.

_____ 8 rest areas are available for shoppers inside the mall.

_____ 9 even though not centrally located, East End Mall can be easily reached by bus.

_____ 10 the owners intend to keep all trees and shrubbery surrounding the mall exactly as they are now.

Exercise R-73

Objective and Directions: see Exercise R-71.

Klondyke Park

Klondyke Park, previously not the kind of place where respectable citizens chose to congregate, provides a fine example of what concerted local efforts can achieve. A vigorous clean-up campaign some months ago by the local churches left the park clean, in good repair, and well-groomed, and recently the caretakers received a letter of commendation from the mayor, praising them for the beautiful condition in which they have maintained the park's trees, flowers, and plants of all sorts.

As a result of the pride which the entire neighborhood now takes in the park, people of all ages feel safe there and it is by no means unusual to see many busy people working or reading there, especially on weekdays. The impression of safety and calm is enhanced by the fact that the authorities have effectively prohibited the use of any motorized vehicles within the park boundaries as well as by the fact that, although not illegal, the playing of radios is firmly discouraged by many of the park's regular visitors. Even dogs are welcome when properly supervised by their owners, as most are.

The grassy areas are for picnics, strolling, and resting, while plenty of larger, open spaces are available for sports and running around. These are well-used by Scout troops which meet in the park on weekends on a regular basis. Scouts can be seen pitching tents, rope-climbing, enjoying strangely-conceived races, exercising, and so on. Furthermore, on almost any Sunday afternoon, there will be some kind of free entertainment, more often than not a band or dance group.

According to the above information

_____ 1 in the past, Klondyke Park's reputation was much more unsavory.

_____ 2 the recent rise in Klondyke Park's respectability was solely due to efforts made by the religious community.

_____ 3 the mayor believes that the park employees are worthy of praise.

_____ 4 work may be done in the park only on weekdays.

_____ 5 the outlawing of motorized vehicles and radios has enhanced the feeling of tranquility in the park.

_____ 6 unsupervised dogs cause the greatest problems in the park.

_____ 7 those interested in active sports must restrict their play to designated areas.

_____ 8 no eating is permitted inside the park's boundaries.

_____ 9 organizations such as the Boy Scouts and Girl Scouts meet regularly in a nearby park.

_____ 10 Sunday park visitors can usually choose between watching Scout troops or enjoying a music or dance group.

Exercise R-74

Objective and Directions: see Exercise R-71.

Expressing Yourself in English

Expressing Yourself in English is an interesting new textbook with some variations from the traditional in its approach. It would seem appropriate for self-study, especially when used in conjunction with the cassette, but is primarily intended for classroom use. Indeed, the text itself contains notes to the teacher, rather than these appearing in a separate teacher's guide.

Each unit contains three readings, all of which, except for those appearing in the ninth and final unit, are illustrated. The teacher's notes indicate that the teacher should refrain from answering students' questions about these readings until each student has worked through all the reading comprehension exercises without help.

Among the book's distinctive features is the fact that it contains a more extensive list of affixes than any other written for this level, while exercises are provided which allow students to be creative with the English they learn. Again, unlike most comparable texts, *Expressing Yourself in English* does not formally introduce the verb *to be* until Unit 3. One hint for teachers and students alike is that students should not expect to be successful with the examinations offered in the body of the text unless they study outside of class and memorize the dialogue that introduces each unit.

In order to keep the price low, the book is paperbound and all pictures and illustrations are in black and white. The textbook will be accompanied by a workbook to be published later this year.

According to the above information

_____ 1 the aim of *Expressing Yourself in English* is to present a more traditional approach to learning English.

_____ 2 although suitable for students who want to study alone, *Expressing Yourself in English* was written to be used in groups.

_____ 3 teacher's notes are available to anyone who buys this book.

_____ 4 the book includes more than twenty-five illustrated readings.

_____ 5 teachers are instructed not to answer any student questions about reading comprehension.

_____ 6 the authors consider knowledge of affixes important in learning English.

_____ 7 exercises are included which allow students to be original and to express their own ideas with the English they know.

_____ 8 the verb *to be* is considered unimportant in this text.

_____ 9 students should be advised that outside study on their part is essential for their successful completion of the book.

_____ 10 textbook and workbook are now available at a very reasonable price.

Exercise R-75

<u>Objective and Directions:</u> see Exercise R-71.

McGaffic College

McGaffic College is a large school which not only boasts a beautiful campus, but also is surrounded by charming rural villages. It offers advantages, such as small classes, individual counseling and private dorm rooms, which few schools of its size can match. The college offers degrees in a wide range of liberal arts fields, though no longer in oriental languages, and has a wide-ranging sports program embracing most of the usual collegiate sports, with the exception of football. In contrast to nearby Perkins College, which requires students to live off-campus, McGaffic houses all its all-male student population in dormitories on campus.

The college has a distinguished teaching faculty and, in addition to highly-qualified lecturers, has at least three artists-in-residence on campus each year. The college's strong liberal arts bias underwent a significant shift in the mid-sixties, when it invested in a new science building, instead of the new theater which many alumni, including two former state governors, would have preferred. However, the policy change seems to have paid off as all of the science departments, with the sole exception of the chemistry department, have had representatives win awards in national science competitions.

Given this success, other policy changes might be expected, but the least likely, in the eighties at least, would be for McGaffic to become coed.

According to the above information

_____ 1 McGaffic College considers itself fortunate in its location.

_____ 2 McGaffic College has many desirable features unusual for a large school.

_____ 3 many students attend McGaffic for its degree program in Chinese.

_____ 4 most exceptional in its inter-collegiate sports program is the
McGaffic College football team.

_____ 5 women students at McGaffic College are required to live in college
housing.

_____ 6 a small number of specialists in their fields may be found at McGaffic
College during any given school year.

_____ 7 many former students did not approve of the college's trend away
from liberal arts in the sixties.

_____ 8 the college has graduated at least two state politicians.

_____ 9 in light of its success in national science competitions, the chemistry
department may have benefited most from the new science building.

_____ 10 McGaffic College welcomes applications from young men and
women throughout the country.

Exercise R-76

<u>TOEFL Practice:</u> Reading Comprehension (Restatement): Time 15 minutes.

<u>Objective:</u> To practice answering questions which are similar to the restate-
ment type questions on the TOEFL.

<u>Questions 1–5</u>

<u>Directions:</u> Read the passage and then choose the <u>one</u> best answer, (A), (B),
(C), or (D), to each question. Write your answer in the blank. Answer all
questions following a passage on the basis of what is <u>stated</u> or <u>implied</u> in the
passage.

As the cost of gas and oil for home heating has gone up, many Americans
have switched from these fuels to wood for heating their homes. In 1973,
approximately 200,000 wood-burning stoves, intended for home use, were
sold in the United States; by 1979, this figure had reached one million; and by
the end of 1981, there were as many as seven million home-owned wood-
burning units in operation in the U.S.

In addition to low fuel bills, many people choose these stoves because their
initial cost is very low (the prices range from $50 kits to $5,000 top-of-the-line
models), and because new technology has made wood fires more efficient,
cleaner, and, therefore, safer than ever before.

One new technological feature of this type is the catalytic combustor which
adds about $100 to $200 to the cost of the stove, but which causes much more
complete combustion of the wood and therefore burns up more of the
pollutants left by incomplete combustion and produces more heat.

A second cost-saving innovation is a device which agitates the wood, increasing the amount of oxygen that reaches the center of the wood pile, and leading to more efficient combustion. The real advantage of this device is that it allows the owner to make use of cheap sources of wood such as dirty wood chips (an industrial by-product) that have almost no commercial value, cost as little as $20 a ton, and burn very inefficiently in furnaces without an agitator.

_____ 1   According to the passage, the number of wood-burning stoves sold for home use

(A) went up five-fold over a six-year period
(B) rose to seven million during the seventies
(C) multiplied thirty-five times between 1973 and the beginning of 1981
(D) increased by 6,800,000 over an eight-year period

_____ 2   According to the author, which of the following is **not** a factor in the recent increase in popularity of wood-burning stoves?

(A) Their greater cleanliness than in the old days
(B) The high cost of alternative heating fuels
(C) The wide range of prices
(D) The relatively cheap cost of their energy source

_____ 3   Which of the following is an example of an innovation in wood-burning stoves?

(A) Dirty wood chips
(B) The catalytic combustor
(C) $5,000 top-of-the-line models
(D) Industrial by-products

_____ 4   Which of the following statements is **not** true?

(A) Wood-burning stoves are safer and more efficient than they used to be.
(B) No factories exist for the purpose of producing dirty wood chips.
(C) Both catalytic combustors and wood agitators save money in the long run.
(D) Wood-burning stoves with catalytic combustors cost between $100 and $200.

_____ 5   The passage states that

(A) many Americans have switched from hydrocarbon-based fuels to wood because the price of the latter has risen
(B) some wood-burning stoves cost up to one hundred times more than others

440

      (C) catalytic combustors increase the amount of pollution caused by wood-burning stoves

      (D) agitators are a cheaper addition to wood-burning stoves than catalytic combustors.

Questions 6–10

Directions: For each of these questions, choose the answer that is closest in meaning to the original sentence. Note that several of the choices may be factually correct, but you should choose the one that is the closest restatement of the given sentence.

_____   6 The components, which are stored separately, are not dangerous unless brought into contact with each other.

      (A) Contact between the components is not dangerous if they are stored separately.

      (B) Unless they are dangerous, the components are stored out of contact with each other.

      (C) The components form a dangerous mixture.

      (D) Less contact with each other is dangerous for separately stored components.

_____   7 Chameleons change their color when emotionally aroused.

      (A) Color changes affect the chameleon's emotional state.

      (B) Emotional reactions effect color changes in chameleons.

      (C) A change in color arouses a chameleon's emotions.

      (D) Chameleons react emotionally to color variations.

_____   8 O. J. Simpson, though a stylist of a completely different sort, has been ranked with Jim Brown as the greatest running back of all time.

      (A) Jim Brown, not O. J. Simpson, has been rated as the top running back in the history of football.

      (B) Jim Brown and O. J. Simpson are considered the foremost running backs in all of football's history.

      (C) Because of stylistic differences, O. J. Simpson will be placed above Jim Brown as a running back in the long run.

      (D) Jim Brown has rated O. J. Simpson as the best running back that he has ever seen.

_____   9 Beth promised her mother that she would have dinner ready by the time everyone returned from the airport.

      (A) Beth is going to stay home and fix dinner.

      (B) Beth and her mother are waiting for everyone to get back from the airport.

      (C) Everyone is going to have dinner before going to meet the plane.

      (D) Beth's mother asked her to promise to be ready to go to the airport on time.

_____ 10 Many parents and educators are convinced that average students are being shortchanged in favor of gifted and handicapped students when it comes to budget allocations.

(A) The feeling of parents and educators is that average students are receiving greater budget allocations than gifted and handicapped students.

(B) According to parents and educators, middle-range pupils are not receiving a fair share of funds when compared with handicapped or gifted pupils.

(C) Parents and educators believe that middle-range students are being favored over handicapped or gifted children who need the benefit of extra budget allocations.

(D) According to parents and educators, the extra budget allocations for the gifted and the handicapped indicate that the average student is being favored in the schools.

Section 4: The Test of Written English (TWE)

Introduction

The TOEFL Writing Test differs significantly from the rest of the TOEFL in that it tests your **production** of English rather than your recognition skills. You will be asked to demonstrate certain kinds of knowledge and ability by producing an essay (suggested length 200–300 words) on a specified topic. You are encouraged to plan your essay before starting to write; space is provided for you to make notes and organize your ideas. However, since you have only **thirty minutes** for planning and writing your essay, it is very important to use the time wisely.

Criteria for evaluating your essay

1 Does it follow a **clear plan** of organization?
2 Does it **answer the question** that is asked?
3 Does it offer **effective support** for the ideas it puts forward?
4 Is there a **clear relationship** between all the **parts** and the **whole** essay?
5 Does it show your **mastery of the language**?
6 Does it show a **variety of sentence types and vocabulary**?

The essay subject you must write about will be **one** of two types:

(a) a two-sided argument where you will usually be asked to outline the two positions, support one of them and justify your decision.

(b) a graph-based question where you will usually be asked to report on the information presented while highlighting or explaining its significance.

It may be seen, then, that in Type (a) you are provided with the issue and you must provide supporting points in a reasonable and well-argued composition. In Type (b), on the other hand, you are supplied with the information and must develop an argument on this basis.

We begin this section by examining a model essay of Type (a), which is followed by a discussion of the characteristics which might make it worth imitating. Then comes an analysis of the steps you are recommended to follow in planning and executing your essay, together with recommendations relating to time constraints and regarding the appropriate exercises for consultation in the earlier parts of this book. Five typical essay topics are included for practice of the steps identified. A similar procedure is then followed for Type (b) essays. The final part contains a number of appropriate essay topics for further practice.

443

Part A: Analysis of Question Types

Type (a): A Two-sided Argument

Exercise W-1

<u>Objective:</u> To become familiar with a TOEFL-type writing question.

<u>Directions:</u> Read the writing question and answer the questions which follow it.

<u>Question:</u> A frequently recurring controversy in recent years has been that surrounding the use of nuclear energy to generate electricity. Summarize the arguments on both sides of the issue and say which side you would favor for your country. Give reasons for your answer.

1 What is the controversy (or argument) which the question asks the writer to discuss? _____

2 Besides summarizing both sides of the issue, what other two points must the writer be sure to include in her/his essay, according to the question?

    A _____

    B _____

Exercise W-2

<u>Objective:</u> To become familiar with an essay written in response to a TOEFL-type Writing Question.

<u>Directions:</u> Read the model essay on page 445 and answer the questions.

1 Are the points made in Paragraph 1 *for* or *against* using nuclear energy to produce electricity? _____

2 List the points which support the main idea in Paragraph 1.

    A _____

    B _____

    C _____

Model Essay

Proponents of using nuclear energy to produce electricity usually put forward three fundamental arguments, two of them economic and the third political. The first argument is that it is potentially cheaper to produce electricity by this means than by any other. The second economic argument is that most of the other ways of producing electricity require the use of non-renewable, and therefore finite, resources such as coal and oil. This brings us to the related political issue: countries which do not themselves possess the necessary raw materials for non-nuclear generation may have to depend excessively on unreliable sources of supply.

The most common argument against the use of nuclear energy is based on safety. The main point here is that, despite the claims made by the nuclear industry, the immediate results of a severe nuclear accident could be so devastating, and the long-term results so insidious that no degree of risk is acceptable. Three-Mile-Island in the United States and Chernobyl in the Soviet Union are recent cases which have strengthened the anti-nuclear position.

As far as my own country is concerned, I believe there are two main reasons why it should not involve itself with nuclear energy at the present time. In the first place, we have ample supplies of both oil and hydro-electric energy from which to generate electricity. Secondly, if nuclear safety cannot be guaranteed in advanced countries like the United States and the Soviet Union, it certainly cannot be guaranteed in my country. Here, nuclear energy would simply be an expensive, imported prestige project. We have many better and more urgent uses for the money.

---

3 What is the focus of Paragraph 2?

_____ A More arguments for using nuclear energy to produce electricity

_____ B Arguments against using nuclear energy to produce electricity

_____ C Examples of countries that use nuclear energy

4 List the points which support the main idea in Paragraph 2. Main idea: Nuclear energy production is not safe.

A _____

B _____

C _____

5 Paragraph 3 has five sentences. Which part of the writing question does each sentence relate to?

Sentence 1 _____

Sentence 2 _____

Sentence 3 _____

Sentence 4 _____

Sentence 5 _____

Exercise W-3

<u>Objective</u>: To analyze the model essay.

<u>Directions</u>: Read the model essay on page 445 again, and then read the following imaginary discussion about this essay between a student (S) who is preparing for the TOEFL and her/his composition teacher (T).

S(1): What is the writer's primary purpose?
T(1): To answer all parts of the question asked.

S(2): What are the parts?
T(2): In this case, three things are involved: summarizing the two sides of the "nuclear energy for electricity" issue; saying which approach the writer would favor for his or her own country; giving reasons for this choice.

S(3): Does the writer respond to all these?
T(3): Yes. Paragraph 1 summarizes the arguments for; Paragraph 2 summarizes the arguments against; Paragraph 3 offers a view in relation to the writer's own country and then offers reasons for this opinion. In short, the first two paragraphs respond to the first point; the third paragraph responds to the other two.

S(4): But surely a candidate must do more than simply answer the question?
T(4): Of course. The first essential is to make sure you address all parts of the question, but that is only the first step. The real objective is to show that you can write good expository prose in English.

S(5): How does the writer do that here?
T(5): In the first place, the structure of each paragraph is clear and easy to follow. Then the relationship of each paragraph to the whole essay is also clear, as is the relationship of the whole to the question asked.

S(6): What makes you say that the structure of each paragraph is easy to follow?
T(6): Firstly, each paragraph has a **topic sentence** (the first sentence in each case, as it happens). This topic sentence is supported, or expanded on, by sentences which respond to questions a reader might naturally ask after reading the topic sentence.

S(7): What do you mean by that?

T(7): Let's look at each of the three paragraphs.

In Paragraph 1, the topic sentence says that there are three basic arguments for nuclear energy. The reader might naturally ask: "What are they?" The rest of the paragraph states what they are.

In Paragraph 2, the topic sentence says that the most common argument relates to safety. The reader might naturally respond: "If the only thing you're going to talk about is safety, what's so special about safety?" The paragraph responds by expanding on the topic sentence and by citing some well-known examples in support of the argument.

In Paragraph 3, the topic sentence (which relates the previous discussion to the writer's own country, as required by the writing task) says there are two major reasons to oppose nuclear energy. Again, the reader might well ask: "What are they?" The writer proceeds to give them.

S(8): I notice that the topic sentences are very closely related to the supporting evidence. How does the writer do that?

T(8): The writer first decided what supporting evidence to use (or, more probably, what supporting evidence he could think of!) and *then* wrote the topic sentences. But, of course, the writer does not want to suggest that she or he could not think of anything else. Expressions such as "two of them economic, the third political" (Paragraph 1), "the most common" (Paragraph 2), "two main reasons" (Paragraph 3) all suggest that these factors have been carefully selected. They do *not* give the impression that they were all the writer could think of – even if they were!

S(9): Is there anything else to notice about the structure of the essay?

T(9): There are what we may call **transitions**. These have to do with how the writer changes from one subject to another when she or he changes paragraphs. They also show how the new topic is related to the old and to the essay as a whole. In the model essay, the first sentence in each paragraph indicates or reaffirms nuclear energy as the topic of the essay (Paragraphs 2 and 3 are obviously related to Paragraph 1). In addition, the topic sentences introduce the perspective to be adopted in each paragraph.

S(10): All right. The structure is clear. Is there anything else that's good about the essay?

T(10): Yes. The tone is appropriate. The question is a serious question; a written answer is required; the examination is clearly associated with entry to a university. In response to these considerations (which are always present in the TOEFL), the tone of the answer is formal (obviously written English and not conversational English, though with some personal involvement since the question calls for a personal opinion), with clear, logical indicators to the reader ("the first", "the second", "the main point", "firstly", "secondly") and some complexities of structure that would be out of place in spoken English. Then again, the task calls for the writer to offer an argument. The tone of quite formal argument is created by the use of such words and phrases as "it seems...", "fundamentally...", "in favor of...", "therefore...", "such as...", "this brings us to...".

447

S(11): So both the structure and the tone are important. But what about the level of English?

T(11): That's important, of course. But remember that only two of the six criteria for scoring your essay refer to the language itself. The other four relate to answering the question which is asked, and answering it in a clear and well-organized way. And remember: if you become accustomed to organizing what you want to say clearly, it will be much easier to use the English you know to the best advantage.

It is certainly not necessary for your essay to contain English as complex as this writer uses. However, if each sentence in your essay has a clear purpose, the complexity of the language will look after itself. The secret is: think clearly and use only a level of language you feel confident with.

S(12): You seem to be saying that the structure of the argument is more important than the English you use, but what if the examiner disagrees with my point of view?

T(12): There are two questions there. First, the English you use. I contend that if you plan your argument clearly, you can much better adapt your English to the level required.

Second, the question of the examiner disagreeing with your opinion. That does not matter at all, so long as your opinion is consistent with the argument you have presented. The examiner will look at the *way* you develop your argument.

S(13): Really? Then, if I can think of better arguments for one side, should I support that side in my essay even if I don't really agree with it?

T(13): Certainly. The writing task in this section has no *right* or *wrong* answers. You must simply show that you can develop your ideas clearly and logically with the best English you are capable of. "Logically", you should choose the side you can support with the best arguments.

S(14): Does the writing task always require you to choose one side or the other?

T(14): No. You might have to comment on information provided by the examiner in a chart or graph. But in those cases, too, what I have said about a clear and logically structured essay, and about tone and language, are equally true.

S(15): With all this talk about structure, topic sentences, supporting evidence, logical progression, and so on, this seems a long way from literature!

T(15): It is. All this has nothing to do with literature, and it shouldn't have! If you were asked to write "literature" you wouldn't have a thirty-minute time limit or a suggested 200–300-word length, even if you were writing in your own language.

Literature often involves breaking rules; here you are only asked to show that you can follow them.

Exercise W-4

<u>Objective</u>: To reconstruct the steps taken by the writer in planning, organizing and writing the model essay on page 445.

<u>Directions</u>: Read the eight steps which the writer followed and complete the information asked for.

Step 1: Understand the question

<u>Note</u>: Remember it is your job to answer *all* parts of this question. Do not get sidetracked and discuss a related issue. Focus on the question and decide what it asks you to do.

Complete the following breakdown of the sample question. In order to answer all the question, the writer must remember to...

A Summarize the arguments on both sides of the issue. The issue is:

_____: for and against.

B Say which side is best for her/his country.

C _____

Step 2: List supporting points for the two sides of the issue

<u>Notes</u>: The focus of the first two paragraphs is clear: one paragraph will be in favor of the issue and the other will be against it. The essay writer must make a good case for each side by giving supporting points which explain and prove the general idea of the paragraph. When working on your TOEFL essay, quickly jot down as many points as you can for the two sides. Then choose the two or three ideas for each side that you think will make a coherent, well-argued paragraph.

Complete the following list of ideas that the writer of the sample essay thought of. (Note: The writer probably thought of other ideas, but these are the points s/he chose to use.)

<u>Issue</u>: Using nuclear energy to produce electricity

For	**Against**
A Cheap	Not safe! Why?
B _____	A _____
_____	_____
C Reliable source of energy to countries without coal, gas, oil, etc.	B Nuclear accidents cause terrible long-term results
	C Nuclear accidents *do* happen. Examples:
	1 _____
	2 _____

Step 3: Decide which side of the argument you will agree with

Notes: Remember, you will not get a higher or lower score based on the side of the issue you support. But, your opinion (stated in Paragraph 3) must be consistent with the ideas you present in Paragraphs 1 and 2; therefore, you should end up on the side of the argument for which you have the strongest supporting points.

In the model essay...

A Which side did the writer end up on?

B Did the writer put her/his supporting points for this side in Paragraph 1 or 2? What reasons can you give for this?

Step 4: Write a topic sentence for the two sides of the issue (that is, for Paragraphs 1 and 2)

Notes: The purpose of the topic sentence of a paragraph is to express the main idea. Be sure that your topic sentences are complete sentences, and that they are general enough to cover the supporting points you intend to include in the paragraph.

In the model essay...

A What are the topic sentences in Paragraphs 1 and 2?

Paragraph 1 _____

Paragraph 2 _____

B Explain the relationship between the topic sentences and the supporting points. How do the topic sentences prepare the reader for what is to follow?

(For help in understanding this relationship, review pages 353–380. As you read through these exercises, notice how the topic sentence – or main idea – relates to the supporting points.)

Step 5: Write Paragraphs 1 and 2

Notes: Remember that the real objective of the writing question is to show that you can write good expository prose in English. At this stage, you must put your topic sentences and supporting points together in such a way as to meet the criteria the examiner will apply. (Review the criteria on page 443).

In the model essay...

Compare the list of supporting points under Step 2 above with the sentences in the body of Paragraphs 1 and 2. What kind of information has the writer added to the sketchy ideas s/he started with?

Notes: One of the ways you can make the relationship between the parts of your essay clear to the reader is by using reference and logical connectors. Review the exercises on Reference (pages 330–352) and the exercises which help you analyze the relationship of ideas in written English (pages 410–429). This latter section is especially helpful because it will remind you of four

450

common ways you can define relationships in your essay: linkers, comparisons, time expressions, and cause and effect.

Step 6: List reasons for your opinion, which will be the focus of Paragraph 3

In the model essay...

A Which side of the issue does the writer favor for her/his country?

_____

(Note that this becomes the topic sentence of Paragraph 3.)

B What reasons are given to justify this opinion?

1 _____

2 _____

3 _____

Step 7: Write Paragraph 3

A Again, look at the model essay on page 445 and take note of the difference between the points listed in Step 6 and the final form of the sentences in Paragraph 3.

B This is the only paragraph which contains the personal pronouns *I, my,* and *we*. This is a good rule to follow. Can you explain why?

Step 8: Check the essay

<u>Notes:</u> If you have planned your essay carefully, you should now have a well organized, well developed composition with a clear thesis and general ideas illustrated with appropriate detail. Since you are asked to write such an essay in thirty minutes, you will now have at most 3–5 minutes for a last-minute check.

If you have time, check your essay for the following:

A Have I indented to indicate where each paragraph begins?

B Have I made any mistakes in grammar or spelling that I can correct? (Review the 10-Point Checklist of Problem Areas in Section 2, pages 134–311. It will alert you to common problems to watch out for.)

C Does each sentence end with the appropriate type of punctuation?

D Have I capitalized the first word in each sentence and any other words that need to be capitalized?

E Could a reader easily put my essay in outline form to show which parts are subordinate and which are superordinate?

Practice Questions

The following TOEFL-type writing questions are for use with Exercises W-5 through W-12. Practice completing all eight exercises with one question at a time. Put all of your work for a particular writing question on a separate piece of paper so that you can see how an essay is constructed from start to finish.

QUESTION #1: It is sometimes argued that many of the world's problems would disappear if people everywhere spoke the same language. By contrast, many people regard the idea of an international language as foolish and impractical. Explain some of the arguments for each side. Say which point of view you agree with and why.

QUESTION #2: Many people believe couples who are young make the best parents because their youth gives them the right kind of abilities for dealing with children. Others argue that older parents have much more to offer. Discuss the advantages and disadvantages of young and old parents. What do you think is the ideal age for parents in most cases? Give reasons.

QUESTION #3: In recent years, scientists have discovered ways of genetically altering animals. Some people say that permitting genetic engineering will improve conditions in the world. Others want to prohibit such engineering and insist that it will cause more harm than good. Compare these two views and explain which policy you think would lead to a better future. Explain the reasons for your opinion.

QUESTION #4: City-dwellers often boast about the advantages of urban living, while the inhabitants of small towns think their way of life has more to offer. Summarize the advantages of these two life styles and say which you think more suitable for someone your age. Explain the reasons for your opinion.

QUESTION #5: Many journalists claim that they can do their jobs properly only if they have complete freedom to report on anything for which they have reliable evidence. Other people object to this unrestricted license, arguing that the press should not be permitted to make public certain types of personal as well as governmental information. Compare these two approaches to freedom of the press and explain which you think might be more appropriate in your country.

Exercise W-5

Objective: To practice identifying what you are asked to do.

Directions: Read the question and indicate the points the writer must deal with in order to answer all parts of the question.

Help: This is Step 1, *Understand the question*. If you are unsure of how to do this exercise, look back at Step 1, page 449.

Time: Remember, when you are taking the TOEFL, you will have thirty minutes to complete the section on writing. In a real test situation you should take about **2 minutes** for Step 1. At first, this will probably prove difficult, but, don't hurry. Your first objective is to understand what you are doing. However, once you understand how to do these exercises, you must aim to finish each one within the suggested time so that you are prepared to complete the TOEFL Writing Section in thirty minutes.

Exercise W-6

Objective: To practice thinking of supporting points for the two sides of the issue (the body of Paragraphs 1 and 2 will comprise these points).

Directions: In two columns, write supporting points for the two sides of the issue.

Help: Step 2, page 449.

Time: Real TOEFL time for this step is about **5 minutes.**

Exercise W-7

Objective: To practice deciding which side of the argument you will agree with.

Directions: Read your two lists of supporting points. Choose the points on each side which will make the best, most coherent argument. Finally, decide which side of the argument you will support in Paragraph 3.

Help: Step 3, page 450.

Time: Real TOEFL time for this step is about **2 minutes.**

Exercise W-8

Objective: To practice writing topic sentences that cover a list of supporting points.

Directions: Write a topic sentence for each of your two lists of supporting points.

Help: Step 4, page 450.

Time: Real TOEFL time for this step is about **3 minutes.**

Exercise W-9

Objective: To practice writing Paragraphs 1 and 2 for a TOEFL-type essay.

Directions: Write Paragraphs 1 and 2 for your essay. Write complete sentences and be careful to make the relationship between the parts of your essay clear to the reader.

Help: Step 5, page 450.

Time: Real TOEFL time for this step is about **9 minutes.**

Exercise W-10

Objective: To practice thinking of reasons which justify your opinion on the issue.

Directions: Look at the writing question again to be sure you remember any special directions for this part of the essay. (For example, sometimes you will be asked to say what *your* opinion is on an issue, but other times, you may be asked to give your opinion about what is best for someone your age, for the leaders of your country, for teenagers, for low-income families, etc.) Note two or three reasons for your opinion.

Help: Step 6, page 451.

Time: Real TOEFL time for this step is about **2 minutes.**

Exercise W-11

Objective: To practice writing the concluding paragraph for a TOEFL-type essay.

Directions: Write Paragraph 3 for your essay. Begin with your opinion and then justify it.

Help: Step 7, page 451.

Time: Real TOEFL time for this step is about **4 minutes.**

Exercise W-12

Objective: To practice checking your essay for mistakes that can be corrected quickly. (Note: This practice will also make you aware of the type of mistakes you tend to make. This awareness should help you avoid those typical mistakes as you write your essay.)

<u>Directions:</u> Proofread your essay and correct the mistakes you find.

<u>Help:</u> Step 8, page 451.

<u>Time:</u> Real TOEFL time for this step is about **3 minutes.**

After you have completed Exercises W-5 through W-12 using Question #1, do the same exercises using Question #2. Then, one by one, work on Questions #3–5.

Type (b): A Graph-based Question

Exercise W-13

<u>Objective:</u> To become familiar with the kind of information included in a TOEFL-type writing question which is based on a graph.

<u>Directions:</u> Read the writing question and answer the questions which follow it.

<u>Question:</u> Comment on the changing trends in family expenditure (use of family income) in the United States indicated by these graphs.

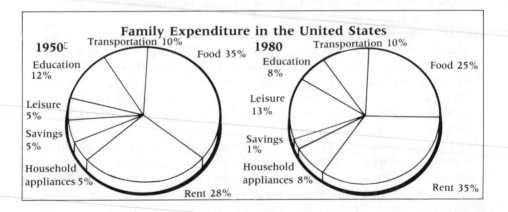

1 What does the question ask you to comment on? _____

_____

2 Which items were lower in 1980 than they were in 1950?

_____   _____   _____

3 Which items were higher in 1980 than they were in 1950?

_____   _____   _____

4 Which item remained unchanged? _____

Exercise W-14

Objective: To analyze a model essay based on a graph.

Directions: Read the model essay and the imaginary conversation between a student (S) and her/his teacher (T) which follows it.

Model Essay

Considering that the two graphs represent the average income use of families separated by a period of thirty years, it might be suggested that the changes indicated are not drastic ones. There are, of course, certain obvious swings, with the relative positions of the two major expenditures, food and housing, being reversed and it is noteworthy that only one category, transportation, has remained constant. However, in my view it is the trends in what we could call the minor categories which suggest that changes of the greatest importance to society are taking place.

Let us, nevertheless, first consider the obvious changes: those in expenditure on food and housing. Food is the first necessity for any family and it is a very encouraging sign that this necessity occupied only a quarter of family income in 1980 compared with over a third in 1950. On the other hand, housing is a necessity only slightly less essential and the proportion of income it took up rose by 25% over the period. Hopefully, this all means that people are eating more sensibly and living in better houses since the two items together continue to represent three-fifths of family income.

The difference of 3% spent on housing and food appears to be neatly offset by the increase in spending on household appliances, which might conveniently be included in expenditure on housing. If we do this, and note that spending on transportation has remained constant, we are left with only 22% unaccounted for in each case. Although that amount may seem relatively unimportant, I believe that it is here that we see the most significant trends.

Leisure expenditure shows far the greatest proportional increase of all categories. Indeed, in 1980, it was approaching a share almost three times as great as only thirty years earlier. At first sight, this might appear an excellent indication that things are improving. The factors which are very worrying, however, are education and savings. It is obvious that extra leisure expenditure is being achieved at the cost of these two vital areas.

To sum up, we may say that basic needs (food, housing, transportation) continued to take up a fairly similar proportion of income in 1980 as compared with 1950, but that expenditure on other areas in 1980 gave much greater importance to immediate satisfaction than in 1950, and much less importance to future considerations. This seems to be a very dangerous trend, for the future of a country depends to a considerable extent on our willingness to save and on our willingness to invest in the education of future generations.

S(1): This essay seems to be organized differently from the other model essay. Why is that?

T(1): Principally because the question is of a different type.

S(2): How is it different?

T(2): First of all, the other question (see page 445) gives the writer two sides of an issue, and the writer is asked to provide evidence for each side and draw a conclusion. Here, by contrast, the information is provided by the graphs, and the writer is merely asked to *comment* on it.

S(3): So in the other essay, the student's main task was to *provide evidence*, while here the main task is to **discuss the evidence** given. I understand that, but how does that affect the organization of the essays?

T(3): Well, in the other essay, the normal pattern would be: the arguments I can give for Side A (Paragraph 1); the arguments I can give for Side B (Paragraph 2); which side I prefer and why (Paragraph 3). In this essay, the normal pattern would probably be: a general trend I have noticed (Paragraph 1); commentaries on details of the information given (middle paragraphs); conclusions, referring back to Paragraph 1 and forward to some wider consideration (final paragraph).

S(4): So the key thing here is to discover some important or interesting trend?

T(4): Yes. That is, some way of reformulating the information and making more general statements from the specific facts.

S(5): What happens if I'm not accustomed to doing that kind of thing? How do I find such trends?

T(5): Almost certainly you'll be asked to compare some kind of numerical information. The important thing is to look for **contrasts** (big changes) on the one hand, and for **consistencies** (little or no change) on the other, and then adopt a **point of view** on this basis.

S(6): Does this writer do that?

T(6): She or he certainly does. She or he compares food and housing, noting their opposite trends, and then does something different from the graph by adding the two figures together. The point of view the writer adopts is that the most important changes are to be found (in this case) among the smaller categories.

S(7): Where does she or he emphasize this point of view?

T(7): As you can see, she or he introduces it in the first paragraph and then returns to it in the conclusion. However, she or he certainly makes sure that the intervening paragraphs (the body of the essay) do not contradict this point of view.

S(8): Does she or he take the right point of view, though, in this case?

T(8): Who knows? There is no *right* point of view in these questions. Another candidate might isolate different information from the same graphs and come to different conclusions.

S(9): If the conclusion itself is not important, then what is?

T(9): Several things: the way the writer relates her or his point of view to the evidence; the way she or he insures that the whole essay should appear to be balanced, reasonable and logically argued and, therefore, a **legitimate interpretation** of the information given.

S(10): What do you mean by "a legitimate interpretation"?

T(10): Well, we've already said that there is no one *correct* interpretation. If the writer offers her or his interpretation and supports it with logical and well-reasoned arguments, these arguments will make it *a* (not *the*) legitimate interpretation.

S(11): Apart from the structure of the essay, what else is good?

T(11): Many of the same things as in the other essay. The **transitions** from one paragraph to another, for example, allow the subject discussed to be changed but the connection to be made clear. For example, the word "nevertheless" at the beginning of Paragraph 2 introduces a contrast with a proposal made in Paragraph 1. The reference to housing and food in Paragraph 3 refers back to Paragraph 2, but the same sentence also introduces the new subject: household appliances. The "significant trends" mentioned at the end of Paragraph 3 looks forward to the discussion of them in Paragraph 4. The introductory "To sum up" of Paragraph 5 refers back to all the preceding paragraphs.

S(12): Anything else, apart from the transitions?

T(12): The general tone, again, is appropriate, with close attention paid to logical argument (including the transitions). Even though, here, the writer expresses her or his opinion quite emphatically, this is done within the constraints of reasoned opinion, rather than by simply insisting on a viewpoint that is supported.

S(13): What if the writer used other information than what she or he found in the graphs to support such a viewpoint?

T(13): That would be inappropriate because it would mean she or he was not addressing the question which refers to "changing trends...indicated by these graphs". Remember that the absolute, inescapable requirement is to address the question. If you observe the first two steps suggested on page 449, you will not lose sight of the question when constructing your essay.

S(14): Unlike the other essay, a lot of this essay consists of reproducing a lot of numbers. Is that desirable?

T(14): Given the topic, it is almost inevitable. The thing to notice, though, is that the numbers are frequently manipulated in some way (combining, comparing, etc.), rather than being simply *reproduced*, and also that after each set of numbers quoted, some general comment (note that word in the question) is offered. Here these comments are usually *opinions*, but they might be extrapolations of the figures or simple observations. The important thing is that they should in some (logical) way go beyond the bare information offered in the graphs.

S(15): The two types of essay seem very different.

T(15): In some ways they are. However, the differences are more a matter of detail. In principle, you can make use of all the attitudes considered in relation to the first essay. Good expository writing is what is required here, too. The different type of question may require a different organization of your ideas and their appropriate expression in English. These two things offer the key whichever type of question you get on the TOEFL.

Exercise W-15

Objective: To examine how the writer of the model essay used the information given in the question.

Directions: Answer the following questions about the graphs and the model essay based on them.

1 Look at the first paragraph. What has the writer decided to put most emphasis on in this essay?
_____ A changes in the major expenditures
_____ B changes in the minor expenditures
_____ C expenditures which remained unchanged
Why do you think the writer found this topic the best one to focus on?

2 The use of family income for food went from _____% in 1950 to _____% in 1980. The use of family income for housing went from _____% in 1950 to _____% in 1980.

In Paragraph 2, what comments has the writer made about

A food and housing in general?
B the trends in the use of family income for these two items?

3 Explain where the writer found the 3% and the 22% discussed in the third paragraph.
In what way does the writer think these percentages are significant?

4 Why does the writer focus on expenditures for leisure, education and savings in Paragraph 4?

5 What is the writer's opinion about the changes that the graphs show?
Based on Paragraph 5, what kind of advice do you think the writer of the model essay would like to give to American families about using their incomes over the coming thirty years?

Exercise W-16

Objective: To practice writing TOEFL-type essays based on graphs.

Directions: Answer the following two questions. Allow yourself thirty minutes to plan, write and check a TOEFL-type essay for each question.

Question #1: Write a report discussing the information given in the charts below on the average American's diet and what you see as the major implications.

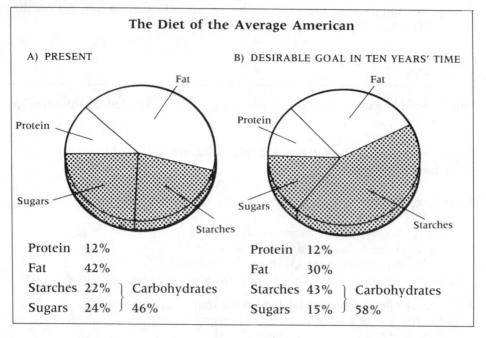

The Diet of the Average American

A) PRESENT

B) DESIRABLE GOAL IN TEN YEARS' TIME

Protein	12%		Protein	12%	
Fat	42%		Fat	30%	
Starches	22%	} Carbohydrates	Starches	43%	} Carbohydrates
Sugars	24%	} 46%	Sugars	15%	} 58%

Question #2: In the world as a whole, an average of 3.9 children are born to each woman. However, this average figure conceals wide variations, some of which are indicated on the chart below. Report on the information given, particularly in light of the contention that stabilization of world population figures would require an average of about 2.0 children per family.

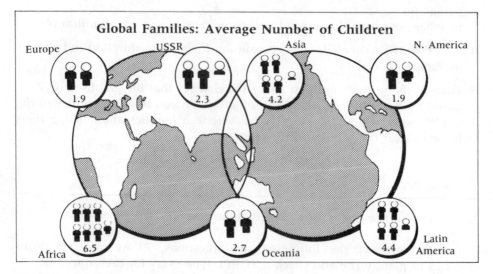

Global Families: Average Number of Children

Europe 1.9 — USSR 2.3 — Asia 4.2 — N. America 1.9

Africa 6.5 — Oceania 2.7 — Latin America 4.4

Part B: Practice Questions

For further practice, answer the following questions. Allow yourself thirty minutes to plan, write and check a TOEFL-type essay for each question.

Question #1: While some people condemn television as a negative influence on the overall mental development of children, others praise it for its contribution to children's education. Specify some of the principal arguments on either side and give your own opinion, with reasons.

Question #2: There has been considerable discussion in recent years about the role of government and the system of taxation. Some people argue that government should stay out of people's lives and should reduce taxation as far as possible. Others say that one of the responsibilities of a government is to guarantee a full life for every citizen even if this means a greater tax burden for some. Outline the arguments on each side and say which approach you think more appropriate in your country. Give reasons.

Question #3: Write an account of the trends you observe in the chart below, and suggest which nation or nations the United States might seek to emulate in this field.

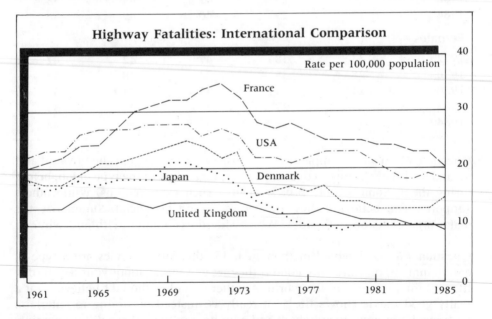

Question #4: Today's super-rich include entertainers such as rock stars, movie stars and professional athletes. Many people believe that the money these top entertainers receive is well-deserved. Others feel that their astronomical earnings are unjust and bad for the society as a whole. Discuss some of the reasons for each of the points of view, say which you agree with and give your reasons.

Question #5: Some employers hire people on the basis of their education and professional training, while others think a prospective employee's previous, related job experience is the most important qualification. Outline the arguments on both sides. Say whether you think education or experience is more important and explain why.

Question #6: Write a report discussing the results of the government's efforts to curb smoking, as evidenced in the table below.

Adult Cigarette Smoking: by Sex and Socio-economic Group

% age smoking cigarettes	Group				
	Pro-fessional	Employers & Managers	Skilled Manual & Services	Un-Skilled Manual	All Persons
Males					
1972	33	44	57	64	52
1976	25	38	51	58	46
1980	21	35	48	57	42
1982	20	29	42	49	38
1984	17	29	40	49	36
Females					
1972	33	38	47	42	42
1976	28	35	42	38	38
1980	21	33	43	41	37
1982	21	29	39	41	33
1984	15	29	37	36	32

Question #7: Today, companies often insist on checking out the physical and mental health of all prospective employees, regardless of the type of job, before hiring them. Some people protest against such examinations, while others support them, believing they are necessary and beneficial. Summarize the major arguments on both sides. Which side do you agree with and why?

Question #8: One school of thought holds that since movies are a type of entertainment, they are only good if they let you forget about your day-to-day life and the problems of the world. Another school of thought believes that a really good movie shows life as it really is; instead of aiming to entertain, such movies attempt to enlighten and educate. Compare these differing points of view, saying which type of movie you prefer and giving reasons for your preference.

Question #9: In many countries, consolidated shopping malls with everything the shopper needs under one roof are replacing the more traditional town center. Many people welcome the arrival of such malls, but others believe they have a bad effect on business as well as on the social life of the town. Summarize some of the arguments on both sides and explain which plan for stores and businesses would be best for your home town.

Question #10: In the United States, there is a well-organized, sincere group of people who defend the right of American citizens to own small arms (for example, hand guns). There is also an opposing group which is equally committed to stopping the purchase of small arms by private citizens. Discuss these positions with specific examples. Which policy would you support in your country? Why?

Section 5: Complete TOEFL Practice Tests

TOEFL Tactics for the Practice Tests and the actual TOEFL

The introduction to this book includes some advice on "TOEFL Tactics". Read through this advice again before using these TOEFL Practice Tests. Also study the following additional "TOEFL Tactics", which are related specifically to the actual TOEFL.

(i) TOEFL Tactics: Using an answer sheet

1 Mark clearly, heavily, and only in the correct place on the answer sheet. Extra marks on the answer sheet may be counted as errors if the test is machine-graded.
2 Erase carefully and completely. Again, the test-scoring machine may read any poorly-erased answers.
3 Mark only one answer for each question. Two answers to one question will be counted wrong.
4 Answer every question. Leave no blanks.
5 Raise your hand and tell the examiner immediately if you accidently mark your answers out of order. The examiner will help you.
6 Raise your hand and speak to the examiner if you think that there is something wrong with your answer sheet or with your test booklet.
7 Do not worry if you do poorly on one section of the test. Poor performance on one section can be compensated for by your performance on the other two sections.
8 Use two hands when you answer the questions. Keep your pencil hand in the correct place on your answer sheet. Use your other hand to keep your place on the questions. Do not hold your test booklet or your answer sheet in your hand. Leave both of them on your desk or table.

(ii) TOEFL Tactics: Guessing

1 Always answer all the questions.
2 Always guess when you are not sure about an answer; you will not be penalized for incorrect answers.
3 Eliminate what you know is wrong. Then, guess among the possibilities that are left.
4 Choose one guessing letter to use when you have no idea about the answer or when you do not have enough time to read the question.
5 Test your guessing ability on practice tests. Find out if your first guess or your second guess is better.
6 Do not leave questions blank even when you think you will have time to answer them later. Mark your best guess on the answer sheet and put a light dot beside the questions you want to reconsider later.

(iii) TOEFL Tactics: Avoiding suspicious behavior

1 The TOEFL office presents very clear guidelines about improper behavior at a test administration in the "TOEFL Bulletin of Information and Application Form". These guidelines clearly state the unacceptability of:

 – taking any test materials from the test room
 – trying to take the TOEFL for another person
 – helping another candidate or accepting help oneself
 – not following the instructions of the test supervisor
 – reading or working on a section of the test during time allowed for a different section
 – making marks in the test book or making notes on the answer sheet
 – bringing any books or dictionaries, notes, recording or photographic equipment into the test room
 – copying test questions or answers
 – cheating in any other way

If it is found you have cheated in any way, the TOEFL office will refuse to score your answer sheet and will not refund your test fee.

2 Most students are honest and have no intention of cheating. If you are one of these students, it is important for you to realize that certain behavior, no matter how innocently performed, is suspicious and will probably cause you to be closely watched by the TOEFL examiner.

cheating	suspicious behavior
Working on the wrong section	Opening the test booklet before receiving instructions to do so Flipping through the test booklet several times Bending over the test booklet very closely as if to conceal something from the examiner
Giving or receiving help	Stretching; leaning back; pushing chair back from desk or table Talking for any purpose at any time Looking around the room Watching the examiner Tapping foot or pencil; hand movements Vocalizations such as throat clearing
Possession of a "cheat sheet"	Bringing extra paper or books to test even if kept in pocket or purse Refusing or failing to place all personal belongings on the floor or wherever the examiner tells you

Taking test books or answer sheet   Hiding material, even playfully or
                                      absent-mindedly
                                      Asking to leave the room during the
                                      test
                                      Standing up or attempting to leave
                                      the room before being told by the
                                      examiner
                                      Failing to hand in any test material
                                      even if not asked by the examiner

3 The repercussions of cheating or attempting to cheat are very serious both for
   the individual and sometimes also for the entire group of students taking the
   test at the same time or at a different administration later in the day.

4 If you maintain a serious attitude before, during, and after the test, you will
   have a good chance of getting your best score.

Practice Test I

Section 1
Listening Comprehension

Time – 40 minutes

In this section of the test, you will have an opportunity to demonstrate your ability to understand spoken English. There are three parts to this section, with special directions for each part.

Part A

Directions: For each problem in Part A, you will hear a short statement. The statements will be <u>spoken</u> just one time. They will not be written out for you, and you must listen carefully in order to understand what the speaker says.

When you hear a statement, read the four sentences in your test book and decide which one is closest in meaning to the statement you have heard. Then, on your answer sheet, find the number of the problem and mark your answer.

Listen to the following example:

You will hear:

You will read: (A) The ambassador enjoyed meeting you and your family.
                (B) You missed the ambassador by a day.
                (C) Earlier in the day, the ambassador met with his family.
                (D) Yesterday's meeting with the ambassador was cancelled.

Sample Answer

Ⓐ ● Ⓒ Ⓓ

Sentence (B), "You missed the ambassador by a day," is the closest in meaning to the sentence, "If you had arrived a day earlier, you would have met the ambassador and his family." Therefore, you should choose answer (B).

Listen to the next example:

You will hear:

You will read: (A) Dave will be the only person driving this time.
                (B) Dave will call the station.
                (C) The party left from the same station as last time.
                (D) Dave is a volunteer fireman at our local station.

Sample Answer

● Ⓑ Ⓒ Ⓓ

Sentence (A), "Dave will be the only person driving this time," means most nearly the same as the statement "Dave volunteered to bring his station wagon so that everyone could go at the same time." Therefore, you should choose answer (A).

1 (A) The boy takes a lot of trips.
   (B) The boy has made several attempts to join the Navy.
   (C) The boy frequently has problems.
   (D) The boy suffers a lot from internal pain.

2 (A) Someone cleaned Susan's car for her when she returned.
   (B) Susan cleaned her car when she returned home.
   (C) On her return north, Susan took out car insurance.
   (D) The car was cleaned while Susan was away.

3 (A) Jack is the probable winner.
   (B) Jack did not win.
   (C) Only Jack spent enough on television advertising.
   (D) The cure for Jack's infection is expensive.

4 (A) All the food is ready and everything must be eaten.
   (B) The children need to eat some food soon.
   (C) The children had mustard with their meal.
   (D) Some children have had a meal recently.

5 (A) Betty didn't pay all the money due.
   (B) Betty's credit card was canceled.
   (C) Betty couldn't find an empty cab.
   (D) Betty needed a receipt for the lab test.

6 (A) Back issues are more expensive.
   (B) I put on someone else's footwear.
   (C) I would not want to pay so much.
   (D) I think his shoes cost too much.

7 (A) The noise of the steam finally stopped.
   (B) One team was below his.
   (C) The final game was played beside the river.
   (D) The last course was a steaming dessert.

8 (A) She said she was astonished.
   (B) She didn't expect to make a speech.
   (C) She was so astonished she was speechless.
   (D) She won two prizes for oratory.

9 (A) The library will be open if the weather is clear.
   (B) You must complete your work by the beginning of next week.
   (C) The library is open every day until the end of the term.
   (D) The library will not be open this weekend for term papers.

10 (A) Don't consult Fred if your problem is mental or emotional.
   (B) Fred never gives free medical advice.
   (C) The prescriptions Fred gives are often not very logical.
   (D) Fred's qualifications for his profession are questionable.

11 (A) Paul will attempt to steal the tests before tomorrow.
   (B) Paul has another week to prepare for his exams.
   (C) Paul slipped in class and will have to miss the next two days.
   (D) Paul missed two days of school just before the exams.

12 (A) This phase of the trip is very difficult for her.
   (B) She is responsible for her present problems.
   (C) The letter she received described the ship's present route.
   (D) She has her own key to the ship.

13 (A) They met their parents after the project was finished.
   (B) They gave their mother and father the financial aid they needed.
   (C) Their meat order had been delivered before their parents arrived.
   (D) Their mother and father worked with them.

14 (A) He hurt her when he got on the bus.
   (B) She felt that he was too sure of himself.
   (C) She thinks that his insult was intentional.
   (D) She made an effort to offend him.

15 (A) Your loan for school will now be more expensive.
   (B) Tuition will be raised by 10.5 percent.
   (C) You have been praised for lending money to students.
   (D) I'm interested in your intuition about investments.

16 (A) Ben's boss is usually late for work.
   (B) Ben gets to work early one day in ten.
   (C) Ben almost never takes the bus to work.
   (D) Ben rarely arrives at work as early as he'd like to.

17 (A) Bill's house has been barricaded.
   (B) The ground in this area can be tilled.
   (C) My new place cost five times more than Bill's.
   (D) I can't find where Bill lives.

18 (A) Dr. Elkins did not complete his lecture today.
   (B) Dr. Elkins was reading when the fire began.
   (C) Dr. Elkins was injured during the fire.
   (D) Dr. Elkins' class was shorter by five minutes today.

19 (A) Amy tripped over that same piece of furniture half an hour ago.
   (B) Amy hasn't stood up for more than thirty minutes.
   (C) Amy doesn't appear to need another drink.
   (D) Amy would like to find a more comfortable place to sit.

20 (A) During the course of the interview, Carl felt sick.
   (B) The interview made Carl feel uncomfortable.
   (C) The recruiting office had a view of the sea.
   (D) The tea served on the cruise made Carl very ill.

Part B

<u>Directions:</u> In Part B you will hear fifteen short conversations between two speakers. At the end of each conversation, a third voice will ask a question about what was said. The question will be <u>spoken</u> just one time. After you hear a conversation and the question about it, read the four possible answers and decide which one would be the best answer to the question you have heard. Then, on your answer sheet, find the number of the problem and mark your answer.

Listen to the following example:

You will hear:

You will read: (A) Jim is beginning to act like an adult.
   (B) Jim will eventually benefit from giving up cigarettes.
   (C) Jim has been having a hard time since he started smoking.
   (D) Jim is becoming a better long-distance runner.

Sample Answer

(A) ● (C) (D)

From the conversation we know that Jim has recently stopped smoking, and that the woman feels that this will eventually help him. The best answer, then, is (B), "Jim will eventually benefit from giving up cigarettes." Therefore, you should choose answer (B).

21 (A) Change her clothes.
   (B) Drive her car.
   (C) Have a meal.
   (D) Type an essay.

22 (A) She feels unable to express an opinion about what's happened to George.
   (B) She isn't speaking to George.
   (C) George is always late for appointments.
   (D) She finds it difficult to tolerate George's behavior.

23 (A) The man has not been asked what he thinks.
   (B) Both speakers think half the staff are very efficient.
   (C) The woman approves of the hotel staff, but the man doesn't.
   (D) The man and the woman disapprove of the hotel staff's attitude.

24 (A) In a theater.
   (B) In a library.
   (C) In a sporting goods store.
   (D) In a bookstore.

25 (A) She's a typewriter repairwoman.
   (B) She's an accountant.
   (C) She's a carpenter.
   (D) She's a typist.

26 (A) Open the window a little bit.
   (B) Bring her a bowl of chili.
   (C) Leave the window closed.
   (D) Tell her how he's feeling.

27 (A) Since Phil moved to Los Angeles, his job standing has improved.
   (B) Phil is not doing very well in Los Angeles.
   (C) Phil has always lived with his father in Los Angeles.
   (D) His father was not satisfied with Phil's work.

28 (A) The man.
   (B) The woman.
   (C) The woman's mother.
   (D) A baker.

29 (A) Dr. Johnson's class is already full.
   (B) The reserved spaces are for faculty only.
   (C) He will give the student a chance after she waits a while.
   (D) No exceptions can be made with regard to registration policy.

30 (A) He was interested in the woman's request.
   (B) He was nervous about lending the woman money.
   (C) He was offended by the woman's inconsistency.
   (D) He acted as if he didn't know the woman.

31 (A) It is one of their favorite places to eat.
   (B) The decor and food are the best around.
   (C) They are both disappointed in the recent changes.
   (D) They haven't been able to find another that they like as much.

32 (A) Put on expensive costumes.
   (B) Leave the city for the night.
   (C) Telephone his younger sister and then go downtown.
   (D) Have a night out with his wife.

33 (A) He must attend a meeting first thing on Monday.
   (B) He is bored with the tour.
   (C) He dislikes meeting people on Mondays.
   (D) He is facing financial ruin.

34 (A) Opening a gallery.
   (B) Losing weight before getting any new clothes.
   (C) Adding up the cost before going shopping.
   (D) Buying some new clothes in a hurry.

35 (A) A movie she has recently seen.
   (B) A book she is reading.
   (C) A political campaign.
   (D) The financial dealings of her cousins in Washington.

Part C

Directions: In this part of the test, you will hear several short talks and/or conversations. After each talk or conversation, you will be asked some questions. The talks and questions will be spoken just one time. They will not be written out for you, so you will have to listen carefully in order to understand and remember what the speaker says.

When you hear a question, read the four possible answers in your test book and decide which one would be the best answer to the question you have heard. Then, on your answer sheet, find the number of the problem and fill in (blacken) the space that corresponds to the letter of the answer you have chosen.

Listen to this sample talk:

Now listen to the first question on the sample talk:

You will hear: Sample Answer

You will read: (A) In the fifteenth century.   Ⓐ ● Ⓒ Ⓓ
                 (B) In the nineteenth century.
                 (C) In this century.
                 (D) About 1910.

The best answer to the question, "When did Americans probably begin sending Christmas cards?" is (B), "In the nineteenth century." Therefore, you should choose answer (B).

Now listen to the second question on the sample talk:

You will hear: Sample Answer

You will read: (A) To celebrate birthdays.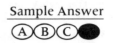
                 (B) To acknowledge holidays.
                 (C) To commemorate birthdays, Christmas,
                     and Easter.
                 (D) To wish others well on almost any
                     occasion.

The best answer to the question, "Which of the following most accurately describes why Americans send greeting cards?" is (D), "To wish others well on almost any occasion." Therefore, you should choose answer (D).

36 (A) She wants to become an English major.
   (B) She wants to apply for a job.
   (C) She wants to discuss a career in teaching.
   (D) She wants to take his course on Faulkner.

37 (A) She's a junior.
   (B) She's a senior.
   (C) She's a graduate student.
   (D) She has completed her studies and is working.

38 (A) Occasionally write questions for Dr. Taylor.
   (B) Give lectures to freshmen.
   (C) Write essays and take tests.
   (D) Attend lectures and take notes.

39 (A) She thinks he needs some assistance.
   (B) She thinks his lectures should be better organized.
   (C) She thinks he's outstanding.
   (D) She thinks he has a lot to learn about teaching.

40 (A) Get a teaching job.
   (B) Write a book on Faulkner.
   (C) Give literature lectures.
   (D) Go to graduate school.

41 (A) Introduce this student to Mr. Faulkner.
   (B) Send each applicant a letter about the job.
   (C) Interview other students and then choose an assistant.
   (D) Hire this student.

42 (A) In Scout troops.
   (B) In the British army.
   (C) In boys' camps.
   (D) At Scout jamborees.

43 (A) To work for the Boy Scouts.
   (B) To write books on military life.
   (C) To become a baron.
   (D) To travel around the world.

44 (A) Training boys as Scouts.
   (B) Training members of the armed forces.
   (C) Boy Scout camps.
   (D) Book publishing.

45 (A) In 1920.
   (B) When he was thirty-seven.
   (C) In 1910.
   (D) When he was eighty.

46 (A) Cook.
    (B) Organizer.
    (C) Author.
    (D) Soldier.

47 (A) In a supermarket.
    (B) In a tobacco store.
    (C) In a drugstore.
    (D) Near a fire.

48 (A) Some medicine and some vitamins.
    (B) A carton of cigarettes.
    (C) Pills for tension and some plasma.
    (D) A cast for her broken arm.

49 (A) She was smoking in bed.
    (B) She was very nervous and tense.
    (C) She was fixing some food.
    (D) She was doing housework.

50 (A) A non-smoker.
    (B) A light smoker who has a small cut.
    (C) A heavy smoker with a broken leg.
    (D) A physically healthy but tense person.

THIS IS THE END OF THE LISTENING COMPREHENSION PORTION OF THE TEST. LOOK AT THE TIME NOW, BEFORE YOU BEGIN WORK ON SECTION 2. USE *EXACTLY 25 MINUTES* TO WORK ON SECTION 2.

Section 2

Structure and Written Expression

Time – 25 minutes

This section is designed to measure your ability to recognize language that is appropriate for standard written English. There are two types of questions in this section, with special directions for each type.

Directions: Questions 1–15 are incomplete sentences. Four words or phrases, marked (A), (B), (C), (D), are given beneath each sentence. You are to choose the one word or phrase that best completes the sentence. Then, on your answer sheet, find the number of the problem and mark your answer.

Example I.   Sample Answer

- - - - - - - or sharks, for instance, the dolphin is
a mammal.

(A) Either fish
(B) When it is like
(C) Being fish
(D) Unlike fish

In English, the sentence should read, "Unlike fish or sharks, for instance, the dolphin is a mammal." Therefore, you should choose (D).

Example II.   Sample Answer

Not until exhaustive tests have been carried out by the
Food and Drug Administration, - - - - - - -.

(A) that a new drug is allowed on the market
(B) is a new drug allowed to be put on the market
(C) there is a new drug placed on the market
(D) a new drug is allowed on the market

The sentence should read, "Not until exhaustive tests have been carried out by the Food and Drug Administration, is a new drug allowed to be put on the market." Therefore, you should choose (B).

As soon as you understand the directions, begin work on the problems.

1 The sun - - - - - - - vast amounts of gases.

(A) gives off   (C) which
(B) with   (D) from

2 If Peter had enough money, - - - - - - - on the trip to Las Vegas.

(A) he would have gone   (C) he went
(B) had he gone   (D) he would go

475

3 Darlene insisted on taking the boat trip even - - - - - -.

   (A) the sea was becoming quite rough
   (B) though the sea becoming quite rough
   (C) although the sea was becoming quite rough
   (D) though the sea was becoming quite rough

4 It has been proven that cockroaches - - - - - - - for several weeks even after their heads have been cut off.

   (A) are surviving
   (B) can survive
   (C) surviving
   (D) that survive

5 - - - - - - - a reservation, it will be impossible to get a hotel room this weekend because of the jazz festival.

   (A) Without you have
   (B) If you have
   (C) Unless you have
   (D) Unless having

6 As fuel prices rose, bus companies raised their fares and - - - - - - -.

   (A) so did the airlines
   (B) neither did the airlines
   (C) so the airlines have done
   (D) neither the airlines did

7 Before the Great Fire of London in 1666, - - - - - - -.

   (A) were most of the dwellings squalid and unhealthy
   (B) most squalid and unhealthy were the dwellings
   (C) most of the dwellings were squalid and unhealthy
   (D) squalid and unhealthy dwellings

8 Payload is an influential factor - - - - - - -.

   (A) that an airplane has for economy
   (B) in determining how economical an airplane is
   (C) to determine airplane economy
   (D) an airplane's economy is determined by this

9 After carrying out a large number of experiments - - - - - - -.

   (A) Alfred Nobel finding the formula for dynamite in 1866
   (B) the formula for dynamite was found in 1866
   (C) it was in 1866 that the formula for dynamite was found by Alfred Nobel
   (D) Alfred Nobel found the formula for dynamite in 1866

10 The party was taken out to see a film - - - - - - - on location in the desert.

   (A) being shot
   (B) being now shot
   (C) while being shot
   (D) that being shot

11 The two friends, - - - - - - -, met by chance on a European tour.

   (A) for many years they had not seen each other
   (B) had not seen each other for many years
   (C) who had not seen each other for many years and who were now getting on in years
   (D) who each other had not for many years seen

12 - - - - - - -, the gorilla has recently been the subject of several in-depth studies.

   (A) It is the primate closest to man
   (B) The primate closest to man, it is
   (C) The fact that it is the primate closest to man
   (D) The closest of the primates to man

13 The sidewinder snake catches lizards - - - - - - - in the sand and imitating a blade of grass with its tail.

   (A) burying itself
   (B) to bury itself
   (C) from burying itself
   (D) by burying itself

14 - - - - - - - after the Second World War that test pilots first attempted to break the "sound barrier".

   (A) It was shortly
   (B) Was shortly
   (C) There was shortly
   (D) Shortly

15 Only after years of intensive work - - - - - - - the riddle of DNA.

   (A) and Crick and Watson solved
   (B) did Crick and Watson solve
   (C) Crick and Watson solved
   (D) but Crick and Watson solved

Directions: In questions 16–40 each sentence has four words or phrases underlined. The four underlined parts of the sentence are marked (A), (B), (C), (D). You are to identify the <u>one</u> underlined word or phrase that should be corrected or rewritten. Then, on your answer sheet, find the number of the problem and mark your answer.

Example I.   Sample Answer

The easiest and <u>common</u> manner of determining
            A

whether gas <u>was present</u> was <u>to use</u> canaries, which
           B   C

were <u>highly sensitive</u> to atmospheric impurities.
         D

Answer (A), the underlined adjective <u>common</u>, would not be accepted in carefully written English; the form <u>most common</u> should be used with <u>The easiest</u> since both adjectives are describing <u>manner</u>. Therefore, the sentence should read, "The easiest and most common manner of determining whether gas was present was to use canaries, which were highly sensitive to atmospheric impurities." To answer the problem correctly, you would choose (A).

Example II.   Sample Answer

People in the United States <u>have</u> recently <u>taken</u>
                  A   B

<u>to traveling</u> to work <u>on</u> bicycle to an increasing extent.
    C   D

Answer (D), the underlined word <u>on</u>, should not be used in carefully written English with <u>bicycle</u>. The preposition <u>by</u> should be used before <u>bicycle</u>. Therefore, the sentence should read, "People in the United States have recently taken to traveling to work by bicycle to an increasing extent." To answer the problem correctly, you would choose (D).

As soon as you understand the directions, begin work on the problems.

16 The United States <u>shares</u> <u>extremely long</u> borders <u>with</u> <u>either</u> Canada and
               A   B   C   D
  Mexico.

17 <u>Some</u> great cataclysm appears to <u>have</u> struck the great Mayan cities at
   A   B
  the height of <u>its</u> glory.
    C   D

18 <u>Although</u> Jack was the <u>youngest</u> of the two boys, he was clearly
   A   B
  <u>more mature</u> than his <u>elder</u> brother.
     C   D

478

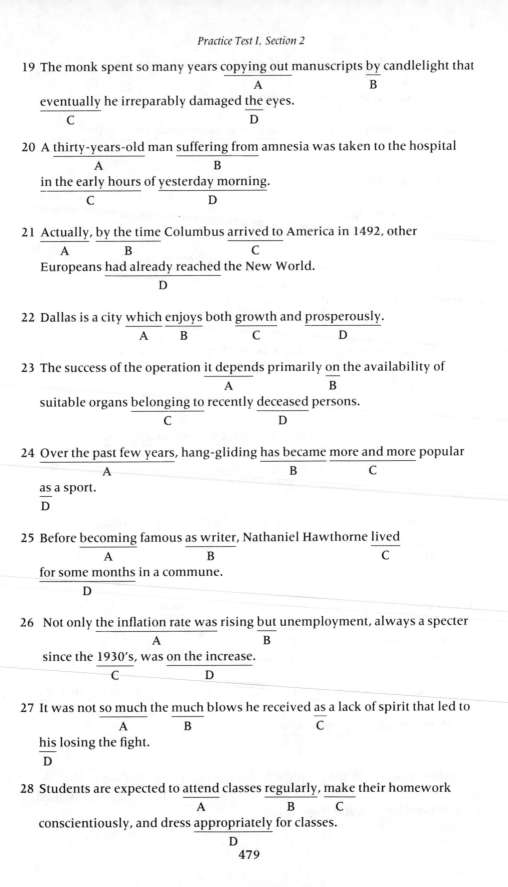

19 The monk spent so many years copying out manuscripts by candlelight that
                                A   B
eventually he irreparably damaged the eyes.
    C   D

20 A thirty-years-old man suffering from amnesia was taken to the hospital
         A   B
in the early hours of yesterday morning.
         C   D

21 Actually, by the time Columbus arrived to America in 1492, other
    A   B   C
Europeans had already reached the New World.
          D

22 Dallas is a city which enjoys both growth and prosperously.
             A   B   C   D

23 The success of the operation it depends primarily on the availability of
                        A   B
suitable organs belonging to recently deceased persons.
             C   D

24 Over the past few years, hang-gliding has became more and more popular
          A   B   C
as a sport.
D

25 Before becoming famous as writer, Nathaniel Hawthorne lived
        A   B   C
for some months in a commune.
      D

26 Not only the inflation rate was rising but unemployment, always a specter
            A   B
since the 1930's, was on the increase.
       C   D

27 It was not so much the much blows he received as a lack of spirit that led to
        A   B   C
his losing the fight.
D

28 Students are expected to attend classes regularly, make their homework
          A   B   C
conscientiously, and dress appropriately for classes.
               D

29 It was likely that a devaluation would occur, and a large one at that, being
     A   B   C   D
   the currency was obviously over-valued.

30 American farmers have historically been extraordinary productive.
                  A   B   C   D

31 During the course of 1981, Pete Rose became the four hitter to achieve
          A   B   C
   as many as 3,600 hits.
       D

32 So many people have burnt theirselves while using matches that the
                      A   B
   scoutmaster has decided to restrict their use.
              C   D

33 Elephants are well-known as the largest land mammals, but they are easy
                      A   B   C
   outweighed by whales.
          D

34 Inevitably, as the hands of the clock move towards and approach zero hour,
               A   B   C
   the contestants become increasingly nervous.
                      D

35 One of the first results of the police investigation were a redesigning of
       A   B   C
   the whole security system.
       D

36 Last year a honor which is rarely conferred was awarded to this scientist,
           A   B
   one of the greatest men of our age.
   C   D

37 The plan had been to go either walking or swimming but the weather was
           A   B   C
   so bad they didn't go somewhere.
             D

38 So impressed were the people with his campaign that they elected he
            A   B   C
   president for a second term.
      D

39 The friendly open manner of Texans is said to reflect its confidence in the

                                              A   B   C   D

American way of life.

40 Mobility is one of the characteristics often demanded of executives, and

     A   B   C

they must accustom themselves to move quite regularly.

                                            D

DO NOT WORK ON ANY OTHER SECTION OF THE TEST.

IF YOU FINISH IN LESS THAN 25 MINUTES, CHECK YOUR WORK ON
SECTION 2 ONLY. AT THE END OF 25 MINUTES, GO ON TO SECTION 3.
USE *EXACTLY 45 MINUTES* TO WORK ON SECTION 3.

Section 3
Reading Comprehension and Vocabulary

Time – 45 minutes

There are two types of questions in this section, with special directions for each type.

Directions: In questions 1–30 each sentence has a word or phrase underlined. Below each sentence are four other words or phrases. You are to choose the one word or phrase which would best keep the meaning of the original sentence if it were substituted for the underlined word. Look at the example.

Example.   Sample Answer

The outcome was that the Allies found themselves in   (A) (B) ● (D)
a far stronger position.

(A) start
(B) implication
(C) result
(D) derivative

The best answer is (C), because the sentence "The result was that the Allies found themselves in a far stronger position" is closest in meaning to the original sentence, "The outcome was that the Allies found themselves in a far stronger position." Therefore, you should mark answer (C).

As soon as you understand the directions, begin work on the problems.

1 When he finally emerged from the cave after thirty days, Schichel was startlingly pale.

  (A) extraordinarily
  (B) frantically
  (C) deceptively
  (D) astonishingly

2 The minister reiterated his intention of resigning.

  (A) repeated
  (B) stated
  (C) described
  (D) reported

3 For decades, Norman Rockwell epitomized the way mainstream America saw itself.

  (A) envisioned
  (B) recorded
  (C) chronicled
  (D) embodied

4 Since an in-house search failed to reveal the culprit, an outside investigation was <u>instigated</u>.

   (A) requested
   (B) initiated
   (C) carried out
   (D) discussed

5 When the parties returned, the chairman announced the <u>findings</u> of the arbitration tribunal.

   (A) intentions
   (B) referees
   (C) decision
   (D) score

6 It was <u>sound</u> advice but the researchers paid little attention to it.

   (A) good
   (B) sensitive
   (C) noisy
   (D) disruptive

7 Walt Disney, the film-maker, also became famous as a great <u>humanitarian</u>.

   (A) investigator into anthropological problems
   (B) producer of human-interest stories
   (C) contributor to the betterment of society
   (D) example of the human race

8 The doctor preferred to resign rather than be accused publicly of <u>infamous</u> conduct.

   (A) unknown
   (B) extraordinary
   (C) mysterious
   (D) disgraceful

9 Americans will <u>eventually</u> have to adapt to smaller, more economical automobiles.

   (A) possibly
   (B) sooner or later
   (C) certainly
   (D) slowly

10 Lyndon Johnson's decision not to run for another term was clearly <u>linked to</u> developments in the Vietnam War.

   (A) responsible for
   (B) identical to
   (C) connected with
   (D) disassociated from

11 <u>Soaring</u> rates of interest have recently made it difficult for young couples to buy their own homes.

  (A) rapidly rising
  (B) very expensive
  (C) slowly rising
  (D) extremely painful

12 Many companies have commented on the government's <u>gratuitously</u> complex labeling requirements for all canned food.

  (A) insistently
  (B) thankfully
  (C) freely
  (D) unnecessarily

13 When Lee Iacocca took over the Chrysler Corporation, he insisted that the changes he would introduce would not be merely <u>cosmetic</u>.

  (A) fanciful
  (B) structural
  (C) superficial
  (D) invented

14 Meteorologists are <u>at odds</u> over the workings of tornadoes.

  (A) mystified
  (B) in disagreement
  (C) up in arms
  (D) in disarray

15 The author lived for years near one of the many <u>creeks</u> flowing into that part of the Ohio River.

  (A) streams
  (B) ponds
  (C) lakes
  (D) swamps

16 Civil-rights marchers in the early fifties often had to contend with the <u>wrath</u> of local residents.

  (A) generosity
  (B) opposition
  (C) dislike
  (D) anger

17 Since Jonas Salk <u>came up with</u> his polio vaccine, infantile paralysis has virtually disappeared from the United States.

  (A) surfaced with   (C) raised the price of
  (B) discovered   (D) elevated

18 Charles Atlas was <u>relatively</u> weak as a teenager.

    (A) amazingly
    (B) dangerously
    (C) comparatively
    (D) congenitally

19 The human ear <u>admits</u> only a very limited range of frequencies.

    (A) confesses
    (B) gives off
    (C) forces in
    (D) lets in

20 <u>Formerly</u> of interest to scientists in relation to its salivary glands, the fruit fly has more recently been important in studies of natural rhythms.

    (A) Originally
    (B) Previously
    (C) Subsequently
    (D) Primarily

21 Stock-market analysts <u>monitor</u> a great variety of financial indicators.

    (A) come up with
    (B) look into
    (C) keep track of
    (D) take charge of

22 <u>While</u> traditional in many ways, Frank Lloyd Wright was a highly innovative American architect.

    (A) Obviously
    (B) Although
    (C) However
    (D) So

23 There were a number of limiting factors on the <u>output</u> of consumer durables in 1973–74.

    (A) outflow
    (B) income
    (C) production
    (D) reduction

24 The Trojans managed to <u>withstand</u> the years-long seige by Agamemnon's forces.

    (A) resist
    (B) rise against
    (C) prepare for
    (D) predict

25 It was in 1665 that the concept of the earth's gravity <u>dawned on</u> Isaac Newton.

(A) interested
(B) appeared to
(C) caught the attention of
(D) occurred to

26 <u>A thorough</u> grounding in math and physics is an essential prerequisite for taking this graduate course.

(A) A solid
(B) A long
(C) An unusual
(D) A hard

27 The effects of the moon's periodicity on sea-creatures are <u>accentuated</u> by vast movements of their environment.

(A) presaged
(B) distinguished
(C) underscored
(D) manifested

28 Vinyl has now largely replaced leather in the manufacture of <u>handbags</u>.

(A) belts
(B) gloves
(C) suitcases
(D) purses

29 Though not lethal to humans, the beautiful crimson-spotted mushroom, Amanita, has been known to drive them <u>berserk</u>.

(A) into hiding
(B) crazy
(C) sideways
(D) unconscious

30 <u>As a general rule</u>, September is the worst month of the year for hurricanes in the Gulf.

(A) Normally
(B) On rare occasions
(C) Invariably
(D) Sometimes

<u>Directions:</u> The remaining questions in this section are based on a variety of reading material (single sentences, paragraphs, advertisements, and the like). In questions 31–60, you are to choose the <u>one</u> best answer, (A), (B), (C), or (D), to each question. Then, on your answer sheet, find the number of the problem and mark your answer. Answer all questions following a passage on the basis of what is <u>stated</u> or <u>implied</u> in that passage.

Read the following sample passage.

People manage to count even when they do not have names for numbers. Early men demonstrated numbers to each other by counting on their fingers, and some primitive tribes still do this. In fact, some tribes have names for only the numbers "one" and "two" and can only indicate higher numbers by pointing to a particular finger. In other tribes, the numbers do have names, but these names are directly connected with finger counting.

Example I.   Sample Answer

Primitive people learn to count by   (A)(B)(C)●

   (A) pointing
   (B) watching more advanced tribes
   (C) naming the numbers
   (D) using their fingers

The passage says that "Early men demonstrated numbers to each other by counting on their fingers." Therefore, you should choose answer (D).

Example II.   Sample Answer

What is the main topic of the paragraph?   ●(B)(C)(D)

   (A) Primitive counting
   (B) Early arithmetic classes
   (C) Differences among primitive tribes
   (D) Names for numbers in different languages

The passage talks specifically about the way primitive peoples count. Therefore, you should choose (A).

As soon as you understand the directions, begin work on the problems.

Questions 31–34

The black-necked stilt has certain features that help it find its prey; ironically, some of the same features make this bird a more likely target of its own predators. Long slender legs allow the stilt to wade into ponds and find aquatic invertebrates, but long thin legs have little utility as weapons; and black-and-white plumage above grayish blue or red legs makes it difficult for the bird to find a hiding place. Essentially the only protection stilts have comes from being alert and fleeing predators. Living in flocks reduces the chance of being ambushed because there are more birds to keep watch. Even with the difficulties stilts face in protecting themselves, there are up to six stilt species and representatives of the birds on every continent except Antarctica.

31 The black-necked stilt's long, thin legs

(A) are both advantageous and disadvantageous to it
(B) find aquatic invertebrates
(C) are its predators' target
(D) are black and white

32 The black-necked stilt protects itself

(A) by using its legs as weapons
(B) by hiding its black-and-white plumage
(C) by wading into ponds
(D) by remaining vigilant and running from its enemies

33 What is the subject of this passage?

(A) The physical beauty of the black-necked stilt.
(B) The distribution of the black-necked stilt throughout the world.
(C) The survival apparatus of the black-necked stilt.
(D) The living patterns of the black-necked stilt.

34 Which of the following statements is **not** true according to the passage?

(A) The black-necked stilt is carnivorous.
(B) The feathers of the black-necked stilt provide it with helpful camouflage.
(C) Black-necked stilts congregate in large groups.
(D) There are no black-necked stilts in Antarctica.

Questions 35–42

In approximately 260 A.D., a massive volcanic eruption buried some highlands of Central America in ash, forcing the Mayan people to abandon this area for decades and up to two centuries in the worst hit areas. The eruption was swift; it occurred in only two identifiable stages, with almost no interval in between. As a result of the lava outlet route being under water, steam explosions contributed to the violence of the eruption, and the rapid cooling of magma to tephra (ash and other materials) by the lake waters created very small particles, which the wind carried long distances. The magnitude of the eruption can be calculated from the three-foot-deep ashfall forty-five miles from the source. One small area in this region was struck by three additional eruptions in the years that followed. These various eruptions differed in terms of the size of the area devastated and the nature of the tephra blasted into the air, but in each instance people showed a dogged determination to reoccupy the lands affected, thereby taking obvious risks but also reaping the less obvious benefits of volcanic activity.

35 A huge volcanic eruption caused the Mayans to abandon parts of Central America

    (A) about 620 years ago
    (B) about 2,250 years ago
    (C) about 1,725 years ago
    (D) about 260 years ago

36 Mayans in the area had to leave

    (A) for about 10 years
    (B) for about 260 years
    (C) in two stages
    (D) for as long as 200 years

37 It can be inferred that the explosion was particularly strong because

    (A) the eruption was swift
    (B) the escape route for the lava was under water
    (C) the magma cooled rapidly to tephra
    (D) the ash forty-five miles from the source was three feet deep

38 The magma was cooled quickly to tephra thanks to

    (A) ash and other materials
    (B) very small particles
    (C) the wind
    (D) the water of the lake

39 The size of the eruption can best be gauged by the fact that

    (A) there was deep ash a great distance from the eruption itself
    (B) the wind carried particles a great distance
    (C) the lava outlet route was under water
    (D) three additional eruptions occurred

40 A sequel which all three additional eruptions mentioned in the passage had in common was

    (A) the size of the area devastated
    (B) the type of tephra generated
    (C) the return of the inhabitants to affected areas
    (D) the obvious risks of volcanic activity

41 The volcanic eruption in 260 A.D. was probably

    (A) swifter than the others mentioned
    (B) larger than the others mentioned
    (C) two centuries before the others mentioned
    (D) later than the others mentioned

42 The inhabitants of the area which had been hit by the additional eruptions

    (A) gained some advantages
    (B) did not take obvious risks
    (C) differed in terms of the areas affected
    (D) were determined to keep their dogs on the land affected

Questions 43–45

As of March first, differential rates will be introduced based on the concentration of people and vehicles in the policy-holder's place of residence. The higher rates applying to urban dwellers are a consequence of the increased risks directly deriving from greater exposure to accidents and theft.

43 The changes introduced on March first involve

    (A) all policy-holders paying more
    (B) city residents paying more than others
    (C) increased risks from exposure
    (D) more accidents and thefts

44 Before March first, urban and non-urban dwellers probably

    (A) paid rates based on their places of residence
    (B) paid higher rates
    (C) paid different rates
    (D) paid the same rates

45 The passage is probably about insurance rates for

    (A) automobiles   (C) personal accidents
    (B) homes in cities   (D) exposure

Questions 46–49

When most people think of Melvil Dewey, they think of the classification system for cataloguing and arranging the books and pamphlets in libraries that he devised in the second half of the nineteenth century. This system classifies books and other publications into ten major categories, each category being further subdivided by number. Dewey was fortunate enough to see the Dewey Decimal System adopted by libraries throughout the world and by 96 percent of the public and 89 percent of the college libraries in the United States, but his work did not end with this success. Dewey also helped found the American Library Association, established the first library school in America, set up the Lake Placid Club, and worked out his own orthography. Dewey considered the spelling system of English a nuisance and a great waste of time, called for the simplification of the language, and insisted that once spelling was freed from complexities and absurdities inherited from the past and made uniform, three years could be saved in a child's education. His zeal was such that he not only used his simplified spelling exclusively, he even would correct the spelling in his mail as he read it through.

46 Dewey's major claim to fame rests on

(A) his founding of the American Library Association
(B) his founding of the Lake Placid Club
(C) his library classification system
(D) his simplified spelling system

47 From the passage it can be inferred that the Dewey Decimal System was adopted by

(A) most public libraries throughout the world
(B) most college libraries throughout the world
(C) all but 4 percent of college libraries in the United States
(D) a higher proportion of public libraries than college libraries in the United States

48 Dewey's objections to traditional English spelling were based on

(A) its simplicity   (C) its inconsistency
(B) its uniform nature   (D) its nuisance value

49 Which of the following can **not** be inferred from the passage?

(A) Dewey's correspondents did not always use his writing system.
(B) Dewey's writing system was adopted in American schools.
(C) Dewey always used his writing system once he had invented it.
(D) Dewey's activities were not confined to inventing a new writing system.

Questions 50–55

Throughout the seventeenth and early eighteenth centuries there were frequent attempts made to develop a universal language. Such efforts, which were by no means limited to a single country, had three major goals. There was a need for an auxiliary language, such as Latin had been, to expedite exchanges of various kinds: scientific, political, commercial. There was a need for a "universal character", that would provide a simplified, rigorous set of symbols capable of expressing all actual and possible knowledge and above all, it was felt, a truly universal language would itself be an instrument of discovery and verification.

50 What is the topic of this passage?

(A) Discoveries in the seventeenth and early eighteenth centuries.
(B) International languages in history.
(C) International cooperation in science, politics, and trade.
(D) The aims behind the search for an international language.

51 The search for a common language in the seventeenth century might best be described as

- (A) international
- (B) limited
- (C) continuous
- (D) universal

52 Latin had previously been particularly useful

- (A) in providing a simplified, rigorous set of symbols
- (B) as an instrument of discovery and verification
- (C) in facilitating a wide variety of exchanges
- (D) since it was capable of expressing all actual and possible knowledge

53 Which of the following best reflects the period referred to in the passage?

- (A) 1750–1830
- (B) 1600–1720
- (C) 1700–1718
- (D) 1700–1810

54 The purposes of the common language sought were predominantly related to

- (A) trade
- (B) science and discovery
- (C) politics
- (D) symbols and instruments

55 It can be inferred from the passage that a "universal character" would consist of

- (A) all possible language
- (B) a scientific, political, or commercial exchange
- (C) an apparatus for discovery
- (D) a set of symbols

Questions 56–58

BLAKE BUILDING
DIRECTORY

Bennington, Frank S. — DDS, orthodontics 202
Boris, Jacqueline — attorney 104
De Paoli, Lawrence — CPA & Notary Public 204
Jackson, Samuel P. — MD, obstetrics 106
Martinez, Maria J., PhD — marriage and family counseling 304
Rutherford, Thomas — architect 302
Thomas, Wm. R. — attorney 102

56 How many floors does the Blake Building have?

(A) 2   (B) 3   (C) 4   (D) 6

57 Which room would someone with a tooth problem probably be looking for?

(A) 202   (B) 106   (C) 304   (D) 104

58 All of the following people could probably help with a tax problem **except**

(A) Wm. R. Thomas
(B) Jacqueline Boris
(C) Thomas Rutherford
(D) Lawrence De Paoli

Questions 59–60
For each of these questions, choose the answer that is closest in meaning to the original sentence. Note that several of the choices may be factually correct, but you should choose the one that is the closest restatement of the given sentence.

59 Undergraduate students must select a major area of study at the beginning of their junior year or after completing sixty hours of credit.

(A) Once at least one of two criteria has been met, undergraduates are required to choose a major.
(B) A major must be chosen between the time an undergraduate completes his sophomore year and when he earns sixty hours of credit.
(C) Undergraduates' major areas of study must be determined by the time they complete either sixty hours of credit or their junior year.
(D) Undergraduates must choose their majors on the basis of the credits earned during their first two years of study.

60 Comets are widely believed to be the frozen debris of the material from which the sun and planets were formed.

(A) A lot of people think that the sun and planets were created from frozen material deriving from comet formation.
(B) Many people share the view that comets are the frozen left-overs from the formation process of the sun and planets.
(C) When the sun and planets were formed, comets gave rise to widespread formation of beliefs.
(D) The belief that comets are formed from the debris left by the formation of the sun and planets is wide of the mark.

DO NOT WORK ON ANY OTHER SECTION OF THE TEST.

IF YOU FINISH IN LESS THAN 45 MINUTES, CHECK YOUR WORK ON SECTION 3 ONLY. AT THE END OF 45 MINUTES STOP WORK AND CLOSE YOUR TEST BOOK.

Test of Written English
Time–30 minutes

Changes in Gross Domestic Product per Head: International Comparison

	Percentages change over previous year										Average annual percentage change 1975–84
	1975	76	77	78	79	80	81	82	83	84	85	
France	−0.3	4.8	2.6	3.3	2.9	0.5	−0.1	1.2	0.3	0.9	0.6	1.8
Germany (Fed. Rep.)	−1.2	5.9	3.2	3.0	4.1	1.0	0.0	−0.6	1.6	3.0	2.5	2.3
Japan	1.3	3.6	4.3	4.1	4.3	3.6	3.1	2.2	2.4	5.1	4.4	3.6
U.K.	−0.6	3.8	1.1	3.6	2.1	−2.4	−1.3	1.1	3.7	2.0	3.9	1.5
U.S.	−1.7	3.7	4.4	3.6	1.5	−1.6	2.4	−3.9	2.0	6.2	1.5	2.0

Directions: You have thirty minutes to write an essay on the following writing question. Read the question carefully and be sure to write about what is asked and not about a different topic. You may make notes and you may check your work and make changes within the thirty minutes allowed.

Question: Gross domestic product (GDP) per head is often considered a good indicator of general economic activity. The table above gives the percentage changes in GDP as compared with the previous year for the United States and four other major countries for the period 1975–1985 (minus figures indicate a fall in GDP), and an average percentage change. Discuss the trends the table suggests.

Practice Test II

Section 1
Listening Comprehension

Time – 40 minutes

In this section of the test, you will have an opportunity to demonstrate your ability to understand spoken English. There are three parts to this section, with special directions for each part.

Part A

Directions: For each problem in Part A, you will hear a short statement. The statements will be <u>spoken</u> just one time. They will not be written out for you, and you must listen carefully in order to understand what the speaker says.

When you hear a statement, read the four sentences in your test book and decide which one is closest in meaning to the statement you have heard. Then, on your answer sheet, find the number of the problem and mark your answers.

Listen to the following example:

You will hear: Sample Answer

You will read: (A) Consideration was given to all   Ⓐ Ⓑ ● Ⓓ
                     suggestions.
                (B) Your idea is worth a considerable
                     amount of money.
                (C) That sounds like a pretty good idea.
                (D) I'm not certain that I like your idea.

Sentence (C), "That sounds like a pretty good idea," means most nearly the same as the statement "I certainly think the suggestion is worthy of consideration." Therefore, you should choose answer (C).

Listen to the next example:

You will hear: Sample Answer

You will read: (A) Ellen quit growing at Pamela's age.   Ⓐ Ⓑ Ⓒ ●
                (B) Pamela is short for her age.
                (C) Pamela and Ellen are the same
                     height.
                (D) Ellen is older than Pamela.

Sentence (D), "Ellen is older than Pamela," is closest in meaning to the sentence "Pamela is quite a bit taller than her sister Ellen was at her age." Therefore, you should choose answer (D).

495

1 (A) The hurrying around made him quite ill.
 (B) He hurried home after he finished his math class.
 (C) He'd like to have a hand in the project if he can.
 (D) He was horrified by the consequences of the storm.

2 (A) Ray quit the football team last year.
 (B) Ray majored in physical education last year.
 (C) Ray has gone out with a majorette for three years now.
 (D) This past year was very hectic for Ray.

3 (A) Her apartment is too far from here to get there by eight.
 (B) I have her address but don't know how to get there.
 (C) I don't have the dress she wants anyway.
 (D) I don't intend to go to her house dressed this way.

4 (A) Rob and Diane got together in Rob's office.
 (B) The justice was caught in the building.
 (C) Rob saw Diane before he got outside.
 (D) Rob caught up with Diane before she left.

5 (A) How much climbing have you done recently?
 (B) What have you been doing in the last few weeks?
 (C) How much work did you have up to last week?
 (D) What have the two of you seen lately?

6 (A) Neither Cathy nor I understand what the sign means.
 (B) Cathy hasn't finished the homework, but I have.
 (C) Cathy and I still have work to do.
 (D) I have read half of the assigned chapters.

7 (A) John is overweight.
 (B) John's going on vacation in a week and a half.
 (C) John won enough money to pay for his vacation.
 (D) John is going to die soon.

8 (A) Jim stopped to have a cigarette.
 (B) Jim couldn't find a match anywhere.
 (C) Jim was given a new cigarette lighter.
 (D) Jim hasn't had a cigarette this year.

9 (A) We have to go to a party after work.
 (B) We're going to throw a party when the house has been painted.
 (C) We went to a huge party after the house was painted.
 (D) We'll go to the party if the house is painted.

10 (A) Jeff will play in the summer tournament.
 (B) Jeff will take his racquet with him on vacation.
 (C) Jeff plans to learn to play tennis.
 (D) Ten of us are taking lessons now.

11 (A) The main event will be presented after class.
   (B) Telephone the principal after class has broken up.
   (C) If an emergency occurs, go directly to your classroom.
   (D) In case of emergency, follow these directions.

12 (A) The airplane was unable to land on time.
   (B) The pilot surrounded the airport for a couple of hours.
   (C) The pilot went around the airport four times in two hours.
   (D) The heavy ground fog meant it took the pilot two hours to land.

13 (A) Mrs. Johnson's injections must be given in her lower limbs.
   (B) Mrs. Johnson should have her medicine before she eats.
   (C) Mrs. Johnson will need an injection after breakfast.
   (D) Mrs. Johnson's electrotherapy should be given when she is going
        to eat.

14 (A) The groom had had too much to drink.
   (B) The goods in the place included deodorant, wine, and cigars.
   (C) The smell of wine and tobacco dominated the room.
   (D) Everyone was ordering wine and cigars.

15 (A) I think the red parts are suspicious.
   (B) I like it, but I've had enough.
   (C) Is it okay if I have two slices this time?
   (D) The color comes from the cuts I had to make.

16 (A) Tom needed to find a job after finishing his studies.
   (B) Even though Tom is strong, the strain was too much.
   (C) Tom is looking for a job with the railroad company.
   (D) Tom helped finish the work on the training track.

17 (A) He will not be able to see tonight's performance.
   (B) He has never made an evening bag before.
   (C) His back injury will keep him out of tonight's game.
   (D) This make backs easily and stops on a dime.

18 (A) The baby is just seven months old.
   (B) Dinner is ready, but the baby's asleep.
   (C) Supper will not cost more than seven dollars.
   (D) We are ahead of schedule for a change.

19 (A) A few students quit school this term.
   (B) There are a surprising number of new faces this term.
   (C) With my new glasses, I can see more students.
   (D) There are not so many new students this semester.

20 (A) Her husband is closer to the stove than Kay is.
   (B) Kay was earlier for the cooking class than her husband.
   (C) The husband is the better cook of the two.
   (D) Kay's husband is beside the Coke machine.

Part B

Directions: In Part B you will hear fifteen short conversations between two speakers. At the end of each conversation, a third voice will ask a question about what was said. The question will be <u>spoken</u> just one time. After you hear a conversation and the question about it, read the four possible answers and decide which one would be the best response to the question you have heard. Then, on your answer sheet, find the number of the problem and mark your answer.

Listen to the following example:

You will hear:

You will read: (A) A restaurant.

Sample Answer

●(B)(C)(D)

(B) A bank.
(C) A supermarket.
(D) A service station.

From the conversation we know that the woman is asking about her bill in a restaurant. The best answer, then, is (A), "A restaurant." Therefore, you should choose answer (A).

21 (A) The room is too small for the audience.
(B) The show is very difficult to understand.
(C) The room is full of theatrical people.
(D) The crowd is very noisy.

22 (A) Karen.
(B) A neighbor.
(C) A professional hairstylist.
(D) A friend.

23 (A) Fuel cannot be transported to the northeastern states.
(B) There are too few houses in the northeast.
(C) People in the northeast are inexperienced in dealing with snow.
(D) Cold weather in the northeast has increased the demand for fuel.

24 (A) Ask the stewardess for change.
(B) Move to another part of the plane.
(C) Sit where there's a breeze.
(D) Extinguish his cigarette.

25 (A) Go out for supper.
(B) Go to the movies.
(C) Have supper and then study.
(D) Get ready for the show.

26 (A) She will be changing jobs soon.
   (B) She will have to accept a reduced salary.
   (C) Her boss notified her that she's been fired.
   (D) She always does the right thing.

27 (A) The man is an exceptional student and will write the exam for the class.
   (B) The student will probably not be able to complete the course.
   (C) The student's request will be granted.
   (D) Circumstances will not permit the student to take the make-up exam.

28 (A) She was apologetic.
   (B) She was well spoken.
   (C) She was very kind.
   (D) She was unforgiving.

29 (A) He's a plumber.
   (B) He's an electrician.
   (C) He's a carpenter.
   (D) He's an interior decorator.

30 (A) Go hiking with her friend.
   (B) Rest and take care of herself.
   (C) Stay at home and do her exercises.
   (D) Catch up with her reading.

31 (A) The man has more work to do on his paper than Edward on his.
   (B) The man himself will speak to Edward about his research paper.
   (C) The man has been talking to Edward about his paper.
   (D) The man has finished more than half of his research paper.

32 (A) Both of them have overcome their fear.
   (B) They are both afraid of high places.
   (C) The woman is still afraid of high places, but the man isn't.
   (D) Both of them prefer high places these days.

33 (A) He doubts David's reliability.
   (B) He's willing to trust David.
   (C) He has confided some of his doubts to David.
   (D) He thinks David will benefit from this experience.

34 (A) In his office.
   (B) In his waiting room.
   (C) In an airplane.
   (D) In New York.

35 (A) Demand a check to cover the difference.
   (B) Get a new television set.
   (C) Find another repairman.
   (D) Ask for an adjustment in his bill.

Part C

Directions: In this part of the test, you will hear several short talks and/or conversations. After each talk or conversation, you will be asked some questions. The talks and questions will be <u>spoken</u> just one time. They will not be written out for you, so you will have to listen carefully in order to understand and remember what the speaker says.

When you hear a question, read the four possible answers in your test book and decide which one would be the best answer to the question you have heard. Then, on your answer sheet, find the number of the problem and fill in (blacken) the space that corresponds to the letter of the answer you have chosen.

Listen to this sample talk:

Now listen to the first question on the sample talk:

You will hear:

Sample Answer

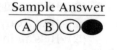

    (A) To attract new members to the Spelunker's Club.
    (B) To gain permission to enter caves and potholes.
    (C) To describe a typical trip through a cave.
    (D) To give new members some useful information.

The best answer to the question, "What is the speaker's purpose?" is (D), "To give new members some useful information." Therefore, you should choose answer (D).

Now listen to the second question on the sample talk:

You will hear:

Sample Answer

You will read: (A) They are only important for the new members.
              (B) They are important to the safety of all spelunkers.
              (C) They must be followed in order to find cave insects.
              (D) If followed, they eliminate any danger involved in spelunking.

The best answer to the question, "What can best be said about the guidelines referred to here?" is (B), "They are important to the safety of all spelunkers." Therefore, you should choose answer (B).

36 (A) Man-made problems for the brown pelican.
    (B) Stages of development in the brown pelican.
    (C) The importance of fish to coastal birds.
    (D) Factors in brown pelican survival.

37 (A) Certain chemical substances are used less.
   (B) More experiments are conducted.
   (C) There are 20 percent more fish.
   (D) There is a greater variety of marine life.

38 (A) At least 20 pounds.
   (B) About 125 pounds every three days.
   (C) It depends on its habitat.
   (D) It varies according to its size.

39 (A) They abandon the eggs after they are laid.
   (B) They teach their babies all the skills they need for survival.
   (C) They are good providers for a limited period of time.
   (D) They weigh 125 pounds when the eggs are laid.

40 (A) It's when the birds become fat.
   (B) It's a period of strenuous exercise.
   (C) It's a crucial learning period.
   (D) It's when the birds are caught for experiments.

41 (A) It prevents them from diving deep enough for fish.
   (B) It is their food until they become successful at fishing.
   (C) It makes them desirable as laboratory animals.
   (D) It keeps them warm and lessens feelings of loneliness.

42 (A) In a fabric store.
   (B) In a clothing store.
   (C) In an appliance store.
   (D) In a laundromat.

43 (A) A formal dress.
   (B) Some linen fabric.
   (C) A graduation gift.
   (D) A dark suit.

44 (A) She doesn't think the store has any dresses in the woman's size.
   (B) She insists that the customer buy a suit.
   (C) She wants the woman to buy a washer and dryer.
   (D) She offers a useful suggestion and information.

45 (A) It must be washed and ironed often.
   (B) It only comes in size twelve suits.
   (C) It is more practical than pure linen.
   (D) It does not require special care.

46 (A) She likes the fabric but not the weight.
   (B) She thinks it is appropriate for the time of year.
   (C) She thinks it is too severe.
   (D) She would prefer to buy a dress that fits right.

47 (A) To recognize unusual student achievement.
   (B) To encourage students to help the handicapped.
   (C) To present some facts about American inventors.
   (D) To discuss a famous person's accomplishments.

48 (A) Her ability as a teacher was almost as amazing as Helen Keller's as a student.
   (B) She had the same handicaps as her student.
   (C) She received her graduate degree in education from Radcliffe College.
   (D) She worked with Helen for a very short time.

49 (A) It was for the most intelligent student in the school.
   (B) It was for a student who wanted to study at Radcliffe.
   (C) It could only be awarded to a blind or a deaf student.
   (D) It was for a student who had succeeded in overcoming disability.

50 (A) They have been able to get scholarships.
   (B) They have learned techniques for public speaking.
   (C) They have been helped by her example.
   (D) They have devoted themselves to reforming the welfare laws.

THIS IS THE END OF THE LISTENING COMPREHENSION PORTION OF THE TEST. LOOK AT THE TIME NOW, BEFORE YOU BEGIN WORK ON SECTION 2. USE *EXACTLY 25 MINUTES* TO WORK ON SECTION 2.

Section 2
Structure and Written Expression

Time – 25 minutes

This section is designed to measure your ability to recognize language that is appropriate for standard written English. There are two types of questions in this section, with special directions for each type.

Directions: Questions 1–15 are incomplete sentences. Four words or phrases, marked (A), (B), (C), (D), are given beneath each sentence. You are to choose the <u>one</u> word or phrase that best completes the sentence. Then, on your answer sheet, find the number of the problem and mark your answer.

Example I.

For centuries, until the first Americans reached the moon, men speculated as to - - - - - - -.

Sample Answer

(A) ● (C) (D)

(A) what did the satellite's other side look like
(B) what the satellite's other side looked like
(C) what looked like the satellite's other side
(D) what like the satellite's other side looked

In English, the sentence should read, "For centuries, until the first Americans reached the moon, men speculated as to what the satellite's other side looked like." Therefore, you should choose (B).

Example II.

- - - - - - - was the center of our planetary system was a difficult concept to grasp in the Middle Ages.

Sample Answer

(A) (B) ● (D)

(A) It was the sun and not the earth
(B) Being the sun and not the earth
(C) That the sun and not the earth
(D) The sun and not the earth

The sentence should read, "That the sun and not the earth was the center of our planetary system was a difficult concept to grasp in the Middle Ages." Therefore, you should choose (C).

As soon as you understand the directions, begin work on the problems.

1 - - - - - - - - as only a second-rate Impressionist painter, Pisarro has recently received high praise from many art critics.

(A) Being long regarded   (C) He was long regarded
(B) Long regarded   (D) Long was he regarded

2 The existence of the inter-maxillary bone - - - - - - - not by an anatomist but by the writer and poet Goethe (1748–1832).

(A) discovered   (C) was discovered
(B) has discovered   (D) has been discovered

3 - - - - - - - associations with left-handedness (sinister) tend to be negative, those relating to right-handedness (dexterous) are positive.

(A) While
(B) In spite of
(C) However,
(D) Indeed,

4 The first NASA sub-orbital space flight was made by - - - - - - -.

(A) a trained carefully African chimpanzee
(B) carefully trained African chimpanzee
(C) an African carefully trained chimpanzee
(D) a carefully trained African chimpanzee

5 - - - - - - - in the Atacama Desert.

(A) It never virtually rains
(B) It virtually never rains
(C) It rains never virtually
(D) Never virtually it rains

6 Although he was already in very poor health, - - - - - - -.

(A) the 1944 Yalta meeting with Churchill and Stalin was attended by Roosevelt
(B) Churchill and Stalin attended the 1944 Yalta meeting with Roosevelt
(C) Roosevelt attended the 1944 Yalta meeting with Churchill and Stalin
(D) Roosevelt with Churchill and Stalin attended the 1944 Yalta meeting

7 - - - - - - -, ozone levels in the ionosphere appear to have dropped recently.

(A) However the reason
(B) It is the reason
(C) What is the reason
(D) Whatever the reason

8 The llama and the camel, though native to very different parts of the globe, - - - - - - - of the same family.

(A) are members
(B) and are members
(C) but are members
(D) they are members

9 - - - - - - - 1932, F. R. Leavis, in his *New Bearings in English Poetry*, placed T. S. Eliot in the forefront of poets writing in English.

(A) So early as
(B) Early as
(C) As early as
(D) As early in

10 Scientists know that the huge Hoba crater in Arizona was made by a meteorite, but they do not know exactly - - - - - - -.

(A) when did the meteorite hit the earth
(B) when the meteorite hit the earth
(C) when did the earth hit the meteorite
(D) when the meteorite the earth hit

11 Deciduous trees - - - - - - - their leaves at regular intervals.

    (A) are shedding   (C) shed

    (B) are when they shed   (D) which shed

12 Henry Ford's introduction of the assembly line vastly reduced the time it took - - - - - - -.

    (A) to make a car   (C) for making a car

    (B) making a car   (D) a car to make

13 - - - - - - - they make show that young children are capable of arriving at surprisingly subtle grammatical generalizations.

    (A) A very mistake   (C) The very mistakes

    (B) Some very mistakes   (D) Very mistakes

14 So successful - - - - - - - that the projected dam was abandoned so that the blue darter snail's only remaining habitat might be preserved.

    (A) was the environmentalists' lobbying

    (B) the environmentalists' lobbying was

    (C) lobbied the environmentalists

    (D) the environmentalists lobbied

15 - - - - - - - surprises many youngsters.

    (A) Butterflies are insects

    (B) Butterflies as insects

    (C) Butterflies being insects

    (D) The fact that butterflies are insects

Directions: In questions 16–40 each sentence has four words or phrases underlined. The four underlined parts of the sentence are marked (A), (B), (C), (D). You are to identify the one underlined word or phrase that should be corrected or rewritten. Then, on your answer sheet, find the number of the problem and mark your answer.

Example I.

    Sylvester Stallone's starring role in *Rocky,* which he
                     A

wrote himself, made he a nationally recognized figure
         B   C

virtually overnight.
        D

Answer (C), the underlined pronoun he, would not be accepted in carefully written English; the form him should be used when an object pronoun is needed. Therefore, the sentence should read, "Sylvester Stallone's starring role in *Rocky,* which he wrote himself, made him a nationally recognized figure virtually overnight." To answer the problem correctly, you would choose (C).

505

Example II.   Sample Answer

   <u>Both</u> Los Angeles and Philadelphia are <u>among</u> the five   Ⓐ Ⓑ ● Ⓓ
    A   B

<u>more populous</u> cities <u>in</u> the United States.
     C   D

Answer (C), the underlined phrase <u>more populous</u>, should not be used in this sentence since more than two items are being compared. Therefore, the sentence should read, "Both Los Angeles and Philadelphia are among the five most populous cities in the United States." To answer the problem correctly, you would choose (C).

As soon as you understand the directions, begin work on the problems.

16 <u>Long before</u> Europeans applied <u>it</u> to firearms, <u>the Chinese they</u> invented
      A   B C   D
  gunpowder.

17 He was a man <u>of extraordinary versatility</u> and <u>became</u> both a <u>lawyer</u>
                  A   B   C
  <u>as well as</u> an engineer.
     D

18 <u>The harder</u> you work, the more likely you are to qualify as <u>doctor</u>
      A   B
  <u>by the time</u> you <u>are</u> thirty.
     C   D

19 In 1936, Jesse Owens <u>proved</u> that he <u>could run</u> <u>more quick</u> than any man
                         A   B   C
  <u>alive</u>.
    D

20 <u>Research</u> <u>eventually</u> demonstrated more applications <u>that</u> had ever been
      A   B   C
  dreamed of.
     D

21 Many centuries <u>prior to</u> the Norman invasion, the Romans <u>have conquered</u>
               A   B
  Britain, and <u>remained</u> there <u>for</u> almost four centuries.
              C   D

22 <u>Being</u> California is <u>the most populous</u> state <u>in</u> the Union, it has the largest
      A   B   C
  <u>number</u> of votes in the electoral college.
     D

23 The telegraph <u>opened up</u> the possibility of almost instantaneous
              A

communication and <u>thereby</u> <u>offering</u> many practical advantages to people in
              B   C

all <u>walks of life.</u>
     D

24 The <u>manufacture and production</u> of steel was one of the <u>industries</u> <u>on which</u>
               A   B   C

the country's prosperity was <u>founded.</u>
              D

25 Antarctica, which is <u>largely</u> covered by ice, <u>receive</u> <u>hardly any</u> <u>rainfall.</u>
              A   B   C   ·D

26 <u>All</u> young men eighteen years <u>of age</u> <u>must</u> <u>to register</u> for the draft.
    A   B   C   D

27 The <u>three</u> largest <u>state is</u>, and <u>has been</u> since Alaska's <u>admission</u> into the
       A   B   C   D

Union, California.

28 As a <u>generally</u> rule, people <u>are</u> not <u>very good judges</u> <u>of</u> their own I.Q.'s.
         A   B   C   D

29 <u>The</u> American bald eagle <u>is</u> <u>a</u> species of particular interest <u>because</u> its
    A   B C   D

symbolic interest.

30 Neil <u>Armstrong's</u> moon-landing provided a <u>very unique</u> moment <u>not just</u>
          A   B   C

for his countrymen but for people <u>all</u> around the world.
                            D

31 As the plane will be arriving <u>shortly</u> at <u>Pittsburgh's</u> airport, passengers are
                           A B   C

requested <u>to fasten</u> their seatbelts.
         D

32 John Maynard Keynes and the <u>economics</u> who <u>agreed</u> with <u>his</u> views
                          A   B   C

focused new attention <u>on</u> labor.
               D

33 Zucchini is a vegetable who can be grown in many parts of the United
               A   B   C   D

   States.

34 New Englanders are an industrious and thrifty people who
                   A   B

   pride theirselves on being individuals of few words.
         C   D

35 Some transplants work only if the replacement organ is took from a close
         A   B   C   D

   relative of the patient.

36 The rattlesnake relishes warmth and find sun-baked southwestern country
               A   B

   roads congenial places to rest, with the result that unwary motorists who
         C   D

   stop are sometimes bitten.

37 Spanish, alike Italian, is largely based on Latin.
        A   B   C   D

38 In common with some other states which impose taxes on raw materials
          A

   "exported" to other areas, Montana imposes a taxes on coal sold elsewhere.
             B   C   D

39 Soaring gasoline prices have reduced American car sizes and the likelihood
   A   B

   is that cars will become even smaller than those producing nowadays.
                        C   D

40 Agricultural pests cause huge losses and raising consumer prices in spite of
                    A   B   C

   all efforts to combat them.
          D

DO NOT WORK ON ANY OTHER SECTION OF THE TEST.

IF YOU FINISH IN LESS THAN 25 MINUTES, CHECK YOUR WORK ON
SECTION 2 ONLY. AT THE END OF 25 MINUTES, GO ON TO SECTION 3.
USE *EXACTLY 45 MINUTES* TO WORK ON SECTION 3.

Section 3
Reading Comprehension and Vocabulary

Time – 45 minutes

There are two types of questions in this section, with special directions for each type.

<u>Directions:</u> In questions 1–30 each sentence has a word or phrase underlined. Below each sentence are four other words or phrases. You are to choose the one word or phrase which would best keep the meaning of the original sentence if it were substituted for the underlined word. Look at the example.

Example.

The demonstrators hurled <u>imprecations</u> at the officials.

Sample Answer

(A) projectiles
(B) insults
(C) garbage
(D) compliments

The best answer is (B), because the sentence "The demonstrators hurled insults at the officials" is closest in meaning to the original sentence, "The demonstrators hurled imprecations at the officials." Therefore, you should mark answer (B).

As soon as you understand the directions, begin work on the problems.

1 The presidency of the United States is often <u>depicted</u> as the world's most strenuous job.

(A) imagined
(B) described
(C) explained
(D) experienced

2 With costs threatening to get out of hand, a <u>ceiling</u> was placed on expenditures in all departments.

(A) minimum limit
(B) cover
(C) maximum limit
(D) roof

3 Recently research has <u>focused on</u> a new approach.

(A) illuminated
(B) discovered
(C) looked for
(D) concentrated on

509

4 The results of the test were quite <u>unambiguous</u>.

(A) clear
(B) doubtful
(C) surprising
(D) illegal

5 Abraham Lincoln was often described by his contemporaries as being <u>an exemplary</u> citizen.

(A) a typical
(B) an imitative
(C) a model
(D) a presidential

6 The original resolution calling for a declaration of independence was <u>bitterly</u> debated by the Continental Congress.

(A) patriotically
(B) acrimoniously
(C) thoroughly
(D) partially

7 <u>For</u> all their protestations, they heeded the judge's ruling.

(A) In spite of
(B) On behalf of
(C) Because of
(D) Without

8 Though he <u>embroidered</u> his tales considerably, there was always a grain of truth in Mark Twain's stories.

(A) lengthened
(B) embellished
(C) repeated
(D) emphasized

9 Secrecy was a <u>decisive</u> factor in the success of the D-day landings.

(A) major
(B) choice
(C) significant
(D) determining

10 She was an <u>unlikely</u> candidate for the position.

(A) unpopular
(B) risky
(C) improbable
(D) unqualified

11 The citizens of Japan were <u>dumbfounded</u> by the appearance off their shores of Matthew Perry's ships in 1853.

    (A) deprived
    (B) delighted
    (C) horrified
    (D) astonished

12 Often regarded by the public as outgoing and sociable, this performer is <u>actually</u> rather shy and retiring.

    (A) in fact
    (B) presently
    (C) momentarily
    (D) nevertheless

13 Davy Crockett was <u>reared</u> in eastern Tennessee.

    (A) born
    (B) well-known
    (C) brought up
    (D) killed

14 Icy roads and poor visibility are familiar <u>hazards</u> in the midwest.

    (A) chances
    (B) dangers
    (C) conditions
    (D) occurrences

15 In 1844, the government refused to <u>purchase</u> Samuel Morse's invention.

    (A) support
    (B) permit
    (C) build
    (D) buy

16 Many immigrants were prepared to work hard and in appalling conditions for the <u>sake</u> of their descendants.

    (A) benefit
    (B) health
    (C) property
    (D) entertainment

17 President Truman's <u>distinctive</u> turns of phrase have led to his being frequently quoted by politicians and political writers alike.

    (A) felicitous
    (B) characteristic
    (C) remarkable
    (D) distinguished

18 In the nineteenth century, poor Europeans seeking to make their fortunes turned to America <u>as a matter of course</u>.

  (A) automatically
  (B) obviously
  (C) traditionally
  (D) resignedly

19 <u>Wigs</u> were worn for a different effect in the eighteenth century.

  (A) collars
  (B) jewels
  (C) cosmetics
  (D) hairpieces

20 Congress <u>wound up</u> its debate on defense appropriations in a blaze of patriotic sentiment.

  (A) concluded
  (B) carried on
  (C) initiated
  (D) interrupted

21 The common shearwater is <u>seldom</u> encountered off these rugged coasts.

  (A) often
  (B) sometimes
  (C) rarely
  (D) inevitably

22 So <u>engrossed in</u> his efforts would Gaugin become that he barely noticed the passing of time.

  (A) delighted in
  (B) frustrated by
  (C) expanded by
  (D) involved in

23 Potential settlers of the new lands to the west were sometimes <u>intimidated</u> by the pioneers' tales.

  (A) encouraged
  (B) frightened
  (C) inspired
  (D) attracted

24 Copper-mining companies complain about the lag between investment and return a view with which stock market analysts appear to <u>concur</u>.

  (A) disagree
  (B) contend
  (C) agree
  (D) conspire

25 Only recently has more attention been paid in the United States to providing special facilities for <u>gifted</u> children.

    (A) adopted
    (B) severely handicapped
    (C) emotionally disturbed
    (D) especially talented

26 Traders from the various European powers <u>vied with</u> one another over the trade routes to the east.

    (A) competed with
    (B) replaced
    (C) followed
    (D) traveled with

27 Railroad authorities in various countries have been <u>irritated</u> by government decisions to hive off profit-making parts of their operations.

    (A) encouraged
    (B) annoyed
    (C) distracted
    (D) worried

28 Contact with the substance may result in copious <u>weeping</u>.

    (A) itching
    (B) burning
    (C) suppurating
    (D) crying

29 The canyon was formed over the course of millennia as the softer rocks were <u>eroded</u> by the action of the elements.

    (A) eaten away
    (B) chewed up
    (C) ridden off
    (D) piled up

30 The <u>upheaval</u> caused by the Cabinet resignations made it difficult for the government to function efficiently.

    (A) slow-down
    (B) resentment
    (C) disruption
    (D) uprising

<u>Directions:</u> The remaining questions in this section are based on a variety of reading material (single sentences, paragraphs, advertisements, and the like). In questions 31–60, you are to choose the <u>one</u> best answer, (A), (B), (C), or (D), to each question. Then, on your answer sheet, find the number of the problem and mark your answer. Answer all questions following a passage on the basis of what is <u>stated</u> or <u>implied</u> in that passage.

Read the following sample passage.

 The term Badlands is often associated with movies because we think of it as the place where the tough, bad guys come from in the westerns. But this area got its name not because of the people from that area, but because of the difficulties and hardships it placed in front of the early American pioneers and hunters. French-Canadian trappers described parts of southwestern South Dakota as "the bad lands to cross."

Example I.

The Badlands got its name from

Sample Answer

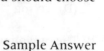

(A) a movie made in that area
(B) the disreputable people who have come from there
(C) the drastic problems it created for people trying to pass through the area
(D) the hard life the first people who settled and farmed there had

The passage says that the area got its name "because of the difficulties and hardships it placed in front of the early American pioneers and hunters" and that it was described as "the bad lands to cross." Therefore, you should choose answer (C).

Example II.

The people who first used the term "Badlands" came from

Sample Answer

●BCD

(A) Canada
(B) South Dakota
(C) the United States
(D) Westerns

The passage says that "French-Canadian trappers described parts of southwestern South Dakota as 'the bad lands to cross.'" Therefore, you should choose (A) as the best completion of the sentence.

As soon as you understand the directions, begin work on the problems.

Questions 31–35

The eyes of human beings are not sensitive to all light, but only that between wavelengths of 380 and 760 millimicrons. This fact prevents us from being aware that our bodies emit electromagnetic waves. These waves are mostly longer than we are sensitive to, but thermographic techniques can translate them into extraordinary color pictures.

Because they are constantly in motion, atoms generate infrared rays and the warmer the atoms are the more active they become. This results in thermographic pictures revealing different parts of the body in different colors: black and blue for the cold parts, green and yellow for the cool or slightly warm ones, and orange and red for those which are hot.

All this has a health application, for such problems as tumors, arthritis, and cancer are shown up as isolated red areas on the thermographic portraits.

31 According to the article

   (A) the eyes of human beings are not all sensitive to light
   (B) light wavelengths vary between 380 and 760 millimicrons
   (C) some light cannot be seen by the human eye
   (D) some people's bodies emit electromagnetic waves

32 Atoms generate rays of light

   (A) because they are infrared
   (B) if they are active
   (C) due to their constant motion
   (D) when they become warm

33 The majority of electromagnetic waves emitted by the human body

   (A) are above 760 millimicrons in length
   (B) vary between 380 and 760 millimicrons in length
   (C) translate into thermographic techniques
   (D) are below 380 millimicrons in length

34 Thermographic portraits show the body in different colors

   (A) only if the patient is suffering from tumors or cancer
   (B) according to the activity of atoms in the different parts
   (C) because some parts are black and blue and others orange and red
   (D) when the atoms are active

35 The atoms in tumors or cancerous areas are

   (A) problems
   (B) isolated
   (C) red
   (D) very active

Questions 36–40

One of the greatest problems for those settlers in Nebraska in the last quarter of the previous century was fuel. Little of the state was forested when the first settlers arrived and it is probable that by 1880, only about one-third of the originally forested area remained, down to a mere 1 percent of the state's 77,000 square miles. With wood and coal out of the question, and with fuel needed year-round for cooking, and during the harsh winter months for heating, some solution had to be found.

Somewhat improbably, the buffalo provided the answer. Buffalo chips were found to burn evenly, hotly, and cleanly, with little smoke and, interestingly, no odor. Soon, collecting them became a way of life for the settlers' children who would pick them up on their way to and from school, or take part in competitions designed to counteract their natural reluctance. Even a young man, seeking to impress the girl he wanted to marry, would arrive with a large bag of chips rather than with a box of candy or a bunch of flowers.

36 What is the main topic of this passage?

    (A) The solution to the Nebraskan settlers' fuel problem.
    (B) Life in Nebraska in the late nineteenth century.
    (C) The importance of the American buffalo.
    (D) Deforestation in Nebraska in the late nineteenth century.

37 Which of the following statements is **not** true according to the passage?

    (A) Nebraska was not a densely-forested state even before the settlers arrived.
    (B) The children enjoyed collecting the buffalo chips.
    (C) The children spent a lot of time collecting the chips.
    (D) Buffalo chips were satisfactory as a fuel.

38 According to the passage, how much of Nebraska was forested when the first settlers arrived?

    (A) About 33 percent
    (B) About 1 percent
    (C) About 66 percent
    (D) About 3 percent

39 The passage implies that buffalo chips were needed

    (A) in greater amounts in summer
    (B) in greater amounts in winter
    (C) only in summer
    (D) only in winter

40 Which of the following does the author **not** express surprise at?

    (A) The children needed competitions to stimulate them.
    (B) The buffalo chips gave off no smell.
    (C) Buffalo chips were the answer to the settlers' fuel problem.
    (D) Young men took bags of buffalo chips to their girl friends.

Questions 41–45

One of the most extraordinary of the people discussed was Kansas City-born Ted Serios, who was in his mid-forties when introduced to Jule Eisenbud, Professor of Psychiatry at the Denver Medical School, in 1963.

Over the ensuing three years, Eisenbud proved that Serios was endowed with an extraordinary ability to produce recognizable images on film of distant objects by merely staring with intense concentration into a camera. These "thoughtographs", eventually numbering several hundred, involved people, buildings, landscapes, or machines and were produced under carefully controlled conditions in the presence of scores of reputable witnesses, some of whom were hostile. The precautions to eliminate the possibility of fraud included medical examinations, X-rays, and tying Serios up in a strait jacket or stripping him naked.

In spite of the rigorous scrutiny to which Serios' efforts have been subjected, not only has no satisfactory explanation for his pictures been offered, but the tests have excluded all the obvious kinds of electromagnetic radiation which had originally been viewed as offering the most likely explanation.

41 Ted Serios was born in Kansas City in

    (A) 1945
    (B) 1918
    (C) 1948
    (D) 1963

42 In order to produce his pictures on film, Serios needed

    (A) several hundred people
    (B) carefully-controlled conditions
    (C) a number of reputable witnesses
    (D) a camera

43 According to the passage, the medical examinations

    (A) consisted of X-rays
    (B) were to keep Serios from becoming ill
    (C) were part of tests to guarantee scientific validity
    (D) required that Serios be stripped naked

44 The paragraph preceding this one most probably discussed

    (A) a general account of a meeting devoted to people with unusual powers
    (B) previous research done by Jule Eisenbud
    (C) how Ted Serios developed his incredible ability
    (D) Ted Serios' Kansas City childhood

45 It can be inferred from the passage that

(A) later studies explained exactly how thoughtography works

(B) Ted Serios has been able to teach several hundred people how to produce pictures using his method

(C) strenuous efforts were made to see whether Serios was using some kind of trick

(D) an obvious type of electromagnetism was subsequently shown to have been the method Serios used.

Questions 46–51

In what now seem like the prehistoric times of computer history, the early post-war era, there was a quite widespread concern that computers would take over the world from man one day. Already today, less than forty years later, as computers are relieving us of more and more of the routine tasks in business and in our personal lives, we are faced with a less dramatic but also less foreseen problem. People tend to be over-trusting of computers and are reluctant to challenge their authority. Indeed, they behave as if they were hardly aware that wrong buttons may be pushed, or that a computer may simply malfunction.

Obviously, there would be no point in investing in a computer if you had to check all its answers, but people should also rely on their own internal computers and check the machine when they have the feeling that something has gone awry. Questioning and routine double checks must continue to be as much a part of good business as they were in pre-computer days. Maybe each computer should come with the following warning: for all the help this computer may provide, it should not be seen as a substitute for fundamental thinking and reasoning skills.

46 What is the main purpose of this passage?

(A) To look back to the early days of computers.

(B) To explain what technical problems may occur with computers.

(C) To discourage unnecessary investment in computers.

(D) To warn against a mentally lazy attitude towards computers.

47 According to the passage, initial concerns about computers were that they might

(A) lead us into the post-war era

(B) be quite widespread

(C) take control

(D) take over routine tasks

48 The passage recommends those dealing with computers to

(A) be reasonably skeptical about them

(B) check all their answers

(C) substitute them for basic thinking

(D) use them for business purposes only

49 An "internal computer" is

(A) a computer used exclusively by one company for its own problems
(B) a person's store of knowledge and the ability to process it
(C) the most up-to-date in-house computer a company can buy
(D) a computer from the post-war era which is very reliable

50 The passage suggests that the present-day problem with regard to computers is

(A) challenging
(B) psychological
(C) dramatic
(D) malfunctioning

51 It can be inferred from the passage that the author would disapprove of

(A) computer science courses in high schools
(B) businessmen and women who use pocket calculators
(C) maintenance checks on computers
(D) companies which depend exclusively on computers for decision-making

Questions 52–56

In order to qualify for a single room in a university dormitory, you must be a full-time student who has completed the necessary number of hours to be ranked as an upperclassman. Applicants for such university housing are required to submit completed applications to the Office of Student Housing no later than the second week of the semester preceding the semester for which they are requesting such housing. Students will be notified regarding the status of their application by the sixth week of classes. Private dorm rooms will be assigned to qualified students on a first-come, first-served basis.

52 According to the passage, private dorm rooms are reserved for

(A) freshmen and sophomores
(B) juniors and seniors
(C) office workers
(D) high-class men

53 According to the passage, students **cannot** have individual living quarters if they

(A) do not carry a full load
(B) are going to graduate soon
(C) apply too early
(D) do not want to share a room

519

54 What kind of student will most probably get one of the rooms referred to in the passage?

    (A) One who applies in the fourth week of classes.
    (B) One who comes to the office and serves on the student council.
    (C) One who notifies the top advisor of his or her interest in private houses.
    (D) One who applies on time.

55 What is the main topic of this announcement?

    (A) Applying to the university.
    (B) Construction jobs available for students.
    (C) Obtaining a one-person college residence.
    (D) Meeting requirements for being a full-time student.

56 Where would this paragraph most likely be seen?

    (A) In a private dormitory room.
    (B) On a university bulletin board.
    (C) In a student's house.
    (D) Outside a new apartment building.

Questions 57–60

    For each of these questions, choose the answer that is closest in meaning to the original sentence. Note that several of the choices may be factually correct, but you should choose the one that is the closest restatement of the given sentence.

57 The congressman pledged support for all legislation aimed at reducing the tax burden on the elderly.

    (A) The congressman has voted for all the bills to help old people pay their taxes.
    (B) The congressman has won the votes of the elderly by pledging to support their tax legislation.
    (C) The congressman promised to back any bills that would increase old people's ability to pay their taxes.
    (D) The congressman called on his audience to support more laws to lessen the tax burden on old people.

58 Admission requirements are sometimes complicated and differ from college to college.

    (A) Each college is required to have its own unique admission policy.
    (B) It must be admitted that requirements are very difficult for students at every college.
    (C) There are complex differences in requirements for students to be admitted from one college to another.
    (D) Every college has its own policy regarding admission.

59 One of the most important requirements for starting one's own business is adequate capital.

   (A) The primary source of success for a new business is adequate capital.
   (B) One's own business constitutes one of the most important ways of making adequate use of capital.
   (C) Adequate capital is one of the basic necessities for anyone going into business on his own account.
   (D) The one essential need for initiating a business venture is adequate capital.

60 Contrary to popular belief, physical adaptation to living at high altitudes is environmental and not transmitted genetically.

   (A) In spite of the widespread opinion to the contrary, it is environmental rather than inherited influences that help people to adapt to living at great altitudes.
   (B) Most people do not realize the role geneticists play in transmitting high-level environmental policy.
   (C) Although it is not popular to say so, beliefs relating to high-altitude living are environmental and not genetic.
   (D) The fact that physical adaptation to high-altitude living can be transmitted from one generation to the next is contrary to what is generally thought.

DO NOT WORK ON ANY OTHER SECTION OF THE TEST.

IF YOU FINISH IN LESS THAN 45 MINUTES, CHECK YOUR WORK ON SECTION 3 ONLY. AT THE END OF 45 MINUTES STOP WORK AND CLOSE YOUR TEST BOOK.

Practice Test II

Test of Written English
Time – 30 minutes

<u>Directions</u>: You have thirty minutes to write an essay on the following writing question. Read the question carefully and be sure to write about what is asked and not about a different topic. You may make notes and you may check your work and make changes within the thirty minutes allowed.

<u>Question</u>: Some schools encourage their students to take part in team sports, such as football, baseball and basketball, while others place greater emphasis on such individual sports as tennis, running and swimming. Explain some of the benefits of each approach and say, with reasons, which you would prefer for yourself.